On Dean W. Arnold's writing . . .

UNKNOWN EMPIRE
The True Story of Mysterious Ethiopia and the Future Ark of Civilization

"I read it in three nights..."

"This is an unusual and captivating book dealing with three major aspects of Ethiopian history and the country's ancient religion. Dean W. Arnold's scholarly and most enjoyable book sets about the task with great vigour. The elegant lightness of the writing makes the reader want to know more about the country that is also known as 'the cradle of humanity.' This is an oeuvre that will enrich our understanding of one of Africa's most formidable civilisations."

—**PRINCE ASFA-WOSSEN ASSERATE, PHD**
Magdalene College, Cambridge, and Univ. of Frankfurt
Great Nephew of Emperor Haile Selassie
Imperial House of Ethiopia

OLD MONEY, NEW SOUTH
The Spirit of Chattanooga

"...chronicles the fascinating and little-known history of a unique place and tells the story of many of the great families that have shaped it. It was a story well worth telling, and one well worth reading."

—**JON MEACHAM**, Editor, *Newsweek*
Author, Pulitzer Prize winner ...

THE CHEROKEE PRINCES
Mixed Marriages and Murders —
The True Unknown Story Behind the Trail of Tears

"A page-turner."

—**GORDON WETMORE**, Chairman
Portrait Society of America

"Dean Arnold has a unique way of capturing the essence of an issue and communicating it through his clear but compelling style of writing."

—**BOB CORKER**, United States Senator, 2006-2018
Former Chairman, Senate Foreign Relations Committee

THE WIZARD AND THE LION
(Screenplay on the friendship between J. R. R. Tolkien and C. S. Lewis)

"Significant historical details are clearly represented and yet [he provides] a well-crafted drama."
—**OXFORD C. S. LEWIS SOCIETY**

"...sincerely impressed."

—**DR. TYLER FISHER**
Magdalen College, University of Oxford

Books by the author are available at deanarnold.org and Amazon.

For information on joining the author on a trip to Ethiopia during the summer of 2020, visit deanslist.info/trip

UNKNOWN EMPIRE

THE TRUE STORY OF MYSTERIOUS ETHIOPIA AND THE FUTURE ARK OF CIVILIZATION

DEAN W. ARNOLD

CHATTANOOGA
HISTORICAL
FOUNDATION

Chattanooga Historical Foundation
2019

Title: *Unknown Empire: The True Story of Mysterious Ethiopia and the Future Ark of Civilization*

Author: Dean W. Arnold

Editor: Daniel P. Bockert
Cover design: Peter Selgin
Interior design: Najdan Mancic

© Chattanooga Historical Foundation, 2019

ISBN: 978-0-98-937793-5
Library of Congress control number: 2019909943

To purchase this book, visit chattanoogahistoricalfoundation.com or contact the author at deanarnold.org

For Dottie

CONTENTS

15

PART ONE
The Barefoot and the Castrated
The Ark for Africa's Greatest Battle with the West

97

PART TWO
Mussolini, Hitler, and Haile Selassie
Questions Undermining the Ethiopian Ark

185

PART THREE
Never Defeated, but Beware the Suicide Demon
Eden, Ethiopia, and Israel

237

PART FOUR
The Oligarchs and the "Unfit"
A False Ark for the West and the True Ark

UNKNOWN EMPIRE

It is the glory of God to conceal a matter.

—Solomon

PART ONE

The Barefoot and the Castrated

The Ark for Africa's Greatest Battle with the West

PROLOGUE

I DID NOT want to ask him *if* the Ark of the Covenant was in Ethiopia. It is a question that is too often asked, and I had already asked the question to a great many people.

As I sat down to interview this theological leader of the Ethiopian Orthodox Church, I wanted to know the answer to the deeper question: *Why?*

Why, if the Ark really does exist, is it in Ethiopia of all places?

"Why didn't God just hide such a relic in a cave somewhere, or let it decompose?" I asked him. "Why, in his wisdom, do you think God decided that this particular artifact would be so preserved by one particular nation? What is the purpose? What is the reason?"

He laughed. Then I laughed. His was not a light-hearted chuckle. It was a sentiment of compassion. He was exhibiting what I have found to be part of the Ethiopian character: a gentle and quiet meekness that disguises an almost incomprehensible confidence.

He smiled again and spoke with hesitation.

"The response...would be somehow difficult for you to accept... or to believe in."

I waited. I hadn't traveled to the country three different times to let him off the hook at this critical point.

"There is a belief or a tradition in Ethiopia," he said, "or a consideration..."

He hesitated again.

"...that Ethiopians are..."

He was right. It was too much to handle right away.[1]

CHAPTER ONE

THE RUNNER CREATED a stir at the starting line of the 1960 Olympic marathon in Rome, land of emperors. This thin Ethiopian caught the attention of his Western opponents. "Oh, well, that's one we can beat," quipped an Australian runner to his teammates.

No black African had ever won a gold medal, not in any sport. Abebe Bikila, twenty-eight, had only started training four years before. He had one other glaring handicap as he waited for the starting gun to fire. He was barefoot.

Bikila had actually hidden in the tent a few minutes earlier to avoid the snickers from his opponents. He had tried running shoes at various times, but they hadn't felt right. Boys in Ethiopia grow up walking and running several miles a day in search of good grazing for their livestock. They never seemed bothered by the blazing sun that the ancient Greeks assumed must be closest to mankind in this land of 'burnt faces,' as they called it (*Aeth* 'to burn' + *ops* 'face'). Many people in 1960 also used the later Latin-Arab term *Abyssinia*, meaning 'mixed,' which shows up even today in the various shades of color and sharp-to-round features across the population. However, the people themselves leaned toward the earlier term, as Greek writings are filled with fantastic compliments of this ancient race. Homer called them the "blameless Ethiopians."[1]

As a child, Bikila spent his days like other barefoot children, caring for animals and attending church school. Like today, they lived in straw-roofed mud huts. The largest building in his village was the church, an institution that likely has modeled heaven for the earthly tribe for over a thousand years. Ethiopia claims one of the most ancient Christian traditions in the world, beginning with the biblical character they call "Bacos," the well-known Ethiopian eunuch of Acts 8 in the New Testament. This secretary of the treasury under Queen Candace was baptized by Philip after asking the apostle questions about the book of Isaiah, which Bacos was reading while sitting in his chariot—adding credence to Ethiopia's claim to 1,000 years of Old Testament worship before the time of Christ.

ABEBE BIKILA RUNS BAREFOOT IN THE 1960 OLYMPIC MARATHON

For the twenty-six-mile race (forty-two kilometers), Bikila wore bright red shorts and a green shirt with the number 11 on it. Video of the Olympic coverage provides a lengthy shot of the odds-on favorite, Russian runner Sergei Popov, looking confident, laughing and joking with a friend as they wait for the race to begin. For a moment the camera shows Bikila's face. The commentator asks: "And what's this Ethiopian called?"[2]

The *New York Times* provides a description of the beginning of the race: "It started at Campidoglio Square, designed by Michelangelo, skirted the Circus Maximus and the Baths of Caracalla, went along the 2,000-year-old Appian Way, and ended at the Arch of Constantine. As the lean, little Ethiopian approached the brilliantly illuminated arch, close by the ruins of the Forum and Colosseum, thousands cheered."[3]

The Roman imagery was highly ironic. Bikila was forced to move to another village at the age of three when the Italian military invaded his country to claim their long-desired colony. Ethiopia was the last holdout for an African continent otherwise completely conquered by Europe. A few years earlier, Italian Colonel G. B. Luciano objected when colonization was being questioned: "I have no intention of degrading the Abyssinian race, strong, intelligent, and noblest among the indigenous peoples, but I insist that in many respects we are superior to it, especially as to civilization, and we should not renounce the supremacy of the white race over these peoples." He continued his thoughts on interbreeding, which he felt "causes the downfall and decay of a superior race."[4]

Bikila was never critical of the Italians. "He was very polite, very humble," said Onni Niskanen, his Scandinavian trainer. "From the bottom of his heart, he was a good man." Niskanen told his family back in Sweden that the Ethiopians were rather quiet but "very nice."

Nevertheless, the people, historically, have never taken a liking to invasion. A few decades before Bikila's village was occupied, Emperor Yohannes IV gave a clear response to the Italians who first demanded they hand over their country for colonial purposes: "How could I ever agree to sign away the lands over which my local ancestors governed?" said Yohannes. "Christ gave them to me."

Conflicts inevitably ensued. The "very nice" Ethiopians had a penchant for castrating both their dead trophies and prisoners of war. In one account, it took eight men to hold down one Italian soldier. "I still have my hands," he said. "When I heal, I want to mow down all the Abyssinians!"[5]

Ethiopia's reputation existed as far back as 50 BC, when it was described by Diodorus Siculus, one of the most reliable ancient historians: "They have never experienced the rule of an invader from abroad, and although many and powerful rulers have made war upon them, not one of these has succeeded in his undertaking."

Ethiopia is "the Land of God," according to other ancient writers, a phrase repeated by a publication approved by the Ethiopian church, which adds: "And she will survive until the end of the world."[6]

In between fighting colonists in the modern era and defeating invaders in the ancient and classical ages, Ethiopia has spent a millennium fighting Muslims on its borders as a majority Orthodox Christian country. However, within her borders, Ethiopia remains somewhat peaceful today with its thirty-five percent Muslim minority (Muhammad allegedly outlawed jihad there when the Christian Emperor Armah took in Muslim refugees.) However, Islamic countries have relentlessly attempted to encroach on every side of the country, making Ethiopia "the island of Christianity" in Africa and the source of the medieval Prester John legend of the only non-European Christian nation in a land of mountains far, far away.[7*]

The TV commentator finally dug up the name of the Ethiopian runner among the sixty-nine contestants. "Bikila, the African, hasn't taken part in international competition before," he noted. *World Sport Magazine* said Ethiopians "run past farmers driving teams of oxen, ploughing the land in much the same way as their forefathers did in biblical times."

This statement was no stereotype. They grow the grain *teff* and make the honey wine *tej*. "We Abyssinians are a poor people with no mechanical support," Bikila said in a later interview. "So we run everywhere on foot. Forty kilometers are nothing to me."

Before the race, one resourceful reporter found a translator and was able to ask a few questions.

"Why do you run barefoot?"

"Habit."

"Will you be able to finish the race?"

"If I were not going to finish the race, I would not start it to begin with."[8]

---

* An asterisk (*) indicates further commentary with the note at the back of the book. A reference number without an asterisk provides only the source or sources used in the previous section.

Bikila may have been a bit energized by the date, September 10, a day before the Ethiopian New Year—September 11 by the calendar. However, liturgically he was indeed running on the New Year, the eve of which was being celebrated back home. Traditionally, a day begins with prayers in the evening before the celebration of the Eucharist the next morning at the house of worship, and that ritual starts with the priest cutting loaves in a side building they call Bethlehem ("house of bread")—all corresponding to the pattern in Genesis 1: "And there was evening, and there was morning—the first day."

Ethiopians also celebrate on this day the return of the Queen of Sheba to Ethiopia after visiting Israel's King Solomon, the two luminaries of ancient Ethiopia. This famous Old Testament story does not include the interesting details in the Ethiopian tradition, which tells us that their visit was so good that they had a son (not beyond the pale for a king with a thousand partners, according to 1 Kings 11). Through this connection, Ethiopia claims to hold the Ark of the Covenant, the golden chest built by Moses, the central object of the Israelite temple and perhaps the greatest treasure in history. Do they? This book will follow the trail.

As the 1960 marathon commenced, Abebe Bikila was not among the leaders. With thousands of spectators nearby, a "mob scene" developed that even the police couldn't dissolve in the short term. Nevertheless, the runners were able to get through the host of excited onlookers and successfully onto the long road.[9]

One by one, the competitors began to fall off the pace like a flock of birds dissolving. Within a few kilometers, two groups of four or five runners each emerged at the front. Bikila was in the second group with the Russian, Sergei Popov, and a New Zealander, Barry Magee. The lead group included a former French soldier, an Englishman, and a Belgian.

Belgium was an infamous pioneer of colonialism. While Britain was establishing colonies from "the Cape to Cairo," France gobbled up North Africa and Algeria. Belgium targeted the Congo. Sometime after 1876, Belgium's King Leopold II sent Henry Morton Stanley on a deep state secret mission inside the Congo. Of the sixteen million people there, only eight million survived the brutality of Leopold's regime.

However, most people only remember the romantic story of Stanley meeting a missing white missionary in the Congo's interior and saying "Dr. Livingston, I presume."[10]

Ethiopia's past success against invaders provided inspiration for African countries in the twentieth century as they fought to gain back their lands from Western occupation and domination.

Many take refuge regarding such harsh views and behaviors by Westerners as being only a thing of the past. But some are still fans of the Belgian emperor: "We need a modern King Leopold to assist the noble savage for a better life," according to a comment on an article by Doug Casey, an author who a few years ago spent weeks as number one on the *New York Times* Best Seller list. "Africans don't have the Protestant work ethic of Europeans," wrote Casey. "The continent has no civilization, no economy, no technology, no military power."

Another *NYT* bestselling author, a Harvard and Oxford scholar, is also quite willing to defend Western civilization: "It's not eurocentrism," writes Niall Ferguson in *Civilization: The West and the Rest*. "It's a statement of the obvious."[11]

A strategic investment advisor, Casey is actually a fan of the continent's future. "Africa is going to be the epicenter of what's happening in the world for years to come" he admits, basing his conclusions on birthrates, which are below replacement level in the West. They are strong but declining in Asia. In Africa, they are booming. These mathematical certainties point to a civilizational shift that we may not have seen since the Northern European barbarians camped across the Rhine river from Roman territory in the fifth century. When the river froze over, they marched across and defeated the Romans and went on to sack the capital of the 1,000-year-old empire. They had no idea their battle would mark the end of an age. "Ethiopia...is regarded by modern Europeans much in the same way as ancient Britain was regarded by the Romans," says Ethiopian scholar Sergew Hable Selassie.[12]

Another commenter on Casey's article understands what is at stake: "If there is not some form of mandatory birth control, we are in real trouble." This might sound like an offhand remark, but the latter part of this book will address in great detail the substance of his comment.

As the Arch of Constantine, illumined by the setting sun, faded from the view of the marathon contestants, a shift began to emerge in the leading groups. The shoeless Ethiopian had moved up from the second group of runners. He had now passed the Russian, the favorite at the beginning of the race. By the fifteenth kilometer, he had reached the back of the leading group, a pack of four that included only those associated with Britain, Belgium, and France.

"And there's that unknown Ethiopian we saw earlier," announced the commentator. "He's called Abebe Bikila. He's barefoot."[13]

CHAPTER TWO

I GOT IN his face and yelled at him. I was upset. My guide as I toured the holy city of Axum had been late several days in a row, and I feared my opportunities would soon disappear if we didn't get a move on it.

His name is Bazien, named after one of the Magi, the three wise men that visited Jesus and gave gifts of gold, frankincense, and myrrh. Ethiopians believe one of the Magi was Ethiopian.

Bazien is the nicest guy you'll ever meet, but he did share the cultural quality called "maambfak" by British scholar Richard Pankhurst, a tendency to always be late. But in typical Ethiopian fashion, Bazien did not return my anger. He was apologetic. He was kind.[1]

The next day, we found ourselves in a small village in the northern Tigray region, enjoying an hour-or-two-long coffee session. Goats and a donkey wandered nearby. We sat on stones with a dirt patio.

Bazien is in his late twenties, tall, striking, a black African with sharp Arabic features. His colleagues call him "The King" because of his royal heritage. He was wearing a white prayer robe, typical of ordained deacons of the church. In this setting, he reminded me of a young prophet.

"Ethiopians come from the tribes of Levi, Judah, and Dan," he told me.

"Who else was Ethiopian?" I asked.

"Enoch was Ethiopian," he replied. "He walked with God."

Bazien was alluding to the cryptic character in Genesis 5 who gets one verse of description—"Enoch walked faithfully with God; then he was no more, because God took him away."

Bazien is fluent in both his tribal tongue, Tigrinya, and Amharic, the national language. He also speaks perfect English, and for good reason. He was raised in Toronto. He moved back to his country of birth four years ago to study at the country's keynote Orthodox seminary. He believes, like all Ethiopian Orthodox, that the Sheba-Solomon story is true.

"Ethiopians don't call themselves Jewish," he said, sipping a small porcelain cup of coffee with no handles. "They followed Old Testament practices in the order of Melchizedek."

Melchizedek, also Ethiopian according to Bazien, is another strange character in the Bible who only appears one time, acting as a priest to Abraham after the founder of Israel wins a key battle. Melchizedek serves him bread and wine (a foreshadowing of the Eucharist) and "blesses" him (Gen. 14:18–19). Abraham responds by treating him as a superior, giving him a tenth of all his possessions, then Melchizedek disappears. The Bible does not provide any hints related to where Melchizedek came from or where he went.

Professor Girma Batu, the man I quoted at the beginning of this book, the vice academic dean of Ethiopia's largest seminary, shied away from articulating Ethiopia's significance, but agrees with Bazien's thoughts on Enoch and Melchizedek.

"It's a position taken by some scholars in the church," Girma told me. "Enoch and Melchizedek lived an ascetic life." He said that the monasticism of Ethiopia preceded even the time of Christ, something that sounded to me like the "school of prophets" discussed in the Old Testament. Today, there are as many as 1,000 monasteries in Ethiopia.[2*]

"Are there any monasteries today that claim to be part of this tradition of Melchizedek and Enoch?" I asked Girma.

"Each and every monastery," he said.

One hundred years before Abebe Bikila's 1960 marathon, England's Queen Victoria sent an envoy to Ethiopia to present the gift of a pistol to the man they called Theodore, also known as "The Barefoot Emperor," according to the title of his biography by Philip Marsden. In Ethiopia, his name was Tewodros. Neither Victoria nor Tewodros knew this gift of a pistol would lead to the murder of a monarch.

Like most Ethiopians, Tewodros attended a church school to learn the basics and the Bible. He was then sent to a convent at Lake Tana for more training in ancient and modern European history, literature, and even some Shakespeare. Along with the pistol, Victoria sent him a royal letter in 1855 upon his inauguration as Tewodros II, Emperor of Ethiopia. Tewodros's return letter was never answered.[3]

British envoy Charles Cameron delivered the initial letter and the pistol. After a full year, Cameron continued to insist that the queen would respond to the request in the emperor's return letter for skilled technicians for Ethiopia's advancement. Tewodros was also hopeful for an alliance between two Christian nations against the Muslim countries on his every side—Sudan, Egypt, and Somalia. Finally, Cameron returned home to inquire about the emperor's letter. When Tewodros learned that Cameron traveled back through enemy Egyptian and Turkish territories, the emperor's suspicions mounted.

Victoria was not simply ignoring him. Christian advancement had to be weighed with the priorities of empire—money and trade. The Suez Canal had recently opened on the Red Sea at Ethiopia's northeast border, but Egypt had built a port in Ethiopian territory at Massawa. France—Britain's greatest rival—had built a port near Massawa at Djibouti. Britain needed access to those waters without depending on France and could not afford to upset Muslim powers.

Tewodros's initial instructions were for Cameron to hand deliver the letter to Victoria, which he failed to do. Tewodros was impatient. The technical skills he needed were not only for civilizing Ethiopia. He needed weapons. Without advanced cannons and rifles, he could not defeat the Muslim enemies on his borders.

When he became emperor, he brought to his court an eleven-year-old prince, the son of a king who fell victim to Tewodros's expansion. This boy would one day be featured on the cover of *Vanity Fair*, the *Time* magazine of its day, sharing the honor with such notables as British Prime Minister Benjamin Disraeli, Charles Darwin, Napoleon III, and Russia's Czar Alexander.[4]

EMPEROR TEWODROS II

The boy's father named him Menelik, meaning "son of the king." More importantly, it was the name of the son born to Solomon and Sheba. Both Tewodros and Menelik—in fact all Ethiopian emperors—claim direct descent from Solomon himself through Menelik I. A 2008 publication of the Ethiopian Orthodox Church says that "Solomonian descent provides a Divine right for their rule and their claim was confirmed by the church." Twentieth century Emperor Haile Selassie was officially declared in the Ethiopian Constitution to be the 225th descendent of Menelik I, son of Solomon.

The emperor and boy developed a Saul and David type relationship. "Although he killed my father," said Menelik later, "he always loved me as a son. He educated me with the greatest care, and almost showed for me greater affection than for his own son." Like Saul confessed to David, Tewodros told Menelik "more than once" that he would follow him as emperor. But the young Menelik's destiny would lie in wait until the fate of Tewodros and Victoria unfolded.[5]

Tewodros impressed Britain early on as a progressive king who announced the end of castration as a military practice. But he grew irritated with European missionaries, their work seeming redundant in an historic Christian nation, a majority of which attended the Ethiopian Orthodox Church. He allowed missionaries to only proselytize the minority Muslims, pagans, and Jews. After more delay, he rounded up several missionaries and demanded they make weapons for him. But they failed to deliver, as they were teachers, not technicians.

Further delay from Cameron led Tewodros to arrest a British missionary to Ethiopian Jews, Henry Stern, who had written a pamphlet calling the emperor barbaric, cruel, and unstable. The king held him at gunpoint, but, instead of killing him, he had Stern "chained and severely treated" and his assistant flogged with bamboo rods.[6]

Cameron finally returned, without the long-awaited letter from Queen Victoria, but begged for more time, offering his own head if the letter did not arrive in two months. Instead, the emperor locked him up in prison. Finally, a letter from Victoria arrived. She instructed Cameron to leave for Massawa, the Egyptian port on the Red Sea. Tewodros was not mentioned. Enraged, the emperor imprisoned a dozen more British subjects. Cameron sent a curt message to the queen: "No release until civil answer to king's letter arrives." Three years after Tewodros's initial letter, Victoria sent a message, simply demanding the release of all of her British subjects. This time, it was Tewodros who refused to answer.

The Ethiopian emperor picked a tough opponent. Britain boasted the largest empire in history, a record that still stands. It needed the Ottoman Empire (today's Turkey) to serve as a buffer with Russia and couldn't risk that strategic piece to help Ethiopia. In addition, cotton was extremely difficult to obtain after the Confederate defeat in the American Civil War. The Red Sea lanes provided Egyptian-Sudanese cotton. Instead of help, Victoria sent to Ethiopia one of the larger European armies to ever touch African soil, 20,000 strong, which began unloading their weapons just below Djibouti, France's Red Sea port, one mountain range to the east of Tewodros's palace. Commanding General Robert Napier navigated Ethiopia's historic wall of defensive mountains by using forty-five Indian elephants, with Armstrong field guns strapped to their backs and sides.[7]

Earlier, Tewodros had beaten to death two of Stern's missionary assistants. His erratic behavior, like King Saul's Jekyll and Hyde behavior toward David in the Bible, forced Prince Menelik, three years before Napier's expedition, at the age of twenty, to escape his mentor's clutches. He reclaimed Shewa, the throne of his father in the province to the south, the region of the future Addis Ababa. A Muslim aristocrat, angry with Tewodros for imprisoning her son, helped Menelik get away by providing a river crossing in her territory. For helping Menelik, her imprisoned son and his companions were seized "in the presence of the King and his nobles and hacked and chopped to pieces," not unlike Saul's murder of the priests who helped David in 1 Samuel 22.

Tewodros killed twenty-nine more Muslim dignitaries, as well as twelve Christian aristocrats. His power was waning throughout the empire. Menelik, once a prince but now a king, discerned the shift in power and sent a letter to Queen Victoria in 1867, asking for Britain's friendship with Shewa. He referred to himself as "King of Kings," an early bit of evidence for his larger ambitions.[8]

No Ethiopian force could match the British army approaching Tewodros's stronghold. Would this be the final conquering that the nation had avoided for millennia? Would Protestant England respect Abyssinia's Orthodox Christian heritage? For now, Ethiopia was being ignored in favor of Muslim merchants. And the fact that a Prester John legend even existed proved how unaware Europeans could be of other Christian people. According to the first English voyage to the "Dark Continent" in 1554, all of the people in Africa engaged in "beastly living, without a God, laws, religion, or common wealth; and so scorched and vexed with the heate of the sunne...they curse it when it rises."

"Without a God" is not accurate for the Ethiopian part of Africa. Most people would be surprised to learn that Africa in fact boasts the *first* Christian empire. "Ethiopia became the second nation after Israel to believe in Christ," stated the Ethiopian Patriarch, Paulos I, to a synod of bishops at the Vatican in 2009.[9]

Ethiopian leaders also say the Archangel Michael himself instruct-ed the party escorting Sheba's son back to Ethiopia to steal the Ark of the Covenant from the temple. On their return voyage, they, and the Ark, flew a cubit above the Red Sea. Maybe so, but where is the proof? "We don't need proof, because it's a fact," a monk at the Tana Kirkos Monastery told a *Smithsonian Magazine* reporter. "The monks here have passed this down for centuries."

Indeed, the ancient roots of the Ethiopian church have been faith-fully passed down by oral tradition since the days of the Ethiopian eunuch. Skeptics abound. Only European man is rational, according to followers of the legendary Western thinker Carl Jung, Sigmund Freud's disciple and chosen torchbearer. In Jung's view, Africans have not reached an evolutionary stage of consciousness that involves cre-ative, critical thinking.[10*]

The scoffers of Ethiopia's oral tradition regarding their early Chris-tian empire ate some humble pie in 1969 when a Greek inscription was uncovered with a proclamation from Ethiopian Emperor Ezana, dated to AD 330: "I, Ezana, King of Axum [Ethiopia], have been given great victory...by the power of Christ God in whom I have believed." This reference is one of nearly ten references to Christ and the Trinity in the inscription.

At first, Ezana minted his coins—one of only four nations minting coins at the time—with the pagan symbols of the crescent moon and disc. But starting in c. AD 330, the coins included crosses—the first time this Christian symbol occurred on any coin, anywhere. When they did appear on Roman coins, the crosses were much smaller than the prominent symbols encompassing the entire back side of Ethiopian currency. One coin even bears the phrase "In this cross you will con-quer," undoubtedly related to Roman Emperor Constantine's famous words from the Battle at Milvian Bridge in AD 312 upon seeing an apparition of the sun with a cross above it and the Greek words: "In this sign, conquer."[11]

Ancient documents also provide no doubt that the Ethiopian Christian empire was dominant by the year AD 356. In that year, Ro-man Emperor Constantius II wrote a passionate letter to Ethiopia's archbishop Frumentius, begging the Trinitarian empire to back his embattled non-Trinitarian kingdom, at that time controlled by the Arian heresy, which taught that Christ was created, not God himself. Frumentius refused. But can such a giant Christian empire, to which the Roman emperor was writing, appear overnight? In fact, estimates of a AD 330 conversion for Ethiopia may be quite conservative. Ezana and his country may have converted years before the first Christian coin was minted.[12*]

What about Rome as the first Christian empire? Emperor Constantine declared Christianity legal for Rome, along with other religions, in AD 315, but it was not made the official religion of the empire until AD 380 under Emperor Theodosius. Ezana's 330 date wins the day. Ethiopia was the first Christian empire. What Patriarch Paulos proclaimed at the Vatican in 2009 was correct.[13*]

All this to say, those early English explorers in Africa were quite mistaken when lumping in Ethiopia as godless. Ethiopian Emperor Ezana built the Church of St. Mary of Zion in the city of Axum in AD 340. Oral tradition says the Ark of the Covenant was transferred there from a synagogue in Ethiopia and has remained in the country ever since.

Might the invading British General Robert Napier want the Ark? The British have always been legendary treasure hunters, and what could possibly be better for the British Museum than the world's most coveted artifact? British explorer James Bruce toured Ethiopia in the 1700s. This giant, swashbuckling adventurer was the first of his kind to provide European exposure to Abyssinia and certainly the most prolific as he wrote five volumes on the subject. He also happened to "acquire" a great many ancient manuscripts for himself and the museums back home. Among his prized collection was the book of Enoch, a mystical Jewish book quoted or alluded to several times in the New Testament (Jude 1:14 cites Enoch directly) and considered historically reliable by other Orthodox groups. While not part of the West's Scriptures, it's in the Ethiopic Bible.

Until this time, Europe only had fragments of Enoch and believed that the full scroll had passed out of existence. In the ancient book,

Enoch talks with angels. We are given names for the nine archangels, including Gabriel, Michael, Raphael, and Uriel. We also learn that evil angels decided to mate with human women who gave birth to giants. And we learn from Enoch that the leading evil angel, Amezarak, taught humans how to cast and resist spells. Kokabiel taught fortune-telling and Tamiel taught astrology.

While much of the strange content in Enoch corresponds with a passage in Genesis 6 that has often been interpreted as describing angels mating with women and producing giants, most Western rationalists, their rank and file busy building the British Empire, consider it laughable. But not necessarily their elite. Ironically, the term "British Empire" was coined by a key founder of science and mathematics, John Dee, who, like Enoch, spent many years talking with angels.

A key advisor and top spy to Queen Elizabeth I, Dee spent his final twenty years focused almost exclusively on contacting angels, or, as one of his manuscripts is entitled: *"A True & Faithful Revelation of what passed for many years between Dr. John Dee...and some spirits."* A spiritual entity he called Uriel gave him prophecies. Other spirits provided hidden insights for science, technology, and astrology. (For those wondering if he was dealing with good or bad spirits, a decent clue given is that all of these angelic discussions led to Dee engaging in wife swapping with his colleague while all four sought esoteric wisdom in the act.)[14]

Dee signed his secret correspondence to Elizabeth as "007," giving the occultist a Hollywood legacy as well. As recently as 1967, the United States' key intelligence service, the National Security Agency, referred to "our man Dee" in its *NSA Technical Journal.* He is described as "a principal advisor to most of the Tudor monarchs of England, and to certain European rulers as well....He excelled in mathematics, cryptography, natural science, navigation, library science, and above all in the really rewarding sciences of those days—astrology, alchemy, and psychic phenomenon."[15]

Dee's work today is known as "Enochian magic." These contradictions in Western society between rationalism and supernaturalism will be explored in later chapters, but, for our purposes at the moment, we can see why the British elite held so much interest in certain Ethiopian artifacts. The Ark would be no exception.

British General Robert Napier had made no mention of the Ark at the onset of his expedition into Ethiopia. While driving his elephants toward Emperor Tewodros's small army, the British commander decided to include the classic operation of divide and conquer in his strategy and contacted the two kings who were Tewodros's greatest rivals. (Ethiopia is home to a number of "kings," many descended from Solomon. The succeeding emperor is not always the previous emperor's relative.) One king was Ras Kassa Marcha of Tigray, the most ancient Ethiopian territory, which included the northern city of Axum, known as the "Ethiopian Jerusalem" and where the Ark-holding Church of St. Mary of Zion resided. Ras Kassa enthusiastically accepted Napier's deal to help him defeat the emperor in exchange for weapons. Menelik, who was mentored by Tewodros, now ruled as the other most powerful king in the country and headed north to meet Napier in the Muslim-held Wollo area, but he returned home under the auspices of celebrating Easter in Christian territory.

Tewodros was left with little help from the remaining Ethiopian leaders and was limited to a small force. The British methodically marched toward his mountain stronghold. Cornered, Tewodros offered to free the British prisoners and make a treaty. Napier refused. When they broke into Tewodros's headquarters, the Emperor of Ethiopia placed a gun to his mouth and shot himself dead. He used the pistol he received from Victoria.

CHAPTER THREE

"NO WOMEN ALLOWED" was hand-painted on a small wooden sign as I approached the monastery in Axum just a few yards from the building that contains the Ark of the Covenant.

A diminutive monk, looking old but spry, helped me in the front door. The building was centuries old, rather stark and plain. It resembled an old medieval fort. In fact, the Ark was said to have resided in this structure for centuries before being moved to today's smaller chapel nearby.

I removed my shoes before entering. Shoes are always removed. No Orthodox service exists, anyplace, where someone with shoes is allowed to enter the building. Ethiopian Orthodox Christians worship God with bare feet or stocking feet—but always without shoes.

These monasteries are old-school institutions, and some issues are non-negotiable. Birth control is one such issue. It is never allowed. The broader church is less vocal, even though it holds the same position. However, the old-school types and monasteries have never wavered: God's first command was to be fruitful and multiply and that has never changed.

In fact, it is this issue that brought me to Ethiopia in the first place. For decades, I watched global birth rates with alarm. The West is doomed to decline over the next century. A woman in the West averages 1.5 children, way below the replacement rate of 2.1 children. I looked for Christian nations outside the West. South Korea, a booming Protestant country, with a rate of 6.0 in 1960, has dropped to an alarming 0.96 rate.[1] Historically Orthodox Russia, now at a still scary level of 1.75, is struggling with all her might to recover from its 1.16

rate of three decades ago. No country in history has ever recovered from a rate of 1.3 children per woman.[2]

Ethiopia averages around five children per woman, as does the rest of Africa, making it the continent of the future. Only Ethiopia has a Christian tradition in sub-Saharan Africa longer than 200 years, or a written language and script that precedes colonization. Therefore, it serves as the spiritual and cultural leader of this ascendant continent. Fittingly, the African Union, Africa's United Nations, is permanently seated in Ethiopia.

Ethiopia may become the future of Christendom. At current rates, there will be more Ethiopians than Russians in fifty years. But maybe not. My professor friend Girma Batu says the numbers are a bit deceiving.

"The high rate in population size is mostly Muslim," he told me, expressing concern that the forty-five percent Orthodox Christian to thirty-five percent Muslim ratio could flip in current conditions. "There are sponsors that want to multiply the number of Muslims. They want to make Ethiopia an Islamic country, a Muslim-dominated country."

It is an unfair fight. Muslims are allowed to have several wives. Ethiopian Orthodox are allowed only one. In addition, Americans and the West are working furiously to bring down the birth rate by advancing contraception across Ethiopia. However, as Muslims refuse to use the contraceptives, Bill Gates and company focus their efforts on the traditional Christians. Of the four ethnic groups with the highest birth rates, only one, the fourth highest and smallest of the four, is Christian.[3]

"They are contributing contraceptive methods and even abortions sometimes," said Girma regarding the population control advocates. "At least one, maximum two children, that's enough, say those who want to be moderns. They are exactly copying the West."

"The biggest things are the modern tools of contraception," says Bill Gates, regarding the targeting of Africa by the Bill and Melinda Gates Foundation.[4]

I learned an interesting tidbit about the small hotel where I was staying in Axum before I hitched a ride that day to visit the monastery next to the Ark. A few months before, Melinda Gates had been a guest at the same hotel.

Most of the country rejoiced upon the news of Tewodros's death, as their Saul-like emperor had clearly gone mad over the years, but not King Menelik, his former protégé. Nonetheless, he proclaimed a public holiday to officially celebrate the historic event. He confessed that he did this only "to satisfy the passions of the people."

"As for me, I should have gone into the forest to weep," he said, in a twist reminiscent of David's musical lament over Saul's death by suicide as the Philistines approached to kill Saul. "I have now lost the one who educated me, and toward whom I always cherished filial and sincere affection," said Menelik. He could not betray Tewodros, and this decision cost him a great bounty of weapons that went to King Ras Kassa instead (*Ras* is a term for nobility). "If I had fallen in with the British army, not only would I have been…presented with the rifles and cannon, but I probably would have been elected and proclaimed emperor," Menelik said. "Now, all is lost, and perhaps another will sit on the throne which belongs to me by right."[5]

However, ambitions for emperor were irrelevant if Britain seized the opportunity to add Ethiopia to its long list of colonial conquests. True to form, a bevy of ancient treasures was seized, including Tewodros's two crowns, his cap and seal, dozens of ancient manuscripts, and an icon of Christ wearing the crown of thorns. These items made their way to the royal castle, Oxford library, and a number of English museums. At the beginning of the expedition Napier promised: "We do not come to conquer Ethiopia, nor to submit her to our rule, but solely to free our brothers, unjustly held prisoner by Theodore." The British general was still over 200 miles from Axum, the Ethiopian

Jerusalem, and no attempt had been made so far to find the Ark of the Covenant.[6]

EMPEROR YOHANNES IV

As Menelik feared, Ras Kassa had the weaponry and power needed to seize the throne. He was soon crowned Emperor Yohannes IV in the holy city of Axum. His path to greatness looked to be sealed when Napier promptly packed up his army and left Ethiopia, keeping his word. Fifteen elephants and 200 mules were required to carry back the Ethiopic treasures he seized.[7]

The British were not comfortable with a black African nation in charge of the Ethiopian coastal city of Massawa, the Red Sea's most strategic port. And they certainly couldn't let their top rival make it a French port. As the Italians also had high ambitions for the area, Britain utilized Italy as a compromise solution, keeping the strategic area in rational European hands. "A bit of treachery," said reporter Augustus Wylde.[8] Throughout Ethiopia's long saga with Italy, Britain always lurked as the hand behind the curtain.

Italy soon followed England's lead and adopted the strategy Napier used to march right into Ethiopia—by finding a rival chief. Italy decided to empower this rival with weapons and then divide and conquer. Menelik now played the spoiler role that Yohannes had played against Tewodros. The Italians had already met with Menelik years before and a visitor described him as "muscular...most intelligent...[with] head and feet naked....He was very friendly, and a fanatic for weapons."[9]

Menelik had been championed for years by Italian envoys as a fellow Christian leader defeating Muslims. "The cross has defeated the crescent," they wrote. With the new developments, secret negotiations commenced for Menelik to get the mass supply of weapons he had so long desired.

Yohannes had his own plans for securing his country. "Steeped in legends of the vast Axumite kingdom which had stretched in ancient times from modern-day east Sudan to western Somaliland, he dreamt of rebuilding a great trading nation which would roll down from the highlands and spill into the sea, a Christian empire in a region of Islam," wrote author Michela Wrong. His primary weapon to control his rival Menelik was a woman. He successfully arranged a marriage between Menelik and a princess of Yohannes's own Tigray region.

Taytu Betul did not agree with her new husband's flirtations with the Italians. It was said that she could not tolerate the odor of Europeans. She was known to be more of an idealist for Ethiopia than the shrewd Menelik, and a "devoutly Orthodox Christian" who, according to the court historians, was "slender" and as beautiful as an angel, "like Saint Mary."[10]

For Menelik's part, Britain's Lord Gleichen reported that he "rises every morning at 3 a.m., goes to early morning chapel, and at 6 or sooner receives reports." Not all of the accounts were so glowing. An Italian envoy called him "one of the ugliest men I have ever seen, but with a very sweet smile."[11]

The Italian may have noticed the scars. "His skin was deeply pitted," wrote a biographer, "the traces of a bout with smallpox. It was a useful mask—a hardened look that belied the subtle, sensitive spirit within. Menelik was not a handsome man, but those who met him remarked on the warmth, kindness, and quiet power in his face."

That same writer mentioned Menelik's "beautiful, intelligent, and kind" eyes, and Taytu's "rare, quick wit." He also suggested that Menelik was unfaithful and Taytu may have poisoned one of those lovers. He concluded: "It was said that while the gentle Menelik was loved, Taytu was feared." Nevertheless, "she was his sounding board and they worked well together," wrote another biographer. Although Menelik's ambitions for the throne tempted him to challenge the new emperor, Taytu, a Tigrayan like Emperor Yohannes, opposed the idea.[12]

One area in which the two kings agreed was conversion of the Muslims, but Menelik used a more moderate approach. When Yohannes converted the Muslim governor of Wollo with his military, the province over time turned back to Islam. Conversely, Menelik marched to Wollo and threw a giant party. "Yohannes beat [Wollo's king] with cannon. I have fought him with [honey wine] and I am certain to defeat him." Although effective, Menelik's eating and drinking with Muslims was a scandal to some.[13]

It should be noted that Menelik was not opposed to forcing his will if necessary. When he later occupied the strategic city of Harar, a Muslim dominated coffee trading post connecting Shewa to the Djibouti Red Sea port, he had the main mosque torn down and replaced with an Orthodox church. "This is not a Muslim country, as everyone knows," he said.[14]

Eventually, Yohannes demanded a visible demonstration of Menelik's loyalty. According to Ethiopian tradition, he was to approach the emperor naked to the waist with a stone on his bare back, ask forgiveness, and pledge his faithfulness. Menelik balked. Besides the humility involved, Menelik also opposed the tribute of cash and 50,000 cattle that was required. Yohannes approached Shewa with a superior army, but to avoid war asked church officials to mediate. This group was headed by his confessor, Abba Germa Sellasie. An agreement was reached, and Menelik came out to meet the emperor.

He came in the prescribed traditional manner, rock on bare back, and "sad and pensive," according to biographer Harold Marcus. "The moment he set foot on the rugs in the imperial tent, Yohannes's cannons 'thundered twelve times,' announcing the downfall of Shewan independence." Yohannes considered Ethiopia united, unaware of Menelik's secret dealings with the Italians.

Yohannes signed a formal treaty with Italy, under Britain's watchful eye, where the new Europeans in Ethiopia promised not to move beyond the coast. Yohannes promised to leave alone the Italian-occupied Massawa port. "I wish only to defend my country," he said.[15]

Italy championed a course of bringing a "civilizing mission" to Ethiopia. Lip service was paid early on to focus on the port of Massawa and the coast, not inland, as anti-colonial sentiment was growing in Rome. The pro-colonizers tried to emphasize the wildlife in Ethiopia, home of the world's largest lions, tallest giraffes, unique baboons, and other exotic creatures. This inventory of the animals was all part of the civilizing mission, as the ninetheenth century was bubbling with scientific curiosity. "Africa draws us invincibly towards it," said a member of the Italian Geographic Society. "It lies just under our noses, yet up until now we remain exiled from it."

Ferdinando Martini, president of the Italian Geographic Society, was a critic of Italy's ambitions for Ethiopia and its northern Red Sea port of Massawa and surroundings, which the Italians renamed Eritrea ("erythros" in Greek means "red."). A prolific writer and member of Parliament, Martini came from aristocratic stock and wrote plays, like his father. He boasted that his iconoclastic views made enemies for him of every political party.

"We are liars," he wrote bluntly. "We say we want to spread civilization in Abyssinia, but it is not true. Far from being barbaric and idolatrous, these people have been Christians for centuries." But voices like Martini's could not stop the movement of settlers beyond the coast and into the heartland. According to Michela Wrong, "The Italians knew the boundaries of their fledgling colony would have to be extended into the cool, mosquito-free highlands if it was ever to amount to anything."

However, a much larger force was driving the encroachment: population growth. Difficult to envision today, during this period Italy was booming with Italians. It had one of the highest birthrates in Europe. In a four-year period around that time, 717,000 Italians left for opportunities in America and Australia, where land was already being gobbled up. The number of emigrating Italians soon tripled. "Italy, a growing number of politicians came to believe, needed a foreign colony to soak up its land hungry." And why send them to another country if they could relocate to Italian-owned land? [16]

Each family received fifty acres in perpetuity if they worked the land for five years. Startup costs and travel were paid for with a three percent loan from the government. Italy loudly proclaimed its declaration of

Eritrea as a new colony in 1891. In 1893, the first nine Italian families emigrated into the highlands of Eritrea, moving beyond the mosquito infested coast.

Yohannes promised "he would grant nothing entailing the cession of an inch of land." A war was brewing. Its first skirmishes began with the successful defeat of 540 Italian soldiers at the town of Dogali. They found themselves surrounded by 5,000 of Yohannes's men under one of Ethiopia's greatest generals, Ras Alula. Only eighty Italians survived what became the Dogali massacre. The rout ignited horror and patriotism in Rome, where a train station, still today, is named Cinquecento, meaning "the Five Hundred." General Alula's fame in Europe led to reporters saying that he was not so black after all, but "more like a brown Englishmen...very good looking."[17]

Ethiopians across the nation rejoiced over the news of Alula's victory—everyone except Menelik. He knew what it meant. "The enthusiasm of the Abyssinians approached delirium," according to one report. Menelik alone "understood the gravity of the situation."

For Italian generals in Eritrea, it was only a bump in the road. Their long-term plan was to bring tens of thousands of soldiers to Eritrea along with the best weapons of Europe. Dogali was no reflection of the future.

Yohannes would not get an opportunity to test the confidence of the Italians to the north. He was forced to look south, where Muslims from neighboring Egypt and Sudan had crossed the border and sacked the second holiest city in Ethiopia, Gondar, the historic home of centuries of emperors. Most of the churches were burned and thousands of Christians were taken prisoner. Yohannes immediately made an about face with his army to address the crisis. He would, as one ancient Ethiopian manuscript worded it, be "baptizing with blood those who had never been baptized with water."

Meanwhile in the south, Menelik was courting Italian officials by providing assistance on scientific adventures in exchange for high-tech weaponry. Menelik was a "fanatic for weapons" and showed "great intelligence and great mechanical ability," his Italian suppliers said. He "perfectly understood their use and importance and also could distinguish the various European makes." In exchange for a few thousand rifles and cannons, Menelik supplied money, servants, mounts, and escorts for the expeditions. He also provided the village of Let Marafya to the Geographic Society as a permanent base of operations.[18]

There was a reason he knew all the European makes. The King of Shewa refused to depend on one source for weapons. He was also dealing with the French in secret. His new territory, Harar, known primarily as a haven for coffee merchants, had begun dealing in weaponry, thanks to being on the direct route from Shewa to the French port of Djibouti. Even Taytu was warming up to her husband's secret deals for weapons. She in fact hoped that Yohannes, her fellow Tigrayan, would stay occupied fighting others so as to keep his attention away from Italian and French intrigues in southern Shewa.

EMPRESS TAYTU

What looked like a possible brewing of hostilities between the Emperor and Menelik never developed. Instead, Yohannes met his death fighting the Egyptians and Sudanese on his southwestern border. "The emperor was shot, first in the right hand, and then, as he again advanced, by a bullet which passed through his left hand and lodged in his chest." His head was placed on a pike back in Sudan's capital of Khartoum. The Ethiopian army tried to keep his death a secret. They laid his decapitated corpse in a way that suggested that he was wounded and recovering. "Unfortunately, the heat of the day speeded decomposition; by nightfall the stench was unbearable, and the truth known."[19]

Menelik received this news on March 25, a few days before the Italians got word. Preparations were made for Menelik's coronation in the capital city of his Shewa region, Addis Ababa, and for a peace treaty with Italy. The great crowning took place in Addis Ababa at the Church of St. Mary on Mount Entoto. Archbishop Matewos, the officiant, commanded the people to be faithful to the new emperor on pains of excommunication. A large feast was held. The emperor wrote to his Italian peer King Umberto: "By the will of God, through the love of the people, the celebration of my coronation was accomplished."[20]

Emperor Menelik also wrote Queen Victoria regarding relations between Ethiopia and all of Europe. Once again, no answer was forthcoming.

More encroachments from the Italians inland from the coast were followed by rationalizations. They only needed "a site with a cool climate for the soldiers at Massawa, as a refuge in the hot months, and nothing else." Menelik decided to sign a treaty with Italy, against Taytu's wishes, that would provide the Italian soldiers with the cool air that they allegedly needed. A line was drawn at Asmara, a city in Eritrea just fifty miles south of the coast and 225 miles north of Axum. However, problems emerged with the interpretation of the treaty, and other European royalty were failing to respond to Menelik's communications.

Meanwhile, the scandalous treatment of the native people in Eritrea created political problems in Rome. Officers "resorted to enthusiastic use of…a whip made of hippopotamus hide that flayed backs raw." Rich Eritreans and esteemed holy men were disappearing at night. One journalist said that their fate was well known. "They are being shot, clubbed, and stoned to death and immediately buried in shallow graves on the outskirts of town." Torture and seizure of all assets were also involved, not for security "but because corrupt Italian officials were greedily intent on confiscating their assets."

At least 800 Eritreans were killed this way, according to reports, merely for the offense of wanting to keep their own lands. One account talked of officers drawing lots for the widow of a man to be executed, another of a cleric begging not to be shot while a soldier fired into the man "cackling like a maniac, [the] police chief smoking calmly as the pit was filled."

The Italian public "had lazily taken it for granted that Italy was doing good in Africa, its enlightened administration lifting a heathen people out of the primeval slime. The Massawa scandal exposed colonialism at its most bestial."[21] Newspapers demanded an investigation, and Rome announced the establishment of a royal inquiry. To help lead the commission, officials appointed the freethinking, outspoken playwright, Ferdinando Martini, who had been championing the Ethiopians' cause as a writer and member of Parliament. The public was elated to have such an advocate on the commission, and the protesters calmed down for a time.

To negotiate the Treaty of Wichala (a town in Ethiopia), as it was to be known, Menelik sent to Rome his most trusted nobleman, Ras Makonnen Wolde Mikael of Harar, a Christian governor and scholar, who built the first church in that Muslim city under Menelik's orders. (Makonnen's many accomplishments would be overshadowed in history by his fathering the future emperor, Haile Selassie, whose given name was Tafari Makonnen). Fluent in several languages, Makonnen was sent by Menelik to become the toast of Rome. By all appearances, an African and a European country were signing a treaty as peers, something unique to history at that point.

After Makonnen returned, a letter from Queen Victoria arrived. She said that she could not answer Menelik's original letter because the Treaty of Wichala required all communications to go through Italy. This requirement also applied to all "other powers and governments." Italy had, for all practical purposes, declared Ethiopia an Italian protectorate, a colony. Most historians concluded this clause of the treaty was the victim of mistranslation. The Amharic language version said "it is possible" for Ethiopia to involve Italy in its communications with all other nations. The Italian version said Ethiopia "consents" to do so.[22]

Accounts say Menelik and his court were furious, certain the mistranslation was purposeful. However, the Italian army, thousands strong, made further discussion, negotiation, and official protesting irrelevant. They simply invaded the interior of Ethiopia in early 1895, disregarding the treaty line at Asmara fifty miles from the port city. The encroachment was halfway into Ethiopia from the coast, 225 miles past Asmara, and included the holy city of Axum, the Ethiopian Jerusalem, and home to the Ark of the Covenant.

CHAPTER FOUR

THE ARK OF the Covenant is the central object in the Ethiopian Church's worship of Jesus Christ. Every one of the tens of thousands of churches in the country use a replica of the ark in its inner sanctum, serving as the table for the mystical body and blood of Christ. You cannot conduct services without an ark.

Once Italy had occupied Axum, the city containing the Ark itself, "No self-respecting ruler of Ethiopia could let such an affront stand," wrote Professor Raymond Jonas in his book on Menelik's military campaign, *The Battle of Adwa* (Harvard University Press, 2011). But Menelik did nothing. He waited. This and other past actions had popularized the phrase: "Menelik is a myth."

Others fought the Italians. For example, Ras Hagos Tafari, an Eritrean leader who years before agreed to help the Italians, flipped sides to lead a rebellion. "One recovers from the bite of a black snake, but...never...from the bite of a white snake," he said. He was crushed in three days.[1]

He had announced that he was fighting for Ras Mangasha, the King of Tigray, son of Yohannes, named successor by the dying emperor. Mangasha was never able to mount a successful effort for the throne, despite having under him the nation's best general, Ras Alula, leader of the Dogali massacre.

The patient Menelik, looking past Mangasha's competing claim to the throne, sent him reinforcements to help in his conflicts with the Italians in the north, but was sorely disappointed when he learned Mangasha simply withdrew, ceding Axum to his opponent. For the Italians' part, their intelligence assured them that the leadership in

Ethiopia was fragmented, always on the verge of civil war, and that a reprisal for their invasion was unlikely. More reports assured them that Menelik could not muster up a large army and would only be able to amass twenty or thirty thousand men, similar to the Italian numbers, but without their technology, weaponry, or training.

Menelik wanted more weapons. He worked with Makonnen in Harar to acquire from the French in Djibouti more cannons, guns, and ammunition. More war materiel addressed to Makonnen was shipped from Germany and Austria, but the British intercepted those efforts. All this waiting strengthened the "Menelik is a myth" reputation. He had wined and dined his Muslim opponents in Wollo rather than fighting them like Yohannes. He was patient with Mangasha rather than crushing a challenger. He allowed Italy to move fifty miles inward from the coast to Asmara when he signed the Treaty of Wichala. This last action even set off Empress Taytu against her husband. According to Italian agent Augusto Salimbeni, she said to the emperor: "Yohannes never wanted to cede an inch of territory: he fought against the Italians [and] he fought against the Egyptians; he died for this, and you, after such an example, want to sell your country?"

EMPEROR MENELIK II

Menelik's reportedly low number of soldiers emptied the threat made by his ambassador in Europe, who said that the emperor was employing the traditional Ethiopian tactic "to entice the enemy into the country and then envelop him with superior numbers." Regarding Taytu's charge of selling off the country, biographer Jonas says "the key question is not whether Menelik could be paid but whether he could be bought. It was a distinction the Italians were about to learn."[2]

The Italian invasion now encompassed over 40,000 square miles, a chunk the size of Ohio (Ethiopia is twice the size of Texas). Italy wanted a swath of land across Africa just like the other powers. "France had Algeria, Britain had Kenya. It was only fair that Italy should have her 'place in the sun,'" wrote Michela.

Besides simply wanting to "keep up with the empiring Joneses," the Italians were motivated to find some decent land. North Africa and Eritrea were "standing on hot, barren rocks." J. A. Rogers paints the picture: "The Roman Wolf now cast greedy eyes upwards to where his rich, fertile neighbor, Ethiopia, lay in the cool, well-watered mountains. Europe had grabbed all of Africa save this prize. He licked his chops greedily. He would finish the job."

Like other colonizing nations, Italy couched its plans for domination in terms of "civilizing" the Ethiopians. "The phrase 'colonial tutelage' was a signature of the doctrine," writes J. M. Blaut in his book on Eurocentrism, "and this conception is found in most history and geography textbooks of the time."

"'Savages' were mental children without qualification. Problematic peoples like the Indians, Ottomans, and Chinese, were thought to be childlike in some respects and not in others," Blaut writes. "Colonial revolts were obviously irrational—were outbursts of childlike emotion."[3]

The *Atlanta Constitution*, watching from across the ocean, gave its assessment of the situation with an obvious allusion to America's Manifest Destiny. Africa "is already carved up and possessed by the three different governments of Europe," it wrote. "The Negro must go, as did the Indian in America."[4]

Anti-colonial activists in the West, along with all of Ethiopia, hoped that the official commission inquiring into Eritrean scandals might reverse the invasion and perhaps even declare an end to the colony. Ferdinando Martini, the liberal commission member on whom activists had put their hopes, shared in a later journal his own experience of the horrors.

Martini described an infamous field outside Massawa called the "Field of Hunger" where helpless natives were sent to die. "Corpses lay here and there...with insects, which snaked their way through limbs twisted and melted by the rays of the sun.... The dead were waiting for the hyenas, the living were waiting for death."

Historian Michela describes how Martini "takes to his heels after glimpsing a group of young Eritrean girls sifting through mounds of camel dung in search of undigested grain, fighting for mouthfuls from a horse's rotting corpse. 'I fled, horrified, stupefied, mortified by my own impotence, hiding my watch chain, ashamed of the breakfast I had eaten and the lunch that awaited me.'"

But when the final report was released months after this horror, Martini made a complete reversal. Michela calls it a "counter-intuitive conclusion" that demonstrated the aristocrat's ability to be "both painfully sensitive and chillingly mechanistic." He also had in his sights an appointment to the governorship.

The report conceded only a dozen executions, but allowed the overseeing General Antonio Baldissera to explain: "It was necessary to strike terror into those barbarians to make them submit." The report concluded that "not an inch of acquired territory should be surrendered" from this "fertile and virgin land...stretching out its arms to Italian farmers."

Martini gives detailed explanations for his reversal in his lengthy memoir, a bestseller in Italy that stayed in print for forty years. "I would have preferred us to never have gone to Africa: I did what little I could, when there was still time, to get us to return home: but now [that] time has passed.... We have started the job. Succeeding generations will continue to depopulate Africa of its ancient inhabitants, down to the last one."

"One race must replace another, it's that or nothing.... we will have to hunt him down and encourage him to disappear, just as has been done elsewhere with the Redskins, using all the methods of civilization—which the native instinctively hates.... Injustice and violence will be necessary, sooner or later, and the greater our success, the more vital it will be not to allow trivial details or human rights to hold us up."[5]

Michela provides the underlying notions for the shocking stance of Martini, who did indeed go on later to become governor of Eritrea: "The views he expressed were the notions of his day, an era in which Darwin's theories of natural selection and survival of the fittest were used to justify the slaughter of Congo's tribes by Belgian King Leopold's mercenaries [and other colonial conquests]. The intellectually and technologically superior white race would push aboriginal tribes into extinction."[6]

Surely Menelik realized that the Italians and Europeans were never going to back down. He had waited. And he continued to wait. Why? Menelik possessed "acute strategic imagination" according to biographer Raymond Jonas. "Sometimes being a leader means knowing what *not* to do."

More weapons were needed. More importantly, Ethiopia was divided, but not as badly as Italy believed. The reports they received were primarily sent by Menelik himself through double agents. As he had hoped, the leaders of Ethiopia had actually united just before Italy moved into Axum. Driven from Tigray, King Mangasha (Yohannes's son) and General Alula traveled south to Shewa. A mile from Menelik's palace, they stopped and stripped bare to their waists and began the formal act of submission to their new emperor. The army (without weapons) and their clergy followed them. As they approached Menelik they bowed to show the stones on their bare backs. Menelik's troops fired guns into the air. Drums beat and horns played. The two Tigrayan leaders placed the stones at the emperor's feet and prostrated themselves. The Axum priests then came forward and all the leaders kissed the cross as a sign of peace. Mangasha's party asked for forgiveness, and Menelik replied simply that they were pardoned. Fifteen minutes of silence commenced to honor the moment, broken by the sound of artillery fire.

Time was needed for gaining weapons and forging unity, and Menelik had gained it. Some historians even suspect the mistranslation of the Treaty of Wichala was no mistake. Indeed, Makonnen had every opportunity to understand and comprehend Italy's misunderstanding of the treaty when he visited Rome. (Jonas calls the claims of mistranslation "a convenient fiction.") But now, having gained time, the leaders were united, creating an historic moment for modern Ethiopia.

The Italians were unaware of the new development and still considered Menelik an ally more interested in arms than war. However, in examining papers seized from the crushed rebel Hagos Tafari and the fleeing Mangasha, Italian officials determined these opponents were not taking independent actions. Menelik had been directing their maneuvers all along, with the intent of a later coordinated attack. The emperor had stayed silent for a long period, gaining time and momentum. But the game was up. The Italians saw the written evidence and now knew for certain he was their enemy, a monster they had created themselves after years of secret dealings. They thought they were creating rivals in Ethiopia, while Menelik was building an arsenal for the empire he would unite.

Trumpets sounded from the top of the mounds in Addis Ababa. The emperor announced the gathering of his army. It was time to fight. The beating of war drums notified men across the country, who gathered with their equipment for soldiering: "Shield, lance, rifle, and ten days' supply of food," writes Jonas. "Horns were filled with red pepper and butter. Cartridge belts were slipped over the shoulder or around the waist. Rifle muzzles were stuffed with scraps of wood or a rag to keep out dirt on the march. Swords were strapped to the right hip, following Ethiopian custom. All able-bodied men answered the call to arms."[7]

Enthusiasm was high, but how many men could the emperor muster? Rome believed it would not be enough. "The Italians were sure that 30,000 troops were the most that Menelik could place on the Eritrean border, and were equally convinced that a trained force of 10,000 could easily handle that number."

Menelik gave his war speech: "Enemies have now come upon us to ruin the country," he proclaimed. "Today, you who are strong, give me your strength, and you who are weak, help me by prayer."

Now Menelik courted the Muslims, focusing on ethnicity rather than religion: "I am black and you are black—let us unite to hunt our common enemy."[8]

The emperor's war council solidified: members included Empress Taytu, considered second most powerful; Ras Makonnen, the scholarly diplomat; Ras Alula, the famous general; and Ras Mangasha, the son of Emperor Yohannes.

Makonnen, who had traveled to Rome to sign the Wichala treaty, made a last effort to find peace with his Italian friends, asking for written confirmation from the emperor of the proclamation. Menelik responded immediately. "I do not want to hear words of peace," he wrote, and ordered Makonnen to deport all Italians from his cosmopolitan city of Harar. Makonnen complied the next day.

Taytu had long been a proponent of war. "I am a woman and I do not love war" she told Menelik after learning about the treacherous treaty, "but rather than accepting this, I prefer war." She was also suspicious of Makonnen, who was still holding out for peace. He was next in line for the throne. Might the Italians have targeted him as the rival they needed to pit against the emperor, as Europe had done before by allying with the rivals of Tewodros and Yohannes? With the submission of Alula and Mangasha, the leadership looked to be united, but the views of the Italians that betrayal was always a possibility could not be dismissed. Had not Menelik himself been willing to deal secretly?[9]

Soldiers gathered from across Ethiopia. They marched northward, led by Menelik and his generals. Although barefoot, they were far faster than any marching army in Europe. They covered 590 miles, longer than Napoleon's march to Moscow and twice as long as Lee's march to Gettysburg or Sherman's March to the Sea.

Blocking the path was an Italian fort at Mekele. The emperor sent Makonnen ahead with his division of several thousand to prevent the enemy from knowing the Ethiopian army's full numbers. Mekele was defended by only 1,000 Italians under Colonel Giuseppe Galliano. Ranking General Oreste Baratieri needed Mekele as a stalling tactic while he built up the Italians' major strategic fort a few miles north of Fort Mekele at the top of the mountains at Adigrat. With only 10,000 men, he could not afford to dispatch any more soldiers to Mekele. However, with each day, more soldiers arrived from Rome to increase his numbers at the Adigrat fortifications. The more Menelik and Makonnen delayed, the stronger the Italian position.

When Makonnen approached the Mekele fort, Galliano could see that his numbers approached at least 30,000. The polite Makonnen sent him a message.

GENERAL MAKONNEN WOLDE MIKAEL

"How are you"

"I am well, thanks be to God," wrote Galliano. "Are your soldiers well? Mine are very well."

Makonnen responded: "In the name of my emperor, I pray you leave this land, otherwise I will be forced to make war. It pains me to have to spill the blood of Christians. Please leave with your soldiers. Your friend, Makonnen."

Galliano believed the rumors that Makonnen was open to betraying Menelik. His messages were laced with suggestions that Makonnen should defect and become emperor himself. "My king has ordered me to remain here and I will not move," Galliano told Makonnen. "Do what you have to do. I assure you I have fine rifles and very fine cannon."

Several days later, Makonnen asked Galliano for a doctor, a Lieutenant Mozzetti, to attend to his wounded from a previous skirmish. Galliano cordially agreed, because he wanted secret information. He got it by serving generous portions of brandy to Ato Gheorgeos, the doctor's Ethiopian military escort on his return to Fort Mekele. As Gheorgeos grew drowsy, he revealed that Menelik's army was in fact over 125,000. He also had artillery "and his aim was to enjoy a drink in the governor's palace in Massawa. In other words, Menelik's goal was to drive Italy not only from Tigray but also from Africa entirely." [10]

Italian intelligence in Addis reported two Ethiopian armies totaling only 12,000 each. Instead, Menelik organized one of the largest armies in African history. Jonas called it "brilliant gamesmanship." Historian George Berkeley described it as unprecedented: "Never, probably, in the history of the world, has there been so curious an instance of a commander successfully concealing the numbers of his army and masking his advance behind a complete network of insinuation, false information, and circumstantial deceptions. [Every] village in every far-off glen of Ethiopia was sending out warriors in answer to the war-drum."

Now that he no longer needed to hide his numbers, the emperor marched his full army to Mekele to meet with Makonnen. An Ethiopian prisoner of war had previously warned his captors: "Menelik's soldiers…they are as many in numbers as the locusts." An Italian officer who was the first to glimpse the size of the army shouted, "Sono molti, molti" ("They are many, many!") And only part of Menelik's forces had arrived. [11]

To compensate, the Italians furiously added to their fortifications. The building of their Mekele fort started by utilizing a church for an ammunition depot. Churchyard tombstones were used for the foundation. A 230-foot wall was then built as the main defense, six feet thick at the top and sixteen feet at the bottom. Previous battles had shown that the Ethiopians had no answer for the European style of fortified strongpoints. Even General Alula could not overcome their fortifications—the Dogali massacre he led took place in the open field.

Menelik and the other leaders rebuked Makonnen for taking so long. While he talked under a white flag and borrowed a doctor, several valuable days were given to the Italians to add soldiers to their main fort at Adigrat and finish the fortifications at Mekele. As retribution, the war council determined that Makonnen's forces would be required to serve on the front line and lead the bloody invasion of the fort.

The attack led to many casualties. Italians shattered glass below, ripping apart the bare feet of many Ethiopian soldiers. Makonnen attacked again the next day with worse carnage and no sign of taking the fort. One thousand men were blocking 125,000, Africa's largest army. Taytu and the council were whispering treason as the reason for Makonnen's initial delay.

"What do I have to do to prove my loyalty?" he pleaded.

"You gave them time to build the fort," they answered. "It's up to you to take it down."

After two more defeats, Makonnen staged a night attack at 3 a.m., raising ladders into the fort. This plan looked to be successful, but the Italians were holding their fire. When they unloaded their cannons and rifles, 600 more Ethiopians lay dead.

Makonnen was ready to end his life, and stood in front of the fort to be shot by the enemy. Instead, Ras Alula grabbed him and removed his fellow general from harm's way. "Coming from Alula, a critic of Makonnen, this was a redemptive gesture," writes Jonas. When the full council gathered, weeping could be heard throughout the camp. Menelik and Makonnen faced each other, tears in their eyes.

"This is a sad day for Ethiopia," said the taciturn Menelik. After some silence he simply said, "This is my faithful subject." He stood and embraced his friend and ally. Never again would Makonnen's loyalty be questioned.[12]

Menelik realized that these direct attacks would not work, so he initiated a siege and targeted the fort's water supply, some say at the suggestion of Taytu. It was a move that would be a trademark for Ethiopia in the future: sidestepping the direct assault for something more clever. Even the quenching of the spring outside the fort had its own foreshadowing of future victory tactics.

Colonel Galliano flew the white flag. The emperor marched 1,000 Italian prisoners through two Ethiopian columns, while the yellow, red, and green colors of Ethiopia were raised above the fort. Menelik's army was marching north toward Adigrat for the final direct confrontation between the full force of both armies.

CHAPTER FIVE

DURING MY INITIAL visits to Ethiopia, I kept looking around for some coffee trees. I have been drinking at least two French press pots of coffee every day for over twenty years, supplied by my local roasting master Ian Goodman, who gets his beans from around the world and often from Ethiopia. Coffee originated in the country's highlands.

We were staying at a friend's house in an Ethiopian village and I mentioned my need to see a coffee tree. He laughed, took me to the backyard, broke off a twig, and handed me some red berries.

One of the more repeated local legends is told as follows. Around the sixth century AD, a shepherd named Khaldi noticed his goats getting excited after eating the red berries off a certain plant. He tried them himself, felt the adrenalin, and took some to a local abbot. (The berries have a large bean-shaped seed inside.) The monks noticed that the berries helped them stay up during their all-night prayer vigils. The movement spread from there.[1]

Ethiopia gained coffee around the same time in history that she lost her Christian allies in Byzantium and Rome. Ethiopian Orthodox Christianity—today called "Oriental Orthodox," along with Egyptian Copts, Armenians, and Christians in Southern India, parts of Syria, and a few other places—split with the Eastern Orthodox and Roman Catholics (at that time united) in AD 451 over bitter disputes regarding the two natures of Christ. Both groups—Eastern and Ethiopian Orthodox—were unbending regarding the teaching still honored today in Bible-believing Protestant churches that Christ was and is "fully God and fully man." Both groups view St. Cyril of Alexandria as the great leader of this view. Cyril led the church's condemnation of Nestorius, who was proclaimed a heretic in AD 431 for teachings considered destructive to Christ as "fully God." Cyril's famous phrase was "One incarnate nature of God the Word."

But a monastic leader named Eutyches pushed it too far. Though a champion of Cyril's teachings, he was condemned twenty years after Nestorius for emphasizing the deity of Christ at the expense of Christ being "fully man." Eutyches himself was proclaimed a heretic at the Council of Chalcedon in AD 451 by the Byzantine and Roman Orthodox. He was also condemned as a heretic by the Oriental Orthodox.

So far so good. But the two groups could not agree on the terminology of just exactly how these two natures of Christ reside in one person. "The divine nature and human nature are not mixing together," I was told by Girma Batu, vice academic dean of the leading Ethiopian seminary. "But at the same time, they are united, in a miraculous way."

A noted scholar with the Orthodox Church in America believes the difficulties can be overcome. "They are virtually the same as us," I was told in an interview with Archbishop Alexander Golitzin, who taught Patristics at Marquette University for twenty-three years and is the author of *Mystagogy: A Monastic Reading of Dionysius Aereopagita.* The archbishop described a series of colloquia between the Oriental and Eastern Orthodox starting in the 1960s. He said these scholars concluded that "we really don't believe differently."

We are not divided "by the substance of the faith," the archbishop said, but rather by which saints are saints, which are anathematized, who is the patriarch of a certain area, such as Alexandria and Syria, and certain specifics of the liturgy.

He said the two churches in Syria—and also Egyptian Copts and Greeks—allow the faithful to commune in each other's churches when necessity requires, and weddings are recognized by both churches. However, many Eastern Orthodox take a different view on the Oriental Orthodox. "Their Mysteries are invalid and...they should be received as non-Orthodox," write the editors at the Orthodox Christian Information Center (OCIC).[2]

Both sides agree that much confusion emerged over the definition of the term *nature*. The Eastern Orthodox used the term in two different ways depending on the context, while the Orientals and today's Ethiopian Christians are what Archbishop Alexander calls "terminological conservatives," sticking with one definition as used by St. Cyril in his famous formula, "One incarnate nature of God the Word." But the OCIC editors reject the view that the Eastern and Oriental Orthodox split over "semantics" and "misinterpretation and misunderstanding." They are concerned that this position leads to a view where "the Fathers of the [Eastern] Church were in error . . ."[3*]

Both Girma and his fellow professor, Jacob Jossi, have little expectation in the short term for unity between the two Orthodox camps in terms of celebrating communion together. Instead of "formal unity," the goal for now should be "functional unity," I was told by Dr. Jossi, who now heads the seminary for the Oriental Orthodox Church in India, a church founded by the Apostle Thomas. Unlike with Protestants and Catholics, where the divide with the Ethiopian church remains wide, meetings between hierarchs of the Eastern Orthodox are more common. The overseer of the leading seminary in Addis Ababa, Archbishop Themotewos (Timothy), told me he attended seminary in Russia and was classmates with current Russian Patriarch Kirill. The late Ethiopian Patriarch Paulos attended the prestigious Eastern Orthodox school in New York, St. Vladimir's Seminary.[4]

After the split in AD 451, the Eastern and Oriental churches grew far apart. Since then, what little interaction Ethiopia has enjoyed with the lands of Rome and Byzantium has largely involved trade. The primary export? Coffee.

The "coffee ceremony" is a major phenomenon in Ethiopia, and I enjoyed several during each of my visits. I saw women on the streets with coffee ceremony setups like hot dog venders at a ball game. But it's not fast food. Once I sat down, I was there for nearly two hours, enjoying the three rounds required by every ceremony. Traditionally, incense is lit and a prayer is said at the end for the barista.

In Ethiopia's cosmopolitan areas, coffee shop chains serve all the espresso drinks we are familiar with, and the largest chain has a green logo that looks a lot like the Starbucks trademark. I asked my friends about this logo. They said that Starbucks sued them and it went all the way to the Ethiopian Supreme Court. They ruled against Starbucks on the basis that coffee was invented by Ethiopia.

The supreme commander of the Italian army in Eritrea was the bespectacled General Oreste Baratieri, who also served as the governor and top political official. He made all of the decisions regarding Italy's occupation in Ethiopia, with overarching authority only from officials in Rome. Like the playwright Martini, his rise involved leadership in the Geographical Society, and he considered himself an amateur African ethnologist. He also admired King Leopold and his efforts in the Congo.

He was a cerebral man who liked to use large words and complex grammar. However, he was not highborn like his three subordinate generals—the handsome Giuseppe Arimondi, who had a "beautiful" Eritrean mistress; the regal but volatile Matteo Albertone, the oldest of the generals; and the book-smart Vittorio Dabormida, a published author on military tactics. All three were aristocrats, unlike their superior, and all three favored aggressive action against Menelik. Baratieri, more hardened than his courtly generals, was wisely cautious and admired his African foe.

Baratieri occupied the strategic town of Adigrat in March 1885. It sits on the highest point of the towering Ethiopian mountain range, part of the great Rift Valley, the barrier that has kept invaders out for millennia. Water drains into the Red Sea from one side and flows to the Nile River on the other. The commander-in-chief for all of Italy's forces in Ethiopia chose to build the best fortifications Europe could design at Adigrat. Each day more soldiers, supplies, weapons, and ammunition arrived from the homeland.

Italian artillery had enormous killing capacity, as was demonstrated at Mekele. Some shells contained shrapnel, thousands of small metal pieces that burst just above the enemy soldiers' heads and killed dozens in one shot. Yes, they were outnumbered by Menelik's army, but the Ethiopians' previously failed attempts to overcome Italian technology convinced Baratieri that his now 20,000 strong army was fully capable of defending Adigrat and defeating Menelik.

Crucial to the effectiveness of the Adigrat fortress was keeping the enemy away from Adwa, a crossroads forty miles to the west. The town sits next to the holy city of Axum, just a few miles further than Adwa.

Explaining military tactics can be complicated. As an analogy, consider the Ethiopians as an army from Texas seeking to reach Seattle, Washington (Asmara and the coast of Eritrea). The direct route is through Denver at the base of the Rocky Mountains. Adigrat is Denver. However, the army could take a left and go westward on Route 66 through the mountains to Los Angeles and travel up to Seattle and miss most of the mountainous travel. Adwa, west of Adigrat and down in the valley, is Los Angeles. Like Route 66, there's only one cut through the mountains to Adwa.

Baratieri was fully aware of this other option. In fact, he made sure that the Italian army secured Adwa from the beginning of the occupation, but Parliament's budget cuts demanded that he trim down his military footprint and Adwa was left vacant.

Nevertheless, the Italian general knew that Menelik would be crushed if he tried to take that western route as it would expose the Ethiopian army's right flank, usually a terminal mistake in military tactics. Armies fight facing forward, just like people. An attack from the front is easily seen, but if someone can sneak up on you from the back or side, it is more difficult. With armies, their cannons and other artillery turn ever so slowly, and supply lines and other support units are also slow to make adjustments. As such, generals spend a lot of time making sure they are never flanked.

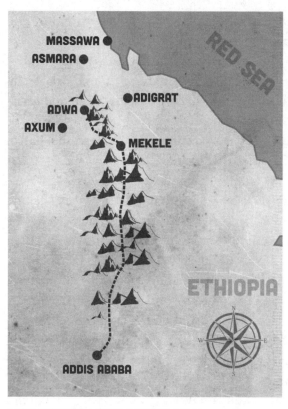

MENELIK'S MARCH FROM ADDIS TO ADWA

Menelik's barefoot army, 125,000 strong, marched with their rifles toward the heavily fortified Adigrat. As they approached, the Italian scouts noticed a movement from the straight path. Indeed, Menelik was making the westward turn toward Adwa. He was exposing his right flank. Baratieri was immediately notified.

However, the Italian commander never advanced to attack Menelik's right flank. The emperor knew exactly what he was doing. He placed at the rear of his army his 1,000 Italian prisoners from Fort Mekele along with thirteen officers and Colonel Giuseppe Galliano. For Baratieri, to destroy Menelik's flank meant destroying his own soldiers.

The army traveled safely to Adwa. Two weeks later, Menelik released the 1,000 prisoners as he had promised to do when the Italians gave up the fort. He was now closer to Asmara (Seattle) than Baratieri. Adigrat sat alone, irrelevant. If Menelik chose to advance on defenseless Asmara and the nearby Massawa port city, then all of the soldiers at Adigrat would be left vulnerable and cut off from supplies, just as they were at Fort Mekele.

Baratieri understood what had happened to him. He was now forced to conduct a humiliating retreat back to Asmara. Or he could march to Adwa and face Menelik in the open field. Neither was a good option, although most of the Italians were confident that they would win with technology over numbers.

"It played well in Europe," wrote Jonas, "where Menelik, always with an eye to international public opinion, could now add shrewd strategist to his reputation as a patient and peace-loving statesman."

Was there anything else behind Menelik's move to Adwa? Yes, he once again avoided a direct confrontation with a clever move to outwit his opponent. Yes, his army had to move regularly to forage for food, and they had lingered a bit too long in front of Adigrat. But something else, something larger, something bigger than armies, may have played a role. The clergy of nearby Axum eventually joined Menelik at Adwa. This is documented. It is also documented that some kind of version of the Ark of the Covenant was brought out for the upcoming great battle. Was it the Ark itself?[5]

Indeed, every bit of help was needed for the Ethiopians at this moment because the Italian generals met in emergency session and made their decision. The full strength of the Italian army would be attacking the Ethiopian army the next day in the open field at Adwa.

The Ark of the Covenant, as described in the book of Exodus, is a chest created in approximately 1500 BC under the direction of Moses. God prescribed the Ark to be built "according to the pattern shown you on the mountain," which made it "a copy of the true one" in heaven (Ex. 25:40, Heb. 9:24). God instructed it be placed in the innermost part of the tabernacle (and later the temple), the area called the "holy of holies" where only the high priest of Israel could enter once a year to offer sacrifices for the sins of himself and the people. (Famously, a rope was tied to his bare foot to drag him back out if the Ark killed him.) The Ark's dimensions were approximately four feet long and two and a half feet high and wide, with permanently attached poles at the bottom, longer than the chest, for transportation by priests carrying the Ark when necessary. It was covered in pure gold. The chest itself was constructed of acacia wood, which the Greek Septuagint translates as "incorruptible wood."

Two angels called cherubim sit on either side at the top of the Ark, also covered with gold, with their wings stretching across the length, touching each other and providing a seat for God himself. The Scriptures describe in several places "the ark of the covenant of the Lord of hosts who sits above the cherubim" (1 Samuel 4:4 NASB). God's feet rest on the earth, which is his footstool (1 Chronicles 28:2, Psalm 132:7–8). The Ark represents the earth and the cherubic seat represents the unseen, unknowable throne of God's actual presence in the dimension called heaven.

Inside the ark were three items: (1) the two tablets of the Ten Commandments, etched in stone, (2) a golden jar of manna, the supernatural bread that rained from heaven, feeding the Israelites for 40 years, and (3) the flowery almond staff of Aaron, Moses's brother, the high priest, which blossomed supernaturally in a contest with competing clerics who challenged Aaron's leadership.

The Hebrew word for *ark* is "aron," which means chest. Our word ark is derived from the Latin for chest (*arca*). We use the same word for Noah's ark, but the Hebrew word for Noah's boat is *tebah*, a chest with connotations of a vessel on water (the same word used for the basket in which the infant Moses was placed).

Moses was raised and trained in Egypt, and objects similar to the Ark are known to Egyptologists. Tablets inscribing a pact between Ramses and Hattusilis were placed at the feet of their respective gods, Ra and Teshup. "Wooden boxes lined with gold were standard artefacts of the religious furniture of the period," says a professor of Egyptology. King Tutankhamen's tomb included a similar chest with carrying poles and winged cherubim-like creatures at the top. At times, the religious chests were interchangeable with coffins.[6]

Synagogues use Ark-like cases to hold their Torah scrolls, hidden from public sight by a curtain decorated with the two cherubim angels. Other religious objects carried on poles by the Egyptians had the same size as the chest but resembled a small ship. This fact may have some relation to our English "Ark-ark" conundrum. Curiously, Ethiopia's traditional text on the Ark of the Covenant also sometimes refers to it as the "belly of a ship."[7]

"The existence of Ethiopia is inter-related to that of the Ark of the Tabernacle," according to a church-approved source. "It's so integrated into the nation's psyche that there's a replica of it in more than 20,000 Ethiopian Orthodox churches," writes Kaye Corbett at *Worldnetdaily*. "It is their source of strength, their reason for living." While skeptics wonder if the actual Ark is in Axum, no one doubts the long history of the tradition. Oxford scholar Edward Ullendorff, perhaps the world's top expert on Ethiopia's biblical history, says the Ark "has formed the centrepiece of the Ethiopian Church service since time immemorial."[8]

A celibate monk guards the building Ethiopians point to for where the Ark is preserved, a smaller chapel that sits outside the St. Mary of Zion Church, originally built by Emperor Ezana in the fourth century. The current guardian is Abba Gebre Meskel, who is sixty-two years old. He is "especially chosen for this blessed duty to serve till the end of his life," according to a church publication. "He is the heir to the office of Azarias, the son of the high priest Zadok, who was appointed by Solomon to accompany his son Menelik I on his return to Ethiopia." Once anointed, the guardian is forbidden for life to set foot outside the chapel grounds. "Abba Gebre Meskel is 100 percent convinced it is the authentic Ark," says his colleague, the temple's deacon, Zemikael Brhane. "It is not only the exact shape described in the Bible, but, moreover, it shines with an enormous light."[9]

According to Oxford scholar Ullendorff, Solomon "dreamed that a great light of brilliance, the 'shekkina,' the divine presence, had left Israel and moved to Ethiopia." Ullendorff was recounting the Ethiopian story of Solomon and Sheba and their son Menelik, preserved in the sacred Ethiopian text called the Kebra Negast, which means "Glory of Kings." A lengthy document, the size of a moderate book by today's standards, the Kebra Negast tells of a woman beautiful of "face" and "stature" named Makeda. We know her as Sheba, the Queen of Ethiopia. Makeda means "not thus"—"Not thus is it good for us to worship the sun, but it is right to worship God," she ultimately tells Solomon.[10]

So many questions arise with the Ethiopian premise: How did they get the Ark from Israel back to Ethiopia? If they stole it, why didn't anybody notice? Under what circumstances did Solomon have sexual relations with Sheba? Is there any suggestion in the Bible that this happened?

Let's start with what we know from the Bible, the primary passage being 1 Kings 10: "When the queen of Sheba heard about the fame of Solomon and his relationship to the LORD, she came to test Solomon with hard questions. Arriving at Jerusalem with a very great caravan—with camels carrying spices, large quantities of gold, and precious stones—she came to Solomon and talked with him about all that she had on her mind. Solomon answered all her questions; nothing was too hard for the king to explain to her. When the queen of Sheba saw all the wisdom of Solomon and the palace he had built . . . she was overwhelmed. . . . King Solomon gave the queen of Sheba all she desired and asked for, besides what he had given her out of his royal bounty. Then she left and returned with her retinue to her own country" (1 Kings 10:1–4, 5b, 13).

Jesus discusses Sheba's visit in the twelfth chapter of Matthew: "The Queen of the South will rise at the judgment with this generation and condemn it; for she came from the ends of the earth to listen to Solomon's wisdom, and now something greater than Solomon is here."

This is the basic information we have on the Queen of Sheba. The Kebra Negast retells the biblical story in great length, along with many other added details and a host of other fascinating bits of theology and mysticism unrelated to the story. According to this traditional Ethiopian text, while sleeping with Sheba, King Solomon dreamed of a "brilliant sun" shining with "exceedingly great splendor over Israel . . . it suddenly withdrew itself and it flew away to the country of Ethiopia, and it shone there with exceedingly great brightness forever, for it willed to dwell there."

We will address the events leading to their bedroom scene in a moment. But according to tradition, Sheba was impregnated and returned to Ethiopia to give birth to their son Menelik, whose name means "son of the king." Menelik seeded Ethiopia's millennia of Solomonic emperors and launched Solomon's Old Testament religion. Menelik did this after returning to Israel as a young man to visit his father. Solomon was very pleased with him, as he resembled his own father, David. After four years, Solomon begrudgingly approved of Menelik's ambition to return to Ethiopia and rule there. Always conscious of continuing his seed into the future, Solomon "gathered together his councilors and his officers and the elders of his Kingdom... 'Come, O ye councilors and officers, let us give him your firstborn children, and we shall have two kingdoms.'" [11]

So, several hundred of the best sons of the nobles and the priests accompanied Menelik back to Ethiopia, including Azariah, son of the High Priest Zadok. Here the story takes an interesting turn.

"And the children and the nobles of Israel, who were commanded to depart with the son of the king, took counsel together, saying: 'What shall we do? For we have left our country and our birth place.'" But Azarias answered them with a larger problem: they were leaving the Ark (which throughout the Kebra Negast is referred to, without explanation, as "Lady Zion"). "Let us sorrow on account of our Lady Zion," replied Azarias, "for they are making us leave her." The nobles agreed: "Verily, she is our Lady and our hope, and our object of boasting, and we have grown up under her blessedness. And how is it possible for us to forsake Zion our mistress?"

Earlier, Menelik had asked his father only for "a portion of the fringe of the covering of the Tabernacle" to take back with him, but the priest Azarias had larger ambitions. "Let us take our Lady Zion," he said. An "Angel of the Lord," later identified as Michael the Archangel, appeared in the night and gave Azarias the plan. He was instructed to go into the holy of holies of the temple with three other men, take the Ark, and replace it with scrap wood. The four men did as they were told and found all the doors to the temple and the holy of holies wide open for them. Azarias left the fake wood in the vacant spot and covered it with the Ark's purple cloth veils. They left with no one noticing.

In a reverse pattern, the flight home of Menelik and his nobles is reminiscent of Israel's flight from Egypt, where the best sons have been lost and the Red Sea is miraculously crossed. "And Michael marched in front as they travelled above the ground to the height of a cubit."

Menelik did not learn of the theft until they left. No one in Israel was aware of the stolen Ark. When Zadok came to Solomon, the king was "sorrowful." He recounted to the high priest his dream of the sun moving from Israel to Ethiopia. "Verily, the sun that appeared to me long ago when I was sleeping with the Queen of Ethiopia was the symbol of the holy Zion." He asked if Zadok was sure that the Ark was still in its place, and the priest replied that the Ark is always covered by veils. Solomon told him to go check immediately.

Zadok "found there nothing except the wooden boards which Azariah had fastened together and had made to resemble the sides of the pedestal of Zion." When Zadok saw this, he "fell forward on his face" and "became like a dead man."

Upon telling Solomon, the king had only one solution to the incident: cover it up. Who would know, since only Zadok was allowed to see the Ark?

"Woe is me!" Solomon cried out, "for my glory hath departed. . . . My father prophesied concerning them," alluding to Sheba's people. Solomon then quotes his father David from Psalm 68:31: "Ethiopia shall stretch out her hands to God."

What about the question of Menelik's conception? Did Sheba and Solomon really have a son? The Kebra Negast provides a long and interesting narrative of the encounter. Solomon gained permission to sleep in the same chamber as Sheba, but in different beds, as long as he promised not to touch her. He agreed to that condition, provided that she agree not to steal anything in his palace, to which she also swore an oath.

At dinner, he secretly fed her a potion that makes one very thirsty. In the middle of the night, she got up, agonizing for a drink of water. She found a convenient pitcher nearby and lifted it to drink a large amount. Solomon grabbed her hand, accusing her of stealing from him, for nothing is more valuable than water: "'Verily, thou hast now become my wife according to the law of Kings'" he said to her. "And she gave herself into his embrace willingly and yielded to his desire, according to that which she had covenanted with him." [12]

Oxford's Ullendorff believes they did have sexual relations. He notes: "The queen 'came to Solomon and communed with him of all that was in her heart' (1 Kings 10:2 GNV). The Hebrew term 'to come, enter' is also used as the technical term for coitus." Ullendorff here references Genesis 16:2 where Sarah tells Abraham, "Please go in to my maid, perhaps I will obtain children by her."

Ullendorff continues: "In 1 Kings 10:13, we are told that 'Solomon gave unto the Queen of Sheba all her desire" (KJV). Ullendorff notes that this statement infers a consummation. He adds that renowned middle ages scholar Rabbi Shlomo Rashi tries to equate "all her desire" with wanting wisdom, but "the very fact Rashi felt impelled to stress this aspect demonstrates quite clearly that he was aware of less innocent embellishments to this verse." [13]

As we shall see later, many questions remain in the scholarly community regarding the existence of the Ark and the possibility of it residing in Ethiopia. But beyond the quibbling of what is or is not literal, the Ark as a theological concept and Old Testament shadow still works quite effectively for Christian worship today. Ullendorff agrees with the Ethiopians that the Eucharist table in the liturgy alludes to the Ark. St. Germanus, the great ninth century theologian whose commentary, at one time, accompanied every liturgy book in Europe, agrees with the Ark's representation as the altar table. [14]

Moreover, every Eucharist table in traditional Christianity contains the three elements inside the Ark: (1) The Ten Commandments are replaced with the Gospel Book, (2) the manna is the bread of the

Eucharist, and (3) the blossoming staff is the wooden cross atop every altar table. (Seasonally, like blossoms, the cross is decorated with flowers for certain feasts.)

In Orthodox churches, the altar area is modeled after the few glimpses of ultimate reality or "heaven" given to us in Scripture, where, like above the earthly Ark-throne, cherubim are constantly giving glory to God. The liturgy of St. John Chrysostom, used by both Ethiopians and Eastern Orthodox, makes the cherubic cry of "holy, holy, holy" a constant refrain. A "cloud" is another constant, consisting of incense below and a cloud of angels above. There are six or seven places in the Scriptures that depict the ultimate presence of God, including the passages of Isaiah 6 and Ezekiel 1 where "the temple was filled with smoke" and "an immense cloud with flashing lightning" was joined by mighty angels who sing continually "holy, holy, holy" in the presence of God.

In Revelation 4 and 5 we see the same throne scene. Angelic beings send incense up to the throne and "never stop saying: holy, holy, holy is the Lord God Almighty." Then the Apostle John sees Christ move from the "right hand of him who sat on the throne" to "the center of the throne" where he offers himself as the new sacrifice.

According to the book of Hebrews in the New Testament, Jesus Christ is now the high priest "at the right hand of the thrown of the Majesty in heaven" and who "serves in the sanctuary, the true tabernacle set up by the Lord" (Heb. 8:1–2). The liturgy here on earth reflects the ongoing, eternal liturgy taking place in heaven.

Ethiopian and other Orthodox liturgical traditions reflect not only the heavenly pattern of worship, but also the key event in history: at the resurrection, two angels (cherubim) sit at either side of the coffin/altar/ark where Jesus was laid (John 20:12). That very slab serves today as the preparation table for the Eucharist at the Church of the Holy Sepulchre in Jerusalem.

Like the altar table of a holy church, Ethiopians believe the related object of the Ark itself has supernatural powers. In the Old Testament, Israel won battles when the Ark was brought out for such extraordinary occasions. Joshua's army defeated the mighty city of Jericho after the

Ark was marched around its walls seven times. The Jordan River parted for crossing when the Ark-bearing priests stepped into the water. When Uzzah reached out to balance the Ark as it looked to be toppling over, he was struck dead in judgment. Jewish commentaries speak of others killed by the sparks emitted from the Ark. When the Ark was held for a time at the house of Obed Edom of Gath, Scripture tells us that Yahweh "blessed Obed Edom and his whole family" (2 Sam. 6:11). Jewish tradition tells us that this included "being blessed with many children" including "six being born at one time."[15]

Many Ethiopians believe the power of the Ark is responsible for Axum erecting what some call the largest single piece of stone ever successfully quarried and erected in the ancient world. This greatest of the Axum obelisks (now broken from a fall) was placed in the early centuries not more than 100 yards from the chapel of the Ark-guardian.

"How you think it was raised up?" the guardian of the Ark asked author Graham Hancock, according to his 1991 book *The Sign and the Seal*. Hancock confessed that he did not know. "The Ark was used," whispered the monk darkly (according to Hancock's penchant for drama). "The Ark and the celestial fire. Men alone could never have done such a thing."[16]

According to the Kebra Negast, the Archangel Michael said he was "commanded by God to be with the Ark forever." Menelik, leaving Israel, was quick to take advantage of this heavenly warrior's presence and used the Ark as a battle help as soon as he re-entered his country. He had trouble with the "city government" and with the Ark's help "laid waste the district" and "blotted out the people and slew them with the edge of the sword."[17]

The Ark has a mind of its own. When the Philistines captured it and placed it in a pagan temple, the idol of Dagon was found the next day on the ground bowing before the Ark. Propped back up, the next morning it bowed down again, only this time with its hands and head broken off (1 Samuel 5). After this incident and a series of calamities, the Philistines hitched the Ark to some animals which by instinct headed immediately back to Israel. The Kebra Negast agrees that the Ark has a volatile nature: "It goeth of its own free will wherever it wisheth, and it cannot be removed from its seat if it doth not desire it."[18]

In that light, as we return to the invasion of Ethiopia by the Italians in the 1890s, the clergy of Axum and Emperor Menelik couldn't just take the Ark outside of its hiding place for the Battle of Adwa simply because they wanted to. The Ark must agree.

Did they bring it out? Iconography of the Battle of Adwa depicts priests carrying an Ark, just as we would have imagined Israel to do against its enemies. We know that at least two replicas of the Ark were brought out for the Battle of Adwa: the Tabot of St. George and the Tabot of St. Mary. But according to another account from Graham Hancock, it was the Ark itself that was used at Adwa. He asked the question to an Ethiopian archpriest serving as a missionary to the British, the Very Reverend Liqa Berhanat Solomon Gabre Selassie. (Hancock, who defaulted on just calling him "Solomon," said his beard was as long as his name.)

Father Solomon was specific with his written answer to Hancock's question. Yes, he said, it had been used over the centuries "as a source of strength against the aggressors...as on the day when Joshua carried the Ark around the city of Jericho, likewise our priests carried the Ark, chanting and going into battle in the glory of God." Then he got more specific: "As recently as 1896 when the King of Kings Menelik the Second fought against the Italian aggressors at the Battle of Adwa in Tigray region, the priests carried the Ark of the Covenant into the field to confront the invaders."[19]

Many Ethiopians themselves do not believe the Ark itself was used for the Battle of Adwa. They believe the original is too sacred. "No, I do not believe it was the original Ark," said theology student Fre Salib. "According to historical sources, priests went out carrying the Tabot of St. George." The March 1 battle happened to be on the feast day of St. George on the church calendar, so no one doubts his tabot was used that day.[20]

Based on current available sources, it is impossible to confirm if the actual Ark of the Covenant, the golden chest used in battle by the Israelites, was brought out for the Battle of Adwa. Perhaps the results of the battle can provide a clue.

CHAPTER SIX

I WAS ABOUT to fly from Addis to Axum. I met with the chairman emeritus of the history department of Addis Ababa University, Ethiopia's largest academic site, and asked him where to visit. His first recommendation was the Abba Garima Monastery, named after St. Garima, which preserves the oldest illustrated Gospel Book in the world, written in Ethiopia's ancient script called Ge'ez. According to the "Acts of Garima," the saint copied all four Gospels and drew the illustrations in one day. The sun stopped to make a longer day for him to complete the task. The book has healing powers, and is read to the sick.

When I got there, an armed guard stood outside the simple little structure housing the 1,600-year-old Garima Gospels, written on goat skin. One little monk watched us in the dimly lit, 300-square-foot building while my guide and I leaned over the ancient book on top of a small table just under some glass. We were inches away.

"Scholars and scientists previously agreed that the Gospels...were written centuries after [Garima's] death," write the authors of *Abyssinian Christianity*. However, "recent radiocarbon dating carried out by Oxford University suggests a date between AD 330–650 for their creation, opening the possibility that the Gospels were actually copied by Abba Garima himself." The *Los Angeles Review of Books* repeats this discovery and exclaims in a 2017 article: "For anyone interested in the history of the Bible...this is very big news."

I have seen some of the ancient Bibles in Britain. The Garima Gospels are older than the Lindesfarne Gospel as well as the renowned Irish Book of Kells. It is only preceded by the Codex Sinaiticus in the British Museum, a third–fourth century work, the world's oldest complete volume of the Old and New Testament, discovered in Sinai, Egypt. However, it is now divided between monasteries and museums in Egypt, Britain, Russia, and the U.S. The entire Garima Gospels have remained in one piece in the same spot for almost two millennia.

When some Anglo-French scholars got wind of the Garima Gospels in 1950, they sent a team to inspect it. The chief scholar, Beatrice Playne, was not allowed inside, so the Gospels had to be brought out to the parking lot for her to examine.[1]

I was more fortunate. Not only was I male, I had a nice beard, and that is high currency among Ethiopians, especially monastics. I was able to interview their top scholar, Father Abraham, about my aim to write a history of their nation. "The founders of Ethiopia descended from Noah," he told me. "It begins from Noah. That is important."[2]

When Emperor Menelik gave his rousing war speech to begin the great march from Addis Ababa to Tigray, he warned that the Italians had come "to change our religion" and then asked for the earnest prayers of all devout Christians in Ethiopia. Historian Michela says that the Italian politicians talked of "Rome's 'civilizing mission,' its duty to bring enlightenment and Catholicism to a region…firmly in the clutches of the Orthodox Church."

General Baratieri's great vision for the Italian colony he administered involved a societal overhaul. "There would be churches, schools, clinics, Italian language classes—an entire cultural infrastructure." He was patient and farsighted. For this reason and others, he leaned toward a retreat from the heavily fortified Adigrat, no longer relevant, back to Eritrea's Massawa port, closer to his supply lines and in a better position to defend if Menelik were to attack.

His generals disagreed. "When they see us they will scamper off," said General Matteo Albertone, the impetuous aristocrat, to one of his officers. Others referred to the Ethiopians as "effeminate." For Menelik's part, he was not interested in tangible proofs of masculinity. "Bring me the man, not the testicles," he commanded his soldiers, continuing Tewodros's prohibition of castrations. From his experience with the Mekele fort, he knew the value of a prisoner.[3]

Baratieri gathered his generals around a small table in his tent for a final strategy session the day before the battle. He had hoped to confirm his notions for a retreat. Instead they all lobbied for an attack, starting with Matteo Albertone, volatile and intemperate, the eldest at 56. The handsome Giuseppe Arimondi shared Albertone's concerns that the soldiers were tired of waiting around and not fighting. The military writer Vittorio Dabormida, who had not yet seen conflict, lifted his prized white-handled saber passionately and said that the soldiers would never understand a retreat and instead must attack. Baratieri laid his glasses on the table and told them he would consider their opinions.

Baratieri's delays disgusted the elegant Arimondi, who enjoyed a local mistress and needed no other outlet. Rather, he mocked Baratieri's unfruitful fortification of Adigrat as "the onanism of the military arts." (The biblical Onan "spilled his seed on the ground" rather than obediently impregnating his wife.)

In Rome, cooler heads did not prevail. That day Baratieri received a telegram from the prime minister, who said that the secretary of the treasury needed a quick victory or their efforts may break the bank. "We are ready for any sacrifice to save the honor of the army and the prestige of the monarchy," he wrote. The telegram helped tip the scales. That evening, Baratieri gave the order to his generals. They would descend the mountains and advance on the small plain of Adwa at midnight, March 1. His words were specific. It would be an advance, not an attack. Baratieri believed that the advantage would go to the prepared defenders, and he wanted Menelik to attack him instead. It was a game of chicken and the stakes were increasing, as the emperor had plans to evacuate the next day, March 2, for other places to forage. Menelik described his army as "starving," according to one account. Who would attack whom, if ever? There existed a small window for Menelik to entice Baratieri into his trap. Italian ambition assisted him.

GENERAL MATTEO ALBERTONE

The regal generals under Baratieri's command knew combat was the place to advance higher both in rank and in politics. Many historians suspect this motive was behind the arguments for an attack. Others wonder if subsequent events that led to an attack were part of a collusion. As for the soldiers, they were in high spirits. Rumors swirled that Menelik's generals would betray him. Estimates of the Ethiopian numbers were deflated. To keep spirits high, the soldiers received daily rations of wine, coffee, rum, and tobacco. "Come Abyssinians! We'll help you find the road to hell," said one of those soldiers enjoying the rations. Officers shared bottles of chianti: "Long live Italy! Long live the king!" Attitudes rarely were based on all the information. Just before the previous siege of Fort Mekele, Colonel Galliano, on the verge of surrender, wrote General Baratieri: "Morale is as high as can be."

General Albertone, the oldest, was selected to lead the advance with his 4,000 men, but Arimonde's and Dobormida's divisions were nearby to prevent the classic military mistake of dividing an army. Albertone's subordinate, Domenico Turitto, reached a strategic pass more quickly than expected. When Albertone caught up, he asked his subordinate why he had stopped. Turitto replied that he had reached his destination. Albertone looked at his map and declared Turitto was wrong. The destination was miles further.

In fact, the map was wrong. Albertone could have easily sent a courier to his superior, Baratieri, to clarify, as there was no hurry. Instead he rashly told Turitto: "Go ahead; I don't want any hesitation." He followed this order with a statement that would cause Turitto to throw caution to the wind: "You're not afraid, are you?"[4]

A few hours later, Turitto was leading half of Albertone's army down a winding mountain path under moonlight. It would have been much wiser to wait for daybreak so that he could see the myriad of Ethiopian tents in the valley just below him. But the general had questioned his courage. At 5:30 a.m. he stumbled into the enemy camp itself, and the Battle of Adwa began. Italy's army was divided.

Menelik's headquarters were located at Adwa's Abba Garima Monastery, home of the Garima Gospels. Reports confirm that the emperor and empress, along with the generals, were in church at 4 a.m. the morning of the attack. An anonymous Ethiopian soldier later gave an account of the emperor and his wife being "deep in prayer" when notified of the attack at 4:00 a.m. Piously, Menelik waited until the service was over to notify his troops to be ready for battle at 5:30 a.m.

The delay on Menelik's part is rightly questioned by historians, but there can be no doubt they were in prayer at 4 a.m. This was Sunday morning, and all Ethiopian Orthodox Christians, even today, begin Divine Liturgy services around 3 a.m., if not earlier, and worship through the night. Liturgy ends closer to 8 a.m., so Menelik certainly did not wait to finish communion once he was informed.

This Divine Liturgy service, taking place at the famous monastery, included clergy from the nearby city of Axum. In short order, the clergy and their arks (real or replicas) chose to follow the soldiers. Reports confirm that holy communion was served just behind the battle lines, suggesting that the interrupted worship service continued on the field. Priests appeared, blessing the assembled troops and hearing confessions. Menelik, Taytu, and their generals also received the bread and wine of communion on the field. The flag was raised toward the icon of Christ.[5]

Empress Taytu stood on the field and "acted like a warrior," encouraging her 5,000 soldiers. "Don't give an inch," she cried. The Italians had less than 20,000 men against Menelik's more than 100,000. The Italians were outnumbered, but the time to demonstrate technological superiority was at hand. Ethiopian artillery had been featured against the fort at Mekele, but was useless against its walls. However, these same quick-firing French-made 57 mm Hotchkiss batteries proved highly effective in the open field and fired even further than the Italian guns.

The Ethiopian infantry conducted a frontal assault. The Italian artillery was able to repel them, but not with the kind of carnage that a fortified position like Adigrat would have availed. A second and then a third wave of Ethiopian soldiers attacked. The mathematics were unassailable, as Menelik knew. Like the Union army against the Confederates, overwhelming numbers would surely win the day. Ethiopia had numbers. One Italian officer counted one hundred multi-colored Ethiopian flags while hearing beating war drums throughout the valley.

Colonel Giuseppe Galliano, the captured commander of Fort Mekele, was back with the Italian army and guarding Albertone's vulnerable right flank. He was impressed by the effectiveness of the Ethiopian artillerymen. After firing a long shot, an adjustment was made, and then the next short volley was finally corrected to fire just right. Their precision caused Galliano to insist that they were not operated by Ethiopians. "It's impossible that they are not Europeans," he concluded. Menelik's patience after years of weapons acquisition and training was finally paying off.

Ethiopian infantrymen were also at no disadvantage. While Emperor Yohannes attacked the Italians with ancient muzzle-loaders, Menelik had equipped his entire army with modern rifles. Popular sources highlight "spear carrying" Ethiopians at Adwa, but if any of his soldiers were in fact without guns, they were put in reserve. While romantic, the spear image reduces the real truth of Adwa, that an African army was using both wits and muscle. However, the Ethiopians did fight with bare feet.[6]

The mass of Africans began to swarm every side of the divided Italians. Not only was Albertone divided from half of his own army in front of him, led by Turitto, but no general behind him could reinforce Albertone's rear, since the Ethiopians had wedged between them. Albertone identified a very effective and strategic spot between two small mountains that he felt was impossible for either army to climb, but soon he saw barefoot Ethiopians scaling both hills.

The Ethiopian "Oromo Cavalry" entered the fray with their fearsome lion's mane headdresses. They collected scrotums on their saddles and word reached the Italian soldiers that Menelik's order to "bring me the man, not the testicles," was only being lightly followed. Reputedly, the cavalry only castrated those soldiers who kept firing their weapons, so a number of accounts describe soldiers tossing their rifles "like madmen" before they were captured. A Lieutenant Pastore shot himself with his revolver to avoid such disgrace. Another man jumped off a cliff, a cigarette still in his mouth. Albertone's division was destroyed. Colonel Giuseppe Galliano, having just returned from Fort Mekele, was killed attempting to protect the impulsive general's flank. Albertone himself was taken prisoner.

Baratieri had three more divisions. The closest army to the current crisis was led by the handsome General Arimondi. As the Ethiopian soldiers approached, one of his men shouted: "They won't get away today!" He turned around to find his general sitting on the ground with his head in his hands. Arimondi was killed shortly after.

"It was no longer a fight but a slaughterhouse," wrote a surviving officer. The initial attacking battalion under Turitto was completely destroyed by 8:15 a.m. Arimondi was dead. Albertone was captured.

The published tactical expert General Dabormida, experiencing his first taste of combat, was left alone for a time. After a lull, some of his soldiers believed that the battle was over and they had won. They ran about firing guns and shouting, "Viva l'Italia! Victory!" But soon they too were flanked and overwhelmed by the enemy. The book-smart general was killed and stripped naked. His white-handled saber was taken to Menelik as a war prize.

Instead of the Ethiopian generals turning on each other, it was the Italians who failed to follow instructions. Albertone was ordered to advance, not attack. His colleagues were instructed to allow no gap in the army as Albertone moved forward. Neither order was followed. In fact, some question whether the three generals colluded against their overly cautious supreme commander and agreed to confront the enemy that day rather than allow for more delay. One man who was later a prisoner with Albertone, Lieutenant Gherardo Pantano, claimed that the general said to him, "You are young and have a better chance of returning to Italy. Remember well what your general is telling you. Tell them that General Baratieri was betrayed by his officers."[7]

Italy lost seventy percent of its approximately 18,000 man army to casualties (dead, wounded, prisoners). Over 6,000 were killed, one-third of Baratieri's army. Though the death count was similar for Ethiopia, it amounted to less than one-tenth of its army. Out of 610 Italian officers, 352 were killed.

Effectively, the battle was won by 9:30 a.m. Baratieri survived but was forced to retreat. His papers and correspondence fluttered across the valley as he struggled to navigate the small rocky path. Adding to his humiliation, his glasses were destroyed in the chaos and he was reduced to being guided by an assistant.

"Horrendous and Colossal Slaughter" proclaimed the headlines when the news hit Rome. Ethiopian soldiers spent the rest of the day stripping the dead of all their clothes, possessions, coins, rations, and anything of value. (Ethiopian soldiers received no pay, so this was standard compensation.) That night the campfires abounded with songs, drums, and celebrations.[8]

A glorious procession took place on March 3. Priests with their tabots were followed by musicians. The parade included the generals and Empress Taytu. Then Emperor Menelik II was cheered as "the man who engineered modern Africa's greatest military triumph," according to Adwa historian Raymond Jonas, "and one of the greatest military victories of all time."

Menelik and Taytu catapulted to celebrity status in Europe and the United States. Sons were named Menelik. Both were pictured on the front of major newspapers, and Menelik was featured on the cover of *Vanity Fair*, the day's *Time* magazine. He shared this honor with Charles Darwin, the Czar of Russia, and other notables. "Africa's Christian Monarch," he was heralded.

Menelik and his military secured Ethiopian independence for more than a generation. "They also gave a stunning lesson to would-be conquerors," wrote Jonas. "Ethiopia's victory established its status as one of the great African nations [and] announced the end of an era in which foreign powers could colonize African territory at will." Or, as Italian survivor Captain Mario Bassi put it, Adwa was "the beginning of the end of the colonial farce."[9]

African Americans were also triumphant. W. E. B. Du Bois called for a new African state, which would include "Negroes," and proposed the name "Ethiopian Utopia." His fellow activist, J. A. Rogers, said Adwa "amazed Europe and heartened Black men everywhere."[10]

"The battle of Adwa was the battle for Africa," concluded Jonas. "Over the next hundred years, European domination would gradually unravel. The history of African sovereignty in the modern world started at Adwa."

Menelik was triumphant, but he also gave shrewd consideration to the wild rejoicing by some, and not others, across the West. Like his isolated mourning after the Dogali massacre and its reverberations back in Europe, the emperor feared blowback. The screaming headlines by Italian newspapers of disaster and carnage inspired not only compassion but also revenge. The *Chicago Tribune* reported that Italy would widen the draft and double its efforts for conquest. Vengeance was a visceral theme.

In fact, Menelik's top general, Ras Alula, architect of the Dogali massacre, requested permission for a cavalry attack as victory unfolded at Adwa. Menelik denied approval. This decision prevented the deaths of several thousand more Italians and likely a near annihilation of the entire army. Historians in hindsight wonder if the emperor was avoiding another Alula-led Dogali massacre. Similarly, Menelik was criticized for not continuing his attack all the way to the coast of Eritrea, which Italy continued to occupy. Today Menelik's choice to head home victorious from Adwa is lauded by most historians as far-sighted.

He had a plan. The Ethiopians took 1,900 prisoners, a massive number in proportion to the Italian army and an indisputable public relations nightmare for Rome. Menelik was embarking on the return trip of the longest major military march in modern history, and he needed his rear protected. Like with Galliano and the Mekele prisoners,

Ethiopia's new prisoners would serve that purpose. More importantly, when he reached Addis Ababa, the emperor would have the great bargaining chip he needed to sign a lasting peace treaty with Italy and Europe.

After divvying up the prisoners to various generals and leaders as the armies headed in various directions, Menelik's main army kept 800 Italian captives. The rest he charged to be treated correctly: "Bring them back to me alive!" he ordered. In fact, the treatment of the prisoners would be important. Too cruel a hand and the propaganda wars in Europe would be lost and perhaps the thirst for vengeance rekindled—enough to ruin the gains at Adwa.

Fifty prisoners died on the ten-week trip that distanced 600 miles along a winding path, from the same causes as many Ethiopians died: hunger, exposure, wounds. Not every overseer was as level-headed as Menelik, as this long march was one of the first times that Africans had the position to rule over white colonialists. In some cases, at watering holes, the Ethiopians drank first, then the animals, then the Italians. Stragglers were beaten, and the troublemakers were hit in the crotch area.

People in villages came out in droves to see the first white men they had ever encountered. Some called them "Turks," and many held cloths up to their noses to block the odor. According to many Italian accounts, the Ethiopians believed white people gave off a distinct and disagreeable odor.[11]

One Italian officer gave his shirt for a chicken, though to the Ethiopians' credit, both groups received the same rations: a few chickpeas and barley each day. Some desperate prisoners found a dead mule and ate the entire thing, including the intestines. At night, the mostly unclothed men slept next to each other "like sardines" in the bitter cold with no tents or blankets. They switched sides every few minutes in unison to make it through the night.

While these circumstances were awful, they were understandable, and not too different from what the Ethiopians themselves were suffering. The bigger problem for Menelik and public perception was the castrations. Of the 1,900 prisoners taken, approximately seven percent were known to have been emasculated. A far greater percentage of those soldiers left dead on the field had been castrated to acquire war trophies.

Giovanni Tedone, a captive, provides details on these ugly events on the day of the battle. He approached a wounded, stripped, and naked colleague who called out to him, and in a gesture of modesty "covered his genitals with his hand to conceal the wound created by his emasculation, which...had taken the scrotum but not the penis." It left only a yellowish patch, and little blood was involved, he said. "Two lateral cuts, and then a cut from the bottom up, and that's it."[12]

Another soldier tells of walking past a pile of bodies and hearing a cry for water. He saw "one of ours" in the pile who was dying and "horrible to say it, emasculated." One pile of forty dead Italians was buried, and the report said twenty of them had been castrated. The Oromo Cavalry decorated their horse's necks with daisy-chained scrotums. Italian prisoners saw scrotums on lances and shields. Tedone's host, when he made it back to Addis Ababa, told him: "At Adwa, I killed eight Italians, and I castrated them." He then revealed a necklace under his shirt with the evidence.

Jonas spends a page explaining that castration is not completely foreign to Europe. Parliament castrated the perpetrators of the Gunpowder Plot in 1605 in England, and a Protestant leader was castrated during the St. Bartholomew massacres in France. He adds that most lynchings in Jim Crow America involved castration.

For many Ethiopian soldiers, the motive for castration was collecting trophies. Others did it for more symbolic reasons. "The Abyssinians explain themselves," wrote a Dutch observer on the march, "by saying that this is how they bring a halt to the enemy's capacity to reproduce."

"In spite of all the laws and edicts," he added, "Menelik can do nothing to abolish this ignoble practice."

On the positive side, good relations were beginning to develop between captor and captive. When they arrived in Addis Ababa, each prisoner was assigned to a host family. Unable as a practical matter to survive outside the city, they were allowed to roam free. Prisoners later wrote of the "abiding memories of kindness" they received from their hosts.[13]

One prisoner was unable to buy a journal of a fallen comrade for sale at a flea market. His host, Ato Gabriel, bought it for him. Prisoner Franciso Frisina sent back to his host soap, canned fruit, cigars, and liquor. He said that he couldn't do enough for the man who was "like a father," and he "promised that he would never be erased from his heart." Many Ethiopians became close friends with Italians. Others became lovers.

"It was a racial turning of the tables that put whites at the mercy of blacks in significant numbers for the first time, opening the door to retaliation and cruel revenge that never came," writes Jonas. These friendships and love stories at the end of the journey apparently overcame whatever damage the initial cruel treatment had engendered. At the diplomatic level, Menelik was able to make a formal treaty with Italy, which included a return of all the prisoners, including General Matteo Albertone. The Treaty of Addis Ababa, signed on October 23, 1896, stated that the former Treaty of Wichala "is and will remain definitely annulled." Italy recognized "absolutely and without reserve the independence of the Ethiopian empire."

Once again, Ethiopia had preserved her reputation as a country never conquered. As one established author wrote: "Ethiopia is considered the longest-lived independent Christian nation in world history."[14]

Eight weeks after Adwa, a team of priests, unarmed soldiers, and relatives of General Arimondi returned to the battlefield to bury their dead. Most bodies were unidentifiable, as they had been stripped naked and some burned. Others had been ravaged by vultures and hyenas. Of the dead, 2,000 soldiers were in a decent enough condition for burial, including the body of General Dabormida. General Arimondi's body was never found. Before they left, the group erected a monument and offered a mass.

Forty years later, Italy placed another monument at the Adwa battlefield, a bust of fascist dictator Benito Mussolini, recent invader of Eritrea and Tigray, who was leading the largest fighting force ever assembled on the African continent. Soon to become Hitler's top ally,

Mussolini brought to Ethiopia 476,000 men, 500 tanks, 350 aircraft, 1,500 artillery pieces, and 15,000 machine guns. The year was 1935, and Italy had not forgotten.

"For the lack of a few thousand men, we lost the day at Adwa," Mussolini said as he prepared to conquer Addis Ababa. "*We* shall never make that mistake."[15]

CHAPTER SEVEN

IN THE ELEVENTH chapter of the book of Revelation, after a thousand years of disappearance from Scripture, the Ark of the Covenant reappears with much grandeur. "Then God's temple in heaven was opened, and within his temple was seen the ark of his covenant. And there came flashes of lightning, rumblings, peals of thunder, an earthquake and a severe hailstorm."

What is happening in these verses? How would Ethiopians interpret this passage? Does it refer to the Ark claimed to be in their country? Why is the Ark in Ethiopia hidden? Why can no one see it? Many may think the reason relates to the question of the proof of its existence, and that is why it is not kept in a museum for viewing. But there may be other reasons.

"The Ark is only a relic," I was told by a top theologian of the Ethiopian Church.

"It's just a relic," a theology student told me. "Christ is worshipped."[1]

In fact, for those with eyes to see, the Ark is everywhere in Ethiopia. This is the case because they believe the true Ark, the fulfillment of everything the Ark stands for, is Mary, the mother of Christ.

The verse in Revelation 11 that mentions the Ark for the first time in the New Testament is followed by this verse: "A great sign appeared in heaven: a woman clothed with the sun, with the moon under her feet and a crown of twelve stars on her head. She was pregnant and cried out in pain as she was about to give birth." Ethiopians believe this is Mary, the fulfillment of the Ark, the greater sign that the Ark foreshadowed.

Many Church Fathers agree. Athanasius the Great, Christianity's leading defender of the Trinity controversy in the fourth century, wrote: "O noble Virgin, truly you are greater than any other greatness. . . . You are the ark in which is found the golden vessel containing the true manna, that is, the flesh in which divinity resides."[2]

Everywhere you look in Ethiopia, you see an icon of Christ or Mary, often both of them. She is in every house, in every church, on buses, on taxis, and around people's necks. Of the approximately 25,000 churches in the country, 15,000 of them are named after the Virgin Mary.

Is this a Catholic influence? Besides the Italians, the Catholics were driven out in the 1500s amid Portuguese attempts to evangelize Orthodox Ethiopia. Devotion to Mary existed long before they arrived. I was told by theology professor Girma Batu that "when the Jesuit missionaries came to Ethiopia in the sixteenth century, one of their missionary leaders by the name of Pedre Paez said 'these people have a special place in their minds for the holy Virgin Mary. So, in order to proselytize them, we need to preach the gospel under the umbrella of the holy Virgin Mary. If you do that, they will be convinced easily. Otherwise, it's difficult.'"

The professor continued: "In relation to the presence of the Ark of the Covenant in Ethiopia, there is a special inclination toward the holy Virgin Mary in Ethiopia. If you want to compare it with the theology of the Orthodox people in Africa—even with neighboring country Egypt, the sister Coptic Orthodox Church—somehow it is different. The holy Virgin Mary has a special place in the heart of the Ethiopian Orthodox Church."

Is there any biblical evidence for the view that Mary is the true Ark, the living Ark? There is the obvious, which the theologians point out. The Ark contained the stone tablets of the Word. Mary contained within her womb the Word of God himself. The contents inside the Ark provide more foreshadowing: "The manna which is in the pot is to be interpreted as the Body of Christ," says the Kebra Negast. "The pot of gold [containing the manna] is to be interpreted as Mary. And the rod which without water burst into bloom indicates Mary, from whom was born, without the seed of man, the Word of God."

Others point to the word *overshadowed* used by the archangel Gabriel to describe what would happen to Mary in order to conceive God the Messiah: "The Holy Spirit will come on you, and the power of the most high will overshadow you" (Luke 1:35). In the New International Version, this word is only used elsewhere to refer to the cherubim "overshadowing" the Ark of the Covenant.

"Luke wove some marvelous things into his Gospel that only a knowledgeable Jew would have understood," writes author and documentarian Steve Ray. "When the ark was completed, the glory cloud of the Lord (the Shekinah Glory) covered the tent of meeting, and the glory of the Lord filled the tabernacle (Ex. 40:34–35; Num. 9:18, 22). The verb for 'to cover' or 'to overshadow' and the metaphor of a cloud are used in the Bible to represent the presence and glory of God....It's easy to miss the parallel between the Holy Spirit overshadowing the ark and the Holy Spirit overshadowing Mary."[3]

While many Protestants today struggle with a deep appreciation for Mary, this suspicion was foreign to the first 1,500 years of Christianity and also not a problem for the leaders of the Reformation. Protestant founder Ulrich Zwingli believed Mary "forever remained a pure, intact Virgin." John Wesley concurred: "The Blessed Virgin Mary...continued a pure and unspotted virgin." John Calvin refused to denounce the ever-virgin doctrine. In his last sermon, Martin Luther asked: "Is Christ only to be adored? Or is the holy Mother of God rather not to be honored?"[4*]

Several times in each Orthodox Church service occurs this exclamation about Mary: "More honorable than the cherubim, and more glorious beyond compare than the seraphim, without corruption thou gavest birth to God the Word." Daily prayers repeat the phrase: "Holy, holy, holy" (invoking the throne room), followed by "through the Theotokos (the mother of God) have mercy on us." These words clearly point to an Ark fulfillment. For this reason, many traditional churches depict a large and central icon of Mary above and behind the Ark/altar table, placing Christ, who is in her womb, precisely in the spot above the Ark where the wings of the cherubim provide a throne seat.

THE QUEEN OF SHEBA (ARTIST'S DEPICTION)

The previously "unknowable" God, for both men and angels, has now become known to men, more so than angels, through his incarnation. This knowledge is intimately entwined with the flesh and blood, the bodily fluids, the sacred body parts, and tender nursing of Mary. The intimacies of birth and motherhood far exceed the only intimacies that most in the reductionist West today are capable of appreciating.[5*] This physical enmeshment with God himself now causes the astonished angels to stand back in amazement at the heights to which mankind has ascended. While they eternally cover their eyes shouting "holy, holy, holy," Mary embraces God himself.

In this context, it is plain to see why the Kebra Negast refers to the Ark almost exclusively as "Lady Zion." The Ethiopian text refers to "the King of Ethiopia and Zion, the Bride of heaven, and her chariot whereby they move. [They] shall continue in the Orthodox faith until the coming of our Lord." This "Bride of heaven" terminology is a natural theme for Ethiopians. They believe they have provided a Bride for God and his representative since Sheba came to Solomon in 1000 BC and, 500 years earlier, when Moses married an Ethiopian. We are told in the Old Testament: "Then Miriam and Aaron spoke against Moses because of the Ethiopian woman whom he had married; for he had married an Ethiopian woman. So they said, 'Has the Lord indeed spoken only through Moses? Has He not spoken through us also?'" (Num. 12:1, NKJV).

The Lord responds by striking Moses's sister Miriam for a short time with leprosy (an ironic case of the skin becoming deathly white). God then states that Moses did indeed hear clearly from the Lord regarding his marriage: "I speak with him face to face, even plainly, and not in dark sayings, and he sees the form of the Lord. Why then were you not afraid to speak against my servant Moses?" (Num. 12:8, NKJV).

Josephus, the authoritative first-century Jewish historian, provides information on Moses's first 40 years in Egypt not recorded in Scripture, giving details on Moses's first marriage before marrying Zipporah, Jethro's daughter (recorded in Exodus 2): "Tharbis was the daughter of the king of the Ethiopians: she happened to see Moses as he led the army near the walls, and fought with great courage....she fell deeply in love with him; and upon the prevalence of that passion, sent to him the most faithful of all her servants to discourse with him about their marriage. He thereupon accepted the offer, on condition she would procure the delivering up of the city.... and when Moses had cut off the Ethiopians, he gave thanks to God, and consummated his marriage, and led the Egyptians back to their own land."[6*]

Second-century Church Father St. Irenaeus confirms the Ethiopian view that Moses's bride serves as a larger symbol for all God's people: "By means of the marriage of Moses was shown forth the marriage of the Word. And by means of the Ethiopian bride, the Church taken from among the Gentiles was made manifest." The most reliable of all early church historians, Eusebius, hints at this relationship between Ethiopia and all gentile Christians when he declares Ethiopia the "first-fruits" of all believers. Bacos, the Ethiopian eunuch from Acts 8 "received of the mysteries of the divine word from Philip in consequence of a revelation, and having become the first-fruits of believers throughout the world, he is said to have been the first on returning to his country to proclaim the knowledge of the God of the universe and the life-giving sojourn of our Savior among men; so that through him in truth the prophecy obtained its fulfillment, which declares that 'Ethiopia stretches out her hand unto God.'"

Early church theologian Origen, a major scholar, quotes the bride in Song of Solomon 1:5 as saying "I am black and beautiful" and urges Christians to dig for the "mystical exposition."

"This Bride who speaks represents the Church gathered from among the gentiles," says Origen, who then puts his own words in the mouth of the black bride of the Song of Solomon: "I am surprised, O daughters of Jerusalem, that you would want to reproach me with blackness of my hue. How have you come to forget what is written in your law, as to what Miriam suffered when she spoke against Moses because he had taken a black Ethiopian to wife? How is it that you do not recognize the true fulfillment of that type in me? I am that Ethiopian.

"I have received the Word made flesh; I have come to him who is the image of God, the firstborn of every creature and who is the brightness of the glory and the express image of the substance of God, and I have been made fair."

Origen then moves to another analogy of the Bride and the Church—the Queen of Sheba, whom he says is also Ethiopian and "black and beautiful." He quotes from 1 Kings 10: "... and she spoke to him all that was in her heart" and relates Solomon to Christ, who "answered all her questions and there was no question that the king left out and did not so answer" (1 Kings 10:2–3). Origen says the Queen of Sheba "came not as a single nation, as did the synagogue before her that had the Hebrews only, but the races of the whole world...the Church that is gathered from among the Gentiles."[7]

A nice summary of the bride theme in Scripture is provided by Presbyterian theologian James Jordan, who, in his exposition on the book of Revelation, explains what is behind the book's finale of a marriage feast. "Three is the number of God. Four is the number of Creation: Father, Son, Spirit, and Daughter," says Jordan. "Those are the four elements that operate in the creation: God the Father, God the only begotten Son, and God the Spirit exist in eternity—and God decides to create an only-created daughter. That's what humanity is:

daughter Zion/daughter Jerusalem. And she is supposed to grow up and marry the son. So there is such a thing as history, and we are in the middle of that.... The bride is supposed to be getting herself ready, growing up."

"What's the plan? The plan is to create a bride for the son," says Jordan. "God creates a daughter, and the daughter is supposed to grow up to be a wife for the son. That's what history is. You want to know what the world is all about? That's it, right there."[8]

PART TWO

Mussolini, Hitler, and Haile Selassie

Questions Undermining the Ethiopian Ark

CHAPTER EIGHT

WHEN WORD OF Menelik's victory at Adwa hit the news in
Italy in 1896, Benito Mussolini was thirteen years old and at school.
"It was a blow to his impressionable mind," writes World War II historian Barrie Pitt. The 10,000 dead "were still hammering around in
his head," and he believed that the Ethiopians had "perpetrated the
most barbaric atrocities on Italian prisoners." In 1935, the fascist dictator used Adwa as the rallying cry for his return invasion of Ethiopia
and the opening salvo for his new Roman Empire. "The great account
opened in 1896," cried Mussolini, and must "be settled at all costs."[1]

Facing Mussolini's giant army from Addis Ababa and the south was
Ethiopian Emperor Haile Selassie, also known as Ras Tafari, his given
name at birth. He was age three when his father, General Makonnen
Wolde Mikael, served as the right-hand man to Emperor Menelik II at
the battles of Mekele and Adwa. As governor of the eastern coffee trading
city of Harar, Makonnen replaced the largest mosque there and built the
first Christian church, according to Menelik's instructions. Makonnen
placed his son under the teaching of a Christian monk, so Tafari was
raised in the faith of Christ.

Makonnen and his young son Tafari were both in the line of Solomon and candidates to be Ethiopia's future emperor. However, Tafari's
father died early. Menelik, instead of choosing Tafari or several other
qualified kings and princes in the country, appointed as the heir apparent
his grandson, Iyasu. Menelik demanded an oath from those watching
the ceremony for the new crown prince: "May those who break this oath
of loyalty give birth to black dogs."[2]

Being named crown prince did not guarantee that Iyasu would become emperor. Tafari was an underrated competitor. Both princes were teenagers when Emperor Menelik II died in 1913. Biographer Asfa-Wossen Asserate, who is kinder to Iyasu than many historians, describes the great contrast. "Tafari [Haile Selassie], who was naturally slight, was a quiet and reserved boy with a studious and disciplined character. Lij Iyasu was the precise opposite: tall and athletic, he was mad about sport and had an aggressive disposition. He shunned reading, preferring to spend his time in bars and brothels." The two cousins did not get along well. Adding to their morals and lifestyles as dividers, the crown prince was also rumored to be courting Muslim leaders to gain support for his future empire.[3]

TAFARI MAKONNEN (EMPEROR HAILE SELASSIE I)

At this time, Iyasu was several inches taller than Tafari Makonnen, and the 5'2" son of Makonnen never got any taller than a "stunted teenager," explains Michela, the Eritrean historian. "With his predilection for sweeping military capes and oversized pith helmets, the effect could be downright comic—from a distance, it looked as though a willful child had been let loose on his father's wardrobe."[4] On the other hand, she mentions his "wizened features" and quotes another biographer who describes his "inner eminence." A later rival warned: "Do not underestimate the power of Tafari. He creeps like a mouse but has jaws like a lion."[5]

Iyasu was losing admiration from the aristocracy for a number of reasons, not least that he was sleeping with some of their wives, daring the husbands to respond. He also displayed petty arrogance. For example, he once ordered his minster of defense, Habte Giorgis, to dismount in his presence. "How dare you address me while you are still on horseback?" he demanded. But as soon as the minister got down from his horse, the crown prince told him, "now you may get back in the saddle."

Tafari, in contrast, had a lighter touch when he later reached the status of crown prince. "Ras Tafari entered the room, dressed in his official robes and with a prince's crown on his head," writes an observer at a cabinet meeting. "He walked up to the war minister and kissed his feet. To try and provoke Ras Tafari I asked: 'Do you really think these narrow shoulders of yours will be strong enough to support such a great land as Ethiopia?' Ras Tafari just smiled benignly and replied, 'I'll find everything easy with masters like you to guide me.'"[6]

When Iyasu remained in Muslim territory during Easter, the Christian priests were scandalized. He had been seen wearing a turban and holding Muslim prayer beads. Then word came that he had built a mosque in the Wollo region, prayed there, and prostrated himself toward Mecca. Menelik's daughter, Zauditu, the crown prince's aunt, reached out to have the future emperor placed under her personal custody and "be brought back to Christ and salvation" under her guidance.

Some historians believe that Iyasu, as officially crowned emperor, would have united the entire Horn of Africa under Islamic law. Alarmed, the leaders of the church and Christian state convened to bring formal charges:

> Lij Iyasu...followed Islamic practice in taking four wives, all of whom came from Muslim homes.

> Rather than trace his ancestry back to the genealogy of Menelik I, he claimed instead to be a descendant in the 40th generation of the Prophet Muhammed.

> He...used government funds to build a mosque.

> Rather than attending the funeral of Menelik II, he played polo instead.

The council of church and state officials was chaired by the same minister of defense whom Iyasu had humiliated by demanding he dismount and remount his horse. The leaders determined that the crown prince had converted to the Muslim faith. As such, he was excommunicated from the Ethiopian Orthodox Church and deposed. His aunt Zauditu was named empress on a temporary basis, as the Ethiopian tradition prefers male rulers. Ras Tafari was named crown prince and the new heir apparent.

Zauditu remained empress for over a decade, but Ras Tafari, as regent, in many ways ran the government. He took the opportunity during this unstable power struggle to strengthen his position to ultimately become emperor, which was still no certainty. In fact, biographer Asfa-Wossen suggests the aristocrats wanted Tafari as a token leader because he was a "political lightweight" who kissed the feet of the nobility: "…it would appear that the princes were after a weak regent without strong dynastic ties, whose strings they could pull. And Tafari Makonnen appeared to fit this bill admirably."[7]

But they misjudged the true stature of the prince. "Ras Tafari had read his Machiavelli," writes Asfa-Wossen. "Over the following 12 years he would gradually manage to eliminate all his opponents." He was "wily" according to biographer Harold Marcus. "So wily was Tafari that no one remarked on his wiliness."[8]

"[Ras Tafari] was endowed with radiant charisma," writes Tafari's longtime legal advisor, John Spencer. "Diminutive, speaking in a low, grating voice, with great economy of gesture, he effortlessly commanded the rapt attention of all who came into his presence. Indeed, his reserved, almost unassuming demeanor seemed to act as a foil to set off his aura of authority."[9]

In 1930, Empress Zauditu fell ill and died of a typhoid-like fever. Barely twenty-four hours later, Tafari made the following statement to the people of Ethiopia: "Proclamation…His Majesty King Tafari Makonnen, on his ascent to the imperial throne under the name of His Majesty Haile Selassie the First, King of Kings of Ethiopia…and so from the Throne of David, to which I am now called, I will watch over you with the help of God's grace."

He was thirty-seven years old. His new name meant "Power of the Trinity." His full name was actually "By the Conquering Lion of the

Tribe of Judah, His Imperial Majesty Haile Selassie I, King of Kings of Ethiopia, Elect of God."[10]

Some, even today, complain that "Lion of Judah" was a name reserved only for Christ. The criticism accompanies many other concerns during his rule, where the modernizing vision of the new emperor clashed with the nation's conservative traditions. And yet his insistence on monarchy over democracy never wavered. Neither did his commitment to the ancient Christian faith of Ethiopia.

Conservatively, Haile Selassie also fought for the term "Elect of God" for his constitutional name, believing he truly was chosen by God for the task. The Constitution also specified that, in the Solomonic Dynasty, Haile Selassie was the 225th successor of Menelik I to ascend the Ethiopian throne. Liberally, he initiated the Constitution himself, a device often rejected by autocrats, and a concept Zauditu refused to implement. A fan of technology, he immediately oversaw improvements in the electric and telegraph systems, cars and road-building, schools, hospitals, and the creation of a central bank independent of Egypt. Even more significantly, he began the process of removing the Ethiopian Church from the oversight of Coptic Egypt's Alexandrian patriarch, calling for Ethiopia's own patriarch, and establishing an autonomous Orthodox church after 1,500 years of dependency.[11]*

At his coronation ceremony, however, Western reporters noted the backwardness. "It is absurd to pretend that Ethiopia is a civilized nation in any Western sense of the word," wrote the *New York Times*, noting that a major commercial center, Harar, "can only be reached by a two-days' mule ride up the circuitous mountain caravan route."[12]

King George V of England revealed that he held the same notion of "the uncivilized Abyssinian" when he greeted Hailu Tekle Haimanot, the Ethiopian representative in London, years before at George's coronation with Queen Mary. The British reports in the file dubbed Ras Hailu as "uneducated." The new king asked Hailu questions through an interpreter:

"Can you speak English?"

"No."

"French?"

"No."

"Arabic?"

"No."

"Well, what *do* you speak?" he asked with some indignation.

"Can you speak Amharic? Gallinga? Gurage?" Hailu asked the king.

"No."

"I am glad to see that we are both equally ignorant."[13]

. In a later diplomatic visit to London via Cairo, the Ethiopian delegation's shoes were the main focus of the newspapers. A *New York Times* headline said, "Ethiopian Royalties Don Shoes in Cairo." While correctly remembering that most Ethiopian soldiers still went barefoot, the reporters assumed this was the first time Ethiopian dignitaries had ever put shoes on their feet.

Great Britain was among the many nations represented at Haile Selassie's coronation in 1930, along with Italy, Japan, Belgium, Sweden, The Netherlands, Egypt, France, the United States, Germany, Turkey, and Greece. The act of anointing was the central element in the ritual. "Just as Zadok the priest anointed King David and Nathan anointed Solomon, so I anoint you with sacred myrrh," the ranking church official proclaimed as he applied the oil. He charged the emperor to faithfully obey "the teaching of the Gospels." Tafari and his wife, Menen Asfaw, the empress, received communion as the new royal couple.[14]

Soon, Haile Selassie would be named *Time* magazine's Man of the Year. He had reached his great goal as King of Kings—"Negusa Negast" in Ethiopia's Amharic language. However, that pinnacle also meant becoming the victim of untold cruelty by one of history's most ruthless dictators and being a central character in the greatest war the world has ever seen.

In 1911, during the time Haile Selassie was about to receive the news of Emperor Menelik's death, Benito Mussolini was revealing his secrets in a journal he wrote from prison.

The young Italian who decried the country's disgrace at Adwa received a five-month sentence for sedition. As a radical socialist and newspaper editor, he had called for the end of the current government and opposed military involvement on the eve of the First World War. "The national flag is for us a rag to be planted in a dunghill," he declared. He also condemned Italy's war against Turkey for control of Libya. In a speech, he called on the Italian people to declare a general strike, block the streets, and stop the trains.[15]

In another speech he was just as adamant: "May the masses cry out with one voice and may their cry resound through the streets and squares of Italy: 'Down with war!' The day has come for the Italian proletariat to obey its vow of old—we won't send a single soldier, we won't give a single penny—whatever it takes!"[16]

Raised by a socialist blacksmith who read Karl Marx's *Das Kapital* to him at night, Mussolini embraced with ease the socialist and free love movement that swept the liberal elite at the turn of the century. Across the Atlantic, feminist and birth control advocate Margaret Sanger, one of the many high-profile free love radicals of the time, boasted of a new religion emerging with no definite name. She said that they were "agnostics, freethinkers, or atheists" and "as fanatical in their faith in the coming revolution as ever any primitive Christian was for the immediate establishment of the Kingdom of God."[17]

Mussolini emerged from prison a socialist star and was feted at a banquet. A man there proclaimed him "The Leader"—the *Duce* in Italian (pronounced "doo-chay")—and the nickname stuck. The socialist press described his style as "fascinating and compelling...his voice like a forest murmur, his gestures like someone haunted by a nightmare." A Socialist Party leader sang his praises: "The party has the good fortune to be led by a man who is upright and honest...

BENITO MUSSOLINI

105

he has incomparable moral force, driven, like all such moral forces, by ruthless logic."

But what kind of morality? With Mussolini, the people generally chose to see only what they wanted to see. The Duce was expelled from his village school for three different knifing incidents. He stabbed a fellow student in the hand who "started to scream, at first with the pain and then at the sight of blood squirting everywhere." The second student he stabbed in the buttocks. The third victim was a woman, but no details are known of the incident.[18]

He provides details of an early sexual encounter while still in school with a girl named Virginia, recorded in his journal from prison. "One fine day, when everyone else in Varano had gone to San Cassiano to listen to some pompous sermon from a friar, I led her up some stairs, pushed her into a corner behind a door and had her on the spot. When she got up she was distressed and crying and started to insult me.... Our affair lasted three months—let's just say it was more a meeting of bodies than of souls."

He also shares that his first sexual experience was, in fact, at a brothel. This tryst and his encounter with Virginia add credence to the reports that the sexually charged Duce was not a classic ladies' man but "shabby, dirty, touchy, and morose," according to an ex-lover from his free love circles. Most of his early sexual activity was spawned at social- ist dances, where it was acceptable within that crowd to find partners, married or otherwise. One such partner, Giulietta, was beautiful and married with a child. "Our relationship lasted for a few weeks until we were found out. Her husband heard about it and ordered his wife to be driven away from the house. She took her little boy with her and joined me in the room where we'd first come together." Another of his married partners had five children.

Mussolini had taken one of his first jobs out of school as a teacher in a small town. His debut as a socialist speaker occurred when he agreed to debate a Christian spokesman in the town. Five hundred people packed the hall. "When the chairman of the discussion asked him to speak, Mussolini got to his feet, asked someone to lend him a watch, and then issued an ultimatum: if, at the end of five minutes, he had not been struck down by the hand of God, this was a proof the deity didn't exist." Seeing that he was addressing citizens living in the center of worldwide Roman Catholicism, some criticism might be expected. Instead, he was warmly applauded.[19]

His teaching stint was not successful. "Parents of the young girls he had seduced stepped in, with brisk determination; they would carry their daughter back home, putting a firm stop to any hopes of marriage with an unruly and notorious young man." His sister, Edvige, however, believed her brother was ready to marry these girls. She said he seemed to want it so convincingly. Mussolini had written an article for an anti-clerical publication, *The Whip*, where he used the pen name "A True Heretic." Parents and church authorities lobbied to have him removed from his position.[20]

Soon, he met his future wife, Rachele, a young blonde, from a town in northern Italy. "She was blooming, buxom, with nice breasts, attractive. I followed her around, paid court to her, she pleased me. One day I got her down on the armchair and, in my usual way, roughly took her virginity."

This time he was ready to marry. "I'm fond of her because she lets me do whatever I want to do," Mussolini wrote. He continued to go to socialist dances and practice free love, but he forbade Rachelle from attending them. As "good socialists," they had no church wedding service. The Duce had a special dislike for religion. "He particularly liked to ridicule Jesus, describing him as an 'ignorant Jew' and claiming that he was a pygmy compared to Buddha.... Any socialists who practiced religion or even tolerated it in their children should be expelled from the party. Mussolini demanded that party members renounce religious marriage, baptism, and all other Christian rituals," writes Jonah Goldberg in his book on Mussolini and fascism.[21]

He was certainly talented. He was an amateur violinist, spoke several languages, was well read, and was a prolific writer. The *Avanti!* newspaper appointed him chief editor, one of the more powerful posts in the country. He was also violent. He beat his wife and, in one encounter, brandished a gun to both Rachele and her mother. They backed off, but a few of his lovers did not. Ida Dalser, who bore the

Duce an illegitimate child, showed up in the street one day outside his newspaper offices. Holding little Benito in her arms, she yelled up to him: "You coward, you pig, you murderer, traitor. Come out if you dare!" A number of people wandered out to see what the trouble was. Mussolini raced down the stairs with a revolver: "That's it, I've had enough. I'm going to deal with you once and for all." Before he could act further, she was led away by police. Leda Rafanelli provided a different type of encounter. They didn't meet in free love circles; instead, she wrote for the *Avanti!* newspaper. A Muslim interested in Sufism, but also a well-read socialist, she entranced the Duce with a more exotic experience. "You made me feel I was in the marvelous and mysterious Orient, with its intense perfumes and its mad, fascinating fantasies," he told her. Early on, he made this proposal: "We shall read Nietzsche and the Koran!" alluding to the most popular philosopher of the day among radicals, Germany's Frederich Nietzsche. Their lengthy affair was upset by her learning he had a wife and child.[22]

"Why have you always lied to me?" she asked.

"You always told me you knew anyway."

"But you always denied it," she countered. "You told me that if I knew you had a wife or you were living with another woman, I would break off our friendship."

"It doesn't matter whether I have a wife or not. She's used to my infidelities. She's a good woman."

In her autobiography, the matronly Rachele Mussolini, who was mother to five of his children, alludes to her husband's serial adultery. "He never denied that he was attracted to women, with one misgiving which one day he revealed to me. 'You will always be the only beautiful woman in my life, because beauty is untrustworthy—it can make even the wisest man lose his head.'"

He got into fist fights with husbands and squarely punched a lawyer he was opposing on political matters. Nevertheless, the Duce was rising to the top of the Socialist Party's leadership and becoming a populist leader throughout Italy. In the same way his wife looked past his infidelities, the Italian nation looked past Mussolini's character in favor of its need for a strong leader. Rather than sexual impropriety serving as a warning, it instead became the central feature of the "myth of Mussolini" that launched his meteoric rise.[23]

These times were chaotic, similar to the late sixties in America, but worse. Europe was reeling from strikes that led to violence, as well as from assassinations, terrorist bombings, and the threat of looming great wars. Italy was unstable. Civil war was a possibility. The times called for a strongman, "which would nurture the Duce as 'the great lover,' 'the alpha male' who was potent in every sense of the term," according to biographer Roberto Olla.

"Many rumors about Mussolini's potency circulated among women—whispered no doubt, accompanied by blushes—during his 20-year dictatorship, and, in the same way, anecdotes, tinged with envy, were bandied about among men." The myth included "Mussolini's closely shaved 'Roman head,' which fascinated women; Mussolini's jutting square jaw; Mussolini with his cat, on his horse, playing his violin, fondling his pet lion, driving his Torpedo, in swimming trunks, with his blazing eyes and powerful naked torso, with the look of gritty determination at the wheel of his racing car or an air of daring at the controls of his plane." His Muslim lover wrote for publication this sentiment on first hearing him speak: "Benito Mussolini…is the socialist of the heroic times. He feels, he still believes, with an enthusiasm full of virility and force. He is a Man."

In the same way that Rachele allowed her husband's smooth words to cover his lies and adultery, the Italian people chose Mussolini's rhetoric espousing peace and the Rule of Law. They were willing to ignore the growing rumors that tactics of violence by "armed squads" were a part of his rising success. "Whenever I spoke to my brother about the phenomenon of the armed squads," writes sister Edvige, his response ranged from "outright and bitter denunciation" to "a lightly condescending irony."[24]

However, the peaceful rhetoric was getting in the Duce's way. His popularity was almost strong enough to propel him to prime minister, the country's top position (above the king, similar to England). But the patriotic, nationalistic call to enter World War I was still stronger. Mussolini had made large promises to his socialist base, many of whom were pacifists. His next move involved treating his fellow socialists the same way he treated his women.

The social radicals of the day all had one intellectual mentor in common: philosopher Frederich Nietzsche. The phrase "God is dead" was made popular by this young thinker. "Christianity remains to this day the greatest misfortune of humanity," he wrote in one of his last books, *The Antichrist*.

Birth control pioneer Margaret Sanger was attending lectures on Nietzsche in London around the time Benito Mussolini was "devouring" a biography of Nietzsche as a young teacher. "No hero or preacher of egoism had as much an influence on him as the philosopher-poet Friedrich Nietzsche," writes biographer Laura Fermi. This German professor called for "the will to power" to replace God and inspired followers to become "supermen," elite thinkers who transcended traditional morality. As Mussolini put it: "Each of us is free to create his own ideology."[25]

Sanger considered Nietzsche a "genius." Agreeing with the German professor's ideas, Sanger called for the end of the "tyranny" of Christian leaders and traditional morality. "Birth control appeals to the advanced radical," she printed in her *Birth Control Review*, "because it is calculated to undermine the authority of the Christian churches." (The same article predicts "the downfall of the church.") Like the Duce, she had multiple sex partners in a given month. She promoted "a new sex morality" with a clear religious goal: "Through sex, mankind may attain the great spiritual illumination which will transform the world, which will light up the only path to an earthly paradise. She advised her sixteen-year-old granddaughter that sex three times a day was "about right."[26]

Her husband, William Sanger, an attorney, protested with Margaret for better wages for women and was even locked up advocating for birth control. But when Margaret fell under the spell of the radical's radical, Emma Goldman, a free-sex anarchist imprisoned for attempted assassination, he scurried Margaret away to Europe to keep the family together. Her next mentor was Havelock Ellis, the celebrated author of a seven-volume series on sex, who also became one of Margaret's lovers. The Sangers divorced. William Sanger called the socialist revolution simply "an excuse for a Saturnalia of sex." Biographer Madeline Gray says William "was sick of hearing Emma hammer away at the idea that marriage and fidelity were among the chief curses of mankind."[27]

Sanger and Mussolini also built upon Nietzsche's words regarding race and breeding. In 1880, Nietzsche wrote: "The testimony must be towards the rendering extinct of the wretched, the deformed, the degenerate." Elites, rather than the masses, should be in charge of re-production, he said, so that "race as a whole [no longer] suffers," noting that "the extinction of many types of people is just as desirable as any form of reproduction."

Nietzsche went insane at age thirty-three. Those years of madness included claims that he created the world. He signed his letters "the crucified one." He died at age forty-four from syphilis. He may have been projecting his own tendencies onto the masses when he said be-fore his madness: "Go through the towns and ask yourselves whether these people should reproduce! Let them go to their whores!"[28]

After losing popularity from being associated with Hitler's ideas, Nietzsche has been resurrected as an esteemed thinker today. Stanford University notes that he is even read "by cultural icons like Shaquille O'Neal and Marilyn Manson." Modern scholars seek to disassociate Nietzsche from the Führer, but there is a similar ring in Hitler's proc-lamation that "the demand that defective people be prevented from propagating equally defective offspring is a demand of the clearest rea-son" and "all great cultures of the past perished only because the origi-nally creative race died off through blood-poisoning."[29]

Who will serve the heroes and Supermen? Nietzsche names the "subhumans" as their natural attendants. Sanger uses similar terms as she called openly for using birth control and sterilization as ways to eliminate "human waste." She agreed that "the noblest and most difficult art of all is the raising of human thoroughbreds." In fact, the masthead of her *Birth Control Review* magazine said: "Birth Control: To create a race of thoroughbreds."[30] Sanger is the founder of Planned Parenthood, the largest performer of abortions in the world and a multibillion-dollar operation today.

In 1925, Sanger hosted a "Neo-Malthusian" conference at the Hotel McAlpin in New York in honor of early nineteenth century anti-population doomsday writer Thomas Malthus, another man admired by Mussolini. At the conference she stated: "Year by year more money is expended...to maintain an increasing race of morons which threatens the very foundations of our civilization."[31]

Malthus taught that population grows geometrically (or exponentially), but resources and food only grow arithmetically (or incrementally). While Malthus himself was not a scientist or demographer—he was an Anglican clergyman—his views fit perfectly with Margaret's desire to make birth control legal for women, as she promoted "weeding out the unfit, of preventing the birth of defectives," and decried war, which kills "not the weak and the helpless, but the strong and the fit." She also quoted with sympathy an activist who called for humans to model animals. "If men insisted that those who were sickly should be allowed to die without help of medicine or science, if those who are weak were put upon one side and crushed, if those who were old and useless were killed, if those who were not capable of providing food for themselves were allowed to starve, the struggle for existence among men would be as real as it is among brutes and would doubtless result in the production of a higher race of men."[32]

"We are not willing to let it be done," Margaret laments. "Mothers' hearts cling to children, no matter how diseased, misshapen, and miserable."[33]

This thinking of the day is known as eugenics, and later became quite unpopular when Hitler used the same premises to conduct his Nazi ethnic cleansing campaigns. Today, followers of Sanger seek to downplay the hundreds of on-the-record embarrassments. But even sympathetic biographers call it "indefensible" and admit that "Margaret's support of eugenics...ultimately cost her some of her reputation," according to Jean H. Baker. "Today, its atrocities have no justification."[34]

Malthusianism was also helpful for Mussolini, who believed that Africans were "inferior." He told the senate in 1919 that "continued population increase would cause misery and hunger because of the poverty of Italy's economic endowments," according to Maria Quine in *From Malthus to Mussolini*. Thus, his solution for Italy's current over-population problem was to invade and colonize.[35]

Mussolini saw high birthrates in Africa and Asia as a threat to the white race. His speeches involved the cry: "Are the blacks and yellows at the door?" "Yes, they are!" came the reply. He also believed that the United States was doomed as the American blacks had a higher birth-rate than whites. Sanger seemed to hold similar notions. In 1939, she designed a "Negro Project" for Southern health officials who "were not known for their racial equanimity," as dryly noted by George Grant in his expose of Planned Parenthood, Sanger's legacy. As one contributor to Sanger's *Birth Control Review* wrote: "It is the lower elements of the population, the negroid aboriginal tribes and the pariahs or outcasts, who are gaining the fastest."[36]

Sanger's same magazine published a favorable review by her lover, Havelock Ellis, of the book *The Rising Tide of Color Against White World Supremacy* by Lathrop Stoddard. Ellis notes that Stoddard chooses to "concern himself mainly with...the maintenance of White suprema-cy." Ellis agrees that "by prejudice of color, we must mostly be on his side in this matter." Ellis also shares his concern about African Amer-icans: "the migrations of lower types, even within the white world, such as those which have worked havoc in the United States, must be rigorously curtailed." Ellis also wrote the preface to Sanger's 1920 book, *Woman and the New Race*. In a later *Birth Control Review* article, Sanger calls for giving "certain dysgenic groups in our population their choice of segregation or sterilization." She also published an article by close friend and advisor Ernst Rudin, who was then serving as Hitler's director of genetic sterilization for the Nazis. It was entitled "Eugenic Sterilization: An Urgent Need."[37]

With Mussolini holding the same Nietzschean and Malthusian views as Sanger, one wonders, if he reached his goal as prime minister, how he might implement his ideas on the Ethiopian people, whose defeat of Italy at Adwa he sought to avenge. In later memos, he would even give orders to "exterminate."[38]

CHAPTER NINE

SECRET AGENTS OF the Italian government followed Benito Mussolini minute by minute, now that he was one of the country's most high-profile figures, head of the Socialist Party, and leading candidate for the country's highest position. They knew about all the affairs. Agent Giovanni Gasti remarked on the Duce's "strong physical constitution, despite his syphilis, which allows him to work uninterruptedly for long periods."

The "myth of Mussolini" was growing at a breakneck pace. His sights were on the top post of prime minister, but he was trapped in his ten years of anti-war leadership among a people in a patriotic fervor for war, like many other nations in Europe.

Gasti also noted Mussolini's "changeable" political views, adding hope that he could be turned into a government informant and collaborator. He had the ability "to change direction and help to undermine institutions and principles that he has hitherto supported and advocated." His Muslim lover, Leda Rafanelli, aware of his personal lies, also saw the ideological wavering. "Far from being tough and intransigent," biographer Olla reports from her memoirs, the Duce "switched opinions and changed his mind easily" and "rapidly abandoned positions which only a moment before had appeared to be unchangeable beliefs."[1]

As late as August 1914, Mussolini wrote an article entitled "Down with the War. We remain neutral." But true to character, he changed his position and penned his reversal in the leading Socialist publication that he oversaw as editor. "The sentiment of nationality exists and cannot be denied," he wrote. He described the old way as International

Socialism. He called for a new "National Socialism." It was necessary "to assassinate the Party in order to save Socialism." He resigned from *Avanti!* and formed the new Fascist Party, the name taken from "fascio," a bundle of sticks bound together to hold an axehead.[2]

"Women prefer men to be brutal," he once said, and he believed the same about his former socialist friends who had removed him from the party for his newfound warmongering. "You hate me today because you love me still," he told them. "You think you can turn me out, but you will find I shall come back again. I am and shall remain a socialist and my convictions will never change! They are bred into my very bones."[3]

Later, Mussolini's fascist squads destroyed socialist newspapers and attacked the *Avanti!* offices. He began writing "quite violent articles" for his new fascist paper and called for a man "ruthless and energetic enough to make a clean sweep of the country." His squads, also called "blackshirts"—because Italian special forces wore black turtlenecks that quickly became vogue among fascists—clashed with communists, socialists, and anarchists at parades and demonstrations. The government stood back, fearing an all-out revolution, some hoping the blackshirts might bring order to the growing chaos.[4]

The government most feared the communist "Reds," who organized a transportation strike on July 31, 1922. Officials looked the other way as the blackshirts broke up the strike, drove the streetcars, kept the traffic moving, and "made the trains run on time." Writes Goldberg, "Mussolini's strikebreaking tactics had a profound effect on the Italian public. At a time when intellectuals all over the world were growing cynical about parliamentary democracy and liberal politics, Mussolini's military efficiency seemed to transcend partisan politics."[5]

The public ignored the fact that the tactics included assaults on the vulnerable and violent abuse, including raping women and "pushing sticks up men's rectums," according to Roberto Olla. "Fascist squads had knifed and beaten many politicians, intellectuals, trade-unionists, journalists, even priests," Olla wrote. "The list of those who had been killed was long." Hitler, a decade from prominence, watched Mussolini at this time and used him as a model for violence. As one newsreel reported it, "Adolf Hitler, only a promising amateur in those days, came to study and emulate the master fascist, Mussolini."[6]

The Duce made a strange peace with the Vatican and had his family baptized. He had not yet become prime minister, but both Church and People had already made their dark pact with a known liar, blasphemer, celebrated adulterer, and suspected murderer. The Pope said he was "sent by Providence."[7]

He still despised the church. A few years before, while making a living as a writer, he produced a highly popular novel about a priest who breaks his vow. Mussolini provided intimate details of all the priest's sexual transgressions. Instead of promoting the church, he proclaimed that "Fascism is a religion." Compared to the competition, "we declare ourselves the heretics," he said. "Spirits endowed with sublime perversity" is what Mussolini said he wanted as he described the contrast: "Christianity said: be mortified.... The Nietzschean superman...wants instead to conquer."[8]

In late October 1922, 30,000 fascist blackshirts gathered in the capital to demand the resignation of Prime Minister Luigi Facta and the appointment of a new fascist government. It is now known as the "March on Rome." Mussolini waited in the city of Milan. The country still looked to King Vittorio Emanuele III as the ultimate head of the military. The king refused Prime Minster Facta's request to institute martial law. Facta resigned, and King Vittorio asked Mussolini to draw up a new fascist government. "Behind the scenes, King Vittorio Emanuele had already asked him to form a new government," writes Goldberg. "But the Duce marched anyway, reenacting Julius Caesar's march on Rome and giving the new fascist government a useful 'revolutionary myth' that he would artfully exploit in years to come. Mussolini became prime minister and fascist Italy was born."[9]

Parliament granted the Duce dictatorial powers for one year (legal according to the Constitution). But within three years, all semblance of a democracy was gone. Mussolini's title was changed from prime minister to "Head of Government." He was no longer answerable to Parliament, and only the king could remove him from the leadership of the military.

His myth involved restoring the Roman Empire. He remembered Adwa. Immediately upon obtaining his dictatorial power, he told his defense ministers: "Take all military and diplomatic steps necessary in order that we may profit from a possible collapse of the Ethiopian empire."[10]

Haile Selassie also remembered Adwa. One of his first initiatives as Ethiopia's leader was the bold action of applying for membership in the League of Nations, the forerunner of today's United Nations.

The League agreed to discipline its ranks and sanction any of its members that attacked a fellow member nation. Along with approximately fifty-two others, Italy was a member and adamantly opposed Ethiopia's entry, the first of any African nation to be considered. Despite the difficulties, Ethiopia was voted in as a member nation by the General Assembly of the League of Nations in 1923. "There was great joy in Addis Ababa," said Haile Selassie. "We thought the Covenant of the League would protect us."[11]

Mussolini had bitter memories of his country's unfair treatment after a great many Italians died in the First World War. Italy was not rewarded at the peace table with the colonial prizes that went to England and France. As the world loomed toward another world war, the Duce was determined to conquer his colonies first.

For years, Italy had been conducting a massive buildup of its army. While some diplomats warned leaders like U.S. President Franklin Delano Roosevelt that the intention of this buildup was for Ethiopia, Mussolini—backed by FDR's ambassador—insisted the forces were to protect the Allies from Hitler invading Austria, the buffer nation between Germany and Italy. The wary U.S. president listened.

FDR needed the Duce. He told Italy's finance minister that he considered Mussolini "his only potential ally in his effort to safeguard world peace."[12]

Mussolini's ambitions hinged on Roosevelt. Were Italy to invade Ethiopia, he believed Britain and France would not enact economic sanctions, required by the League of Nations, without Roosevelt's participation. Sanctions "would be crippling," according to historians Philip Cannistraro and Brian Sullivan. "Italy could suffer economic collapse, defeat in East Africa, and the subsequent dishonor of watching Germany seize Austria. Mussolini, and probably Fascism, would be finished."[13]

American diplomats in Europe continued to warn Roosevelt of Italian plans to attack Ethiopia. To counter these suspicions, Mussolini beefed up his ongoing public relations campaign in America, resting primarily on columns he wrote for the Hearst newspaper chain. In fact, they were written by his longtime Jewish mistress, Margherita Sarfatti. She was attractive, married with children, well educated, spoke several languages, and was perhaps the primary creator of fascism and the "myth of Mussolini." Sarfatti wrote his biography *Duce,* which was printed in nineteen languages and sold millions of copies. She understood the appeal of a book that readers suspected was written by someone who had personally partaken of the sex symbol. She also helped him arrange his encounters with hundreds of sexual partners.

"Mussolini cultivated an impression of being married to all Italian women," writes Goldberg. That mythmaking by Sarfatti made itself a surreal reality when millions of women donated their gold wedding rings to the state as Italy found itself in financial turmoil. Along with being depicted as a violinist and bare-chested model, the versions of the symbol now included the swordsman who could ski, hit tennis, and swim. He played with children and was photographed with flowers and animals. The propaganda was ingenious, "even more so than the system created by Hitler and Goebbels in Germany," writes Sarfatti biographer Olla. "But all these things revolved round or sprang from the idea of Mussolini's sexuality, the image of him as a great lover."

When Winston Churchill's wife, Clementine, met Mussolini in 1926, she noted his "beautiful golden brown, piercing eyes.... He fills you with a sort of pleasurable awe." Churchill himself called him the "Roman genius" and "the greatest law-giver among living men."[14]

MUSSOLINI

Mussolini and his mistress, Margherita Sarfatti, were unsure if their propaganda was as effective with President Roosevelt. They wrote another article for Hearst's American newspapers comparing FDR's New Deal to the fascist corporate state. The Duce dispatched U.S. Ambassador Breckinridge Long to send his sentiment of "great personal admiration" for the president. FDR replied to Long: "There seems no question but that Mussolini is really interested in what we are doing, and I am much interested and deeply impressed with what he has accomplished and by his evidenced honest purpose of restoring Italy, and seeking to prevent general European trouble."[15]

Roosevelt's distant relative, Teddy Roosevelt, Jr., later a general for FDR, visited Rome, and Sarfatti made a point to entertain him at her mansion. As the two began a contest quoting Rudyard Kipling, Teddy was surprised Margherita knew more of the English poet than he did. He later met with Mussolini, but neither face-to-face encounter warmed the Roosevelt nephew, who concluded that Americans "would never consent to a dictatorship."

Sarfatti turned her attention to the American press and arranged an interview of the Duce with *New York Times* reporter Anne O'Hare

McCormick. The resulting headline: "Il Duce insists the chief aim of Italian policy is peace."

"I *will* peace; I *need* peace," Mussolini was quoted as saying—speaking in clear English according to McCormick. "We must have peace. You say the people look to me to save the peace of Europe. Well, they are right. Italy will never start a war." McCormick revealed her vulnerability to the myth: "By default of other leadership, Rome rides toward her ancient place," she wrote, "and rides with a certain fresh magnificence."[16]

The propaganda was working in Europe, as Mussolini determined through his private channels that if he attacked Ethiopia, Britain and France would only post official diplomatic protests. They would not enact economic sanctions. Accordingly, he began to dispatch tanks, guns, and soldiers by the tens of thousands to the Suez Canal toward the Horn of Africa. Ambassador Long had continued to tell FDR that the buildup was to fight Hitler, and the president disagreed and told him so. When reports emerged that over 100,000 members of the Italian army were headed to Ethiopia, Long was forced to admit the obvious. He then excused the invasion plan as the cost for preventing Italy from joining forces with Hitler in Europe.

Long fell ill, and FDR replaced him with Alexander Kirk, who finally began feeding accurate reports to the president. Meanwhile, Britain and France polled the public and saw the overwhelming popular support for sanctioning Italy upon an invasion of Ethiopia. The British Cabinet held an emergency meeting. Warships sailed to the Mediterranean with threats to blockade Italy and shut the Suez Canal. The Duce guessed they were bluffing. The deciding card still lay with Roosevelt, who now had all the information. He sent secret letters to Mussolini pleading with him to stop the invasion. Angered, Mussolini threatened war against Europe as well as Ethiopia. He now viewed FDR as an enemy.

Sarfatti argued with the Duce against the invasion. She was even making plans to leave Italy, fearing economic collapse and political disaster. She told a friend that "it is the beginning of the end."

"Why do you say that? Do you think we are going to lose this war in Africa?"

"No, I say it because, unfortunately, I think we will win, and he will lose his head."[17]

Sarfatti later wrote a tell-all entitled *My Fault*. There was little repentance in the book, even though she, more than any other, can be attributed to creating Mussolini and his image. She was no hero. Boratto, the Duce's chauffeur, referenced the activities overseen by the highly educated mistress as "worthy of a brothel." Those liaisons included, in later years, an arranged affair with Sarfatti's teenage daughter. "Shapely and pretty," said Boratto. "I only realized later why she was so often with them." Sullivan confirms the perverse liaison, noting that Mussolini had spent time with little Fiammetta Sarfatti since she was a toddler. The chauffeur's observation was confirmed by the maid: "He remains attached to the mother because he's in love with the daughter, who's crazy about him."[18]

Sarfatti's mythmaking avoided the less impressive details. The trysts with various women included sex on the office carpet and sex standing up with his boots still on; encounters every day, but sheets changed every three days; another mistress who helped her mother run a brothel; sometimes more than two were in the room; and that he had gonorrhea as well as syphilis.[19]

More notably, Sarfatti's myth was not necessarily true. He sometimes required a Viagra-like drug. He couldn't handle alcohol. His sister chided him for refusing to view a dead body. He melted from certain smells, including ether and incense. In his 50s, Mussolini's tertiary syphilis caused him serious gastrointestinal spasms. He developed an ulcer and vomited blood. When Sarfatti was no longer useful, Mussolini claimed he could not perform well during their first few sexual encounters because of her Jewish scent: "this terrible smell they have."[20]

Sarfatti escaped a few years later to South America, but her sister and other Jewish relatives were carted off in cattle cars from Italy to the Auschwitz concentration camp in Hitler's Germany. It was to Hitler that Mussolini looked when Britain, France, and the United States threatened to block his invasion of Ethiopia. He made a deal over time not to interfere with a possible German aggression in Austria. He invaded Ethiopia with 476,000 men, 500 tanks, 350 aircraft, 1,500 artillery pieces, and 15,000 machine guns. His commanding general, Emilio de Bono, mounted a white horse and rode into Axum, the holy city, home of the Ark of the Covenant.

I MET GABRIEL on the streets of Axum during a recent trip while I was sipping coffee. He was nineteen, and was finishing up his civil engineering degree after studying algebra, trigonometry, and advanced calculus. He attends the University of Axum, which has around 15,000 students and within which English is spoken exclusively in the classroom.

Gabriel's family and friends, and pretty much everyone else in his community, attends church several times a week. Usually it's a simple morning service from 6 to 8 a.m. On feast days, they will arrive at church at 3 a.m. and stay until 9 a.m. This devotion is typical of all those in his neighborhood, he says. For Ethiopian Orthodox across the country, seventy-eight percent say they attend church at least weekly, compared with ten percent of Orthodox Christians in Europe and thirty-one percent of Orthodox Christians in the United States. And ninety percent of Ethiopian Orthodox say religion is "very important" to them, compared with fifty-two percent in the U.S. and twenty-eight percent in Europe who say this.[1]

Gabriel's parents did not know each other before they were married. The way it is traditionally done is a man will notice a young woman, usually a teenager, and tell his parents of his interest, and Gabriel's father's case was typical. The future groom's father will contact the "matchmaker" in the village, an elderly man. He and the prospective husband's father then sit down with the young woman's parents and discuss the possibility of marriage. The girl is never consulted. If everyone approves, then the young man meets with the girl and gives her a ring of promise. A few weeks later, they are married.

During those intervening weeks, the future bride and groom meet and get to know each other. Gabriel told me that this period is when sexual relations commence. "They can't do it on the wedding day as they will be too tired from all the festivities."

After their sexual relations, just as we read about in the Old Testament, the man will bring to his parents and the elder a blood-stained cloth to show that the woman was a virgin. If she is not a virgin, and the man is a deacon planning to become a priest, he cannot become a priest. And, as a deacon, he is not allowed to enter the church altar for the rest of his life.

Gabriel does not expect to be married until he is at least twenty-five. The girl will be nineteen or twenty. (His grandmother was fifteen and had fifteen children.) It is possible that his arrangement will be similar to his parents, but modern ways may mean that he gets to know his future wife before introducing her to his parents. In his parent's case, they never had a conversation with each other until they pledged to be married.

Haile Selassie gathered his army in Addis Ababa and watched his barefoot soldiers march by in procession. Unlike the ten-to-one advantage at Adwa, the emperor had 100,000 less soldiers than Italy's 476,000, and 200 outdated artillery guns to Italy's 1,500. The Duce had hundreds of airplanes. Ethiopia had three.

"We watched the curious procession," said *Times* of London reporter George Steer. "What could they do? They thought they could do everything."

Indeed, Haile Selassie said Mussolini's "formidable problem is the indomitable spirit of the Ethiopian people." All Ethiopians were aware that they had never been colonized. An invasion had never ultimately succeeded, not in all of history. Ethiopia is "the Land of God," according to an official church publication, "and she will survive to the end of the world."[2]

In 525 BC, Persian conqueror Cambyses defeated Egypt and then invaded Ethiopia, but was repulsed by Ethiopian armies, particularly their archers, who reduced the Persians to cannibalism. Alexander the Great conquered many regions, including Egypt, but chose to avoid Ethiopia. The Romans, too, stopped at Egypt and Meroe (today's Sudan), and Axum was spared. An advisor to an Egyptian Ptolemy king, as he prepared to invade Ethiopia in the second century BC, remarked: "Why futilely announce an impossible task?" The earlier referenced church publication comments on its belief that all invaders are doomed, saying any anti-Ethiopian force "has hurried their own downfall, and will do so in the future."[3]

Amharic, the common language for all Ethiopians, originates with the Amhara ethnic group. The word means "Free People."[4] Ethiopia's ancient liturgical language, known as "Ge'ez," derives from the Agazian ethnic group. Agazian also means "Free People," and "Lord of the Free" is inscribed in Ge'ez on one of the famous ancient stone pillars—also called obelisks or stelae—erected a stone's throw from where the Ark is kept in Axum.

That stela, or obelisk, was seized by the Italian occupiers. Having been broken into five pieces a millennia before, it was taken piece by piece to Rome and reassembled. Like the occult Nazis, the Italians were known to desire such objects. Were they seeking the Ark? Author Enrico Cernuschi states that the fascist government was aware of a cryptic map in the obelisk, a notion also discussed in Ethiopian tradition. While they attempted to break the code, lightning struck and damaged the stone map just two weeks after it arrived in Italy. Meanwhile, later reports indicate the Ark may have been secreted away by Ethiopian clergy during this period, as they had done in former times of persecution. The most notable secondary location was an island monastery at Lake Tana. Long before Italian forces could secure the area, Italian Minister of Popular Culture Alessandro Pavolini traveled to Lake Tana and boarded a water landing craft. "One can only speculate why he took the risk of getting there as soon as possible," writes an investigator at *HistoricMysteries.com*.[5]

Two weeks after Mussolini's obvious and brazen invasion, the League of Nations voted to enact economic sanctions, in accordance with the charter's by-laws, for any aggression against a member nation. However, it was only an "arms and credit" embargo and did not include the most important item—oil—and that is what mattered. Mussolini admitted to Hitler that an oil embargo would have forced his immediate retreat. The United States, not a member of the League—even though its then-president, Woodrow Wilson, envisioned it—was under no compulsion to follow Britain and France, and League members decided to wait to see what FDR would do before including oil in their sanctions.[6]

MUSSOLINI AND HITLER

Much was at stake. If the League did not take firm action against Mussolini's African campaign, how could they tell Hitler not to invade European members of the League? For his part, Mussolini was convinced he could win the League over if it appeared that the war was won, the occupation inevitable, and any effort by another nation to stop it was a pointless adventure. He needed a quick victory and doubled his troops and forces.

Like the final moments of Adwa before the giant conflict, General de Bono was playing a game of chicken with Haile Selassie. He did not want Italy to appear as the aggressor when combat began. However, he reluctantly messaged the Duce: Haile Selassie "is ordering too many prayers and fasts to give us reason to think he wishes to attack us," he wrote. "We ourselves must take the initiative."[7]

And yet, the emperor was indeed making plans. He radioed the empress: "Since our trust is in our Creator and in the hope of his help, and as we have decided to advance and enter the [Italian] fortifications, and since God is our only help, confide this decision of ours in secret to the Abuna [archbishop], to the ministers and dignitaries, and offer up to God your fervent prayers."

Mussolini took to his balcony to make speeches, where he often stated that he had "brought civilization to triumph over barbarity" and "Italy wants peace for all." Haile Selassie, now an international figure, received letters from across the world. "Ethiopia must not lose courage, for [God] will fight on her behalf and send His angels to protect her," wrote one woman. Another from California said the whites "are not as civilized as they loudly assert themselves to be."[8]

Mussolini and Haile Selassie embodied the moral contrast. The Ethiopian emperor never created a scandal involving infidelity. His day began at 5 a.m. with a half an hour of morning prayers. He observed all of the Church's fast days, and he worked late into the night. A British journalist noted that "it was a marvel to me how this frail little man—the exact opposite of the brawny Italian dictator—could cram so much work into twenty-four hours."

An impatient Duce replaced General de Bono with General Pietro Bodoglio. The wary Italian soldiers advanced southward to the Tekeze River and waited with caution—they had heard the reports of Ethiopian castrations at Adwa and believed it could happen again. The emperor's General Ras Imru aligned his troops across a mountain crest, and Italian Major Criniti "ordered his tanks to smash a way through them. The tanks lumbered forward and the [Ethiopians] engulfed the steel monsters in a mass of human flesh—preventing the crews from using their machine guns and tearing the tracks off...when dusk fell almost half of [Criniti's] men lay dead or wounded on the battlefield."[9]

When night fell, the Italian commander had lost. This success was an important moral victory for Ethiopia and the first time the massive Italian army withdrew. Badoglio was forced to message an enraged Duce. Ethiopian forces then smashed into Badoglio's right flank. A great Ethiopian counter-offensive began that lasted for another three weeks.

The former ambassador, Breckinridge Long, was notified of unusual anger in Mussolini's speeches. He wondered with Sarfatti if he were about to take some rash action. Was it true, he asked her, that the Duce was as inflamed as he appeared? She said the Duce was under enormous strain. She said she had never seen him lose control like that in public. Long begged her to tell him such public displays were dangerous.

In fact, secret communications were taking place at that time between Mussolini and his generals to commit one of the twentieth century's great war crimes. An incident with a downed plane provided the pretext. Italian pilot Tito Minniti experienced engine trouble and was forced to land behind enemy lines. His plane was surrounded as he fired his machine gun. When he ran out of ammunition, he was captured and killed. Before he died, three of his fingers were cut off and he was castrated. His head was displayed in a nearby village. Mussolini and the Italian press were quick to once again accuse the Ethiopians of being "savages."[10]

The Duce ordered his generals to use chemical weapons to drive back the Ethiopians. General Ras Imru describes the first incident: "I had just crossed the Tekeze River—a group of planes appeared on the horizon...however, the aircraft did not drop bombs, but instead curious looking canisters, which burst open the moment they hit the ground or the water. Before I could grasp what was happening, hundreds of my men had been sprinkled with a strange liquid and were screaming in pain. Their bare feet, hands and faces were covered with blisters. Those who had drunk from the river writhed around on the ground for hours in their death throes...I had no idea what to say to them or how to combat this burning, deadly rain."

The chemical is known as mustard gas. After its horrid use in the trench warfare of WWI, it was universally outlawed in the Geneva Protocol of 1925, which Italy signed. Soldiers whose skin comes into contact with the clothing of other soldiers are also affected with injury and death. It penetrates clothes, so more than exposed skin is contaminated. It causes temporary blindness, blisters in the respiratory system, and can turn the skin blue, orange, red, and pink. Some forms cannot be seen and have no smell. It is a persistent, lingering weapon that can be effective on the ground for weeks.

A nurse serving in WWI described the pain: "They cannot be bandaged or touched. We cover them with a tent of propped-up sheets. Gas burns must be agonizing because usually the other cases do not complain, even with the worst wounds, but gas cases are invariably beyond endurance and they cannot help crying out."[11]

Thousands of soldiers were contaminated and left dead or wounded. Civilians were sprayed along with soldiers. Hospitals were bombed. A Red Cross official called it a "veritable hell." The reports alarmed the international community, but Italy's propaganda program simply denied the reports.

Unlike the Adwa campaign a generation before, the Italian public was not divided over this war effort. The elite were poised to enrich themselves. The common man viewed Ethiopia and its fertile lands as the means to better his way of life. In his early speeches announcing the colonial effort in Ethiopia, Mussolini inspired his people to seize their rewards: "sirens sounded, church bells pealed throughout Italy and the population was seized with a fit of nationalistic frenzy. Shouting and cheering, many of them rushed into the streets and squares in a passionate, patriotic stampede, comparable only with the demonstrations before Caesar in the days of the old Roman empire."

The reports of war crimes were dismissed. Despite these horrific chemical attacks, the Ethiopian army somehow continued to score victories. The Italian light tanks struggled against the Ethiopian infantry, which shot through the weapon slits in the armor. General Ras Kassa succeeded in dividing the Italian army and was headed toward a strategic advantage. "Wave after wave of Ethiopians surged forward to attack the Italian fortifications, and there was a good deal of bloody hand-to-hand fighting," according to A. J. Barker of the Royal Military College of Science. Italian casualties were heavy: sixty officers and 1,000 soldiers. "It left the Italians distinctly uneasy," said Barker, "so much so now that Mussolini began to consider the possibility of a compromise peace."[12]

Months earlier, Roosevelt passed legislation empowering him as U.S. president to enact an oil embargo on Mussolini, the one action that could stop the war. But the Italian propaganda machine trumpeted victory in Abyssinia and duped the international community into believing Italy's triumph was imminent. Breckinridge Long, with Sarfatti's encouragement, lobbied FDR to drop the embargo idea. Stronger pressure came from the president's moneyed advisors.

The Duce did not like compromise. His response to the Ethiopian surge was to drop more poison gas. Hundreds of planes dumped more than 1,000 tons of the "terrible rain" on the Ethiopians and their land over a period of several months. Two of Mussolini's sons flew planes and helped drop the gas canisters, with phosgene and chlorine now used along with mustard gas. Soldiers fled as their bare feet interacted with the chemicals. "The Duce shall have Ethiopia," General Rodolfo Graziani famously pronounced, "with or without the Ethiopians."[13]

Still the Ethiopians surged forward. Cannistraro and Sullivan capture the drama: "Badoglio escaped catastrophe by the barest margin," they write. "The marshal's men had advanced too confidently; one Italian division was cut off and surrounded. The Ethiopians poured all their reserves into the gap this created. By [evening], Badoglio was in despair—his only apparent option was to order a general retreat. To do so meant abandoning huge supplies of ammunition to the enemy. Without those munitions, Badoglio could not defend Eritrea. The Ethiopians would flood into the colony, and any Italians who survived the rout would be driven into the Red Sea."

"Nonetheless, Badoglio ordered a withdrawal. He saw no alternative. Fortunately for him and for Mussolini's regime, the marshal's staff refused to obey. They simply could not bring themselves to set in motion a massacre of Italian soldiers. They argued strenuously with their commander until he reversed his order. At daybreak, bombers took off with their deadly loads of poison chemicals. For twelve hours they dropped tons and tons of mustard gas on the advancing Ethiopians. On the ground, the Italian forces fought grimly to hold their positions. A day and another night of bloodshed followed. Finally...the Ethiopians fell back."[14]

General Ras Imru escaped death while moving his 10,000 men across a now poisonous river. When they reached their destination, gas wounds and desertions had thinned his army to 300 men. He arrived in Addis Ababa to learn that Emperor Haile Selassie had abandoned the capital. The war was lost by all accounts as 150,000 Ethiopians were dead compared to less than 25,000 Italians.

With the war appearing to be an inevitable Italian route, President Franklin Roosevelt decided to halt the sanctions process. Oil would flow. "On this occasion, once again, the interests of American capital invested in oil companies made sure the profitable Italian market was protected," writes Olla. The League of Nations "noted" and "deplored" the fascist invasion but viewed it as a "fait accompli," according to Barker. Vittorio Emanuele III was proclaimed the new emperor of Ethiopia.[15]

CHAPTER ELEVEN

THROUGHOUT HISTORY, ETHIOPIAN emperors fought to the death to preserve their 3,000-year-old empire. That was certainly Haile Selassie's plan. In fact, in defending their last stronghold of Addis Ababa, he hurried to the palace roof and began firing an anti-aircraft howitzer as one of his aides watched, stunned that Haile Selassie knew how to operate it.

The emperor's next move was confusing to some, especially the European observers. He traveled to Lalibela, a haven of Ethiopian Christian monasteries and a UNESCO World Heritage site renowned for its churches hewn entirely from rock, a centuries-long process. He prayed with the monks for three days. "This was a useless and dangerous diversion," writes secular British historian Barker. "Yet the impulse reflects the strange and complex character of the Ethiopian emperor...he knelt and began to pray. For two days the head of an empire which was about to topple sought to renew his spiritual strength, and during this time not a morsel of food or a drop of water passed his lips."

Just before Addis Ababa was given up, the emperor summoned his Imperial Council and announced his plans to defend the capital. To his shock, the council told him he must leave the country as his death would destroy the spirit of the people. He must survive for Ethiopia to fight another day. The emperor flatly refused.[1]

Biographer Asfa-Wossen Asserate explains the role then played by the emperor's top general: "Ras Kassa requested a private audience with the emperor. Once they were alone, he impressed upon his cousin that he should leave Ethiopia," he wrote. "And because the Italians might be liable at any moment to cut the railway line, there was no time to lose: the emperor should depart at the earliest opportunity." The *Times* of London correspondent watched him depart the meeting. "He was dressed in khaki as a general. His aspect froze my blood. Vigor had left his face, and as he walked forward he did not seem to know where he was putting his feet. His body was crumpled up, his shoulders drooped; the orders on his tunic concealed a hollow, not a chest."

He departed for the ship *Enterprise* at Djibouti, but the train was stopped halfway by a military escort led by Tekle Hawariat, who had written the Ethiopian Constitution. "He boarded the train, strode into the emperor's compartment and told Haile Selassie: 'Your Majesty, an Ethiopian emperor does not leave his country in the lurch!" He called him a traitor and coward. "But his attempt to get Haile Selassie to reconsider at the eleventh hour was to no avail," writes Asfa-Wossen, who also notes that later, during another tumultuous time, Tekle Hawariat himself chose safety by exile.

The British ship's captain noticed the emperor looked very tired and had "a hunted look in his eye." Asked whether his safety could be guaranteed, the captain replied "as safe as the Bank of England." This statement brought a hint of a smile, the emperor's first in a long while. "I have seldom been impressed by any man, black or white," the captain said later, "and his consideration, courtesy, and above all his dignity, has left a very deep impression on every officer and man in my ship."[2]

The emperor's dignity remained because he was not fleeing the country for his safety. Like at Mekele and Adwa, he was avoiding the direct confrontation his enemy preferred, and was attacking instead with a clever alternative. At Fort Mekele, his father Makonnen and Emperor Menelik blocked the spring that watered the fort rather than continuing an attack on the fortification. At Adwa, Menelik and Makonnen circumvented the heavily fortified Adigrat stronghold and instead drew the Italians out into the open field, a clever strategic move that impressed tacticians across the world. Like these two great Ethiopian military leaders, Haile Selassie was choosing to avoid a direct confrontation.

He was headed to fight for his country at a higher level, where he would be mocked, insulted, physically threatened, and blocked at every turn. His Imperial Council had in fact charged him to appear before the League of Nations itself and plead the case of the Ethiopian people. No head of state had ever addressed the League. Haile Selassie had just appeared on the cover of *Time* magazine as its Man of the Year. Such an appearance in Europe, by a now internationally famous world leader, would be a terrible embarrassment to Britain, France, and the nations working with all their skills to cover up the failure of the League to follow its charter. But Western Europe greatly feared the rising German superpower and was willing to betray Ethiopia to keep Mussolini from joining forces with Hitler.

Meanwhile, the Duce gave the greatest oration of his career, entitled "The Proclamation of the Empire." The six lions on the grounds of the Ethiopian emperor's palace were shot dead. In Rome, the famous artist Martini sculpted "The Hero Subdues the Lion of Judah" while a mosaic by the artist Sironi praised "The Triumph of Italy." Mussolini's title was changed from Head of Government to Founder of the Empire. He spoke from his balcony: "Ethiopia belongs to Italy! It belongs by deed, since our victorious troops have occupied it, and by right, since the Roman sword has brought civilization to triumph over barbarity."[3]

The Allies expected Emperor Haile Selassie to concede the defeat and solve their many problems. Mussolini was demanding such a concession, and the Italian propaganda was effective in persuading Europe that Ethiopia had given up on a hopeless effort. However, an appearance before the League of Nations on the world stage by the Ethiopian emperor himself would destroy that clever deception.

A serpent has been the enemy of Ethiopia since its very beginnings. It takes the form of a giant snake in its legends and acts in a more sinister ideological form to its West, with the ability to kill not just the body, but also the soul.

EMPEROR HAILE SELASSIE I

As I traveled with my guide Yirga to the Debre Damo Monastery, an hour outside Axum, he asked an offhand question. "Mr. Dean, do you like to take hikes?"

I wasn't sure what hiking had to do with the monastery, Ethiopia's oldest, built on a spot that had previously been a site for ancient serpent worship.

"I don't really like to hike," I told Yirga, "but I can do it if necessary." He nodded his head, said nothing, and exchanged glances with our driver. As we approached a several-acre rock formation that juts immediately upward from the ground and walked past the donkeys and goats along the path, we arrived at the entrance to the Debre Damo Monastery. In fact, there was no entrance—on the ground. The entrance stood some 300 feet straight up a cliff. At the top, a monk in an orange robe and hat crouched, holding on to a single rope.

"You will have to hike up the rope," Yirga informed me.

As a consolation, someone tied another rope to me that might prevent a full fall if I were to let go. Hopefully the person holding it at the top would not let go. I began my ascent, criticizing my fifty-three-year-old gray-bearded self for being out of shape. Halfway up, my heart was beating too fast. I was trapped between continuing upward and retreating back down, not sure if I could do either, and sincerely wondering if I would survive. Many people were shouting from the top and the bottom, some in English but most of it unintelligible. A group of young Ethiopians were laughing.

Debre Damo was founded by St. Aregawi in the sixth century, one of the famous Nine Saints of Ethiopia who covenanted together in Byzantium to travel to Abyssinia and start a monastic movement. When Aregawi first climbed the cliff, he had similar problems as mine. Just as he was about to fall to his death, according to church tradition, a giant serpent coiled down from above, grabbed him up, and helped him reach the top. Icons of this snake as he assists Aregawi are showcased throughout Ethiopia.

A serpent is depicted on one of Axum's famous obelisks. According to legend, the first king of Ethiopia was the son of a serpent, his father a python, his mother human. His name was Arwe, and the worship of this human reptilian included offering each day a beautiful young girl as a sacrifice. According to a church publication, this first king was the thirty-fifth descendent of Adam. Some of these kings lived 300 or 400 years. After forty years of the first king Arwe's tyrannical rule, a warrior named Angabo plotted to kill him by poisoning a sheep the king ate. Angabo took over as the new king and married Arwe's sister. The Tarich-Negus chronicle provides the line of Ethiopian kings from Arwe to Menelik I, Solomon's son.[4]

For my part, I prayed for help to make it up the cliff. I even hoped a giant snake might help me out. Finally, with a bit of encouragement and rope-pulling from up top, I made it over the cliff after about a half hour of struggle. The youngsters cheered. Yirga then took me to the monastery chapel where we took off our shoes before entering. We met a leading monk there named Abba Kiros who showed us some ancient manuscripts. He told me St. Arwegawi was the son of a king. The saint chose this spot for his monastery because "this location was shining, more than seven times the normal sunshine. Then the serpent helped him, and he brought him upright. It was a very big serpent. About thirty meters."

I had many questions for him. He was used to skeptics.

"I told you that we have a lot of miracles, no matter what people say about it—scientists, believers, unbelievers."

I asked him if he had any other information about the giant snake that once lived there.

"The serpent is still alive," he said. "Underground."[5]

While a girl-eating serpent-king no longer haunts Ethiopians, the serpent of European rationalism attacks the ancient Christian civilization in a much more dangerous and destructive way. Unlike the generous Ethiopian scholar's view toward oral history, Western logic is harsh and insists on scientific rigor. Its ruthless demands for analytical truth attack the very soul of the Ethiopian religious practice, and more particularly, the existence of the Ark of the Covenant.

"The history of the world travels from East to West, for Europe is absolutely the end of history," wrote the great Western rationalist Frederich Hegel. The East for Hegel and his ilk did not include Africa, a people that European rationalists still considered under "childlike" and "traditional" mindsets.[6]

It was under this backdrop that I entered a classroom of the Holy Trinity Theological College in Addis Ababa and prepared to speak to 100 graduate students about my intentions to write a history of their great country.

"From whose perspective will you write it?" asked several students, with a tinge of indignation. "Will it be an Ethiopian perspective, or European?"

Were they asking me if I was going to demand Western rationality and logic in my assessments? Or were they saying something else? It wasn't the first time I had been confronted with the issue.

Left: Ancient Ethiopian coin with Christian cross

Below: Manuscript of Book of Enoch shown to author, archived at Institute of Ethiopian Studies, Addis Ababa

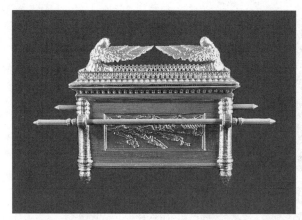

Left: Depiction of the Ark according to description in Book of Exodus

Below: Author's guide in Axum, Yirga Fis-seha, with chapel for Ark of the Covenant in background

Top and middle: Barefoot Ethiopian armies

Bottom: Italians return after Battle of Adwa to consecrate monument to fallen soldiers

Top: Author drinks coffee in Adwa with mountain of Adwa battlefield in background

Right: Monument to Mussolini placed by the dictator at the site of the Battle of Adwa

Above: Edenic scene in Ethiopia at Take Tana

Below: The Obelisk of Axum in Rome before its return to Ethiopia

Left: The Meditation Room at the United Nations

Below: Executed Mussolini hanging upside down (second from left) along with his mistress, Claretta Petacci (third from left)

Above: One of many icon murals common in northern Ethiopia. *Left side of mural:* St. Aregawi helped up the Debre Damo cliff by the giant serpent. *Right side:* the Virgin Mary and Christ child with two archangels

Below: Icon of the Ethiopian coffee ceremony

Top left: St. Garima, who copied the oldest surviving illustrated Bible, the Garima Gospels

Top right: Another icon of St. Arwegawi and the giant serpent

Left: Author struggles to reach top of the cliffs of Debre Damo Monastery

Above: Young worshippers in the unplugged village of Gororo

Below: Orthodox Christian worshippers dressed in white during Timkat feast (Theophany) in Addis Ababa

Ethiopians celebrate Timkat Festival (Theophany) in Addis Ababa.

I was challenged in the same way by Dr. Teclehaimanot Gebreselassie when we met over a cup of coffee in the basement of what used to be Haile Selassie's palace. Trained at Northwestern University in Chicago, the former chairman of the History Department at Addis Ababa University mapped out on a napkin the three monasteries that I should visit while in Axum. Then he challenged me not to be "Eurocentric." Asked what that meant, he referred me to the work of an Ethiopian professor at Dayton University with a doctorate from France. Messay Kebede's paper on Eurocentrism makes some interesting points, but the main idea is that historical development should not always be measured by "progress" or by economic or technological advancement. Other standards exist by which to measure history. He notes that the Ethiopians have had an interest very different, if not more important, than the Europeans: preserving traditional Christian beliefs while surrounded by antagonistic cultures. By this measure, they have performed quite well, says Messay, whose references to Marx suggest he is not necessarily coming from a perspective friendly only to conservatives.[7] One might sum up his views with a famous quote from Mahatma Gandhi: "There is more to life than increasing its speed."

"The development of commerce would not have stopped Islam," writes Messay. "On the contrary, a trading society would have quickly succumbed to Islamic appeals. From the viewpoint of non-Westernized Ethiopians, Ethiopian history is therefore a success story. Ethiopians sacrificed wealth and the refinements of civilization, even opted for isolation, to make sure they remained faithful to their vocation."[8]

All this information I juggled in my head when discussing issues of Ethiopian history with my Ethiopian friends, always hoping I would be viewing things from an Ethiopian perspective.

I sat down over coffee with two friends who were students at the seminary: Bazien, the Toronto transplant they call "The King," and Elias, the student coordinator for 3,000 seminarians.

"What do you make of things like the snake of Debre Damo, which to the modern mind seems crazy?" I asked, showing my willingness to question Western rationalism.

"In the West they like to say there is one fact, and that's it," said Bazien, a deacon and clergyman. "But for me there is both allegorical and historical facts. I mean, the worship of the snake was found there in Debre Damo. So that cannot be overlooked. We do see a minimizing of the serpent god, as being a tool used by the God of Abraham. Allegory could be put into place. Or history. It could be both. It depends on the culture of the people."

I was listening. I sort of got it but sort of didn't. At the risk of showing my Eurocentric perspective, I asked the million-dollar question: "But would you say it is true?"

To help their dilemma, the Ethiopian Church calls the story of Arwe, the first king and reptilian, a legend only. However, the story of St. Arwegawi is read aloud in church annually, as prescribed by the church calendar, the definitive action for whether a story should be believed. So, the big snake helping the saint up the cliff is a legitimate faith challenge.

Bazien was not willing to discount the story. "I don't specifically say one or the other. As a history, it very much could be. But me, being 1,500 years later, I cannot say directly with a full answer, but both are possible."

Elias, shorter with glasses, and a chemical engineer, was less nuanced in his answer. "It's all true for me," he said. "If I believe the talking donkey story in the Bible, why not? It's possible. Anything is possible for God. The Church affirms it and accepts it. And if is found in the Church, it is right."[9]

Elias was getting at the real issue: science—or what we see—versus revealed religion. The Bible says we live by faith, not by sight. Traditional Christians—Orthodox, Catholic, Ethiopian, and modern Protestant believers in the Bible—all choose to believe what is written and revealed over what science theorizes. We all hope that certain alleged facts are not incontrovertible proofs to contradict the faith. We hope they are still only alleged, and time will prove otherwise. "Faith does not go well with scientific proof," said Ethiopian Patriarch Paulos I. Even Europe's top Ethiopic scholar, Oxford's Edward Ullendorff, when discussing the possibility of archeological confirmation of the Sheba story, acknowledges that such confirmation "has indeed happened to many other Biblical stories."[10]

Science really has no way of proving or disproving whether a giant snake helped a man up a cliff at Debre Damo Monastery. However, Elias and Bazien get some help from ancient history. Reputable scholar Diodorus Siculus, a Greek in Sicily, reports in the first century BC that Ethiopia battled against snakes that were "30 cubits long" and ate oxen, bulls, and elephants. And almost as if Bazien and Elias had slipped him a twenty-dollar bill, he adds: ". . . it is not fair to doubt the word of the Ethiopians or to assume that the report which they circulated far and wide was a mere fiction."[11]

Did a snake help a man up a cliff? The answer has few consequences for most Christians worldwide. But the bigger question of the Ark of the Covenant is much different. All Christians share in the belief of Moses's golden box. All Christians acknowledge this object as central to Old Testament worship of Yahweh God. All Christians understand its powers. Does it really exist today? Could it really be in Ethiopia? This question has tangible—and fascinating—ramifications.

Bazien and Elias have no doubt about the Ark of the Covenant's existence in Ethiopia. Neither does their professor, Girma Batu. It's like an American doubting the existence of George Washington or the Declaration of Independence (which, unlike the Ark, you can actually go and see, but, for me, it was quite faded and almost impossible to read). Some observers are not so enthusiastic about Ethiopia's Ark claim. Eritrean historian Michela Wrong expected a more sophisticated answer when she asked the question to a manager of a computer school in Tigray. "Where else would it be?" he replied.

"What is unnerving about the Queen of Sheba legend is that it is not a quaint historical tale," Michela writes, noting that the claim that Ethiopia's emperors are descended from Sheba and Solomon was actually enshrined in the country's Constitution. Haile Selassie "was still insisting on his direct link with the deity in the middle of the 20th century, era of television, the combustion engine, and the jet plane."[12]

Dr. Randall Price's weighty criticism of Ethiopia's Ark claims are more substantial than mere modernistic contempt. He uses historical and biblical evidence to make his argument against it. "Regardless of what is in the Axum chapel," he writes in his book *Searching for the Ark of the Covenant*, "Ethiopians still believe it is the Ark." He is a card-carrying Bible believer, professor at Liberty University, founder of World of the Bible Ministries, and producer of the video "The Bible on Trial: Beyond a Reasonable Doubt."

He is described as a Christian Zionist, having taken 107 trips to Israel and directed excavations at the Qumran Plateau, site of the Dead Sea Scrolls. He has authored thirty books and written for the magazine *Israel My Glory*. He is solidly credentialed with a doctorate from the University of Texas in Middle Eastern Studies.

Price's first argument is that there is no written documentation of the claim of the Ark being in Ethiopia until the end of the thirteenth century. When this documentation does appear, it deals with a conflict between two dynasties, one claiming Jewish lineage from Moses's wife and the other claiming to be descended from Solomon and Sheba. "Jews were a threat," writes Zionist Price, who rejects what he calls "replacement theology."[13]

"The view that Christianity replaced Israel as God's chosen people is the perspective in the Kebra Negast," he writes. "This viewpoint supports a medieval date of the legend's origin and points to a political and religious rivalry as its cause." Thus, Price and others place a fourteenth century date on the composition of the Kebra Negast, 2,500 years after Ethiopians allege it was written.

One of the strongest arguments for the Ethiopian Ark story is the existence of the "black Jews" in Ethiopia, a group also called Beta Israel or "Falasha Jews." Today there are just a few thousand hidden in the northern mountains, but these Jews were once a dynasty in Ethiopia—for a short time—500 years ago. Why are they there? How did they possibly get there? According to highly credentialed Ethiopian scholar Sergew Hable Selassie: "The existence in Ethiopia of a Jewish religious community, the Falasha, with all its archaic ritual and religious practices, is a fact." He goes on to quote another scholar, Samuel Mercer: "They know nothing of the Babylonian captivity nor of the Talmud, but they live according to the laws of Moses and they call themselves the House of Israel." Their authenticity was confirmed in the 1980s when Israeli rabbis deemed the Falashas as true Jews, making them eligible for the Law of Return and Israeli citizenship, one of the reasons for their dwindling numbers.

Price is unfazed by this anomalous sect of Jews in Ethiopia and sees no connection to the Ark or the Solomon and Sheba story. He says Ethiopian Jewry is 600 years old at the most, citing the work of Dr. Steven Kaplan of Hebrew University, *The Beta Israel in Ethiopia.* Therefore, the Kebra Negast and its Solomon and Sheba Ark legend can be traced to a political and religious conflict in the fourteenth century after Christ, says Price.[14]

Price has impressive credentials. It would be difficult to out-credential him in areas related to where the Ark resides today. But there is, in fact, a scholar who can do this, and his views are friendlier to the Ethiopian claims. British scholar Edward Ullendorff taught himself Hebrew and Arabic at age fifteen, received his doctorate from Oxford, studied also at St. Andrews and Hebrew University, and edited manuscripts at the Cambridge Library. To honor the late professor, the British Academy established the annual Edward Ullendorff Award in 2012 for scholarly distinction in Semitic Languages and Ethiopian Studies.

Unlike the Zionist Randall Price, Ullendorff may have run afoul of zealous Israelis during his years at Hebrew University where he was known to show compassion to the Arabs in Jerusalem and was often found discussing Palestinian politics. He titled his memoir *The Two Zions*, tipping his hat to the Ethiopian Jerusalem.

In his works, Ullendorff never comes out directly to give his opinion on an Ethiopian Ark, but he goes out of his way to be generous to such a view. He clearly loves Ethiopia, calling its beauty "stark and overpowering" and its people "a handsome race, elegant, subtle, and nervous." That last quip was likely related to his years in Ethiopia during troublesome times. In a picture with Haile Selassie, he notes that of the eleven leaders he was standing with, at least six had been murdered. He said the emperor's "slight figure was in marked contrast to the overpowering impact of his personality."

Ullendorff also had a bit of a sense of humor. Along with many books on Ethiopia, the ancient Ge'ez language, and the book of Enoch, he wrote *The Bawdy Bible*, which explores the Hebrew Bible's "unabashed outspokenness" on sexual matters.[15]

While Price sees a negative implication in the fourteenth century being the earliest mention of the Ark in Ethiopia, Ullendorff views this event with a glass-half-full attitude. This first mention in the late Middle Ages comes from Abu al-Markarim, a priest in the Coptic Orthodox Church in Alexandria, in his noteworthy work, *History of Churches and Monasteries of Egypt and Some Neighboring Countries*. Apparently, Abu al-Markarim found a way to get a glimpse of the Ark: "The Abyssinians possess the Ark of the Covenant, in which are the two tables of stone inscribed by the finger of God with the commandments which he ordained for the children of Israel. The Ark of the Covenant is placed upon the altar, but is not so wide as the altar; it is as high as the knee of a man and is overlaid with gold."

Ullendorff looks at this description and compares it with passages in Exodus 25 and Deuteronomy 10. "This description clearly shows the marked resemblance to the Old Testament Ark of the Covenant," he concludes.

Regarding any documentation of the Ark before this first-known event with Abu al-Markarim in the late 1300s, Ullendorff uses a creative angle to reach his belief of a much earlier existence. He notes that the Old Testament priesthood rituals in the country, the Ethiopian Ark claim, and the "consciousness of having inherited from Israel the legitimate claim to being regarded as the chosen people of God"—all these must have evolved in a solid way before the accepted dating of Christianity coming to Ethiopia in AD 325. According to Ullendorff, this conclusion means Ethiopian Ark ceremonies took place at least 1,000 years earlier than Price's fourteenth century date. Why does Ullendorff believe this? Because in those days, no Christian society wanted any association with Jews and Judaism. "For it seems difficult to imagine that a people recently converted to Christianity (not by a Christian Jew, but by the Syrian missionary Frumentius) should *thereafter* have begun to boast of Jewish descent and to insist on Hebraic customs and institutions." For Ullendorff, this means that the Ark phenomenon was a part of Ethiopia well before the fourth century.[16]

CHAPTER TWELVE

WHEN MY ETHIOPIAN tour guide, Yirga, announced that we were heading to the Pantelewon Monastery, I figured it would not be too long of a trip, as the map showed that it was only three miles from where I was staying in Axum. He failed to tell me that we were not driving, but walking, and that the building sits atop a hill that might be considered a mountain. At least it wasn't a cliff like Debre Damo, but the "hike" was much longer.

As it was a Sunday, along the way we saw Ethiopians headed to church by the thousands—mostly young people, an unusual sight for this Westerner. All of the women were wearing white head coverings, and many of the men wore white prayer robes. The dynamic crowd moved with a certain rhythm. Drumbeats, though more modest and subtle than what we would expect in Africa, are an important part of the ritual walk up the hill to the various churches that are being attended on higher ground. Services last for hours.

Upon reaching the very top of the small mountain, Yirga took me to the chapel and showed me several eight-inch diameter holes in the natural rock flooring just outside the entrance. They were used for animal sacrifices before the site was Christianized, he told me, and the blood flowed into the holes. When we visited the monks, I was shown old crosses and crowns, and specifically a rock fragment on which was ancient lettering. The Sabean script reads "DMT" and provides the earliest documentation known for the "Damat" civilization that existed in Ethiopia either before or alongside the ancient Axumite empire. There also exists an incense burner with "BR" inscribed on it.

Were these people Jewish or part-Jewish? Dr. Bernard Leeman and other scholars suggest that "BR" stands for *Hebrew*, which stems from the Biblical name Eber, Abraham's ancestor. As ancient languages did not have vowels, BR is how Eber is configured in the Hebrew script. Leeman contends that this inscription is the world's "oldest mention of the Hebrew people." He recruits Ullendorff into his corner, stating that the Oxford scholar "believes that maybe half of Ethiopia's population was Israelite when Christianity was introduced."

Ullendorff agrees with the sceptic Randall Price that the Kebra Negast was published in the fourteenth century and its purpose included a confirmation of the Solomonic empire in Ethiopia. (Church authorities also agree.) However, "its author, Yeshaq of Axum, was thus mainly [a] redactor and interpreter of material *which had long been known* but had not until then found a coordinating hand, an expository mind, and a great national need," Ullendorff writes. "The Kebra Negast is not merely a literary work, but—as the Old Testament to the Hebrews and the Koran to the Arabs—it is the repository of Ethiopian national and religious feelings."[1]

Other scholars have pointed out that the Kebra Negast omits the story of Solomon's two sons and their divided kingdom, evidence of a missing Ark too important to leave out unless the Ethiopians left Israel before that event happened and the first writer of the Kebra Negast was, therefore, too far from Israel to hear the story. "The earliest part is a totally Israelite...document known as the Sheba-Menelik Cycle and appears to have been originally recorded in Solomon's reign," writes Leeman. "The second part, the Caleb Cycle, was probably written in AD 520 on the eve of the Christian invasion of Jewish Yemen."

The Jewish kingdom in Arabic Yemen, just across the Red Sea from Ethiopia, serves as an effective tool for Price to throw a mortal dagger at the Ark theory. He points to scholastic work stating that the Queen of Sheba actually lived in Yemen, not Ethiopia. And, in fact, the Bible never associates the queen who visited Solomon with Ethiopia or Cush. We are only given the descriptor "Sheba" in the Old Testament. In the New Testament, Jesus refers to her as the "Queen of the South."

"...Sheba as an Ethiopian is mythical," writes Price. "Historians agree that she was not from Ethiopia but was from Saba in southern Arabia (modern Yemen) and ruled over the Sabeans." In this view, Sheba is the same word as Saba, where we get Sabean. Price also points out that Axum was nonexistent in Sheba's day and, even if one looks to nearby Meroe (Sudan) as the ancient Cushite civilization of Sheba, it too "was too small to support an empire."

Ullendorff equivocates a bit on the issue. "It scarcely matters very greatly whether we have to seek the queen's home in South-west Arabia [Yemen] or in the horn of Africa [Ethiopia]," he writes. He seems less interested in attaching Ethiopia's Ark claim to the Bible and more interested in simply enjoying the legend for its own sake.[2]

This mortal wound regarding the location of Sheba is seconded by Graham Hancock, author of the highly popular *The Sign and the Seal*. He relays his conversations on the matter with a friend, British scholar Dr. Richard Pankhurst, a leading historian of Ethiopia and founder of the Institute of Ethiopian Studies at Addis Ababa University. In my several visits there to meet with the Institute's current director, Pankhurst's large photo loomed prominently over the waiting area.

As a historian, Pankhurst could not accept the Kebra Negast, says Hancock, "particularly since the homeland of the Queen of Sheba had almost certainly been located in Arabia and not in Ethiopia at all."

To clarify, Hancock asked Pankhurst a direct question: "Do you think there's any possibility that what they say might be true?"

"Frankly, no. No possibility at all. As a matter of fact, Axum didn't even *exist* in the period when this was supposed to have happened. It simply wasn't there."

Pankhurst noted that Axum wasn't founded until the second or third century BC, 700 years after the Solomon and Sheba story of the Bible.

"Well," said Hancock, "that rather puts paid to the whole story doesn't it?"

"Yes," said Pankhurst.

Then, he did some equivocating of his own. "I expect it's just feasible that the Ark could have been brought up to some other place in

Ethiopia which later got mixed up with Axum in the traditions that have been handed down. There are, however, many other fallacies, anachronisms and inaccuracies in the legend—which is why no historian or archaeologist worth his salt has ever been prepared to spend time investigating it."

GRAHAM HANCOCK

Pankhurst throws a lot of water on the Ark claim, but scholars like Ullendorff were still able to show a more generous spirit on the matter. Meanwhile, Graham Hancock seized on Pankhurst's olive branch that the Ark may have reached Ethiopia centuries later by other means. We will look at his investigation later.

Hancock is a bit of a phenomenon. He has sold over five million books, including *Magicians of the Gods*, *Supernatural*, and *Underworld: The Mysterious Origins of Civilization*. He deals in speculation, openly and unabashedly. Nevertheless, his 600-page work on Ethiopia and the Ark is highly documented with the best available sources. I've read it carefully, more than once, and I've studied separately many of the primary sources he cites. His scholarship is conscientious and accurate. Critics, however, are rather harsh. It is true, he spends a decent part of the book chasing some strange connections between the Ark, the Knights Templar, and the Holy Grail. What the critics fail to appreciate is that he makes it clear, all the way through, when he is speculating and going down an adventurous rabbit trail, and when he is being factual. It's carefully done.

He does make the book fabulously entertaining. In all my years, I've come across very few authors like Graham Hancock who can use story structure to make nonfiction a thrilling read. This not only takes talent, it takes a heart of service and is a labor of love for the reader. I have some of my own bones to pick with Hancock, as I will share later. But as a fellow writer, I can only admire what he has achieved.

Price does not agree with Hancock's views. Ullendorff has a clear disdain for him. The popular author's case with the proper British scholar was likely not helped when Hancock's book became an international bestseller in 1992. One paper called it a "first class detective story" and the *Seattle Times* dubbed it "a great intellectual detective yarn."

I suppose yarns are not what certain scholars are looking for, not in circles where academic protocol is what determines credibility. Ullendorff told the *Los Angeles Times* that *The Sign and the Seal* was "a sad joke." Despite the dispersions, Hancock emerged in an instant with far greater name recognition than any other expert on Ethiopia. For whatever reason, a retired Ullendorff decided to take the gloves off and end his formal friendliness and generosity toward the Ethiopian Ark theory. Hancock must be confronted.

"I wasted a lot of time reading it," Ullendorff said.

The *Los Angeles Times* reporter asked Ullendorff, "Does anybody really know what lies behind the curtains of the chapel?"

"They have a wooden box, but it's empty," he said. "Middle-to late-medieval construction, when these were fabricated ad hoc."

"How do you know?"

"I've seen it," said the 72-year-old scholar, who failed to share that fact during his many decades of writing up to that point. "There was no problem getting access when I saw it in 1941."[3]

Ullendorff's comments, and Price's exposure of the Arabian Sheba, pose some difficult challenges for those like me attempting to view the country's history from an Ethiopian perspective. Nevertheless, as a believer in revealed religion, I am used to waiting out certain debunkers until the facts conform to the ancient teaching. Although historical and scriptural support looked to be waning, I saw nothing in the Scripture that contradicted the Kebra Negast. I decided to keep waiting.

Price does not attack Hancock for his popularity. The Liberty University professor has peddled 30 books himself over the years. He disagrees with some of Hancock's biblical interpretations. For the Ark theory, he resorted to a bit of ridicule. "The Kebra Negast attributes magical powers to King Solomon, as well as the ability to talk with birds and animals and to create a flying vessel as a gift for the Queen of Sheba," Price says. "The archangel Michael flew over Menelik's party and parted the sea so they could march on dry ground. The legend states that the Ark destroyed all of Egypt's idols as it flew overhead, and that without the Ark to magically supply Solomon's wisdom, he became foolish and idolatrous."[4]

This rant is strange for a man who founded the World of the Bible Ministries. The good book tells us that Solomon does, in fact, turn idolatrous later in life. The Ark, according to the Bible, destroyed Philistine idols when they came near, an animal talked to Balaam in the book of Numbers, and Elijah flies in a chariot. Angels already caused a group to pass over the sea on dry ground at least once in history, according to the Bible. Arguably twice. The Bible man seems to have a problem with miracles. I don't.

However, Dr. Price made my quest much more difficult when citing a verse about King Josiah in the Old Testament. The materials I had read all stated that the Ark generally disappears from the Old Testament after Solomon. It basically is not mentioned. This is one of the very curious matters for biblical scholars that helps raise eyebrows and give some traction to considering the Kebra Negast theory. But the key words are "generally" and "basically," because there is one verse that does in fact mention the Ark. And it only takes one. This verse deals with a historical period 350 years after Solomon and Sheba.

In one of the last parts of the Old Testament (chronologically), King Josiah gives this command to his priests in 2 Chronicles 35:3: "Put the holy ark in the house which Solomon the son of David, king of Israel, built. It shall no longer be a burden on your shoulders."

Here, in 622 BC, King Josiah commands the Ark to be placed back into the temple. This contradiction to the Kebra Negast's claim of the Ark leaving Jerusalem and going to Ethiopia 400 years earlier, a contradiction to the story so beloved and embraced by my Ethiopian friends, did not simply create a problem related to believing in miracles. This conflicting testimony was Scripture itself, indicating the existence of the Ark in Jerusalem, not in Ethiopia. For me, either the Bible is true or the Kebra Negast is true.

When I first met Professor Girma Batu, overseeing 3,000 students as vice academic dean of the Holy Trinity Theological College, we had lunch at one of Addis Ababa's nicer restaurants. "Lucy," it is named, after the alleged prehistoric human bones discovered in Ethiopia. He is the scholar mentioned at the very beginning of this book, and he is polite and gentle, like most Ethiopians. He is also highly credentialed. After a nice meal and a time of getting to know each other, I shared my dilemma.

"I want to believe the Kebra Negast, the story about Sheba and Menelik and their bringing the Ark to Ethiopia. But the Bible says in 2 Chronicles 35:3 that King Josiah had the Ark brought out. Therefore, the Ark was in Jerusalem, not Ethiopia. I can't get past that."

He nodded his head and said nothing.

CHAPTER THIRTEEN

HAILE SELASSIE WAS snubbed by the British elite. Upon departing from the French port of Djibouti on the British ship *Enterprise*, he sailed two days to Jerusalem, where he dispatched a telegram to the League of Nations announcing his need for a time of exile. He waited to announce his intentions to address the League of Nations itself. He then sailed toward England. But the British exchanged his ship for a more ordinary vessel to downplay the emperor's landing, a ruse by the British royalty to avoid giving him a formal reception.

In a private meeting with Britain's foreign secretary, Haile Selassie requested a meeting with King Edward VIII. "The British monarch stubbornly refused to receive the emperor at Buckingham Palace," wrote Asfa-Wossen. "The prime minister, Stanley Baldwin, also went to great lengths to avoid meeting him. *Time* magazine referred to Haile Selassie as 'The Lion Incognito.'"

Upon learning the emperor's intentions, the British government exerted all of its diplomatic means to keep him from traveling in person to Geneva, Switzerland, to plead Ethiopia's case to the League of Nations. "Tell your Emperor," Foreign Minister Anthony Eden informed Haile Selassie's ambassador, "that no head of state has ever addressed the League—it would be unprecedented! The emperor really must not appear. It would compromise his imperial dignity."[1]

Mussolini insisted that there was no resistance left. "I have dismantled the government of Ethiopia," he wrote to the League of Nations. "The representatives of a vanquished country should not be present in the Geneva assembly." Haile Selassie said the opposite in his press statements: "It has been evident that world opinion has been in part duped." Guerilla warfare was being fought against the Italians all across the country, he said, only one-third of which the Italians occupied. Even that "can only be defended by the air force and . . . mustard gas."

"Italy also distributes leaflets from the air," Haile Selassie said, claiming "that the Imperial Ethiopian government does not exist, and presents me to the public as if I have abandoned my responsibilities and mission. By means of such sinister acts, it consistently strives to mislead and misinform the people."[2]

League members were cornered. On the one hand, they were working with all their might to keep Mussolini happy and away from Hitler. The joining of forces of these two dictators might defeat the Allies in a world war. On the other hand, betraying a smaller nation like Ethiopia ruined the moral authority of the League to act against the Führer if he invaded European countries as he had been threatening. "Hitler had been observing these events carefully," write Cannistraro and Philips. "Mussolini had defied the League, disregarded French pleas, withstood British threats, frustrated Roosevelt's political maneuvers, and gone on to smash the Ethiopians on the battlefield. Hitler's admiration for Mussolini soared, while his contempt for the Western democracies increased."

"The whole world lives in fear of imminent war," Haile Selassie's Ethiopian advisor in Britain told him. "As a guest, Your Majesty should not be involved in anything that would give the impression that Your Majesty was participating in politics." He also told him that member states were discussing whether the emperor had any authority left and if on that basis he could be barred from Geneva. "Your Majesty should know that British lawyers are searching for ways to prevent you or your envoys from appearing at the League."

Haile Selassie refused to back down. "I will not lose hope in the return of my country's independence because I believe that, in the end, God's judgment will eventually visit the weak and the mighty alike, according to what each deserves." He embarked on the trip to Geneva, even though "the times were insecure," as he noted. "We passed through France, and while we stayed in Switzerland, the two governments afforded us the utmost protection and care. Security agents joined hands and stood around us like a fence so nobody could come close to us...motorcycle police rode on our left and right to offer protection."[3]

Just before the emperor was scheduled to address the great assembly, a letter was read from the podium: "Italy considers it an honor to inform the League of Nations about her efforts to civilize Ethiopia," the official statement asserted. "Italy sees this as her sacred duty." As speakers were called on for discussion, not only was oil still not part of the official sanctions, but the matter being discussed on the floor was the removal of the sanctions altogether. Haile Selassie was asking for financial help to fund the resistance movement in Ethiopia.

It was now time for the African spokesman to address the world. He prepared his speech in French, but, at the last minute, reached for his Amharic script to deliver this historic speech in his native tongue. "Haile Selassie stood before the microphone in the great assembly hall in Geneva. There was a breathless hush as the eyes of all present turned to the slight, diminutive figure in a voluminous black cloak. But the President, M. Van Zeeland, had hardly given him the signal to speak when pandemonium broke out in the auditorium. The uproar was caused by twenty or so Italian journalists booing, jeering, and yelling insults at the emperor."

"As Haile Selassie stood there impassively, waiting for order to be restored, Titulescu, the Romanian chairman, jumped to his feet and shouted: 'A la porte les sauvages! ('The savages are at the door!')." More mayhem broke out, and it took ten minutes for the Swiss police to remove the agitators. As soon as they were ejected, the emperor began his speech:

"I, Haile Selassie I, Emperor of Ethiopia, am here today to claim the justice which is due to my people and the assistance promised to it eight months ago when fifty nations asserted that an aggression had been committed...I assert that the problem submitted to the Assembly today is a much wider one than the removal of sanctions. It is not merely a settlement of Italian aggression. It is collective. It is the very existence of the League of Nations." He turned to the delegates and asked them not to recognize an Italian conquest. "Representatives of the world, I have come to Geneva to discharge in your midst the most painful of the duties of a head of state. What reply shall I take back to my people?"[4]

The emperor's solemn speech was greeted with enthusiastic applause. "Everyone agreed that it was a great speech," wrote *Time* magazine, "one of the noblest, most factual, irrefutable, and moving ever made before the League of Nations."

MUSSOLINI

That same month, Mussolini ordered that any Ethiopians who were captured and did not surrender must be executed. An Italian paper applauded: "The crack of the firing squad's rifles was a burst of defiant Fascist laughter at the world that so sanctimoniously condemns us, a shot of defiance to the powers who imposed sanctions on us." The emperor explained what was happening: "Mussolini began to jeer and insult the League of Nations, [saying] its charter and procedures were useless pieces of paper and that the League was a useless forum for bickering. As a result of these abusive and inflammatory words, many countries began to shiver visibly."

The great nations were listening to Mussolini. Less than two weeks after Haile Selassie's historic speech, the Ethiopian resolution in the League of Nations was defeated. Sanctions were officially dropped in all areas of commerce, including oil, the most strategic and important. The British fleet was recalled from the Mediterranean. The emperor's words were "totally without effect on Geneva's sleek, hard, slippery statesmen," wrote *Time*. Haile Selassie "had a pathetic faith in the

League of Nations," said Barker. "Mussolini's victory over the emperor and the League of Nations seemed to be complete."[5]

However, the small nations were listening to Haile Selassie. His boldness in appearing before the League broke all tradition in the pattern of relations between European and African peoples. "It is the value of promises made to small states that their integrity and their independence shall be respected.... In a word, it is international morality that is at stake," said the Ethiopian spokesman for greater Africa and all third world countries. Then he delivered a powerful statement, but also ironic for an Ethiopian, as we shall later discover. "Apart from the Kingdom of our Lord, there is not on this earth any nation that is superior to any other."[6]

Ghana's president was furious with the League, which he said had "declared war on me personally" and he condemned the "wickedness of colonialism." Later assemblies were ominous. "These were wretched days at Geneva," noted Britain's League representative Anthony Eden, a future prime minister. "One morning during an Assembly session about Abyssinia, I suddenly heard a report and saw a figure fall on the benches at my right hand," he wrote. "A Czech spectator had shot himself dead after a cry of warning, apparently about the fate of small countries. His death was a message to his countrymen sealed with his life."

Mussolini was intent on getting Haile Selassie to formally concede his defeat. "It is because of you that I am unable to obtain recognition for Italy's claim on Ethiopia," the Duce said in a delivered message. "Sign a statement and release your claim over Ethiopia in favor of me." Financial compensation was implied for the emperor who now lived in a cold, small country home in Bath, England, a world away from his former palace life with many servants.

"I rejected whatever gifts, material benefits, or political positions that were offered to me to enhance my personal well-being," he wrote regarding his time in exile. "My faith lies in the justness and power of the Almighty God."[7]

Italian General Rodolfo Graziano intended to carry out to the full the Duce's wishes for more executions. He spared the life of General

Ras Imru, who went to a prison in Italy, but his two sons, who led an attack on Addis Ababa, were executed, both shot in the town square. Ras Kassa's two sons, Dejazmatch Aberra and Demazmatch Asfa-Wossen Kassa, were also taken to the highlands and summarily executed. Archbishop Abuna Petros, accused of inspiring these young officers to attack the Italian strongholds, was executed publicly in the Addis marketplace. Mussolini was in a rush for formal recognition. "It took us seven months to conquer the empire," he declared. "But to occupy and pacify it will take far less time." Graziani then launched a campaign with the vague title, "Operations of the Great Colonial Policy."

Haile Selassie, in his autobiography, describes this operation, beginning with stealing "an ancient and historic obelisk, which a previous emperor erected 1600 years ago." Executions, including that of the Archbishop Petros and other Ethiopian clergy, were named, noting that the archbishop was killed for his refusal to excommunicate Ethiopian soldiers who did not surrender. Prisoners were tortured and burned at the stake, along with "the deliberate arson of St. George Church in Addis along with other churches." Relatives were denied the bodies of slain soldiers and instead the Italians "stacked the bodies and burned them like waste." Unmarried women and those women left with deceased husbands were taken "to concentration camps as prostitutes."[8]

But the people of Ethiopia were not asking their emperor to back down on the world stage. A captive in Addis wrote to him of their renewed hope "when we learned about Your Majesty's appearance before the League of Nations holding the scepter of Solomon in your hands." Another leader in Ethiopia wrote "even if we do not have arms, we prefer to die as heroes fighting with sticks and stones rather than dying in cold blood."

The stories of valor are numerous. General Afework refused to receive treatment after being hit with an artillery gun, even though the wound developed gangrene. He feared his men would lose heart if he left the battle. Forty-eight hours later, he collapsed dead on the field and, as he predicted, the troops scattered. Another officer relayed the story of a general whose army was destroyed. "He and two of his servants, three people all together, were surrounded. A white came to him and asked: Are you Dejasmatch Balcha? When he said, yes, I am, the white man said, surrender your arms and untie your pistol belt. Dejasmatch Balcha said, 'I am not here to surrender my arms,' and he killed the white man; then, he and his two servants died instantly without having much suffering."[9]

Another captured Ethiopian had a bullet still in his head, with not long to live. They interrogated him."Who are you?"

"The commander of a thousand men."

"Why don't you lie down on that stretcher? The Italians do not harm their prisoners."

"I prefer to die on my feet. We swore to the emperor that we would capture your positions or die in the attempt. We have not won, but we have died."

He then pointed to the valley scattered with dead bodies. "Look!"

Another general, Gebre Mariam, as his army was destructing, ran into the center of the fighting and was shot and killed while celebrating his martyrdom for the Bridegroom and shouting, "Today is the day of my wedding!"

Some did give in. "We surrendered our arms to the Italians when they came because we thought they were protectors of the weak and lovers of justice," wrote one survivor. "But now we see indescribable injustice being done to us." Haile Selassie refused, in part, to officially acknowledge Italy's victory because he had no belief in a humane occupation. In fact, he spoke of the opposite, and rightly so, with General Graziani wiring orders like the following: "We must continue with the work of total destruction."

In fact, when the emperor first left his country and sailed to Jerusalem to telegram the League of Nations, he wrote that he had "chosen to take the road to exile in order that our people shall not be exterminated." Mussolini and the Italians routinely rejected the accusations, but the emperor invoked the words "extinction" and "exterminate" several times, and discussed the concept in a meeting with the Archbishop of Canterbury: "We know the Italians are out to destroy our race," he told the head of the Anglican church. "For the last 3,000 years Ethiopia has been struggling against paganism. Yet, it is a sad commentary that, today, it is denied its own freedom by another Christian people."

"This is a question which has deeply affected my conscience," the archbishop told Haile Selassie. "I beg you not to rub salt into it." He noted that "we heard the Pope of Rome had declared legitimacy and recognized the Italian occupation of Ethiopia." Then he promised to meet with the British prime minister "to inform him of the Italian objective to exterminate your race."[10]

These were bold charges. In fact, Italian General Graziani had said "the Duce shall have Ethiopia, with or without the Ethiopians." Could extermination have indeed been the Italian goal, similar to Hitler's goal to rid Germany of the Jews? Official transcriptions of Mussolini's orders to his generals, obtained years later, helped provide the answer.

"8th July 1936 (Top Secret): To Field Marshal Rodolfo Graziani: Authorization renewed to carry out systematic campaign of terror and *extermination* against rebel natives and those supporting them. Maximum retaliation only way to bring situation under control in short time. Confirmation awaited. Mussolini."[11]

These were the days of eugenics, and words like extermination were not foreign to scientists looking to purify certain races. The word was also not unknown to Hitler, Mussolini, or the colleagues of Margaret Sanger in America, who targeted the hapless Negroes and other "unfit" people.

CHAPTER FOURTEEN

SANGER WAS CONCERNED for her Negro project. In 1939, she wrote: "We do not want word to go out that we want to exterminate the Negro population, and the minister is the man who can straighten out that idea if it ever occurs to any of their more rebellious members."[1]

In fairness to Sanger, the context involves her recruiting Christian pastors, "colored ministers with social service backgrounds, and with engaging personalities" to travel the country promoting birth control. "The most successful educational approach to the Negro is through religious appeal," she said. Recruiting ministers was in response to a message from one of the Negro Project directors, Proctor & Gamble heir Dr. Clarence Gamble: "There is great danger that we will fail," Dr. Gamble said, "because the Negroes think it a plan for extermination. Hence, let's appear to let the colored run it..."[2]

Was their plan to exterminate? Or were they reacting to the blacks' fears of being exterminated? Either way, the language is disconcerting. Many other Sanger quotes allude to an extermination mentality, and one's pause on the question should not include a belief that Sanger was incapable of such thinking. She wrote in her book *Woman and the New Race*: "The most merciful thing that the large family does to one of its infant members is to kill it."[3]*

In the previously mentioned book *The Rising Tide of Color Against White World Supremacy*, reviewed by Sanger's lover Havelock Ellis in her *Birth Control Review*, Ellis shares his concern that colored people in America— "the migrations of lower types, even within the white world, such as those which have worked havoc in the United States, must be rigorously curtailed." If total extermination for African-Americans was not the goal, partial extermination has been the result so far. When abortion first became legal in New York City in 1970, forty-three percent of the abortions of city residents were performed on non-whites and forty-six percent on whites, and ten percent on Puerto Ricans, even though only twenty-one percent of city residents were black and seventy-seven percent white.[4]

MARGARET SANGER

The numbers nationwide are difficult to obtain today. To provide an objective analysis, Life Dynamics Incorporated conducted an exhaustive study in 2011. The report listed all 3,000 clinics in the country that perform or refer for abortions and used the census to identify the white and minority breakdown of every zip code where the clinics exist. Of the 116 zip codes with more than one population control facility, eighty-four were disproportionately minority zip codes. What this data means is that, when the abortion industry places multiple facilities in a zip code, that zip code is more than two-and-a-half times as likely to be disproportionately minority as not. In other words, minorities (e.g. African American, Hispanic) make up thirty-five percent of the U.S. population, but a zip code with more than one clinic has a seventy-four percent chance of being in a disproportionately minority area.

In Texas, for example, which has ninety-four zip codes with at least one population control facility, only twenty-two are not disproportionately black or Hispanic. In Connecticut—a state thoroughly dissimilar from Texas in size, culture and geography—there are twenty-one zip codes in which population control facilities are located and only six are not disproportionately black or Hispanic. In Tennessee, there are three Planned Parenthood clinics. The black population in that state is 16.4 percent, but, in the zip codes of Tennessee's three clinics, the black population is forty-two percent, fifty-three percent, and fifty-six percent. The targeting seems more effective with African Americans, whose percentage of the U.S. population decreased slightly from 2000 to 2010, while Hispanics, as a percentage, grew by twenty-five percent.[5*]

Planned Parenthood's historic African American targeting has not escaped the concern of popular culture. NFL player Benjamin Watson said Planned Parenthood was founded to "exterminate blacks" reported *Fox News*, which quoted the Baltimore Ravens wide receiver as saying in 2016: "We [as minorities] support candidates, and overwhelmingly support the idea of having Planned Parenthood and the like, and yet, that is why she created it...the whole idea with Planned Parenthood and Sanger in the past was to exterminate blacks, and it's kind of ironic that it's working."[6]

Mussolini's orders to exterminate Ethiopians may have been intended for certain parts of the population or for only those rebellious members. Or, had he had enough time, perhaps he would have exterminated a race with the same intentions as Hitler.

We do know that Mussolini was keenly aware of birthrate realities. While he promoted Malthusian fears of overpopulation in Italy in his early radical years, upon becoming prime minister, he made a complete 180-degree turnaround. Regarding the saying, "the Italian population [is] like a river overflowing its banks," he now insisted, "[It] is not true!" In his famous Ascension Day Speech in 1927, the Duce warned of economic doom: Italy's "cribs lay empty," he cried, "while the country's cemeteries grow full."[7]

Why the sudden change? Firstly, he envisioned "an imminent reproductive war between races which superior species were destined to lose because of their reluctance to breed," according to Maria Quine's dissertation *From Malthus to Mussolini*. Secondly, he was persuaded by the science. Malthusianism made little sense, and is denounced by many scholars today. A "monstrous doctrine of unreason," notes widely published British historian Paul Johnson, who criticized the

Malthusians as "not men of action" but men who sat in their studies creating hard-headed and relentless "mumbo jumbo."[8]

Malthus's premise was that population doubles every twenty-five years while food and resources grow by only a few percentage points. He failed to account for human ingenuity and higher production rates. Mussolini pointed out that Italy had far more food in the 1930s than it did with far less people fifty years earlier. Like many scientists awakening today, the Italian demographers warned the Duce that depopulation spelled economic doom. "Far from bringing misery, as Malthus had contended, excess population contributed to economic development," according to Italian economist Achille Loria.[9]

Rather, more children leads to more economic growth and more productive labor. Italian sociologist Corrado Gini explained how it works on the ground, as conveyed by Quine: "Laborers in industry and agriculture with no family or few children, he argued, lacked the motivation needed to endure long hours and bad pay. Prolific fathers made the most 'productive, deferential, and obedient workers' because they faced the difficult task of maintaining a large brood of dependents." Single workers, on the other hand, were more likely to demand better conditions and go on strike and "showed a destructive propensity." Poverty was an "effective inducement" for workers, according to Gini, a notion as old as Solomon's proverb: "It is good for workers to have an appetite; an empty stomach drives them on" (Proverbs 16:26).[10]

Mussolini was also following another of Solomon's insights: "A large population is a king's glory, but without subjects a prince is ruined" (Proverbs 14:28). Mussolini wanted an empire and needed a larger army. He passed laws to reach that goal. Bachelors who refused to marry and have children were heavily taxed and prohibited from holding public office. Women were given generous maternity leave. Public employees received bonuses with each child. Abortion and birth control remained illegal. A "Prolific Mothers of the Year Award" was given after recommendation letters were received from throughout the country, with the Duce choosing the finalist and presenting the award. A declining population was "demographic decadence" that led to "bestial corruptions" the Italian government now asserted. Countries that refused to grow were "destined to become a weak and degenerate 'eunuch' race."[11]

Margaret Sanger was appalled by Mussolini's "Battle for the Birthrate," as it was called in Italy. She traveled there to campaign for birth control and spoke out against the Duce's more brazen comments about women. He said, ". . . you cannot point to any single instance where a woman has created anything that has been passed down to posterity." In response, Sanger never got around to actually naming any famous female accomplishments. Instead, she gave an ironic biblical response: "Women never created anything?" she fumed. "What about babies? What about you, Signor Mussolini. You would not be here to rant and shout, nor we to read and fight, if women had never created anything." She was echoing 1 Corinthians 11:12: "For as woman came from man, even so man also comes through woman; but all things are from God."

She gave one more example, and continued the irony. "As to women not being creators—shame on Mussolini! Has he forgotten his history? Where are his religious teachings? Does he not know that the Virgin Mary, all by herself and without assistance of man (according to legend) created the leader and founder of Christianity," she said of the religion she hoped to destroy. "This was an act of creation which has changed our civilization for the past 2000 years. Is this not enough?"

Despite all of Mussolini's efforts, the birthrate in Italy did not increase. Sanger, while visiting Italy, promoted birth control to an underground movement, "and this is perhaps, in large measure, responsible for the fall in the birth rate," she claimed. Scholars suggest the reason was related to Italy's great wars in Ethiopia and Europe. Regarding another swipe by Mussolini that "women have no wills of their own," Sanger was also outspoken. "The women of Italy are silently telling Mussolini what they think of him. They are telling him that there can be no life unless they will it..."[12]

On this last point, Sanger was 100 percent correct. The battlefield of the future, and for civilization itself, will be fought in the hearts and minds of its women.

General Rudolfo Graziani, under orders from Mussolini for the "extermination against rebel natives" in Ethiopia, decided to put a positive face on the Italian regime there and distribute money to the needy at a celebration for the birth of the prince of Naples. The ceremony "was attended by almost all the top-ranking Italian authorities...the poor, of whom there were some 3,000, had just begun to file past the long white table on which the [coins] were piled, when a hand grenade hurled by someone hidden in the crowd exploded just above the gate of the palace. A second later, another bomb burst in the midst of the Italian group and Graziani fell, wounded in the back. In the next few minutes, seven more were thrown."

The police "opened fire immediately. The firing went on for three hours, and when it stopped the compound was littered with bodies. But the worst was yet to come. Later that afternoon, hundreds of blackshirts...gathered around the palace and then made for the native quarter of Addis Ababa. There they embarked on a systematic massacre, drenching the [homes] with petrol, setting them alight and shooting the inhabitants as they emerged from the blazing huts. While this hate ran riot the police kept out of sight, and the massacre went on for three days."[13]

Graziani and Mussolini's army did not spare the clerics. An estimated 1,500 to 2,000 monks and clergy had escaped to the Debre Libanos and other monasteries. All were executed, "exterminated at the hands of the enemy." The monastery was burned to the ground, "its treasures looted, and the entire vicinity abandoned and neglected."

Ethiopian official Yohannes Iyasu wrote to Haile Selassie describing these horrible events: "Commanders and soldiers and also young men were rounded up and executed by machine guns without committing any crime. Their wives were raped and their children were burned alive after being gathered in a house. What came as a great astonishment was the fact that those who submitted themselves to the Italians were the first to be killed.

"They say Ethiopia is their property and the Ethiopian people their slaves. They force us to kill each other... They point out that, 'From now on Ethiopia is for the Italians. It should not be called Ethiopia. From now on, only the white race will be entitled to live in Ethiopia. The black race, from now on, will not be allowed to live here.'"

The emperor read letters like these from his small living quarters in England. He was alone, as his wife, suffering from rheumatism, found the clammy English climate intolerable. She left for Jerusalem with their son, Sahle Selassie. "Our life in Bath was very hard," the emperor said. "We also encountered great financial difficulties. Some... had spread rumors that we had taken a great deal of money with us when leaving the country, but it is a complete lie." What money they did have lasted one year. The rest "we used to help the exiles."

A British film company offered him nearly $2 million in today's money to participate in a movie on his life entitled "Escape Under Cover of Darkness." He politely declined. His wife was forced to sell her jewelry along with the imperial silver tableware they had smuggled out, which included the imperial initials and crown.[14]

Mussolini contacted Haile Selassie. "I have heard of your financial predicament. I am willing to buy you a palace in a country of your choice and in addition, to give a million guineas to you so that together with your family, you can live in peace for the rest of your life off the interest of the original deposit." Again, he asked him to sign a release acknowledging Italian victory. Again, the emperor refused. "The history of Ethiopia will not be despoiled by a guinea stained with the blood of Ethiopians," he responded.

Haile Selassie was out of money, cold, and alone in a dark place. "That winter the financial situation became so strained that there wasn't even enough money for coal," writes his biographer Asfa-Wossen. "A fire was lit in only a single grate."[15]

The barefoot runner could see two competitors behind him and three in front. Abebe Bikila's shoeless feet pounded the concrete while he continued racing for Ethiopia alongside Roman landmarks in the 1960 Olympic Marathon.

After many miles, he had already passed the favorite, the Russian Sergei Popov, along with New Zealand's Barry Magee. Ahead of him were Englishman Arthur Keily, Aurèle Vandendriessche from Belgium, and a third man he could not identify. He wore number 185, so it wasn't the runner his Swedish trainer, Onni Niskanen, had specifically warned him about, Rhadi Ben Abdesselam, the man who gained recognition in cross country as a runner under the French flag. Niskanen considered Rhadi to be the top threat, despite the popular regard for the Russian. Niskasen warned Bikila to specifically watch out for Rhadi, number 26. This man ahead of him wore number 185, so that was a relief. But who was he?

The marathon ended at the Arch of Constantine immediately next to the Roman Colosseum—all of these structures reminded Bikila of the Italian army that invaded his home village in Ethiopia when he was three years old. He did not want to suffer defeat in the land of his invaders.

Bikila was a soccer player before he ever considered running. But he traveled twenty kilometers to work and Niskanen had "seen this soldier running from Sululta to Addis and back everyday and hit upon the idea of letting him try a marathon." Bikila was interested, his daughter says, because he had seen the nice outfits the 1956 Olympians wore and the trips they enjoyed, so he decided he would also be an Olympian. "He said this only to become a laughing stock to his colleagues," she writes. "He secretly vowed to himself to work hard and to prepare himself for the competition."[16]

His mother did not approve. She believed Olympic dreams were distracting him from a more steady and promising career path. She decided the solution was for him to get married. A wife and family would encourage him to stop wasting so much time at the track. She arranged a marriage with the much younger fifteen-year-old Yewibdar Wolde Giorgis, an accepted practice in Ethiopia. Biographers describe it as a happy union. They remained married their entire lives.

Author Paul Rambali recounts this exchange between Bikila and a female American runner.

"What's your wife's name?"

"Yewibdar."

"Yewibdar? That sure is a funny name," she blurted. "Oh, I'm sorry. How did you meet?"

"She from village. Parents choose. Parents find bride."

"That's how they do things in Ethiopia, the parents arrange everything?"

Abebe nodded.

"Where I come from, it's us that chooses. You know. You can marry whoever you want. If he asks you."

She paused.

"I wish my parents had arranged things for me," she said. "I got a little baby, you see, back home, only I ain't supposed to say nothing, because the baby ain't got a father, legally speaking.

"They told me not to talk about it with anyone."[17]

Bikila and Yewibdar were married on March 16, 1960, just a few months before his Olympic marathon. Now he had a chance to win a

medal in the Olympic games. There had already been some discussion of Ethiopia not competing in the 1964 Olympics due to their lackluster performance in Rome. The marathon was the last event, and still, no Ethiopian had ever won an Olympic medal of any kind. Three runners were in front of him. If he could only pass just one.

ABEBE BIKILA

183

During the race, they ran by an obelisk on their right, the very one Mussolini had stolen in 1937 and taken back to Rome, the "Obelisk of Axum." The stela stood eighty feet tall, was made from 160 tons of granite, and was over 1,600-years-old. Bikila found the inner strength to make a move. He increased his pace.

Biographer Rambali quotes a radio commentator: "This really is a surprise. After holding the first two places for nearly an hour, the British entrant Keily has dropped back along with the Belgian Vandendriessche, and it seems that the two Europeans have surrendered the lead to two unknown runners."

"It's an astonishing sight, I must say. The Ethiopian, Bikila Abebe, is running barefoot! There's no more than a yard or two between them and that's how it has been for the last 15 minutes."[18]

He and the unknown runner were head to head in the lead. Who was this number 185? As they made their way toward the final stretch, Niskanen got a message to Bikila. His competitor had been given the wrong number at the beginning of the race. In fact, he was neck and neck with the one athlete Niskanen feared the most, Rhadi Ben Abdesselam.

Both runners had seen the doctor that morning, and Rhadi later gave an account of his chance occasion to look at Bikila's bare extremities, propped up for the doctor to examine. "I was amazed at his feet," said Rhadi. "The soles of his feet were thick and black as coal. I remember that I wanted to touch his feet, the hard skin of which resembled, by its consistency, the tires of big military trucks. I was sure that he would feel nothing. But on the contrary. The hard skin was very sensitive."

Bikila looked up at him as soon as as his skin was touched, although Rhadi said "I hardly brushed it with my finger."[19]

Earlier that year, Rhadi had won the international cross country championships. He had once represented the French people, but, in fact, was not running for France this time. He represented a North African country. The two leading runners, Rhadi and Bikila, served as a poignant symbol for shifts taking place in what will become a post-European civilization.

PART THREE

Never Defeated, but Beware the Suicide Demon

Eden, Ethiopia, and Israel

CHAPTER FIFTEEN

ON A FLIGHT from Addis to Axum, I handed a book to my traveling partner, Alex, who had plenty of time to examine it. I thought it was compelling. He handed it back to me and rolled his eyes.

The book was *Eden: The Biblical Garden Discovered in East Africa* by Gert Muller, a German researcher. It pinpoints Ethiopia as the area that the Scriptures describe as the Garden of Eden. Many Ethiopians hold this belief.

I met Alexander Campbell, or Alex, who was twenty-five years old, at the one Eastern Orthodox Church in Addis Ababa. I was twenty years into the Orthodox program but he only had about a year under his belt. He was a former member of the Presbyterian Church in America, a proper fit for someone of Scottish heritage. He has the classic Viking looks, a warrior's build with red hair and beard, and he explained to me early on that his Campbells are directly related to Hamish Campbell, the right-hand man of legendary Scotsman William Wallace. Alex took his heritage seriously, perhaps too seriously, and I was observing with interest how his first trip to Africa might affect his "white and proud" worldview. He decided he needed a summer trip to observe Africa first hand, and we kept getting together for coffee and struck up a friendship. He asked if he could go with me to Axum. I had a sense he might be complicated, but I was glad to have a partner.

Muller's thesis for an Ethiopian Eden is built around the second chapter in Genesis that describes the location, with Ethiopia mentioned in verse 13:

10. Now a river went out of Eden to water the garden, and from thence it parted, and became four heads.

¹¹· The name of the first is Pison: that is it which compasseth the whole land of Havilah, where there is gold.

¹²· And the gold of that land is good: there is bdellium and the onyx stone.

¹³· The name of the second river is Gihon: the same is it which compasseth the whole land of Ethiopia.

¹⁴· And the name of the third river is Hiddekel [Tigris]: that is it which goeth toward the east of Assyria. The fourth river is Euphrates. (Genesis 2:10–14, KJV)[1*]

Alex joined me during an extensive interview with Girma Batu, the vice academic dean of Ethiopia's keynote seminary. (He runs the academic program, as the formal title of dean is held by the archbishop.) We met in a little stand-alone boardroom next to an outdoor café. Girma bought our lunch. We discussed the Eden theory in particular.

The river Gihon is accepted by almost all scholars as the Nile. Josephus and others confirm this view. Girma echoed the Ethiopian church's belief:

"In the church's tradition, there is a perspective among the scholars that Eden is around the river Gihon. Why Gihon? It has a biblical foundation."

"Did you say Evegorian?" I asked.

"River Gihon," Alex whispered.

"What about the Tigris and Euphrates rivers mentioned in the same passage?" I asked. "Wouldn't that point instead to the Middle East rather than Ethiopia?"

In fact, this theory is the one most commonly held today regarding the location of Eden. One river points to the area of the Nile and Ethiopia. But two rivers from the Middle East are named. So, two is better than one. Two rivers by those names today flow through Syria, Iran, Iraq, and Turkey. In ancient times the region was known as Sumer, the land where Nimrod founded Babel and the area Abraham left to find the Promised Land.

Girma provided what sounded like a good answer to my question of whether two rivers were better than one. Unfortunately, I had a difficult time understanding him, which was a bit embarrassing for me. Girma arguably has a better mastery of certain parts of English than I do. He is fluent in several languages compared to my one. They speak English alone in their classrooms. The problem for me was not the English, but the accents. With Ethiopia's eclectic European influences of Portuguese, Italian, French, and British—along with 71 tribal languages—the combination becomes difficult to decipher.

But not for Alex. For some reason, he had an ear for such things. I already knew this by the time of our interview, so I turned to Alex.

"Did you catch that?"

"Yep."

"What is he saying?"

He explained it to me. (I had already apologized to Girma and other Ethiopian friends many times, explaining my admiration for their linguistic acumen and my ugly American shortcomings.)

"He is saying that the names 'Tigris' and 'Euphrates' in Genesis refer to different rivers than what are today called Tigris and Euphrates in the Middle East," Alex explained. "So, it is the Gihon, the Nile, that matters, because Genesis gives a place name, Ethiopia, a geographical location associated with that river."

"Ah," I said. "So that becomes the trump card of the four rivers mentioned in Genesis, because it gives place names that it flows around, like Ethiopia and Havilah?"

"Yep."

People name new cities and rivers after old ones, and this concept is key to remember when trying to decipher the codes of the early Genesis chapters. For example, I met a guy the other day in the Bible Belt area of the American Southeast who told me that he was raised in Rome and educated in Athens. Sounds like a sophisticated European type. Actually, he was born and raised in Rome, Georgia, a small city an hour north of Atlanta, and studied at the University of Georgia, an hour west of Atlanta in the city of Athens, Georgia.

What if someone told you an ancient civilization once existed somewhere between Memphis and Philadelphia? We might all think of someplace between those two American cities, maybe around West

Virginia or Kentucky. In fact, both cities—Philadelphia and Memphis—are names of ancient Egyptian cities. So, the information you received was about Egypt, not the land of Appalachia. Girma was explaining to us that the first Tigris and Euphrates rivers were closer to Ethiopia and the Nile than to the land of Abram. Centuries after those rivers were named, the founders of Babylon decided to name their rivers after those two rivers back in the old country.

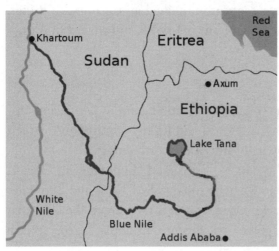

THE SOURCE OF THE NILE

Alex was translating well, but he was not buying the theory. The King James Bible uses the word Ethiopia in the Genesis passage above, but the underlying Hebrew word is "Cush." Alex subscribes to an Arabian Cush theory for this verse. In fact, there is indeed a Cush in Arabia, which we will discuss shortly.

Alex was starting to enjoy the ancient city of Axum with its two-hour coffee ceremonies served twice a day by beautiful women in traditional, brightly colored dresses. But I had an agenda. I announced that we were going to find a village somewhere in Ethiopia that has worshipped Jesus Christ for 2,000 years but still has no electricity. I loved this idea. It breaks through the stereotype that enlightenment comes to African cultures only after missionaries bring power and the Protestant religion. No electricity? Then those Africans must still be pitiful pagans.

Ethiopia blows that stereotype, and I was fixed on finding the village that would make my point. My inner football coach was driving me. A reluctant Alex consented. Bazien served as our guide as we took a bus out of Axum for two hours to a smaller town, with the plan to travel even further to find our unplugged village. Yirga and Bazien had talked and settled on the perfect community that met my criteria— there were less out there than I realized.

On the way, I learned more about Alex's background. He was maybe a little more radical than I thought. "I was 'Alt-Right,'" he told me, "which is a huge term that covers everything from Nietzschean atheists to traditional Christians just worried about multiculturalism. I listened to podcasts. I read books. I came at it from a very Calvinist worldview. My particular niche was called kinism."

I looked up kinism. Wikipedia's first sentence is as follows: "Kinism is a white supremacist interpretation of Christianity."

Alex said that he wasn't that radical. "Kinism raises people's ire, but it wasn't anything like National Socialism or something more extreme, which I never approved of. I sort of sympathized with some of the grander metanarratives but never shaved my head or joined the skinheads."

However, he did attend some meetings with Matthew Heimbach, a year or two older than Alex and the founder of the Traditionalist Workers Party, whose mission statement is "Fighting for the rights and self-determination of Whites in America." Heimbach was recruiting people for a big march in Charlottesville to protest the removal of a Confederate statue. Alex had plans to go, having been told it would be a peaceful protest. But then one of the organizers changed his stance and starting talking about bringing guns. That was a bit much for Alex, and the young father of three, with another soon to arrive, decided to forgo the event.

At a Louisville rally, the burly and bearded Heimbach was arrested for shoving black student activist Kashiya Nwanguma. The video went viral. Heimbach pleaded guilty to a lesser harassment charge to avoid jail time, but he remained committed to the cause: "White Americans are getting fed up and they're learning that they must either push back or be pushed down," he said. Heimbach again made national news when he was arrested for assaulting both his wife and the cofounder of his Traditionalist Workers Party. According to the *Washington Post*, Heimbach was "accused of attacking his wife and choking his white nationalist group's co-founder unconscious after the pair caught Heimbach having an affair in a trailer, authorities said."[2]

It was one of the year's more bizarre stories. Heimbach was having an affair with the wife of cofounder Matt Parrott, age thirty-five. Parrott's wife wanted out, and they "set up" Heimbach to see if he would make an advance while Parrott documented it. They all lived in an Indiana trailer park, a communal move to advance their religious and political interests. So Parrott and Heimbach's wife stood on a box outside the trailer window and Heimbach was caught propositioning Parrott's wife. However, the box broke and Parrott, Heimbach, and Heimbach's wife found themselves in a physical altercation that led to Heimbach's arrest.

But there's more, enough to make Jerry Springer proud. Parrott is the stepfather, from a previous marriage, of Heimbach's wife, making Parrott the father-in-law of sorts to Heimbach, and making Heimbach an adulterer of sorts with his mother-in-law. *Vice* news called it "among the most incestuous—not to mention confusing—love triangles of all time."[3]

Before this situation, when Heimbach and friends arrived in Charlottesville, the crowd of people waving Confederate flags—and a few swastika flags—were confronted by angry progressives. Before officials could quell the growing riot, a self-identified white supremacist drove his car into the crowd and killed Heather Heyer and injured forty more. Alex dodged a bullet by deciding to stay away.

Alex, Bazien, and I hitched a ride to a village just below a monastery. We had plenty of time for conversation. Alex's Arabian Cush theory, which provides a way to push the Edenic Cush reference in Genesis from black Ethiopia to Abraham's lighter Middle East, is rooted in a verse in Habakkuk 3:7: "I saw the tents of Cushan in affliction, and the curtains of the land of Midian did tremble" (KJV).

Midian is known as Northern Arabia, where Moses stumbled into his father-in-law, Jethro. Centuries earlier, Abraham also journeyed there. (The area was named after his son, Midian.) *Easton's Bible Dictionary* says of this verse in Habakkuk: "Probably a poetic or prolonged name of the land of Cush, the Arabian Cush."[4]

So, there *is* an Arabian Cush. But scholars generally conclude that most of the references to Cush in the Bible refer to the Cush south of Egypt, what the King James Version and the translators of the Greek Septuagint concluded was "Ethiopia," the land of burnt faces described by Homer.

This view is supported by the fact that the Jews did not have a word in Hebrew for Cush, something they would have had were it from Arabic origin. Instead, the first instances came from Egypt. An artifact in a museum in Florence, Italy, the Buhen stela, which dates to the reign of Pharaoh Seti I in the thirteenth century BC, refers to a region known as "Kas" and "Kash." Other texts from the sixteenth to the eleventh centuries BC refer to this region as "KSH," without vowels."⁵

ETHIOPIAN ICON OF ADAM AND EVE

Easton's Bible Dictionary says the meaning of Cush causes "not a little controversy," but then provides a seemingly fair and neutral assessment of the various views. Muller implies that a possible black Adam is at the heart of the controversy. *Easton's* admits that the Hebrew term Cush "generally applied" to "the southern limit of Egypt, Ethiopia...with which it is generally associated." The *New Bible Dictionary* agrees, concluding that "'Cushite' is usually taken as 'Ethiopian.'" Muller makes a similar conclusion: "Every time the land of Cush is mentioned in the Bible, which incidentally is 30 times, the primary interpretation of the southern neighbor of Egypt is far easier to make than the secondary interpretations of West Asian locations."⁶

Why prefer the Greek Septuagint's and King James Bible's "Ethiopia" to the modern versions' "Cush"? The answer hearkens back to why traditional Christian churches like the Eastern Orthodox use the Greek Septuagint translation in the first place. Published in the second century BC, scholars preferred it over the Hebrew manuscript used today by modern translators, the Masoretic Text, published 1,200 years later in AD 950. Traditional translators saw the obvious—scholars looking at a text 1,200 years earlier had better access to the meaning of the original text. They also trusted the handing down of manuscripts by Christians rather than Jewish rabbis with a bias against Christianity.

Orthodox priest John Peck notes that many of the discrepancies between the Septuagint and Hebrew Masoretic texts affect Old Testament messianic prophecies: Isaiah's "Behold, a virgin shall conceive" in the Septuagint becomes "the young woman is with child" (Isaiah 7:14). The Psalmist's "They pierced my hands and my feet" becomes "like a lion, my hands and my feet" (Psalm 22:16).[7]

For the proper rendering of the word "Cush," the Septuagint Jewish scholars in the second century BC, living at or near the time of these actual ancient lands, chose "Ethiopia." They were confident that Cush referred to the great land Homer and the Greeks discussed, often with high praise. Almost all modern Bible translations, relying on the much later Hebrew manuscripts, use Cush for Ethiopia. (The Revised Standard Version even calls Isaiah's "virgin" a "young woman.") However, the King James translators stuck with "Ethiopia," as they also consulted the Septuagint and St. Jerome's Latin Vulgate in translating the Old Testament. All English translations before the King James Version also use "Ethiopia," adding credence to the Eden-related verse of Genesis 2:13 as indeed alluding to today's Ethiopia.

In fact, the testimony of the most ancient of historians, both Greeks and Egyptians, serves as some of the more persuasive evidence of an Ethiopian Eden. One of the most reliable ancient scribes, Diodorus Siculus, writes the following: "Now, the Ethiopians, as historians relate, were the first of all men. And the proofs of this statement, they say, are manifest. For they did not come into their lands as immigrants from abroad but were natives of it." He cites historians Agatharchides of Cnidus and Artemidorus of Ephesus. Just to drive home his point, Diodorus adds that knowledge of the Ethiopians as the first humans "is conceded by practically all men." It is a pity that we do not have more manuscripts of the lost histories of ancient Ethiopia. An Egyptian captain named Philon toured Ethiopia in the third century BC. We know that he described his entire journey in a book entitled *Aethiopicus*. But it has not survived. Another adventurer named Ariston also wrote a book, which is lost, as was the book of his successor Dalion, used as the source for Eratosthenes and other geographers. A century later Bion, Aristocreon, and Simonides wrote books about Ethiopia, all of which are also lost today.[8]

However, Egyptian works do survive that discuss adventures into the land of Punt, described as southeast of Egypt, where Ethiopia sits. Punt is also called *Ta Netzjer*, which means "The Land of God." In this ancient material, which describes Egyptian Queen Hatshepsut's commissioned expedition into the sacred country, the God Amun (the Egyptian Zeus) says the following: "I gave you Punt in its entirety as far as the land of gods, God's Land. No one trod the terraces of myrrh...it is a sacred region of God's land. Moreover, it is a place of my recreation."[9]

This land of the gods parallels what the Greeks say about Ethiopia. In the *Iliad*, Homer, the earliest Greek author, writes in the 800s BC: "Zeus went yesterday to Oceanus, to the blameless Ethiopians for a feast, and all the gods followed with him." Homer writes in the *Odyssey*: "Poseidon had gone among the far-off Ethiopians...the furthermost of men, some where Hyperion sets and some where he rises." Greek historian Herodotus makes a similar association: "The inhabitants worship Zeus and Dionysius alone of the Gods, holding them in great honor," thus backing, or nearly so, the Ethiopian claim of longtime monotheism.[10]

Diodorus notes that "the Egyptians are colonists sent out by the Ethiopians...and the larger part of the customs of the Egyptians are, they hold, Ethiopian." Diodorus adds that Egyptian hieroglyphics came from Ethiopia and that the Pharaoh's priests learned their sacred trade from them as well.[11]

Any speculation as to whether Punt, the land of Egypt's gods, the original "Land of God," was Ethiopia proper was put to rest in 2010 when scientists used DNA technology to examine baboon genetic material in Egypt acquired from the Puntite civilization. "The team studied the baboon mummies in the British Museum," wrote London's *Independent*. "By analyzing hairs from these baboons using oxygen isotope analysis, they were able to work out where they originated....Although isotope values in baboons in Somalia, Yemen, and Mozambique did not match, those in Eritrea and Ethiopia were closely matched."[12]

What of the first river, the Pishon, mentioned in the Genesis passage just before the Nile and Ethiopia? Scholars have little to say about it. We only know that it "winds through the entire land of Havilah, where there is gold." If we believe it is near the second river, the Nile and its source, Ethiopia, then Diodorus again is helpful: Ethiopia "contains large gold mines, where the gold is secured in great quantities..."[13]

Where is Havilah? Again, little is known. Genesis 10 tells us that Havilah is the son of Cush. Therefore, it is likely that the place names Havilah and Cush would be near each other. According to one Bible dictionary, the Adal region located in East Africa, and its port city Zaila, is believed to take its name from Havilah. Other geographers note that Benjamin Tudela, the twelfth century Jewish traveler, claimed that the land of Havilah is confined by Abyssinia on the west. Local traditions near Ethiopia and the Gulf of Aden in the Red Sea also assert that Furra, a queen of the Havilah Gadire clan, ruled in East Africa. In fact, the section of the Red Sea between Ethiopia and Yemen, the Gulf of Aden, has been known to be associated with Eden. The *Online Etymological Dictionary* says that Aden is derived "ultimately from Akkadian *edinnu* 'plain,' which some think also is the root of Biblical Eden." A modern geography notes the following regarding a local legend about the town of Aden on the Red Sea coast: "It states that Aden may be as old as human history itself. Some also believe that Cain and Abel are buried somewhere in the city."[14]

The medieval French rabbi Rashi identified the Pishon with the Nile, likely because of a belief that all four rivers of Eden were in that region of the world. The *Jewish Heritage* magazine identifies the Gihon and Pishon as the Blue and White Nile.[15]

Our car arrived at the foot of a small mountain ridge in our quest for the unplugged village. We walked up toward the entrance of the long path to the monastery. A dozen curious teenage boys accosted us along the way. We learned later that they had never seen a white man before—Bazien said they were calling us Chinese. We looked over the valley and my heart sunk. There, below us, was a long row of towers with power lines. Asking a monk who was making his way back home, Bazien learned that the power lines had been built only two weeks ago, and served both the town below and the monastery on the mountain.

Now what?

The boys who had gathered around us overheard our conversation with the monk. Some of them were from a village called "Gororo," which still did not have power. It could only be reached by foot, an hour away. They told us their church had a service that evening. The three of us took council and decided to make the journey. We hadn't come all this way for nothing. The boys, in jeans and t-shirts, barefoot, led us along the rocky path as we dodged sheep and goats. The un-plugged village of longtime Christianity awaited us.

We stopped for coffee at a home along the path. A young mother with traditional dress and head covering lit the fire and began roasting coffee beans picked from a nearby tree.

Alex had been doing his homework. "Girma said the Gihon river trumps the others because it mentions a geographical area, Ethiopia," he said as she lit incense, part of the ceremony. "But the same passage says the Tigris River 'goes toward the east of Assyria.'"

He sipped some coffee with satisfaction.

Assyria was indeed an empire in the Middle East, and that would point to the view of a Mesopotamian Eden. I shared with him what

Gert Muller says about that in his book. The actual word in the Hebrew is "Asshur." The King James Version says Assyria. Newer translations like the NIV say "Ashur."

Muller acknowledges that, in this case, the primary interpretation
for a mention of Asshur would be the area of that name in the Middle
East. But he points to another Asshur in Cush that might also serve as
the referent in Genesis 2. In this case, however, the place named Asshur
is never mentioned in the Bible.

The explanation revolves, once again, around the mirror image of
geography and names, the Athens, Greece, and Athens, Georgia, conundrum, or Memphis, Tennessee, and Memphis, Egypt. Muller contends there was an Asshur in Cush. Why? Because so many of the early
biblical Cushite names such as Sheba and Dedan were used again a few
generations later in Arabia. Even though Asshur isn't mentioned in the
earlier Genesis names, Muller believes he did exist in Cush, and the
Asshur of Arabian/Mesopotamian Assyria was yet another borrowed
name.

"It's either another Cush closer to Asshur or another Asshur closer
to Cush," writes Muller. He chooses the latter.[16]

So, if the Asshur of Genesis 2 is near Cush, and Havilah, where the
Pishon River flows, is also near Cush, then where in the Cushite area
are the Tigris and Euphrates Rivers mentioned in Genesis 2? Muller's
search begins with the actual Hebrew. Tigris, in Hebrew, is "Haddekel"
and Euphrates in Hebrew is "Parat." Both have etymologies, descrip-
tions of word origins, that might describe a river. Josephus gave the
meaning of Haddekel as "swift, with narrowness." Abarim Publications
says "sharp, swift...sharp rapids." Mueller identifies a river of that description in Northern Ethiopia, the Tigray region. The Tekeze River,
the very waterway we have mentioned throughout this book dividing Eritrea and Ethiopia, crossed several times by Italian troops, is, in
places, a swift river with rapids. The Tekeze River Whitewater Rafting
company serves tourists for just such an adventure. (Oddly, Muller
refuses to make any connection between the similarity of the words
"Tigris" and "Tigray.")

The meaning of Parat (Euphrates) is to bear fruit. Josephus defines it as "dispersion" or "flower." Muller identifies a river further north in Eritrea for this stream. The Mareb River contains a delta with heavy silt, and this body of water is key to a very fertile area of land in the region. Certain ancient historians associate the Euphrates with greater Ethiopia. "There is a story that the Nile itself is the Euphrates," writes Greek historian Pausaunias in the second century AD, "which disappears into a marsh, rises again beyond Aethiopia, and becomes the Nile."[17]

Alex was not impressed with Muller's arguments.

Meanwhile, during our coffee ceremony, which can take up to two hours, we had plenty of time for conversation. Bazien shared his views of an Ethiopian Adam, and his belief that the ancient Ethiopian language of Ge'ez is actually where the Hebrew language is derived. He talked about Moses's Ethiopian wife and Melchizedek as Ethiopian.

"Is God an Ethiopian?" Alex asked.

"Enoch walked with God," Bazien said, without missing a beat. "And he was Ethiopian."

Neither looked at the other; they just made little quips as they drank coffee and watched the pretty mother with a baby on her back organize her coffee setup on the dirt courtyard.

"Has your family always been Christian?" I asked her.

"Yes," she said, through Bazien's translation. She told us that her family attends church every Sunday from midnight to 8 a.m. and also on feast days and for baptisms and funerals.

I was told Ethiopians can cite seven generations of ancestors on each side. When I asked her about that, she looked at her mother with an anxious laugh. She wasn't able to get to seven generations.

"Was your family Jewish before they were Christians?" I asked.

"We practiced Old Testament teachings," she said.

We gave her 100 birr, a nice sum for a village mother, and proceeded on to the village of Gororo as it grew dark. They were celebrating the feast day of their church, named for the three Hebrew youths in the fiery furnace (Daniel 3), so the entire village was congregated around the building where we were headed. Bazien assured the leaders that these two white men, the village's first ever, were Orthodox Christians. "That's all they want to know. They don't care about distinctions between Eastern and Ethiopian Orthodox," he said. "They just want to know that you're not Catholic."

We had purchased white prayer robes a couple of days earlier, so we were able to enter the sacred building—men only as the women listened from the outside—and began enjoying a several-hour visual and audio feast, nondigital, analog, and authentic. Colorful icons covered the walls. Vested young men everywhere sang with power, held prayer sticks, and rattled sistra-like instruments. About every fifteen minutes the big drums were brought out, and an animated rhythm and dance episode commenced. Then they retreated to softer chants. We were crammed into a small space—most of the circular building was reserved for the priests. We operated from a foyer-like semicircle.

At 2 a.m., we exited into almost pitch darkness. As we did, I noticed something that distressed me, but I waited to tell Alex and Bazien. For the moment, it was time for a feast. Hundreds of people sat down on logs outside the church building. They gave us a log of honor. A dozen village elders in orange robes and square hats spoke while we ate meat and gravy and drank traditional beer in huge cups that they kept filling to the brim—it's a compliment to make it overflow.

I asked for an interview and spoke with a lay leader who wore an out-of-place baseball cap with his white prayer robe. Bazien translated.

"This church was burned down by the communists," he told us. "Most families lost more than one person."

"How old is this church?"

"Fifth century. Before that, no formal church but places of prayer from the time of Christ."

"What about before Christianity?"

"We practiced Old Testament religion," he said, careful, like the young mother, not to say Jewish. "The Queen of Sheba was born nearby."[18]

Alex had eaten and drunk his fill and was rested. He was looking for a place to sleep. But I had not finished my purpose and was pressing forward toward my goal. I chose then to tell Alex and Bazien what had bothered me when I exited the church building. At the top of the door was a single light bulb, attached to a long cord. I learned that power had in fact come to the village that very day.

For Alex, that was good enough. Bazien was a flexible Ethiopian, and they don't fight small battles. But I was insistent. We had not yet found the unplugged village. Bazien told me that there was one more village church, an hour further by foot, a sister congregation with the same feast day who was also worshipping through the night. Problem solved. The teenage boys were willing to lead us on the path, this one rockier and steeper, with dangerous cliffs below us, and, unlike the earlier hike that day, in the pitch dark.

Alex bit his lip and followed. We headed to a light in the far distance, in hope that it would be the village and church we sought that has never had power in its millennia of worshiping Jesus Christ. In my many walks and travels with Alex, I learned more about his spiritual trek, which I will detail in a bit, a journey where he gained more light on himself and other nations as he experienced Christ in the Orthodox liturgy.

Using Genesis 2 to identify the Garden of Eden in Ethiopia faces two types of objections on a higher level than arguing river and place locations. Firstly, many object to the idea that geographical locations have any similarity to the original after Noah's Flood rearranged the earth's topography. This objection can be overcome by asking, then, why God through Moses even attempted to describe the location of Eden. If the rivers, Ethiopia, Asshur and other specific spots had no meaning, why include them? The implication, therefore, is that in Moses's day, the rivers and place names of Genesis 2 referred to rivers and countries known to Moses's generation.

Secondly, some conclude that Genesis 2 describes a "mystical" paradise, a more ethereal and heavenly state, and that Eden does not refer to any particular spot on the earth. This would contradict the view of many Church Fathers. John Chrysostom, a giant of early church teachers, interprets Eden, like most Fathers, as both symbolic and literal. Likening the rivers of Eden to the church altar and the Eucharist, he writes: "A fountain went up out of Paradise sending forth material rivers, from this table springs up a fountain which sends forth rivers spiritual." But directly refuting modern commentators who distrust the historicity of Genesis and prefer only a spiritual interpretation, Chrysostom writes: "Blessed Moses registered even the name of this place [Eden], so that those who love to speak empty words could not deceive simple listeners and say that Paradise was not on earth but in heaven, and rave with similar mythologies."[19*]

The Genesis 2 passage not only provides the rivers as evidence of an Ethiopian Eden, but it also mentions gold, which we already showed was very prominent in ancient Abyssinia, and a hefty part of Sheba's gifts to Solomon. After gold, the passage lists "bdellium." A bit of a mysterious substance, it is only mentioned in one other place in Scripture. Manna, the bread from heaven that the Israelites ate in the wilderness, is described as having the color of bdellium. Since we don't know what manna looked like, this description is not very helpful. The Septuagint translates bdellium as "anthrax," a precious stone. The St. Pachomius Library translation of the Septuagint describes anthrax as "a dark red gemstone, possibly a ruby or garnet…"

The highest quality of garnets in the world come from East Africa. The fourth of the twelve precious stones on the vestments of Israel's high priest was a red garnet, representing the fourth son, Judah, who corresponds with Aries, the first sign of the zodiac and the first month of the ancient new year (Mars/March). Also fascinating, but not really related, is Muller's tidbit quoting a gemstone company: "Noah, it is said, used a garnet lantern to help him steer his ark through the dark night."

After gold and bdellium, the third substance listed in Genesis 2 is onyx. Though found in Ethiopia, and in abundance in Africa, it does not add much to our discussion unless onyx, "shoham" in Hebrew, can be translated as malachite, which Muller attempts to do, but we will leave this discussion for another time. (Malachite is, in fact, a particular commodity of Ethiopia.)[20]

Also found in abundance in Ethiopia are the following items listed in the ancient book of Jubilees, accepted by early Jewish scholars, which expands on Genesis: "And on that day when Adam went forth from the Garden, he offered as a sweet savor an offering, frankincense, galbanum, and stacte, and spices in the morning with the rising of the sun from the day when he covered his shame" (Jubilees 3:27).

All of these plant-related items sacrificed by Adam point to an Ethiopian, rather than Middle Eastern, Eden. The book of Jubilees was written by Jewish scholars in the second century BC. Though not part of the Jewish, Catholic, or Orthodox canon, it is considered reliable by many, quoted by several Church Fathers, and part of the Ethiopian Bible. The only full manuscripts are from Ethiopia, but several Dead Sea Scroll fragments confirm its reliability. Jubilees also provides directions to Eden from Northern Africa up the Nile to Ethiopia. The map starts at the Mediterranean Sea, then "extends west to Afra, till it reaches the waters of the River Gihon, to the banks of this river. And it extends toward the east, till it reaches the Garden of Eden" (Jubilees 8:15).

Writes Muller: "Jewish scholars of the second century BC concluded, based on Genesis, that the Garden of Eden was located in East Africa. This can be concluded from reading the book of Jubilees," he says. "There was no reason for later scholars not to know about the real location."

"The Garden of Eden is the holy of holies" says Jubilees 8:19. This language is a direct allusion to Israel's holy of holies in the temple where the Ark was kept. The oldest written Eucharistic service of the Church, the Liturgy of St. James, calls the atrium of the Church of the Holy Sepulchre in Jerusalem the "holy garden," an allusion to Eden, but also a reminder that Jesus himself is evoking Eden in allowing himself to be confused with the gardener upon his resurrection.[21]

When Alex and I discussed the Eden in Ethiopia theory with our professor friend, Girma, he brought up, curiously at the time, the fact that the Israelite kings were crowned in Jerusalem at the spring called Gihon. This tidbit made more sense as I learned that Solomon, himself crowned at Gihon, made a conscious effort, along with Moses and the rest of Israel, to model Jerusalem and the temple after the Garden of Eden.

"In Genesis humans spoke directly with God when they were in the Garden of Eden," writes Muller. "Building a temple was a way of re-opening the direct line…" The tabernacle and temple rises up to the holy of holies in a terrace-like form, similar to how ancient Punt modeled its temples after Ethiopia's terraced farmland. Egypt's Queen Hatshepsut considered Punt, the "Land of God," to be the "holy of holies" and called their Egyptian temple modeled after Punt the "place of first things." The priests of Israel attached pomegranates to the hems of their robes, attached them to the top of the temple pillars, and wove them into temple curtains. The word pomegranate stems directly from "garnet" and is the only fruit represented—and one of the few images— in Solomon's temple design.

"A temple was essentially a mini-Punt or a mini–Garden of Eden," writes Muller. "All deities were, therefore, of Ethiopian origin." The Jubilees map says the Gihon "extends toward the east, till it reaches the Garden of Eden." The Bible says the Garden is "in the east," and Greek writers referred to Ethiopians as the people with burnt faces who were closest to the sun, which rises in the east.[22]

The etymology of Gihon is "to burst forth." Muller thinks he's found the ultimate source of this Edenic river: "The Gihon does indeed burst forth from a spring at Gish Abbai near Lake Tana." Graham Hancock cites a scholar who calls a spring at Lake Tana "Giyon." *National Geographic* reports on the people who live near this spring. "The Gihon [is] yet another name for the Blue Nile and one with strong biblical connotations. To the people in these villages set smack in the gorge, the Nile was one of the four rivers that flowed out of Eden at the beginning of the world."[23]

Alex and I were headed to a similar small Ethiopian village, this one without roads, so one must travel by foot. In the middle of the night, using iPhone flashlights (no cell coverage of course), we started to make our way up the giant hill where we could see faint lights from the church. We assumed they were not manmade.

The liturgy of John Chrysostom, observed each Sunday by both Eastern Orthodox and Ethiopian Christians, had made an impact on Alex over time. It says God's salvation is for "all peoples" and repeats over and over again (18 times) that God "loveth mankind." Each service ends with "For God is good and he loveth mankind." Alex talked about John Chrysostom, the giant fourth century church father who composed commentaries on nearly the entire Bible and, though patriarch of the New Rome, Constantinople, ended his life in exile and poverty for denouncing the worldliness of the emperors.

"He was awesome," said Alex. "He was a firebrand for saying 'look, men of every tongue, tribe and nation worship in this church.' And that's the way it should be. He was real big on that."

Alex heard the Beatitudes recited in every liturgy. This emphasis on humility affected him over time and softened his ethnic pride and nationalism. He still has some pride. "Oh yes, this is where I come from, these are my desires, my likes and dislikes, based on my genetics and upbringing. But it's not a competition. It just has to be put in its proper place, which is way down the list of priorities."

Alex had not yet joined me in sharing enthusiasm for the Ethiopian Eden theory, but he was beginning to warm up to the Ethiopians, of which I will share more. He also had a later encounter back in the United States that is worth sharing. Matthew Heimbach, the poster child for white nationalism who made the headlines of the *Washington Post*, moved to a town in the U.S. near Alex and began visiting his church. He recalled that Alex had attended some meetings a couple years back and told him he was so glad to find "one of us" at the church.

I ENTERED THE National Museum of Ethiopia. This institution is famous for its exhibit of "Lucy," the three-and-a-half-foot-tall missing link, half-ape, half-human set of bones found in Ethiopia, dated according to the museum's brochure at 3.2 million years old and celebrated at her discovery as the oldest human remains ever found.

A large body of science agrees with the "Out of Africa" theory for the geographical location of man's origins. But it also has its vocal opponents. "The whole 'Out of Africa' myth has its roots in the mainstream academic campaign in the 1990s to remove the concept of Race," says Australian historian Greg Jeffrey, cited by Stephen Strong in his article "DNA Evidence Debunks the Out-of-Africa Theory of Human Evolution." Jeffrey adds, "When I did my degree they all spent a lot of time on the 'Out of Africa' thing but it's been completely disproved by genetics."[1]

We will look at the DNA evidence he references. Stephen Strong himself is an Australian who champions the idea that his Aboriginal peeps down under are actually the first humans. He makes some decent points, likely because the scientific consensus is that the second oldest migration is out of Australia. But Strong's strident arguments demonstrate what a minefield this whole subject can become when racial agendas are in play.

When I discussed the Out of Africa theory with Alex, he pointed me to a scientific paper written by two Russians. Many Russians, of course, share Alex's Viking ancestry. And in fact, Strong cites these Russian authors in his refutation. "A very recent paper on Y-chromosomes released in 2012 by Anatole A. Klyosov and Igor L. Rozhanskii, strongly supports the existence of a 'common ancestor' who would not necessarily be in Africa. In fact, it was never proven that he lived in Africa."[2]

What's at stake here? Bragging rights for ethnic groups, of course, but also grant money and department funding for professors. A theory for European, Russian, or Siberian origins (they all exist) might be suspect for racist reasons. A theory promoting Africa might be reverse racism, a feel-good liberal agenda.

I met the guide at the Lucy museum, an elderly Ethiopian gentleman named Yosef who has worked there for many years. We sat down for an interview. I asked him about the Ark of the Covenant. Is it in Ethiopia? He spoke softly and said he has concerns about the fact that the Ark is mentioned later in the Old Testament, 300 years after Sheba and Solomon's day. He changed the subject. He wanted to talk about "ancient civilizations."

"The Egyptian gods came from here," he said. "Before history began. Before the Pharaohs."

He mentioned Moses's wife as being Ethiopian—and "definitely" Melchizedek. Regarding Eden, he said that "one of the rivers is Gihon. It is the Blue Nile. The Pishon is the White Nile." He talked about Cush being the son of Noah, adding the captain of the other ark to the list of famous Ethiopians.

"The founders of Ethiopia descended from Noah," I was told by the prominent scholar and monk when I visited the Abba Garima Monastery and asked advice on writing a history. "That is important." Professor Girma was less adamant on the view of an Ethiopian Noah. "Noah's ark was in today's Turkey, I think, or Armenia. It is better to say Noah landed here for a certain period of time, and one of his sons came to Ethiopia."

"So, you are not saying Noah lived in Ethiopia?"

"He did for a certain period of time."

His student Elias was more open to an Ethiopian Noah. He said the location in Turkey is too arid, and an area like Lake Tana matches a watery flood narrative. Of greater importance, he noted that Ethiopia is a more strategic and central geographic spot for Noah's three sons to spread out across the world. But he wasn't advocating it as strongly as the Eden theory.

I asked my museum guide Yosef about the Lucy exhibit. He changed the subject.

I looked into Lucy. She sounds like a nice gal, but she has some real issues. Dr. Donald Johanson announced her discovery in 1974, and a tour of the bones—a skull with about 40 percent of her skeleton—was exhibited across America. Lucy became an overnight sensation. What we weren't told is that Johansen originally found what looked like a pile of scattered rocks and pieced them together to create his ape-human. One of the knee joints was found two miles away, seventy meters deeper in the ground. One of the vertebre was proven to belong to a baboon. Two scientists in the *American Journal of Physical Anthropology* explained in scientific lingo that Lucy's bones are "compatible with a significant degree of arboreal locomotion." In other words, Lucy lived in a tree. She was likely a monkey.[3]

It never helps in the arguments for this feminine missing link to learn how Lucy got her name. As Johanson and friends dug into the Ethiopian ground to get some bones, they were listening over and over again to "Lucy in the Sky with Diamonds," a song inspired from countless acid trips by the Beatles.

Fortunately for the Out of Africa proponents, the theory is in no way dependent on Lucy. Before we get to genetics, the two scientific disciplines of paleontology and linguistics also point to an East African origin for humanity. The most diverse skulls on the planet hail from Ethiopia. The length of the long bones (shin to thighbone) that scientists look for to indicate age also point paleontologists to an East African origin. Linguistics looks for the highest point of diversity to indicate age, and this brand of science concludes that the other races with less diversity would have stemmed from the original, most diverse culture. In fact, studies indicate that the most diverse area in terms of language is Africa. Phonology, a branch of linguistics, reaches the same conclusion: the original people would be expected to be the most complex, to have the most phenomes—the number of sounds in a group of languages. The least phenomes are found in the Americas, the furthest distance from the area with the most sounds—East Africa.[4]

"MITOCHONDRIAL EVE" BEGAN IN ETHIOPIA

Science made a leap in its ability to determine the age of cultures with the discovery and use of mitochondrial DNA. This DNA science "has become a more definitive source of information about past population movements than the traditional tools of archeology and linguistics," writes Harvard scientist David Reich. He credits the beginning of mitochondrial DNA studies with professors Alan Wilson and Rebecca Cann, who (along with coauthor Mark Stoneking) wrote a seminal 1987 paper, "Mitochondrial DNA and Human Evolution." In a 1992 article in *Scientific American*, "The Recent African Genesis of Humans," Wilson and McCann wrote that "all humans today can be traced along maternal lines of descent to a woman who lived about 200,000 years ago, probably in Africa." Reich mentions the name she came to be known by: "Mitochondrial Eve." He notes that "the lower genetic diversity of non-Africans compared to Africans reflects the reduced diversity of the modern human population that expanded out of Africa…"[5]

Reich is one of the rising stars of DNA genome research, in part for his credentials, but also for being an excellent communicator. His online videos lucidly explain chromosomes, mutations, and exactly how scientists calculate the age of ancient bones. He has an agreeable, positive, and enthusiastic way about him—Mr. Rogers meets the Science Guy, without the bowtie.

Part of Reich's enthusiasm is his belief that we have only scratched the surface. We are on the cusp of an "ancient DNA revolution," he declares. Mitochondrial DNA got only 1/200,000th of the genome, he says, while new "ancient DNA" techniques can extract the entire genome. "The first five ancient human genomes were published in 2010," he writes. "By August 2017, my laboratory alone had generated genome-wide data for more than three thousand ancient samples."[6]

What have we learned from all this new data? I could not tell from one of Reich's twenty-minute videos whether he was saying that the new research debunked the Out of Africa theory or confirmed it. I watched it three different times and still couldn't figure it out. Was this highly intelligible professor just not communicating well, or was the obfuscation on purpose?

"David is an eloquent advocate" of the new science, says John Novembre, a computational biologist who studies population genetics at the University of Chicago. But another colleague perhaps explained why David was not so eloquent on the Out of Africa question. Reich's ancient DNA findings are "absolutely sort of mind-blowing," says Barry Cunliffe, an archaeologist and professor emeritus at the University of Oxford. "They are going to upset people, but that is part of the excitement of it."[7]

What was Reich's bottom line? All the excitement is over the fact that ancient human migrations were not as simple as we once thought. People didn't always live in the same place most of the time, with a large transplant on the rare occasion. They moved around a lot, similar to our age. "What the study of ancient DNA has now shown is that the past was no less complicated than the present. Human populations have always turned over," he says. It is "a story about how our interconnected human family was formed, in myriad ways never imagined."

So, the ancient DNA of Europeans includes Asians, Africans, early Americans, and even some Neanderthals, Reich explains. "We are all in this together" seems to be the key point to his highly publicized book *Who We Are and How We Got Here: Ancient DNA and the New Science of the Human Past*. Unlike in his videos, his book seemed much clearer regarding the Out of Africa theory. "What they found is that the deepest branch of the tree," he writes, "is found today only in people of sub-Saharan African ancestry."

This sounds like an endorsement. But the discerning reader must look more carefully. Reich is also squirrelly in print. In fact, he refers to a deeper branch than what the mitochondrial DNA scientists found. His ancient DNA research is uncovering that deeper branch. "Human beings today largely descend from a much later expansion from Africa," says Reich. He calls this later expansion a "bottleneck event" where, somehow, the millions of people on the planet got bottled up in Africa, were reduced to just a few, and then suddenly left Africa again for non-African places. But this information does not mean that the earlier people in Africa before the bottleneck were always from Africa.[8]

It really is difficult to determine Reich's view on the Out of Africa theory. The confusion, I suppose, allows him to get fans and support from both sides of the equation. *The Financial Times* decided he did stick with the now traditional scientific theory of African origins. "Africa was the original cradle of humanity," are the words the *Financial Times* uses to represent Reich's views. But he never actually says that, and a thread on the topic seven pages long at the *Anthrogenica.com* forum proves that such confusion remains.

What Reich does say is that the new ancient DNA research shows that humanity shares a common ancestor in two places. The first occurs a million or more years ago, and he remains agnostic about the geographic location of this DNA Adam. The second common ancestor, the one caught in a bottleneck, he identifies as definitely African who "occurs around 160,000 years ago, the date of Mitochondrial Eve." Or maybe we should call him "Mitochondrial Noah."

Reich provides another fun tidbit for non-Darwinian Ethiopians. Much of his book discusses new revelations related to his view that ancient mankind actually interbred with Neanderthals, the predecessors of our species, Homo sapiens. Neanderthals had two-thirds the brain size of Homo sapiens. "When we tested diverse present-day human populations, we found Neanderthals to be about equally close to Europeans, East Asians, and New Guineas, but closer to all non-Africans than to all sub-Saharan Africans."

In other words, Europeans have more ape-like Neanderthal genes than Ethiopians. "We reached these conclusions however we analyzed the data. This is the pattern that would be expected if Neanderthals had interbred with the ancestors of non-Africans but not Africans," Reich concludes. He then adds, "...the probability of these findings happening by chance was less than one in a quadrillion."[9]

Yosef, the guide at the National Museum of Ethiopia, had his own way of allowing Adam, Noah, and Lucy—metaphors for ancient archeology and genetic theory—to work together for a common cause.

"Do you believe in evolution?" I asked him.

"I have no answer about evolution versus creation."

"What do you think about Lucy?"

"She's getting younger and younger. Other discoveries are coming in. There are many ways of coming into existence."

"What are your views about coming into existence?"

"My interest is in those ancient civilizations that go along with the Old Testament. I like Lucy because we are getting much information on the Nile civilization."

"So, you like the archeology because it brings in resources?"

"It's helpful for the development of our people. There is a big money fortune for us, whether we believe in it or not."[10]

A few months after our return to the U.S., Alex was shocked to see Matthew Heimbach and a few others from his community visit his Orthodox Church. The white rights activist—the subject of a lead *Washington Post* story, and a known national figure—had navigated his legal woes and was free to move on with his life. He and Alex caught up with each other, and, in the account below, given to me by Alex, Heimbach said that he was glad to see "one of us" at the church.

After several long conversations where Alex shared with Heimbach his own spiritual journey past kinism and racial pride, Alex made his position clear. "I'm not one of you" he told Heimbach. Alex urged him to move past his previous activism stage and pursue true Christianity and its teachings, like "love your enemy," as promoted in the ancient church.

On the following Sunday, Heimbach met at length with the church leadership. As he left, he said to Alex: "I've decided to follow your advice." Alex reports that Heimbach made the decision to disassociate himself from all ties to racially controversial organizations.

Vice news reports similar comments. "I decisively failed at my original mission which was to be a voice for working class white folks," Heimbach said, "and ended up in the middle of the most humiliating white trash spectacle of the year. I'm just focusing on my responsibilities and duties, to my family—and God."

For Alex himself, the Ethiopians made a difference in his views. "They aren't all about technology and material progress, and all this other stuff. They believe in the power of story and 'myth'—in a good way." Alex is still very conservative, very traditional. He is the oldest of nine children and has several himself already, with no plans to prevent future blessings. He is unbending in confessing Christian beliefs and moral teachings, no matter how controversial or offensive to the modern mind.

"I started to get their concern about giving in to a Western mentality," he told me. Then he read *The Paradise of the Holy Fathers*, a synaxarion by Athanasius the Great, and realized how surreal the Eastern Orthodox stories could be. He was "impressed by the Ethiopian commitment to believing crazy hagiography." Alex shared an example from Athanasius of a woman who was turned into a horse for not taking communion for five weeks in a row. "She had to be doused with holy water to be restored." In another example, St. Anthony finds Paul of Thebes in the desert just before he dies. He laments having no shovel to bury the saintly father, but two lions appear, use their claws for the operation, and then leave the two saints in peace. Along the way, Anthony has a short chat with a satyr, a creature that is half man, half goat.

"So, what happened when I went to Ethiopia, I felt like I fit in extremely well with them because our view of the world is actually very similar. They have a pre-modern, still very ancient worldview. We have the same metaphysical basis for understanding the world and the same way of living," Alex said. "For example, their women dress modestly, and they go to church regularly and so on. They have all this reverence and piety."

"Almost all of my fellow white Americans—I can't talk to them about the same things I talk about with these guys. These guys get it. It's like 'Yeah, this is disgusting. This is degenerate. I can't believe this is happening in America.' And they agree. I realized—these guys have figured out what matters, and they agree with me. And I thought, these actually are the kind of people that I really wished lived in America."[11]

A donkey trotted past us and headed up the steep hill to the church of the unplugged village. Alex, Bazien, and I, along with the half a dozen teenage boys, trudged our way to the top. We reached our goal. This church and village, named Mulle, has never known electricity. Candles lit the area (albeit, along with a couple of battery-charged floodlights). We took off our shoes and worshipped with them for an hour.

Then we were asked to join the clergy in a separate outbuilding. One deacon cooked us mystery meat as we tried to catch a few minutes of sleep. But the outbuilding's floor was slanted, being part dirt and part sharp rocks. We were also given raw honey, served out of jars with bare hands. Alex at first refused, but then chose the way of politeness. (He was sick for the next few days.)

I interviewed the priest, Father John, who appeared to be about forty years old. Bazien translated.

"How did you get here?" he asked. "It's not easy, even for many Ethiopians."

We agreed and thanked him. "Who is it that you worship?" I asked.

"We worship the Father, the Son, and the Holy Spirit."

"For how long?"

"For 2,010 years."

"Were you Jewish before that?"

"Before becoming Christians, we sacrificed sheep to God the Father," Father John said. "It was different than Jewish. We followed the order of Melchizedek and still do now, sacrificing bread and wine."

"Are you concerned about power coming to your village, with ungodly messages coming from the TV and radio?"

"No. With everything there is good and bad," he said, barely viewable in the dark, cave-like building. "Many here are fond of the lifestyle that is said to be in America. But everything comes with a price."

He paused. "So, we pray for you in America."[12]

CHAPTER SEVENTEEN

MUSSOLINI'S GENERALS WERE under orders to extermi-
nate all Ethiopians who were resisting the Italian invasion. As they continued with their executions and poisonous gassing, the exiled Ethiopian leader in England prayed by a small fireplace in a residential home,
the only source of heat for a king who once reigned from a palace.

Emperor Haile Selassie wrote to the League of Nations, now with
a tone of desperation. "Dear members of the League…What kind of
crime have we committed that led you to reject us?" He then asked a
question that became a prediction: Does the League "really want to
discard the Charter which justifies its very existence, and, by doing so,
commit suicide?"

At Christmas, during this dark period, the emperor gave one of his
greatest speeches, broadcast by radio to his suffering Christian people
in Ethiopia. "There is no greater day of gratitude and joy for Christians
than celebrating the birthday of our Savior Jesus Christ. On this day
of happiness, every Christian, by meditating on [Christ's] life and the
work he accomplished for all of us, tends to forget the trials he faces
and the sadness that breaks his heart.…

"When he sacrificed himself at Golgotha for the atonement of our
sin, he prayed with his last breath for the forgiveness of those who had
tortured him, saying, 'Father, forgive them for they know not what
they do.' Shame on those of us who are Christians and do not follow
the way of the savior of the world, whose life was filled with kindness,
humility, and martyrdom.…

"Since our childhood, our innermost thoughts have been overwhelmed by the mysterious deep spirit of the divine infant's birth,

which is not only expressive but also glorious and inscrutable. Likewise, no matter what one's reputation, whether one's accomplishment is great or humble, tiresome or fruitless, in the journey of life, the mystery of Bethlehem dominates our spirit."

A year after this Christmas speech, two high-ranking officials sent a letter with an encouraging report that the people were standing resolute and strong because of two key factors. "The first is the reputation of Your Majesty, which has captured the heart of the people. The second is the prophecy that has been told in [every tribal language] throughout the whole country that the enemy will not rule our country for more than three years."[1]

Due to General Rodolfo Graziani's ruthless campaign of atrocities, even the Ethiopians who had taken loyalist oaths to Italy were turning away and joining the insurgent guerilla movement. These people now "were convinced that the Italians intended to exterminate them," writes A. J. Barker. in *The Rape of Ethiopia, 1936.*

During Ethiopia's earlier counterinsurgency, the Duce's son-in-law, Galeazzo Ciano, returned to Rome to explain the difficult situation, but also to implore him to seek better relations with Nazi Germany. At this time the Italian currency was plummeting, and Britain, France, and the U.S. were all threatening significant sanctions. Mussolini followed Ciano's advice and met with the German ambassador. In this meeting, plans were made for Hitler to help Italy in a war against Britain. The Duce described the relationship as "an axis around which all the European states could collaborate," and thus, the Axis Powers were named. Meanwhile, Mussolini would allow Hitler to invade European countries.

Hitler first took over the Rhineland, that part of Germany seized by the Allies after World War I. Britain and its Prime Minister, Neville Chamberlain, looked the other way. Then, as so many feared, Hitler invaded Czechoslovakia and Austria to his immediate south. Again, the European nations did nothing, confirming Haile Selassie's prediction that the failure to protect member nation Ethiopia would lead to the League of Nations committing suicide.

The Nazi aggression only further distanced Ethiopia from any hope of rescue. "From here on, it was a short step for the League of Nations to more or less abandon Haile Selassie to his fate," concludes Barker.

However, in September 1939, Hitler invaded Poland, an aggression that was the last straw for Britain, and forced the Allies to act. Mussolini aligned himself with the Nazis: "Blackshirts!" he cried in a speech at Rome, "I have brought back from Germany and my conversations with the Führer a lasting impression. The friendship between our two countries, which we have consecrated in the formal political alliance of the Rome-Berlin Axis, is now implanted in our hearts forever."

The many years of appeasement had failed. Chamberlain was replaced with the new Prime Minister, Winston Churchill. "Italy entered the Second World War as an ally of Nazi Germany," writes Asfa-Wossen. "Overnight, Haile Selassie was transformed from a forgotten exile languishing in a sleepy spa town in the West Country into a key figure on the stage of world history. Soon after, he found himself a passenger on an aircraft flying to the Sudan."[2]

On a return trip to Ethiopia in 2017, I arranged to meet my friend, Professor Girma Batu, the one I ate lunch with at the Lucy Restaurant, and with reluctance shared my problem with believing in the Ethiopian Ark tradition. As I had told him, the Ark is referenced in the Old Testament 300 years after Solomon, making it difficult to believe it came to Ethiopia during the time of Solomon and Sheba's son.

I struggled to find his office and the seminary where he teaches. GPS in Ethiopia is not always accurate. Beyond that, my cell phone did not work the entire time I was in the country. After an hour's delay, I headed to a coffee shop with Wi-Fi to get my directions using my laptop. That didn't work either. Stumped, I approached two Ethiopians next to me, shared my dilemma, and asked for help. I had Girma's phone number, and so they were able to call and notify him of my whereabouts. I had no doubt that these two young men would exhibit the classic Ethiopian kindness.

After sharing a few cups of indigenous Ethiopian coffee with Girma, I brought up again my biblical problem. Directness is a character trait, for good or bad, that I picked up from my theologian father who passed up his second calling as a football coach. Biblical dilemmas must be confronted.

Girma listened to me talk about how the Scriptures record King Josiah ordering the Ark to be brought out, 300 years after it was supposedly brought to Ethiopia. He nodded his head and continued his usual, pleasant expression. He was in no rush.

After a long pause, he spoke.

"Dean, have you read the passage in 2 Chronicles 35 about King Josiah?"

"Yes."

"Did you read the entire chapter?"

"Yes, several times. It says they brought out the Ark."

"It says that Josiah asked them to bring out the Ark. Does it ever say that they actually did so?"

I had to think about that. It wasn't a question I had thought about, not an angle I had considered.

I went back to study the passage. He was right. King Josiah gives the order. The rest of the passage discusses all sorts of things that the priests do to restore temple worship, as the good king had commanded, in what is known as "Josiah's reform." But it never says that they brought out the Ark. The silence is deafening, especially considering that the Ark is such a central piece in the rest of Scripture—during those times when it is, in fact, actually around. Whenever it moves, there are great parades, processions, and convocations. The high point of King David's life, it can be argued, is when he dances before the Lord as the Ark is being moved to Jerusalem. In those earlier stories, the movement of the Ark is described in detail. By contrast, the book of 2 Chronicles drops the matter with no explanation. Girma was right. It made no sense for the Ark to never be mentioned again.

Josiah gave his command to bring out the Ark in 622 BC. We know this date because the Bible says it was "in the eighteenth year of the reign of Josiah." Only four years earlier, the prophet Jeremiah made a declaration that seems to fit with no Ark actually appearing before Josiah during this period: "'In those days, when your numbers have increased greatly in the land,' declares the Lord, 'people will no longer say, "The ark of the covenant of the Lord." It will never enter their minds or be remembered; it will not be missed, nor will another one be made.'" (Jer. 3:16).

Jeremiah shares these words after 300 years of biblical silence on the Ark. The spirit of his declaration fits with the idea that the Ark had been gone a long while and would remain gone. Given this major prophet's decree, it makes more sense that Josiah's priests did not bring out the Ark, despite Josiah's desire to include it in his restoration. None of the details in the Bible of the Josiah reform make mention of the Ark being taken into the temple. Only Josiah's order is recorded.

PROFESSOR EDWARD ULLENDORFF

Having successfully navigated this biblical problem, it now became necessary to focus on the challenge that Dr. Edward Ullendorff presented when he claimed that he saw the Ark and that it was a medieval fake. He named the year as 1941, a time when the Ark was held, not in today's special chapel, but in the nearby St. Mary of Zion Cathedral. We do not know where, specifically, the Ethiopian church leaders stored the actual Ark in the cathedral. But we *do* know that, as with all churches, St. Mary of Zion had a tabot, an ark replica, used by the priests in their closed-off holy of holies to prepare the Eucharist. This ark replica is brought out only on a few feast days. Could this be what Ullendorff claims to have seen?

Scholar Sergew Hable Selassie recounts a nineteenth century episode of a priest from the Caucasus named Dimotheos who claimed to see the Ark. According to Sergew, Dimotheos's description proves he was shown a fake ark. The church refused his initial demands to see it, causing him to appeal the matter to the emperor who decreed his right to view it. "During this time it would have been possible for the [guardian] to substitute and other Ark and present it to Dimotheos as the true Ark," writes Sergew.

A *Smithsonian Magazine* reporter looked into the matter of who could view the Ark and in a 2007 article quoted the Ark guardian on the policy: "No king or patriarch or bishop can ever see it, only me," he said. "This has been our tradition since Menelik brought the Ark here more than 3,000 years ago."

The reporter, Paul Raffaele, did his due diligence and interviewed Abuna Paulos I on the matter, the patriarch himself. "Can you believe that even though I'm head of the Ethiopian church, I'm still forbidden from seeing it?" he said with a shrug. "The guardian of the Ark is the only person on earth who has that peerless honor."[3]

Given these firsthand quotes, it is difficult to believe that Ullendorff was allowed to see the actual Ark. It was a replica.

Ullendorff told the *Los Angeles Times* that he wasn't surprised that Graham Hancock was denied permission to see the Ark. He called Hancock a *parvenu* (which, admittedly, I had to look up: "A person of obscure origin who has gained wealth, influence, or celebrity").

"You need to be able to speak their language, classical Ge'ez," Ullendorff said, regarding the credentials necessary to be an Ark viewer. "You need to be able to show that you're serious."[4]

I have little doubt that Ullendorff believed with sincerity that he was allowed access. But his Ge'ez skills would never be enough street cred for him to surpass the patriarch himself in such privileges. Instead, our proper British professor seems to have convinced himself that he was part of the "in crowd," like a visitor to an urban dance club who performs the white man's overbite in ignorant bliss.

When Ullendorff's judgment is not clouded by that parvenu, Graham Hancock, he tends to express a number of views friendly to the

Ethiopian Ark theory. I quoted him earlier when he said it doesn't really matter whether the Queen of Sheba was from Ethiopia or Arabia, but he follows that comment by saying that the rich forests in Ethiopia favor Africa over Arabia—because the biblical passages reference much "fine timber" that she brought for Solomon's house and the temple.[5]

Ullendorff also points to a strong source, cited by many ancient historians, for an Ethiopian Sheba—the record of Josephus, the reputable first century-Jewish scholar. Josephus refers to Sheba as "the Queen of Egypt and Ethiopia." Ullendorff believes this is a reference to the ancient empire Nubia—also called Meroe— today's Khartoum in Sudan, where Ethiopia's Blue Nile meets the White Nile. Nubia/Sudan borders Egypt and Ethiopia. Regarding Josephus's remark, Ullendorff says, "Even though this is probably intended to cover Nubia-Meroe rather than Abyssinia proper, it does show a concentration on an African, instead of an Arabian, origin." Given the British professor's views, the *Los Angeles Times* reporter gives a curious critique of Hancock, stating that "In fact, biblical scholars consider Sheba to be Arabian, not African." And yet, the primary biblical scholar the reporter interviews, Ullendorff, suggests the opposite.[6]

Girma provided me with some breathing room for a Nubian Queen of Sheba. He said that the Bible's use of Ethiopia (Cush in some translations) refers to a far larger area and empire than today. But "any reference to Ethiopia in the Bible refers to today's Ethiopia," he insists. "There is a church decision about that. But today's Ethiopia is very much narrower than the historical Ethiopia." He said that the Greeks and Homer referred to Ethiopia as the place "from where the sun rises to where the sun sets—it's just to say, Ethiopia is a big country." In other words, the Ethiopian empire at one time included Nubia and the White Nile, as well as parts of Yemen across the Red Sea.

Early church scholar Origen discusses the issue and refers to Homer's description of Ethiopia as "the uttermost parts of the earth." Origen compares this phrase to Jesus's statement that the Queen of the South came from "the uttermost parts of the earth" to visit Solomon. Church Fathers Gregory of Nyssa and Gregory the Theologian also subscribe to an Ethiopian Sheba.

Not much of a groundswell of support exists for an Arabian Sheba. "In Ethiopia, the tradition of the Queen of Sheba is much stronger than in South Arabia," writes Sergew Hable Selassie. "Let us not deny all the ancient traditions in Ethiopia if we are not able to put anything better in their place."[7]

My Axumite guide, Yirga, took me to the traditional site of Sheba's palace. It is located beneath Makeda Mountain, the same name given for the queen in the Kebra Negast. Among the ruins of the foundation, near the center, is an altar area. He said the deepest layer contains bone and charcoal that tested to 1000 BC by carbon dating. I never asked for a reference, but I always found his assertions reliable. Graham Hancock provides a differing account. He was taken to the same site in the 1980s by an employee with the Ministry of Culture, Berhane Meskel Zelelew, who told him—proudly, according to Hancock—that he was looking at the Queen of Sheba's palace.

"Has any archaeology ever been done on the site to test the legend?" Hancock asked.

"Yes, in the late 1960s the Ethiopian Institute of Archaeology conducted some excavations here," Zelelow said.

"And what was discovered?"

Berhane made a "mournful" face. "The opinion was that the palace was not sufficiently old to have been the residence of the Queen of Sheba."

Hancock wrote this account in 1992. But a report from Berlin in 2008 announced an update related to the archaeology finds. "Professor Helmut Ziegert, of the archaeological institute at the University of Hamburg, has been supervising a dig in Aksum, northern Ethiopia, since 1999," reported *Fox News*. Working from the same Makeda-Sheba location, the professor said: "From the dating, its position and the details that we have found, I am sure that this is the palace."

News outlet *nazret.com* provided more details: "The University said scientists led by Helmut Ziegert had found remains of a tenth century BC palace at Axum-Dungur under the palace of a later Christian king. There was evidence the early palace had been torn down and realigned to the path of the star Sirius," *nazret* reported. "The team said evidence for this included Sirius symbols at the site, the debris of sacrifices and the alignment of sacred buildings to the rising-point of Sirius, the brightest star in the sky."[8]

Other facts point to an ancient Jewish presence in Ethiopia. Ullendorff discusses the evidence of animal sacrifice in ancient Christian practice, who, for a period of time, continued this Old Testament ritual. Dr. Richard Hull of New York University says that Ethiopia's Falashas are the only Jews to continue to practice animal sacrifice centuries after Judaism stopped the practice following the destruction of the Jerusalem temple in AD 70. The Falashas observe neither the later Jewish feasts of Purim nor Hanukkah. The Falashas themselves claim to have been in Ethiopia since 1300 BC. They are the "last surviving practitioners of genuine 1st Temple Judaism," says Hancock.

The Falashas are part of the Agaw people. (An 1820 account describes Jewish prayers recited by the Agaw Felashas in a language no one could understand.) The Christian Agaws still practice Old Testament washing ceremonies. All Ethiopian Orthodox Christians retain a great number of Old Testament practices, including circumcision, kosher dietary laws, and both Saturday and Sunday Sabbaths. Axumite archaeology extracts no pig bones.[9]

Marcus Daoud writes in *The Liturgy of the Ethiopian Church*: "It is unlikely that the Hebraic forms were anywhere more faithfully kept preserved than in the Ethiopian service…" On this point, Ullendorff quotes an Eastern European Jew living in Addis Ababa: "I was simply overwhelmed at how 'Jewish' everything was," he exclaimed. "What does it remind you of if not a Sabbath morning in an orthodox synagogue? I found among the various Ethiopian amulets things very close to my own phylacteries and small scrolls. I was exhilarated to discover the high holy days also falling in September, the Sabbath being celebrated on Saturday, and time reckoned from sunset…"

The Ark parades in Ethiopia look like processions in the Old Testament says Ullendorff, "the singing, dancing, beating of staff or praying sticks, rattling of sistra, and sounding of other musical instruments remind one forcefully of the scene in 2 Samuel 6 where David and the people are dancing around the Ark."

Ullendorff believes that the Bible passage in Zephaniah 3:10 points to an Ethiopian Jewish community in the seventh century BC: "From beyond the rivers of Ethiopia, my worshipers, the daughter of my dispersed ones, shall bring my offering" (NKJV). Sergew sees a similar date for an Ethiopian Jewish diaspora based on Isaiah 45:14: "...the merchandise of Ethiopia...will make supplication to you, saying: 'God is with you only...'" (NRSV). Also interesting is the dating of Ethiopia's favorite verse from Psalm 68:31: "Ethiopia shall soon stretch out her hands to God" (KJV). Traditional scholars believe that David wrote this Psalm in 1045 BC. If so, the story of the Queen of Sheba turning to the one true God does take place "soon," just a few years later.[10]

A preponderance of the evidence now seemed to point to an Ethiopian Ark. However, another Bible verse confronted me that jarred my ability to accept the Kebra Negast story. And just to make it more complex, it all depends on how you define "Bible."

CHAPTER EIGHTEEN

ON JUNE 10, 1940, Benito Mussolini made his announcement: "Italy has entered the war as the ally of Germany." Three days later a "Mr. Strong" left the coast of England for Egypt in a Sunderland flying boat.

Restoring the monarch in Ethiopia would put pressure on the Axis powers. Churchill wrote to his foreign minister: "I am strongly in favor of Haile Selassie entering Ethiopia."

Mr. Strong—a.k.a. Haile Selassie—was headed to the Sudan to prepare for a return to Abyssinia with the help of Britain and the Allies. "Although France had been invaded by the Nazis," wrote the emperor, "we took the risk and flew over its skies to Malta." When the entourage reached Egypt, they rested for a time and walked to the Nile River. "We were moved by deep feelings of nostalgia. In fact, we cupped our hands, scooped up some water, and sipped a little."

In Sudan, the British demurred on any immediate action. Italy still had 300,000 troops and 200 planes in Ethiopia. Impatient, the emperor arranged for 10,000 leaflets to be airdropped. At the top was the verse from Psalm 68: "Ethiopia shall soon stretch out her hands to God."

"I will sit on my throne once again," Haile Selassie assured the world. "This is the day God has willed." In a radio broadcast he assured his people. "Your sacrifices have borne fruit... Your major weapon was your innate heroism, and your hope was the God of Ethiopia." To those Ethiopians still siding with the enemy he said: "Hereafter, if you continue to be Italy's instrument, you will leave behind only infamy for your descendants."[1]

British commanders in Sudan continued to stall. Fortunes turned for Haile Selassie when Churchill dispatched to the scene a young major, Orde Wingate, a 37-year-old military star and Zionist idealist who had lived in a kibbutz in Israel. The aggressive officer dreamed of entering the liberated Ethiopian Jerusalem on a white horse. "The gung-ho, Zionist British major and the Ethiopian emperor hit it off right from the start," writes Asfa-Wossen. "In Haile Selassie—the Lion of Judah, who could cite King Solomon and the Queen of Sheba in his lineage—Wingate had found his true lodestar, and from this moment on, he was determined to do everything in his power to restore the emperor to his throne."

HAILE SELASSIE

When they first met, Wingate read a prepared statement: "Sire. In 1935 fifty-two nations let you and your country down. That act of aggression led to this war. It shall be the first to be avenged."

He organized a resistance movement across the border near Lake Tana at the source of the Blue Nile, the spot some believe to be the Garden of Eden. Wingate and the emperor then led a caravan of 18,000 camels that joined an eclectic group of 2,000 soldiers—Sudanese, Kenyans, Somalis, South Africans, and Nigerians—a foretaste of Haile Selassie's leadership a few years later on the continent. Wingate named the fighting expedition "Gideon Force" after the Israelite warrior in the book of Judges. A British advisor described the journey: "First Wingate, then the Emperor (on horseback) then if you please the High Priest with his venerable beard, gallantly paddling along on foot through the African bush with his black robes flapping and his prayer book in hand."[2]

Wingate and the emperor's small army joined forces with the soldiers gathered at Lake Tana and moved toward Addis Ababa as another British army, led by General Sir Alan Cunningham, marched to the capital from the south. The nation was aflame with the news that their emperor was returning. Again, the British delayed. Cunningham messaged Wingate to wait until the area was safer. Haile Selassie had waited long enough and insisted the Gideon Force move forward. "We ought to do what our forefathers have done. We must return to our native country and die there."

The prayers of Ethiopians everywhere were answered when Mussolini made his next move. The Italian army, now facing other confrontations in Europe, abandoned the capital, to the delight of the people. The British were alarmed, however. Of the 100,000 people living in Addis, 40,000 were Italian civilians, and an uprising could involve violent reprisals.

Haile Selassie returned to his capital city on May 5, 1941, exactly five years to the day that the Italian army entered. Tens of thousands cheered. The emperor rode in a convertible guarded by cavalry officers, and Wingate followed on his white horse. "We could not control our tears and deep emotion," Haile Selassie said. "We were welcomed by priests dancing to the tunes of religious hymns...We entered the church to express our gratitude to our Creator, and stayed there until services were over."[3]

After a twenty-one-gun salute, the emperor mounted the podium to address the crowd. "No human lips can express the gratitude which I feel to the merciful God who has enabled me to stand in your midst on this day," he said, "of which angels in heaven nor creatures on earth could neither have thought or known about.

"Mussolini tried to exterminate the Ethiopian race.... The blood and bones of those who were killed with spades and pickaxes, of those who were split with axes and hammered to death, pierced with bayonets, clubbed and stoned, of those who were burned alive in their homes with their little children, of those who perished of hunger and thirst in prison, have been crying out for justice.

"People of my country, Ethiopia! Today is a day in which Ethiopia is stretching out her hands to God in joy and thanksgiving.... Let not our rejoicing be in any other way than in the spirit of Christ. Do not return evil for evil. Do not indulge in the atrocities which the enemy has been practicing," he said. "Take care not to spoil the good name of Ethiopia by acts which are worthy of the enemy."

That day and thereafter the people listened to their Christian emperor. The British had misjudged the situation, and their fears of retribution and violence were unwarranted. Haile Selassie assured his people justice would come and called for them to join the Allied armies. "As St. George killed the dragon...let us unite with our allies to stand against the godless and cruel dragon which has newly risen and is oppressing mankind."[4]

The dragon did indeed meet his fate. Confidence in Mussolini plummeted in Italy upon the news of his failure in Ethiopia. Later, the Allies' bombing of Rome left the people in search of food. The Duce was forced to summon the Grand Council, not called since the beginning of the world conflict, to regather the nation's confidence. The council cast a 19-to-8 no confidence vote for the waning dictator. The Duce ignored it. The council also voted to restore the constitutional powers of the king. That afternoon, the two leaders met, as their regular weekly meeting was on the schedule. Mussolini headed to the royal palace of King Vittorio Emanuele III and began to explain what happened at the war council. He was interrupted.

"My dear Duce, it's no longer any good," the monarch told him. "Italy has gone to bits. You are the most hated man in Italy." As he left the palace, the king had him arrested. He was deposed and placed under house arrest.

A few days later, a German commando unit of the Waffen-SS secretly flew into Rome, rescued the Duce, and set him up as puppet leader of German-controlled Northern Italy. A tearful Mussolini said, "I knew my friend Adolf wouldn't desert me."[5]

He brought his current mistress from Rome, Claretta Petacci, age 20. The 60-year-old Duce met her in elite social circles. He summoned her prominent mother, Giuseppina, to his office and demanded "Is your daughter pure? Keep her under surveillance....Whoever has the privilege of being close to Mussolini cannot have boyfriends." He later asked the mother's permission to be the young girl's lover. In an act symbolic of how an entire nation sold its soul for a season, she gave her approval. "The idea that she will be near a man like you is very comforting to me."

The mother then regularly invited Mussolini to spend nights at the family's 32-room mansion. She placed mirrors on the walls and ceilings of Claretta's bedroom. The myth of Mussolini was still alive, although in reality he was "bald, fat, short-sighted, and sickly," wrote Olla, who relays that the Duce liked to strangle women with a scarf. He also told Petacci that, his entire life, he could only be aroused by thinking of prostitutes.[6]

Soon Northern Italy was under invasion, and Mussolini and Claretta fled to neutral Switzerland. According to journalist Christopher Stevens, "Italian partisans stopped the truck in which Mussolini, disguised in a Luftwaffe uniform and clutching a suitcase of cash, was hidden under a pile of blankets. In the next truck, they found a terrified Claretta. The pair were driven to the village of Mezzegra where, on April 27, 1945—two days before Hitler committed suicide—the death sentence was quickly pronounced on them both."

Accounts vary as to how they were shot and killed, some more romantic than others. Cannastraro and Sullivan conclude that he was likely shot as he lay asleep. What we do know for certain is that both their bodies were found riddled with bullets about a mile from the village where they were taken.[7] The next day they were moved to Milan and strung up by the ankles upside down on a rusty girder at an Esso gas station. Mussolini was 61.

Claretta was not wearing underwear when she died," writes Stevens. "To preserve her decency, some of the older women in the crowd knotted her skirt between her legs before she was suspended like a slab of meat, next to the body of her lover."[8]

Mussolini met the end he deserved. As narratives typically go, the character with opposite traits might be expected to meet a different fate. It was not to be. In fact, it can be argued that Haile Selassie's ending was worse than that of Italy's dictator.

In the decades following Mussolini's death, Ethiopia continued to be attacked by Europe and the West, in a fashion even worse than the invasions of 1890 and 1935. But what could possibly be worse? At Adwa, Ethiopians repelled an attempt to conquer them. With Mussolini,

Ethiopia survived an attempt to exterminate part or all of the population.

Only one thing could possibly be worse than being conquered, worse than being murdered en masse. Today, Ethiopia has already experienced this worse thing—to a great degree— and continues to be confronted by this spiritual and psychological force, imposed from the West, that seeks to destroy them. The demon's name is suicide.

Two runners had taken sole possession of the lead in the final stretch of the 1960 Olympic marathon. The barefoot Ethiopian Abebe Bikila raced neck and neck with the soldier Rhadi Ben Abdesselam, who wore 185 instead of his listed number of 26. But Bikila now knew his identity. He was the competitor to be most feared, according to Bikila's trainer, Onni Niskanen. Bikila fought with all of his determination to keep up with the swift runner.

The radio commentator captured the drama: "Rhadi was down as number 26, but, for some reason, he's wearing number 185," he noted. "Rhadi came from nowhere to win the international cross-country championship earlier this year."

Abebe Bikila, nearing a possible victory, wanted to please Emperor Haile Selassie. He had been quoted as saying: "My life belongs to His Imperial Majesty."

Bikila served in Haile Selassie's Imperial Bodyguard, one of several thousand soldiers charged with protecting the capital of Addis Ababa. It was his intention to impress the emperor. Like Haile Selassie, he was a devoted Orthodox Christian, observed the feasts, fasted every Wednesday and Friday, and faithfully followed the traditions of his faith and nation. "I wanted the world to know that my country, Ethiopia, has always won with determination and heroism," Bikila said.[9]

However, when he finally met the emperor in person prior to the 1960 Games, the exchange was uncomfortable. He and the other marathon contestant, Abebe Wakjira, were brought to the emperor by the Ethiopian Olympic Committee chairman. Bikila had only recently been selected for the race after replacing the country's top runner, Wami Biratu, who broke his ankle in a soccer match. During one of the training runs, Bikila was timed breaking the world record, but no one took the results seriously.

The emperor was no stranger to the Olympic games. He first attended in Paris in 1924, the year Scotsman Eric Liddell won a gold for Great Britain as recounted in the Oscar-winning film *Chariots of Fire*. Decades later, Haile Selassie gained Ethiopia its own chance to compete in the Olympics. Their first opportunity was four years previously in 1956. No one won a medal. The competitive emperor wanted a victory.

Bikila's running partner, Wakjira, describes the first meeting in detail: "The emperor asked who was who and then he saw us. Both of us were very thin and he said: 'Who are they?' [The chairman] said we were the marathon runners and he replied: 'How can such thin people win?'"

The official responded by sharing Bikila's recent record-breaking time. "I didn't ask you for their times," Haile Selassie barked. "I asked you whether they could win or not!"

They flew to Rome the next day. Wakjira was asked if he was nervous about his first flight. "No," he said. But he admitted that he and Bikila "were nervous about the shoes." National pride was at stake. Writes Bikila biographer Tim Judah: "There now came the question of shoes. They generally did not run with shoes, but there was, hovering in the background, the question of national prestige. If they ran without shoes, it might seem as though the Ethiopians were too poor to afford them."

Adidas, the shoe sponsor for the 1960 Olympic games, had only a few pairs left when they arrived. Bikila's daughter says that they had to go buy some. "He wore the new sneakers around for a few days before the competition started in order to break them in," she writes in her book, and "his feet developed painful blisters. This naturally made him worry as to how he was going to go through 42 kilometers of race. No solution seemed to be in sight. He considered the matter at length and there was only one thing to do, run barefoot."

"To [his Swedish trainer] Niskanen," she added, "who had promised victory for Ethiopia, the fact of Abebe's running barefoot only struck him as inviting defeat."[10]

As they neared the end of the marathon, Bikila looked down and saw that Rhadi was wearing new white Adidas. They ran past the Circus Maximus on their left in the direction of the balcony of the Piazza Venizia, where Benito Mussolini delivered so many of his famous speeches. The course then took a hard right and they headed in the direction of the Termini train station adjacent to the Piazza dei Cinquecento, which was named in honor of the 500 Italian soldiers killed by Ethiopian General Ras Alula's troops in the Dogali massacre. However, before they would reach the train station, the finish line awaited them at the Arch of Constantine, built by the first Christian emperor of Rome, whose domain became officially Christian just a few years after Emperor Ezana decreed Ethiopia the first Christian empire.

Rhadi had been a soldier in the French army. However, he was not running for France, even though in the past he had run under the French flag. He now represented Morocco, his native country, colonized by France, but having gained its independence only four years before. The two Africans—from the East and West coasts of the great continent—served as a symbol for the future of the globe. They had both passed all of the European favorites, just as Africa was in the process of throwing off its colonial yoke. They also represented the growing continent of the future.

"Then, he was racing for France," said the radio analyst, "but now he's in the national colors of his native Morocco. Bikila, the African who's been right up there behind him for the last 10 kilometers, hasn't taken part in international events before. He gave his occupation as . . . a private in the Imperial Bodyguard of His Majesty, Emperor Haile Selassie I. Well, the emperor can certainly be proud of his bodyguard today. Barefoot or not, he's managed to outpace some stiff competition."[11]

Only a thousand meters remained. Either of these two finalists could win the gold medal at the 1960 Olympic games. If the barefoot Ethiopian could find a way to finish first, he would accomplish perhaps the greatest feat in the history of all sports.

PART FOUR

The Oligarchs and the "Unfit"

A False Ark for the West and the True Ark

CHAPTER NINETEEN

ON MAY 5, 2009, a handful of the West's richest men met in Manhattan to discuss what they considered the most dangerous, most critical threat to the planet.

Those attending included Bill Gates, Warren Buffett, Ted Turner, George Soros, and David Rockefeller, Jr. Their concern was related to population. Was it the appalling decline of fertility in Europe and Western nations that brought the billionaires together? Indeed, Mussolini's goal of sixty million Italians was never reached. The nation peaked in 2010 at fifty-nine million and now steadily decreases. With a birthrate of 1.2 children per woman, far below the 2.1 replacement rate, Italy is slated to be the oldest nation in Europe in 2050 and the world's second-oldest after Japan. It will cease as a country in a century or two.[1]

The crisis in the West is not confined to Italy. The United States has similar unsustainable birthrates and only current immigration numbers keep the rate above Italy's for now. In 200 years, the German language is likely to pass out of existence. *Demographic winter* is a term now being used to describe this death spiral. "The Death of the West is not a prediction of what is going to happen, it is a depiction of what is happening now," writes author and 1996 Republican frontrunner Pat Buchanan, who uses only United Nations statistics to prove the case in his 2002 book *The Death of the West*. "This is not a matter of prophecy, but of mathematics."[2]

And yet, population increase was the key to the ascendancy of the West. "...the growth of Europe's population in the eleventh century and thereafter is seen as proof that medieval Europe was healthily advancing," writes Chicago scholar J. M. Blaut in his work on Eurocentric history. "Civilization, as we have seen, is about cities," echoes *New York Times* bestselling author Niall Ferguson, who points to having a growing population as the key. "No previous civilization had ever achieved such dominance as the West achieved over the Rest."

"If, in the year 1411, you had been able to circumnavigate the globe, you would probably have been most impressed by the quality of life in Oriental civilizations," says Ferguson. "By contrast, Western Europe in 1411 would have struck you as a miserable backwater, recuperating from the ravages of the Black Death—which had reduced population by as much as half..."

In 1500, "the biggest city in the world was Beijing, with a population of between 600,000 and 700,000. Of the ten largest cities in the world by that time only one—Paris—was European, and its population numbered fewer than 200,000.... Yet by 1900 there had been an astonishing reversal. Only one of the world's ten largest cities at that time was Asian and that was Tokyo. With a population of around 6.5 million, London was the global megalopolis."[3]

In 1913, Europe had more people than China. At that time, Europe and the U.S. comprised thirty-three percent of the world's people. In 2003, that number declined to seventeen percent. Today, it is twelve percent. "Is decline and fall the looming fate of Western Civilization 2.0?" asks Ferguson.

The prospects are grim for stopping the march toward extinction. Low birthrates cause a "vicious circle," according to the Organization for Economic Cooperation and Development (OECD). "Fewer children today imply fewer women of childbearing age twenty years from now, so the cumulative momentum of current low birth rates will be difficult to reverse." Though still mathematically possible, "such a recovery would be unprecedented in human history."[4]

Fewer young workers means fewer people supporting the pensions and health care of the older generations. Riots in Greece and other parts of Europe are rooted in these now lopsided Western economies. The U.S. may not be far behind. "You can't keep going with this completely upside-down age distribution, with the pyramid standing on its point," said a spokesman for the Population Reference Bureau. "You can't have a country where everybody lives in a nursing home."

Unlike the West, Russia is keenly aware of its predicament, as it strives to recover from the 1.16 birthrate that existed when communism was overthrown in 1991. The government now offers incentives for children, the equivalent in U.S. dollars to a lower middle-class income. Parents of seven children are awarded a medal, the Order of Parental Glory. Russia has instituted a national holiday on September 12, Day of Conception or Procreation Day—the people call it "Make a Baby Day"—where citizens get the day off to produce children. The birthrate rose to 1.71 in 2013 and continues to increase. About 1.9 million babies were born in Russia in 2015, up from 1.5 million in 2005. "The rise is slight, but it is still a rise," said a hopeful President Vladimir Putin.[5]

So, is this the threat that Bill Gates and friends gathered to solve? No, it was something else. And what caused this great reversal for Western society? Simply put, Margaret Sanger defeated Benito Mussolini in perhaps the one area where he was correct—opposing the misleading and destructive teachings of the Malthusians and their population and resource fearmongering—although Mussolini's motive was not a biblical desire to be fruitful and multiply and create more image-bearers of God. He wanted an empire. Along with Italy, Sanger also defeated the rest of Europe and the United States. She also sabotaged their Christian morals, thus reaching the goal printed in her *Birth Control Review* to "undermine the authority of the Christian churches."[6]

Sanger, of course, is the founder of Planned Parenthood, the largest performer of abortions in the world. But her greatest accomplishment for her cause was the day she met Dr. Gregory Pincus at a dinner in 1951. Pincus had worked for the Rockefeller-funded Kaiser Wilhelm Institute for Biology, exposed for sterilizing hundreds of French African children and closely associating with the Nazi eugenics program. The meeting led to Planned Parenthood agreeing to fund research by Pincus to develop Sanger's longtime dream of a birth control pill, which was first licensed in 1960. By 1970, forty-three percent of American women were already taking this revolutionary method of contraception.

Concludes Pat Buchanan: "Historians may one day call 'the pill' the suicide tablet of the West."[7]

If the oligarchs who met in 2009 in Manhattan did not address the looming crisis of demographic winter, regarding what grave matter did they deliberate? What did they pinpoint as the key geographical target for the world's largest, most dangerous threat?

Africa.

A Nigerian biomedical scientist working in London calls this new campaign against Africa an attempt at a "new protectorate" from "our new colonial masters." In her book, *Target Africa: Ideological Neocolonialism in the Twenty-First Century*, Obianuju Ekeocha insists that these Western elites are imposing their own morals on others. African leaders "do not need interference from new colonizers; in fact, they must resist if they are to retain everything they hold dear."[8]

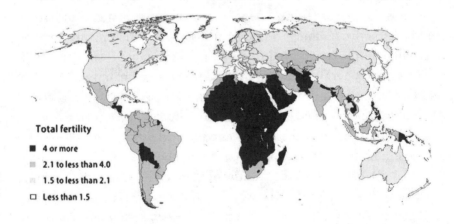

Total fertility
- 4 or more
- 2.1 to less than 4.0
- 1.5 to less than 2.1
- Less than 1.5

More details will follow on the curious agenda of Bill Gates and his wife, Melinda, and the efforts of those dedicated to defeat him, such as Miss Ekeocha. To better understand today's great battle between the West and Africa, we must first finish the story of Haile Selassie, the spiritual leader of Africa. A great hero in his early reign, the latter part of the emperor's life revealed much more of his complex, sometimes noble, sometimes destructive character.

The mother of the future emperor of Ethiopia, Haile Selassie, miscarried nine times before she finally gave birth to a child. When Ras Tafari Makonnen's mother was near to delivery, according to a well-known story in Ethiopia, a hermit came to see his father, Ras Makonnen, and assured him that the boy would survive. "He will rise to become the ruler of Ethiopia and govern the whole country with a firm hand. He will bestow greatness and pride upon Ethiopia and make it renowned the world over. But ultimately he will destroy everything he has built with his own hands and leave the country in ruins."[9]

Would Italy once again be the force behind Ethiopia's ruin? After World War II, Italy was never again in a position to look beyond its borders. Another world power, always lurking in the shadows of Ethiopia's conflicts, emerged as the new threat to end the nation's more than 3,000 years of never being colonized. A memo circulating in the British Foreign Ministry office stated: "It is difficult to believe that the restoration of the former Ethiopian Empire as an independent state is a practicable political aim. That empire survived as long as it did, only because the three Great Powers bordering on it—Great Britain, France, and Italy—were unable to agree on its control." A British war department memo stated the same position.[10]

In public, Great Britain formally recognized Ethiopia as a "free and independent state," according to the official Anglo-Ethiopian Agreement, ratified in 1942. Haile Selassie also kept a straight face in public, referring to his currently benign occupiers as "our true friend, Great Britain." However, he had learned firsthand that Britain's plans were to take over the countries left behind by Italy, the entire region known as "Italian East Africa," which included Libya, Somalia, and, most importantly, Ethiopia. These countries would be added to the British Empire's surrounding colonies of Egypt, Kenya, Sudan, and many others comprising nearly half the continent. Later, Haile Selassie named a specific British officer for his evidence, a Brigadier Maurice Lush, "who led a political group which had sinister intentions toward our country. They spoke publicly that the purpose of their coming was to rule Ethiopia."[11]

The diplomatic war began when General Cunningham moved his headquarters into the Menelik Palace. Haile Selassie moved back into his original palace, built in 1930. Cunningham asked the emperor to meet him at the Menelik Palace, but Haile Selassie knew that such an action would acknowledge the British commander's superior rank. Instead, the emperor invited the ambitious general over to receive a military decoration honoring his great service to Ethiopia, and Cunningham agreed.

Britain's desire to control the country soon became evident. Military and police efforts were overseen by Cunningham. The Ethiopian currency was changed to the British shilling. Cars were instructed to drive on the left side of the road.

The United States, meanwhile, was growing wary of Britain's control, and concluded that England was about to "establish a protectorate over Ethiopia." Haile Selassie discerned the opportunity and sent a letter to President Roosevelt, assuring his full support of the U.S. and Allied powers in all of their war efforts. FDR provided a cordial response, noting that Ethiopia "has gained its independence and self-government." Three years later, the two world leaders met for the first time in Egypt. When Winston Churchill, the prime minister of England, got wind of the meeting, he rushed to Cairo.[12]

FDR hosted the emperor aboard the USS Quincy. They discussed port access for Ethiopia, financial help, and Haile Selassie's desire to take part in drafting the charter of the United Nations, in line to replace the League of Nations, now defunct as predicted by the emperor. They exchanged gifts. Roosevelt gave the Ethiopian leader four military jeeps. For the President, the emperor opened a small box containing a four-inch globe, designed by the palace jeweler, made with shimmering 24-carat gold. It depicted their summit location by the Suez Canal. He also gave FDR a gold cigarette case. Haile Selassie's American advisor, John Spencer, described FDR's "genuine enthusiastic response."

After the meeting, Haile Selassie was informed that Winston Churchill wanted to see him. A meeting was quickly arranged. "This was in fact the first ever occasion in which the two leaders came face-to-face," writes Asfa-Wossen, but "the encounter was brief and chilly. When a member of Churchill's staff asked the emperor what points he wished to discuss with the prime minister, he replied: 'None.'"[13]

Haile Selassie's extraordinary diplomatic skills led to an agreement with the United States' Transcontinental and Western Air (later known as TWA) to develop their own national carrier, Ethiopian Airlines, which is today the largest air carrier in Africa. Relations eventually blossomed into establishing a U.S. military base in the region, providing not only protection and a symbol of friendship, but a handsome financial contract for the struggling postwar country.

The British learned from a spy who regularly visited Haile Selassie's court that the emperor was making plans to announce the expulsion of the British military from Ethiopia. To save face, the British Foreign Office informed the emperor that it planned to withdraw Britain's forces from the country. "Haile Selassie professed great sadness at the news," writes Asfa-Wossen. "He wished further to record his warmest thanks for their help in the past and up to the present." However, "as it turned out, the emperor had been aware all along that his supposed confidant was a British spy." It was a scheme the emperor planned from the beginning, successfully engineering the British departure without making a public statement.[14]

Author Michela Wrong notes that the withdrawal provided evidence of Britain's prejudice toward the black Africans. It matched, if not exceeded, the Italians, who passed racial laws during Mussolini's occupation far worse than the laws enacted during Menelik's day. "Conjugal relations" were forbidden between races, marriages annulled, and no Italian could adopt or give his surname to a mixed-race child. Eritreans in the north of Ethiopia were barred from cinema, restaurants, bars, and hotels, and they were required to use separate clerks at the post office and banks. "Long before segregation was adopted as an official credo in South Africa," writes Michela, "Eritrea had already tasted the delights of apartheid. In its day, it was the most racist regime in Africa."

Upon British occupation, Europeans applied pressure to reverse the laws. "This is very tedious, not an important subject," huffed British legal advisor Colonel E. J. Maxwell. According to historian Alemseged Tesfai, when the Italians left, despite the laws, they had produced thousands of mixed-race children. "I don't know of a single recorded incident of a British official fathering a mixed-race child," notes Tesfai. "Not one."[15]

Strengthening his independence from Europe as well as his relationship with the United States, Haile Selassie became Ethiopia's ambassador to the world. He was the first Ethiopian emperor to trod on the soil of another country and the first to fly in an airplane. He visited more nations than any head of state in his time and set foot in every country of the world except New Zealand and Fiji. Fellow Africans were inspired by the leader who overcame fascism, so impressed by this nation that never allowed colonial rule.

At the end of World War II, all but three African countries were still European colonies. With Haile Selassie as their inspiration, they began to throw off the colonial yoke one by one—first Libya, then Sudan, Morocco, and Tunisia, followed shortly after by Ghana and Guinea. In fact, 1960 became known as the "Year of Africa," as seventeen colonial territories gained their freedom. Within two years, another eight reached independence.

In his autobiography, South African leader Nelson Mandela describes during his visit to Ethiopia the impression that the emperor made on African liberators. "I had never seen a black pilot before," he wrote. "How could a black man fly an airplane? But a moment later I caught myself: I had fallen into the apartheid mindset, thinking Africans were inferior and that flying was a white man's job.... Here, for the first time in my life I was enjoying black soldiers commanded by black generals applauded by black leaders who were all guests of a black Head of State. It was a heady moment. I only hoped it was a vision of what lay in the future for my own country."[16]

Ras Tafari's next demonstration of leadership led to being viewed as the father of the newly liberated nations of Africa. He helped establish a United Nations economic commission that led to a more ambitious vision for the Organization of African Unity, with twenty-eight countries attending the founding assembly in Addis Ababa. Ghana's President Kwame Nkrumah lobbied strongly for a common government, a common army, a "United States of Africa." As this vision for one country out of many dissolved, Haile Selassie was still determined to make the gathering a success. "Even the most impassioned pleas could not alter the Ghanaian president's resolve, and the meeting seemed on the verge of imminent failure. At the eleventh hour, however, Haile Selassie took Nkrumah's oppenent, Guinea's Sékou Touré, to one side. Clutching his hand, the emperor looked deep into his eyes and addressed the president of Guinea: 'Mon fils, je vous prie' ('My son, I beg you.'). . . . Moved by this intervention, Sékou Touré replied: 'Oui pére, je vais essayer.' ('Yes, father, I will try.')" His fatherly appeals reconciled Touré and Nkrumah, and he persuaded the President of Ghana to return to the negotiation table.

The gathered leaders agreed to a charter for the Organization of African Unity, also called the "Africa of fatherlands." Instead of an army, a common defense committee was established. Annual meetings, which still convene today as the AU (African Union), were scheduled with Addis Ababa as the permanent location for this region of the UN. "A milestone in the history of Africa," Asfa-Wossen said. "And the skill in having reconciled the most conflicting opinions was one of the greatest foreign policy triumphs of Haile Selassie. It earned him the soubriquet 'the Father of Africa.'" Nelson Mandela called the five-foot two-inch Ethiopian the "African Giant."

In marked contrast to his time in exile, on his first return trip to England, Haile Selassie was greeted at the station by the queen, the rest of the royal family, and Prime Minister Winston Churchill, showing their new realization of Ethiopia's strategic importance. Red curtains and carpet decorated the platform along with fresh flowers. Nevertheless, whether shunned or celebrated, Haile Selassie was able to overcome the intrigues of Britain and its ambitions to overtake his empire.

Instead, he inspired a movement that led to the downfall of the world's greatest empire, along with the unraveling of its colonial rule.[17]

Decades later, Haile Selassie's fame continued as the subject of the lyrics of reggae icon Bob Marley, who spent years inspiring cult followers of Ras Tafari, known as "Rastafarians," with words like the following from the song "Blackman Redemption":

> Coming from the root of King David,
> Through the line of Solomon,
> His Imperial Majesty is the Power of Authority:
> Spread out, spread out, spread out . . .

Marley himself was baptized an Ethiopian Orthodox Christian by Archbishop Yesehaq, who said a weeping Marley had committed to the church's teaching on monogamy. The singer died seven months later.[18]

Marcus Garvey helped spawn the Rastafarian movement in Jamaica in the 1920s, foretelling the emergence of the return of Christ in the form of a black man. After a long drought in Jamaica in 1930, just as news reports of Crown Prince Ras Tafari's coronation as Emperor Haile Selassie reached the Caribbean island, rain began to pour from the heavens. Followers of Garvey pointed to Haile Selassie as the fulfillment of the book of Revelation. When the Ethiopian monarch visited Jamaica years later, a reverse sign was given: days of rain ended, clouds parted, and the sun appeared just as his plane landed. Crowds invaded the airstrip. To keep control, officials were forced to cancel the day's events. Despite the efforts of Jamaican authorities, Rastafarianism, with its signature dreadlocks and ubiquitous marijuana, continued to thrive.

The emperor was kind to the cult members, but insisted he was not the messiah, speaking in his odd but often-used first person plural: "We are not God. We are not a prophet. We are a slave to God." He dispatched priests to Jamaica to expand the Ethiopian Orthodox Church there. Likewise, Rastafarians made pilgrimages to Ethiopia en masse. The emperor provided a settlement for them at the city of Shashamane, which retains a small Rasta community to this day.[19]

The extreme adulation of the emperor was uncomfortable for some and was considered blasphemous by others. Despite his clear statements to the Rastafarians, the accolades for the emperor grew rather awkward during Haile Selassie's first visit to the United States. After meeting with the president, he was the subject of a parade in Manhattan where tens of thousands lined the streets to see him. The ten-car motorcade was drenched with confetti so thick that the emperor could barely see. After the ticker-tape parade, he visited U.S. Congressman Dr. Adam Clayton Powell's Abyssinian Baptist Chuch in Harlem, who greeted him "in the name of the 700,000 Afro-Americans of New York City, men and women of every faith, belief, and disbelief." You are "the symbol around which we place all our hopes, dreams, and prayers that one day the entire continent of Africa shall be as free as the country of Ethiopia." A 200-member choir then sang from Handel's *Messiah*, with an eerie emphasis on the repeating refrain: "And He shall reign forever and ever."

Conservative Ethiopian activist Ermias Kebede is a fierce critic of Haile Selassie's reign. The messianic complex was compounded, according to Ermias, by associating the title "Lion of Judah" with the emperor himself "and not with Jesus Christ, its rightful owner."

"He trusted in the League of Nations over God," writes Ermias, who believes that Ethiopia immediately repelled Italy at Adwa because of its obedience. However, Mussolini was allowed to win for several years in the 1930s because of Haile Selassie's disobedience.

Ohio professor Messay Kebede [no relation] provides a softer critique from a less conservative, more intellectual perspective. He sees Haile Selassie as failing to be far-sighted in the ideological realm: "Ethiopia had won the battle against colonialism on the battlefield," he writes, but "lost it in the classroom of modern education, the very place where the Ethiopian youth were supposed to glean the secrets of the West." In 1950, only seventy-one Ethiopians were studying in the United States. By 1973, that number was 10,000. Not only that, but 300,000 American students have studied or worked in Ethiopia over the years through programs like the Peace Corps.

The programs and stubbornness of Haile Selassie led to two terrible outcomes: the end of the 3,000-year monarchy in Ethiopia and the genocide of its people. The dangerous classroom ideas that Messay identifies were Marxist-Leninist. Ermias focuses on moral degradation, what he calls "the intense indoctrination of the Ethiopian youth with the western philosophy, coupled with the deliberate abrogation of religious instruction in all schools."[20]

While the emperor did, perhaps unwittingly, allow these destructive Western ideas to enter his country, he himself remained a devout Christian his entire life. His fasting was non-negotiable, even during diplomatic meals, and his early morning routine and prayer life a constant, his commitment to the Church unwavering.

As American students poured into Ethiopia and Ethiopian young people studied abroad, what were the messages given and received regarding traditional morals? The seeds of the sexual revolution were flourishing in the West. In Ethiopia, the message was the same as always—traditional views on sex and marriage, traditional male and female roles. Even today, adultery and homosexuality are illegal. Men gather on a separate side of the church from the women, who cover their heads.

"Women are still regarded with profound suspicion by the Ethiopian church, largely because of our ability to ignite a dangerous passion," writes Melissa Twigg for *The Daily Beast*, who seems to keep a sense of humor. She traveled to where the Ark was once kept at Lake Tana. "There are many young monks on the island, and they are still learning," she was told. "Women cannot be allowed to inflame their passions." Such guidelines were particularly important in guarding the Ark. "The safest solution…was to ban all women from most Ark-related religious sites," said Melissa. "This inexplicably includes female animals, with only roosters, billy goats and male pigs allowed near certain sites."[21]

Ethiopia has over 1,000 monasteries and, therefore, one of the richest monastic traditions on the planet. A monk on one tiny island did not leave it for twenty-five years. Another monk remained silent for thirty-five years. A famous saint stood on one leg and prayed for seven years. Promising young men learn four different types of chants for church services. The lower-level chant can take up to fifteen years to fully learn. It is not uncommon to memorize the entire Bible. Some experts take thirty to forty years to memorize certain Church Fathers and stories of saints. "Ethiopian monasticism throughout the ages has been the greatest culture-creating factor of this country," writes Oriental Studies professor K. Blazewicz at Warsaw University.[22]

I asked professor Girma Batu about an Ethiopian tradition called "Quine," a level of linguistic and spiritual expertise reached by only a few scholars who study a collection of mystical poetry.

"It has not been translated," he told me.

"I've heard they don't want it to be translated."

"It would be very difficult to translate. It is very mystical, very poetic. Do you have that kind of tradition in your culture?"

I couldn't think of one.

"Even the minor things in there, if they want to insult you, they may praise you. You might say, 'Oh, thank you!' but they are insulting you. There are some hidden and strong ideas in Quine, not easy to understand by ordinary people like us."

"The Quine people are different people. They are considered philosophers in our tradition. It is theology at the same time. Strong, rich theology."

Girma discussed how Ethiopians avoid the liberal theological mumbo-jumbo of the West and how a biblical expert in their culture must live a righteous life. "Theology is mysticism. Mysticism is theology. Theology is not a profession. Theology is not a knowledge construction. A theologian is not a specialist. The ancient church tradition says—the Ethiopian tradition says—if you are going to call him a theologian, he must be a saint, such as St. Athanasius, St. Basil, St. Chrysostom. There is no distinction between mysticism, spirituality, and theology."

ACROSS THE ATLANTIC, Ethiopian students watched as American students embraced the sexual revolution. The phrase was created by Wilhelm Reich, a deputy director at Sigmund Freud's Austrian clinic. Reich's name was scrawled on walls during the 1968 student uprisings in Paris and Berlin. Copies of Reich's books *The Sexual Revolution* and *The Mass Psychology of Fascism* were thrown at police.

Eventually to be known as the "father of free love," Reich moved to New York and spent much of his career doing Marxist-oriented research in an attempt to merge the atheist views of Freud and Marx. Reich coined the term "orgone"—from "orgasm" and "organism" for "a biological energy he said he had discovered, which he said others called God." He was also a self-admitted pervert, sharing in his journals as a young man compulsive sex, incest, and, in one entry, a description of the day he masturbated while stimulating a horse's genitalia, which excited both himself and the horse. "From then on, I did this every day," he writes in his autobiography, *Passion of Youth*.[1*]

The contrast between Ethiopia and the West could not have been more stark. "[Reich's] major finding was that masturbation and the religious life were incompatible," writes Dr. Lasha Darkmoon, "which is why he advocated masturbation as the most effective means of eradicating the religious instinct, which he regarded as the ultimate evil."[2]

"What Reich discovered was a fundamental truth," writes *Culture Wars* magazine editor and prolific author Dr. E. Michael Jones. "Either masturbation destroys your prayer life, or prayer destroys your ability to enjoy masturbation. The two forms of activity are psychically mutually exclusive."[3]

Not only does "sexual liberation" sap a man spiritually, says Jones, but it also destroys his will to fight. "By the 1970s, pornography had become one of the psychological weapons of destabilization and control in the CIA's arsenal of covert warfare," writes Jones, author of *Libido Dominandi*, a 643-page expose of sexual liberation as political control. He details various operations, such as in Portugal, where Ambassador Frank Carlucci, later to become a CIA director, distributed mass amounts of pornography in Lisbon to quell the revolution there in 1974. According to author Jonas E. Alexis, Israelis broadcasted pornography over Palestinian TV stations after their invasion of Ramallah.[4]

Jones gives great detail on the psychological operation of the Allied powers after WWII to further destroy Germany as a fighting people when 500 tons of pornography by 149 different publishers were shipped over the border from Austria in 1949. German authorities protested, and a still-traditional populace was outraged but could not stop the effort. "The transformation of the psychology of the average German is the main task of the military government," said David Levy, a New York psychologist charged with screening all artistic materials entering Germany. Levy was under the U.S. Department of the Control of Information, formerly known as the Department for Psychological Warfare.[5]

The authoritarian father was the primary target of the operation. Levy said forced behaviors on children, such as shaking hands, bowing, and other "correct" behaviors created a "passivity" in children that resulted in "aggression, hardness, and even cruelty in German adults." All these inverted teachings stemmed from Reich's perverted sexual playbook: "Suppression of the natural sexuality in the child, particularly of its genital sexuality, makes the child apprehensive, shy, obedient, afraid of authority . . ."[6]

Ethiopian students in Haile Selassie's day did not, by and large, adopt the sexual permissiveness of their Western counterparts. Looming behind those studying in the U.S., when they returned to Ethiopia, were hundreds of thousands of male and female monastics who had renounced sex altogether to fight for the things of God. The returning students, however, did adopt, in great measure, the primary political philosophy being championed in American classrooms: Marxism-Leninism.

Student Germame Neway was representative of the movement. He received a scholarship to study in the U.S. from Crown Prince Asfah Wossen, Haile Selassie's first-born. Germame attended the University of Wisconsin and, later, the Ivy League's Columbia University in New York. "He studied the history of the American Revolution, immersed himself in Locke's and Hobbes' theories of the state, and avidly read the works of Marx and Engels . . ." He returned to his country with the enthusiasm to implement land reform and, as the new governor of Wolaita, distributed farmland to the people.

The emperor summoned him to answer for his communist-like activities. Why was he upsetting the country's tenant farmer system? "Because I am governor, and people have nothing to eat because they have no land," he answered. Germame was moved to another region, where he filed formal complaints with the emperor regarding eight new hospitals never put into operation due to failed bureaucracy. At some point, the talented but exasperated young leader decided to plan a coup to overthrow Haile Selassie.[7]

The emperor seemed to be more interested in his image than the country's welfare. An Ethiopian leader was severely rebuked by Haile Selassie when his picture appeared in newspapers with U.S. President John F. Kennedy. The emperor sent shipments of coffee to the British after a natural disaster there while Ethiopians struggled to eat. The country was ruled by "paternalistic principles," according to Asfa-Wossen Asserate. "Haile Selassie basked in the renown he enjoyed around the world, but all the while he ignored the fact that things were far from ideal within his own country."[8]

Another young rising star, Workneh Gebeyehu, developed the same concerns as Germame. He rose through the military, led a company of Ethiopians in the Korean War, and, though still young, became the emperor's chief of staff. The two were often seen deep in discussion late into the night. But during a trip with the emperor to the Soviet Union in 1959, Workneh decided to broach his concerns about the plight of the country, and implored the aging Haile Selassie to step down in the near future in order for the crown prince to become his successor. The sixty-seven-year-old emperor responded in his trademarked first person plural:

"Workneh, up to now, we had thought you had reached the necessary level of maturity for your important role. But now we are dismayed to find that you are, in fact, still a child. We shall continue to exercise the power that the Almighty has vested in us to the end," he said. "And besides, have you ever heard of anyone voluntarily relinquishing his power?"

CROWN PRINCE ASFAH WOSSEN

Workneh related this statement to a confidant and concluded that "this person is very short-sighted. He neither has any vision for Ethiopia, nor does he wish the country well."[9]

Germame Neway's brother, Mengistu Neway, ran the Imperial Guard, which consisted of 5,000 soldiers. He was able to convince his brother as well as Workneh, the chief of staff, to join him in his plot to overthrow the emperor. On a day when the emperor had gone to Brazil, the three arranged for the top dignitaries of the country, including Crown Prince Asfah Wossen, to come to the headquarters of the Imperial Guard, under the pretense that the empress had fallen ill. The dignitaries were arrested, the telephone lines cut, and the national bank and radio taken over. The crown prince then broadcast a message to the people over the radio that a new government had been formed with himself as the head. By his tone, the people struggled to determine whether he spoke under coercion of the Marxist instigators.

Marxism-Leninism was, by that time, primarily associated with the Soviet Union. However, Marx himself was a product of the West, born in Germany and educated in Britain. His funding came from his colleague, Friedrich Engels, a wealthy owner of British factories.

Regarding Russia's switch from a Christian monarchy to Marxist Bolshevism, this was not all voluntary. Author James Perloff details the West's empowerment of revolution mastermind Leon Trotsky, facts brought to light to the academic community in the 1970s by Stanford scholar Antony Sutton, who traced the work of famous New York and European financiers: "Jacob Schiff and Federal Reserve founder Paul Warburg ran Kuhn, Loeb & Co.—the Rothschilds' New York banking satellite," writes Perloff. "Schiff supplied $20 million in gold to Trotsky, who sailed from New York [to Russia] with 275 other terrorists on a passport obtained through pressure the bankers put on the Wilson administration." Today, that $20 million in gold is equivalent to half a billion dollars.

Perloff shows that the West assisted Bolshevik leader Vladimir Lenin as well. "In Germany, Warburg's brother Max helped persuade the government to provide millions to Lenin and allow him to cross Germany with other revolutionaries in a special train."[10]

In Ethiopia, the three Western-influenced Marxist revolutionaries were able to rally thousands of protesting students to their cause, also under the influence of Western thought. But the people, in general, were not willing to defy their emperor. The army did not join the side of the coup. Most importantly, the Church stood clearly in favor of Haile Selassie. Patriarch Abuna Basilios called for the excommunication of all those who supported the revolution.

The army fought the Imperial Guard. After three days of battling in the streets, tanks surrounded the palace that had been taken over by the two Neway brothers and Workneh, where they held captive the fifteen ministers, generals, and nobles. The coup had failed. The emperor's son-in-law, Captain Dereje, marched toward the palace balcony. "In the name of the emperor, I call on you to surrender!"

Mengistu Neway stood on the balcony, but, before he could talk or surrender, his brother Germame appeared from behind him and shot dead the approaching captain. The tanks began to assault the palace without mercy as the two brothers used machines guns to execute their prisoners, which included the emperor's longtime father-confessor, the secretary of commerce, and an elderly prince of Tigray. Several captives evaded execution by playing dead until the gunners entered the room a second time. Only one survived, a brigadier general. The crown prince, held in a separate third-floor room, was not killed. The three murderers escaped through the garage complex and eluded capture.

The emperor flew back to Ethiopia the following day, and the people celebrated the victory, although 2,000 had died in the three days of fighting. When Haile Selassie appeared in the plane's doorway, the crowd cheered. His son, Asfah Wossen, greeted him by falling on the ground and begging his forgiveness.

"Get up!" his father barked. "We would have been very proud of you if we were coming to attend your funeral." That day he publicly pardoned his son for his part in the attempted coup but remained suspicious. (Years later, the crown prince admitted that he was not coerced into participating in the rebellion.) A week later, the Neway brothers were arrested in the southern part of the country. Before they could be seized, Germame shot his brother in the head and then killed himself. Workneh was discovered under a bridge and killed several police officers before his machine gun ran out of bullets. He pulled out his pistol and killed himself, just after invoking the name of the emperor from a century before. "Tewodros has taught me something!" he cried.[11]

One hundred years before, British Queen Victoria gifted Ethiopian Emperor Tewodros with a special pistol. She did not intend for it to cause his suicide, but her invasion of Ethiopia was no doubt a contributing factor. Gifts from the West can sometimes lead to suicide. Some of these efforts, as we shall see, are in fact designed to cause suicide.

With the gift of Marxist philosophy, the blame cannot be placed completely on the West. Firstly, in contrast to other gifts of suicide that we will later discuss, the West itself was not united on Marxist philosophy. Its proponents were largely in academia. Secondly, class envy and government incompetence played a large role in Ethiopia's adoption of Marxism. However, the result was indeed mass murder and attempted national suicide.

Haile Selassie refused to change, despite the clear warning of civil unrest that the coup had revealed. His stubbornness jeopardized the continuation of 3,000 years of Ethiopian emperors. He refused to name a successor, despite the fact that he had fought years before to amend Article V of the Constitution to require his own sons, not just any descendants of Solomon, to be first in line to the throne. "There will be no change in the system of government or in the government's programs," Haile Selassie announced just after the coup, not "the slightest deviation from the path."[12]

Part of the reason for Haile Selassie's success over the coup was his accessibility to the people. When not traveling, he spent a great deal of time mingling with crowds throughout the capital, cutting ribbons for opening ceremonies, and dedicating new hospitals. In contrast to the aloof European monarchs, Haile Selassie was a visible leader in Ethiopia. His hands-on approach reflected a micromanagement style that he pulled off, in part, due to raw talent. "He stored personal information about thousands of individuals away in his brain: he knew the names, faces, positions, functions, tribal connections and family relationships of officials, military officers or students," writes a German scholar who ran the Ethiopian National Library. "For the population it was a matter of course that the Elect of God should have supernatural qualities, but for officials it was deeply portentous, and it kept them constantly in a state of apprehension."[13]

Although he had the ability to use all the details, failures, and mistakes stored in his head to remove officials, John Spencer, his United States advisor, notes an Achilles heel for Haile Selassie—his inability to remove subordinates, despite ongoing failures. He could be selfish yet generous, "courageous and cowardly, remorseless yet forgiving. The Emperor...was a fascinating split personality."

Spencer acknowledges that centralizing everything into the emperor's control enabled him to "bring Ethiopia far down the road toward the twentieth century." Despite the unrest in the country, Ethiopia "compared with the best Africa had to offer..." But he had done it by ignoring local and regional powers, and this nearsighted notion, along with an aging monarch losing his edge, caused the breakdown of government. A year after the coup, the top five aristocratic leaders of the country gathered to present a formal memorandum to the emperor imploring reform. All of the key positions were appointed by Haile

Selassie. Nothing of significance proceeded without his approval. The five nobles warned of "the danger of revolution increasing." The emperor ignored the warning and relocated them.[14]

After several more years of stagnation, criticism emerged from a region Haile Selassie could not ignore: the United States. President Nixon cut the amount of military spending in Ethiopia in hope that it would prompt reforms. When that failed, Nixon sent word to his ambassador that "the emperor must be prevailed upon to see that he bears absolute responsibility for ensuring an orderly and beneficial succession." Spencer recounts an incident where Haile Selassie was again asked why he had not named his son, Crown Prince Asfah Wossen, as heir to the throne. "Why should we?" the emperor snapped. "He has already been on the throne!"[15]

The United States now threatened to move its military base out of Ethiopia into another African country. Haile Selassie countered with two measures. Firstly, he finally named a successor: his grandson, twenty-year-old Prince Zera-Yokab, who was studying at Oxford. But the appointment of such a young man only convinced most observers that he planned to rule another twenty years, until he was 100. Secondly, Haile Selassie took a trip to the Soviet Union. While such a move worked when he flirted with the Russians in 1959 as the Cold War was more clearly in focus, in 1973, other priorities, such as Vietnam, were of concern to Nixon and his cabinet. When Nixon consulted Secretary of State Henry Kissinger on the matter, who had endured the emperor's many visits to Washington, Kissinger said "my experience is that Haile Selassie does nothing unless it is that he makes the most boring toasts of anybody I have ever heard."[16]

The U.S. bet that the Soviets would not help Haile Selassie, who was asking the Russians to stop backing the Somalis on his border, where tensions were brewing. The Russians refused and, instead backed those plotting to destroy the emperor. The United States moved its military base from Ethiopia to Kenya.

The eighty-year-old began to show his age. The prime minister now had to repeat information for the emperor whose memory was, at one time, almost supernatural. At a state dinner for Zaire with President Mobutu, he asked a server who the guest of honor was who was sitting across from him.

When his minister of public works arrived at the palace, the emperor asked his aide, "Who is that man?" On a visit to China, his first and only, he kept pointing to various places he had visited many times before.

After the attempted coup of 1960, Haile Selassie stopped trusting anyone, even those closest to him. His policy of managing everything worked to a certain degree, for a few years, while he retained his mental gifts. "The trouble was that it was no longer 1960," wrote Spencer. "The power which the Emperor now collected came into the hands of a man now approaching eighty but unable to exercise it, while clinging to the fantasy that he was doing so. What is perhaps surprising is that the coup of 1974 had been delayed so long."[17]

The slow, steady, somewhat silent movement to topple the monarch was hastened by three years of drought. Pictures and video footage of starving children in Ethiopia hit television screens across the world. Haile Selassie was not quick to address the crisis in his own nation. An Ethiopian student in Germany details his encounter with the emperor, who was making his last trip out of the country. As he arrived, student protestors held signs. "Haile Selassie—Go Home and Feed Your Starving People!" The student, who had conducted a fundraiser a few days before to help the famine victims, was summoned to the emperor's suite to translate the protestors' pamphlets. After some mildly unfavorable remarks related to his fundraiser, Haile Selassie slipped the student a $100 bill and asked him to fetch some Vitalis hair tonic. The student got to keep the change.[18]

Between 40,000 and 80,000 Ethiopians starved to death between 1972 and 1974, according to some estimates. Haile Selassie visited the starving regions in 1974, but it was too late to heal the public relations damage, especially when it came to light that, in 1973, the government had shipped 200,000 tons of grain overseas.

In 1974, the Ethiopian military began arresting members of the cabinet. The aging emperor did nothing. This "creeping coup," as it has been called, developed slowly, with no names associated and difficult to pinpoint. But, unlike the 1960 attempt, it was backed by a groundswell of popular support. After various branches of the military joined the effort, a name emerged. The junta called itself the "Provisional

Military Administrative Council—for short, the "Derg," the Amharic word for committee.

As his government officials were arrested and led away one by one, the emperor remained silent. Why? Was the once courageous man now a coward? Was it senility? Spencer believes the master diplomat still hoped for some last-minute development, akin to when Hitler's invasion of Poland caused the Allied powers to rally to Ethiopia's cause overnight.

The center broke for the emperor's support when the head of the Ethiopian Orthodox Church refused to support him. On the Feast Day of the Ethiopian New Year, September 11, Patriarch Abuna Theophilus addressed the public. Instead of honoring the emperor in his customary way, he asked for God's blessing on the "revolutionary movement." That same day, nine princesses were taken away to prison by the new revolutionary government officials, and their heads were shaved. They shared two mattresses in the dungeon-like cell. The men who had already been arrested endured worse conditions, so packed together that they took turns sleeping on the dirt floor. A few hundred prisoners shared one toilet. Bibles were confiscated, and no books of any kind were allowed.[19]

The next day the emperor was arrested and taken outside to a light blue Volkswagen Beetle. The soldiers pointed to the back seat. Haile Selassie looked at the little Volkswagen and said, "What? In here?"[20]

He was taken to the Menelik Palace where he continued to receive meals from the palace kitchen by a few attendants, and, by some accounts, believed he still governed Ethiopia. The nice conditions were provided so that Derg officials could interrogate him about Swiss bank accounts with millions that they needed for their revolution. Questioned intensely for months, Haile Selassie denied the secret accounts, which turned out to never exist.

Over time, the low-profile chairman of the Derg, General Aman Andom, lost his power when a young protégé named Mengistu Haile Mariam grabbed control in a process that led to forty executions within the leadership. Aman himself put a gun to his head, dressed in full military regalia, before Mengistu had a chance to torture and kill him. The nameless Derg now had a face and Mengistu proved to be one of the twentieth century's bloodiest leaders. He was present and in leadership during the killings after Haile Selassie's arrest.

On the evening of November 23, 1974, two months after the emperor was taken away, the sixty-one male prisoners—cabinet members, generals, aristocrats—were handcuffed two by two, told they would be released, and taken to a courtyard. "Why are we being handcuffed if we are to be released?" shouted Ras Mesfin. "You're going to kill us!" As one of those handcuffed, Mekbib Damte, watched his cousins walk by, he broke down and wept. All sixty-one were lined against a wall. The floodlights were turned on so that the assassinations could be filmed.[21]

One of those executed was Ras Asserate Kassa, the president of the Imperial Crown Council and father to the student in Germany who received the emperor's $100 bill. The young Asfa-Wossen Asserate (not the Crown Prince Asfah Wossen) remained in Germany as a scholar and wrote a biography of the emperor, an important source for this book.

On one of his last days in 1975, Emperor Haile Selassie looked out from his porch balcony as tears streamed down and said, according to a personal attendant, "O Ethiopia! Do you ever harbor ill will toward me? Is it not true that I have strived for you?"[22] His personal attendant entered Haile Selassie's bedroom the next morning to find him dead, a pillow out of place beside his head, and a strong smell of ether. Death by suffocation was suspected, but no autopsy was conducted. Years later, court testimony revealed his body was placed under the floor in the palace bathroom directly beneath the toilet.

MENGISTU, DERG CHAIRMAN

Mengistu did not allow a Christian burial for the monarch. "Each day, when he felt the call of nature, he could express his feelings for the Emperor of Ethiopia," Michela adds, "in the crudest way known to man."

When Mengistu became the formal chairman of the Derg, he immediately conducted his violent campaign to eliminate all dissidents and political enemies, modeling his regime after the

Soviets. "We are doing what Lenin did," said colleague Asrat Desta. "You cannot build socialism without Red Terror." That terror would soon end Desta's life, who was shot dead on Mengistu's orders while leaving a meeting with the dictator, who claimed Desta attempted a "fascist coup." Thousands more were executed in the first few months of 1977, including the Patriarch of the Ethiopian Orthodox Church. The Derg professed atheism, and Christians were persecuted. Raping women became a regular practice. Torture was common, including the prying off of fingernails, one by one. A rope named the "Mengistu necktie" was used to slowly strangle victims or to gain confessions. Other Derg officers utilized foot-whipping devices, smashing victims' feet into stumps, permanently crippling thousands. The torture machines are on display today at the "Red Terror" Martyrs' Memorial Museum in Addis Ababa.[23]

If families wanted to retrieve and bury their loved ones, they were forced to pay a large and difficult sum for the "wasted bullet"—another common practice during the Red Terror. The head of the *Save the Children Fund* in 1977 said that "1,000 children have been killed, and their bodies are left in the streets and are being eaten by wild hyenas...You can see the heaped-up bodies of murdered children, most of them aged eleven to thirteen, lying in the gutter, as you drive out of Addis Ababa." Amnesty International estimates the number of murders was as high as 500,000 during Mengistu's regime. Another 500,000 died from starvation, which Derg officials blamed on a drought, but others note that the drought started months after the famine was already well in progress. (This crisis was the inspiration for the 1985 "We Are the World" Live Aid fundraiser featuring Michael Jackson, Lionel Richie, and many others.) Heritage Foundation scholar Michael Johns points to Mengistu's communist agricultural policies as the cause for the great famine, thus making the Ethiopian dictator's total casualties approach one million. This massacre was a worse genocide than what an outsider like Mussolini had inflicted on Ethiopia. And it was done by Ethiopians to themselves, a humiliating and suicidal tragedy. "Haile Selassie affected the youth with Western philosophy and his harvest was weeds," wrote Ermias Kebede. "The covenantal nation turned into a bloodbath." Asfa-Wossen Asserate gives his solemn assessment: "After seventeen years of military rule, which saw Ethiopia cut adrift from all its historic and traditional values, torn asunder from its cultural roots and with all its institutions destroyed, the country was on its knees. From this point, Ethiopia could sink no further."[24]

The end of Haile Selassie also marked the end—apart from a miraculous turn of events—of the 3,000-year-old history of Ethiopian emperors, beginning with Solomon and Sheba's son, Menelik I. However, all through these years of destruction during the time of the Derg, the Ethiopians marched forward in a war to victory—a more important war, a conflict that involved a mighty showdown with the West. No military power, no great leader had foreseen this mighty confrontation. For the third time in a century, a barefoot Ethiopian army triumphed over its Western counterpart. Why? How?

It was not the same kind of army that defeated the Italians. Nor was it the same kind of army that rose up in the northern Tigray region—where Axum and the Ark resides—to finally abolish the bloody Derg regime after its seventeen-year reign from 1974 to 1991. In that conflict with the Derg, the Tigray People's Liberation Front (TPLF), led by former Marxist Meles Zenawi, gained momentum after years of guerilla warfare against Mengistu, when the Soviet Union began crumbling in the late 1980s.

After several military confrontations, Mengistu, seeing that his popular support had disappeared, evacuated Addis Ababa and fled to Zimbabwe, where he still resides today in exile as an octogenarian. (He was convicted of war crimes in absentia.) Overnight, the leadership changed to a Tigray-led government that allowed religious freedom and a degree of free speech. And yet, the authoritarian nature of Prime Minister Meles's party and government remained controversial through his death in 2012 to today.

However, during this intense struggle, Ethiopia was winning a greater war, and winning exceedingly. What was this war? Author David P. Goldman comments on how civilization has generally missed this greatest of conflicts along with their own stunning defeat: "The chattering classes have nothing to say about the most unique and significant change in our times," he writes.[25]

It has been alluded to several places already in this book. Ethiopia's barefoot army in this war is its historic, growing Christian church, worshipping with no shoes, standing strong on traditional morality, and never wavering from its position to follow God's first commandment to be fruitful and multiply. Birth control is officially a sin.[26*]

Demography is destiny. Political and economic power follows population growth, just as a burgeoning European population overtook China and Asia after medieval times to become the most powerful civilization in modern times. During the Derg years, Ethiopia as a nation, as a barefoot army, pulled off a strategic maneuver—wittingly or unwittingly—that compares to Menelik's ability to avoid the Italian's temptation to directly attack their European-designed fortress. Instead, Menelik made a brilliant sideways move to the open field of Adwa. Similarly, Haile Selassie chose not to continue fighting Mussolini's army directly, but made an asymmetrical diplomatic move to address the League of Nations and ultimately helped lead an Allied victory over Italy and the Axis powers.

Europe and the West have attacked Ethiopia in various ways over the decades: physical invasions, British attempts to form a protectorate, and Marxist ideology, to name a few. Ethiopia allowed the last invasion—communism and atheism—to play itself out without direct confrontation. When it collapsed, Christian Ethiopia easily recovered. More importantly, Christian Ethiopia, unlike the West, continued its traditional lifestyle. Ethiopia continued to have children.

From 1974 to 1991, Ethiopia's birthrate grew from 7.1 children per woman to 7.2. The population grew healthily from twenty-seven million to fifty-one million. During that same time, Italy's population remained stagnant. Italy's 2.4 birthrate in 1974 dropped from above replacement level (2.1 children) to an unsustainable 1.3 children per woman in 1991. No country has ever recovered from this level. Social scientists refer to this 1.3 rate as the "low fertility trap."[27]

At the time of the Battle of Adwa in 1896, Italy boasted thirty-one million people, twice as many as Ethiopia. Today, Ethiopia has doubled

Italy's declining population of fifty-nine million. Like the castrations of Italian soldiers after Adwa, Italian men have once again been castrated, some by pills and various contraception methods, others by the more literal version of vasectomy. In the days after Adwa, a Dutch observer explained the motivation of castration: "The Abyssinians explain themselves by saying that this is how they bring a halt to the enemy's capacity to reproduce." They have done this again to the Italians, only on a much larger scale.

In fact, the leader of Italian colonization just before Adwa, Ferdinando Martini, advocated exterminating the Negro the same way the Americans did the Indians: "Succeeding generations will continue to depopulate Africa of its ancient inhabitants, down to the last one," he wrote a century ago. He never lived to see his rationale for colonization backfire with such grandeur.[28]

Britain's numbers are similar to Italy's, as its population was more than twice as large as Ethiopia's in the 1890s (thirty-three million to twelve million) and like Italy remained stagnant from 1974 to 1991 as the birthrate declined from 1.9 to 1.8. Britain's numbers today of sixty-six million (with the help of immigration) pale to its African rivals. Ethiopia, without help, grew from twelve million in 1896 to 110 million today. No country in Europe has a birthrate close to the replacement level of 2.1 children per woman. Birthrates and population numbers are all declining. "For the first time in recorded history," writes Goldman, "prosperous, secure and peaceful societies facing no external threat have elected to pass out of existence."[29]

Goldman sees this development as religion's triumph over rationalism. "Reason itself seems to betray us in this investigation, for precisely those parts of the world that succeed in extirpating faith through the instillation of the cult of reason seem most committed to demographic extinction." He notes that the German population will drop 98 percent in 200 years. The German tongue will disappear, as will Polish, Italian, and numerous other European languages. "People of faith have children, and people without faith tend not to," Goldman writes. The trend "will turn the world into a fundamentalist theme park."[30]

Not only has Ethiopia surpassed its European rivals in population, the continent Ethiopia serves as spiritual and cultural leader has also surpassed the West and the rest of the planet. We are in the midst of a giant civilizational shift. Africa is the continent of the future. And that is why Bill Gates gathered several billionaires in New York in 2009 to discuss the matter.

CHAPTER TWENTY-ONE

AT THE BEGINNING of this book, I wrote about a key point in my interview with Professor Girma Batu, vice academic dean of Ethiopia's largest Orthodox seminary, the Holy Trinity Theological College in Addis Ababa, with an enrollment of 3,000 students.

I asked him why. "Why, if the Ark really is here, does it exist in Ethiopia of all places?

He spoke after some hesitation. The answer is not something an Ethiopian will offer in the normal course of conversation. It takes some prodding.

"The response…would be somehow difficult for you to accept…or to believe in," he said.

I waited.

"There is a belief or a tradition in Ethiopia," he said, "or a consideration…"

I will share his answer shortly. First, he referred me to an author, already quoted briefly, who resides in Washington D.C., someone he called an Ethiopian "activist": Ermias Kebede. Ermias articulates radical views about Ethiopia's role in the world and in history. This special role of Ethiopia is not that the country holds and preserves the original Ark of the Covenant built by Moses at Mount Sinai—an object that in biblical times blessed those near it with fertility. This we have already been told.

We have already learned that Ethiopians believe the Queen of Sheba was from Ethiopia and that biblical, historical, and archeological evidence seems to back this theory. This teaching is key to their national identity, but not the answer to this question of their unique role. We also have seen that Moses was married to an Ethiopian woman, and both this marriage and the Solomon-Sheba union serve as a type and symbol of the entire bride of Christ, comprised of the gentile nations of the Church. But this is also not the answer to my question for Girma. We have also looked at the belief that the Garden of Eden itself was located in Ethiopia. This theory is fascinating, and the evidence is compelling. But neither is this extraordinary feature the answer to the question of Ethiopia's special situation among the nations of the world.

PROFESSOR GIRMA BATU

To answer the question, we must first discuss Ethiopia's longtime relationship with the city of Jerusalem. Top Ethiopian scholar Richard Pankhurst, British founder of the Institute of Ethiopian Studies, states that an Ethiopian church has existed in Jerusalem since the twelfth century AD. Graham Hancock, who talks about being buddies with Pankhurst, speaks of a twelfth-century Ethiopian monastery housed on the roof of a small chapel, within walking distance of the Church of the Holy Sepulchre in the Old City.

But he also refers to an Ethiopian presence in Jerusalem as far back as the fourth century AD. In fact, St. Jerome, considered the most learned of the Latin Fathers, mentions daily encounters with Ethiopian monastics. He lived in Palestine in the fourth century and died in Bethlehem.[1]

Of course, we know about the story of the Ethiopian eunuch in Acts 8. He visited Jerusalem but did not live there. However, another Ethiopian eunuch, likely a prefiguring of the more famous eunuch, did, in fact, live in Jerusalem 500 years before Christ. His story is told in Jeremiah 38. The prophet Jeremiah, as a Christ figure, had been captured and cast into a dungeon before being thrown into a well and left to die.

According to Jeremiah 38:7–9 (NASB): "Ebed-melech the Ethiopian, a eunuch, while he was in the king's palace, heard that they had put Jeremiah into the cistern…[He] spoke to the king, saying, 'My lord the king, these men have acted wickedly in all that they have done to Jeremiah the prophet whom they have cast into the cistern; and he will die right where he is.'" (NASB)

So, in a foreshadowing of the future Messiah's burial and deliverance, the eunuch went out to rescue Jeremiah: "Then Ebed-melech the Ethiopian said to Jeremiah, 'Now put these worn-out clothes and rags under your armpits under the ropes'; and Jeremiah did so. So they pulled Jeremiah up with the ropes and lifted him out of the cistern…" (Jer. 38:12–13, NASB).

So, from the time of Christ, we see a significant Ethiopian presence in Jerusalem during Old Testament times every 500 years. From the eunuch of Acts, back to the eunuch who saved Jeremiah, then Sheba and Menelik, and finally Moses's family. But there is yet another significant presence, according to Ethiopians, even 500 years prior to Moses. And this biblical reference coincides with the first time that Jerusalem is mentioned in the Scriptures.

This seminal instance is the strange appearance in Genesis 14 of the prophet, priest, and king, Melchizedek, whom the keepers of the Ark today believe was an Ethiopian. After Abraham defeated an army, this character, acting in a role superior to the founder of the Israelites—still known as Abram—held the title of King of Salem, the root of the word Jerusalem: "Then Melchizedek king of Salem brought out bread and wine. He was priest of God Most High, and he blessed Abram, saying, 'Blessed be Abram by God Most High, Creator of heaven and earth…who delivered your enemies into your hand.' Then Abram gave him a tenth of everything" (Gen. 14:18–20).

According to Ethiopian activist Ermias Kebede, "From the time of Melchizedek to this day, the Ethiopians have maintained a continuous presence in Jerusalem and a sustained pilgrimage from Ethiopia—the land of their ancestors, Adam and Eve—to Jerusalem." In fact, in his book about the Garden of Eden, Gert Muller notes that the original land grant to Abraham in Genesis includes Ethiopia: "To your descendants I have given this land, from the river of Egypt to the...Euphrates" (Gen. 15:18 NKJV). The Christian Standard Bible renders "river of Egypt" the "brook of Egypt" and the *Brown-Driver-Briggs Lexicon* provides "underground stream" as one definition. Muller believes this Hebrew word points to the source of the Nile: Ethiopia.

"These historical facts show vividly the strong spiritual and physical affinities the Ethiopians have for Jerusalem deep in their hearts from time immemorial," adds Ermias. "They underscore the truth that Ethiopians consider Jerusalem as their place of birth, because of Melchizedek, who is the Patriarch of Ethiopianism. This is confirmed by the word of the Psalmist who said, 'Glorious things are spoken of you, O City of God [Jerusalem]...Behold, Philistia, and Tyre and the Ethiopians: These were born there'" (Psalm 87:3–4).[2]

Ermias also adds that Jesus himself carried the genes of Ethiopia/Cush, or closely so, as the line of Christ included four people descended from Cush's father, Ham. These are the women Tamar, Rahab, Bathsheba, and Ruth. Ruth is famous for sneaking up to her future husband Boaz while he was sleeping on the threshing floor. "Ruth approached quietly, uncovered his feet and lay down" (Ruth 3:7). According to comments in The Voice translation of Ruth: "The Hebrew euphemism 'to uncover the feet' is a sexual expression." In the Bible, bare feet sometimes refer to the private parts. "It's an invitation for marriage. I'm inclined to think this was a more intimate situation than we normally think," says Presbyterian theologian Dr. James Jordan, regarding the Ruth-Boaz encounter. "It's my interpretation that uncovering the feet there probably is the euphemistic rather than the literal."[3]

We find similar biblical passages. Jerusalem is compared to a prostitute that "hast opened thy feet to everyone that passed by" (Ezekiel 16:25, KJV). The Bible speaks of a woman's child "which comes out from between her feet." (Deut. 28:57, NKJV). David told Uriah, the husband of Bathsheba, another Hamite in the line of Christ: "Go down to your house, and wash your feet." Uriah responded, "Shall I then go to my house to eat and to drink and to lie with my wife?" (2 Samuel 11:8,11, NASB) Bare feet can have a double meaning in the Bible, and the barefoot Ethiopians bring their own layered message.

Ermias Kebede, in fact, is the one author I could find in the English language who provides some detail about this unique and special role for the nation of Ethiopia, which I will now reveal. But it should be first noted that, despite this emphasis on the longstanding relationship with Jerusalem over the millennia, neither Ermias nor the Ethiopian Orthodox Church have favorable things to say about the people who actually live in Jerusalem. The Kebra Negast refers to them as "the crucifiers" who are "blinded in heart and enemies of the righteous." Of course, the same sacred Ethiopian text tells us that Solomon had a dream where the sun, a metaphor for God's promise, left Israel due to their disobedience and relocated to Ethiopia. Section 108 of the Kebra Negast captures the tone throughout with its very chapter title: "Concerning the Wickedness of the Iniquitous Jews." It also insists "don't call us Jews!"—a sentiment I heard several times from Ethiopians, who prefer to say that, before Christianity, they "followed Old Testament practices."

Scholar of African Judaism Richard Hull notes that the Falasha Jews living in Christian Ethiopia found themselves isolated and, for their own part, "refused to eat food prepared by non-Jews. [But] local Christian communities began to see these strange people as possessing supernatural powers...evil-eyed, with the power to turn themselves into flesh-eating hyenas and prey upon the population at night."[4]

I never heard this kind of rhetoric from Professor Girma Batu, but he did, as a stereotypical Ethiopian, meek and understated, explain to me just what kind of role Ethiopia plays on the world stage:

"There is a belief in Ethiopia, or a tradition in Ethiopia, or a consideration, that Ethiopians are a chosen people," he said. "That is why I said it is hard to see for you."

"Even better than the Jews?" I asked.

"Even better than the Jews."

There was a pause. I let that concept sink in for a bit.

"There are many books written about this, especially by Ermias Kebede," Girma continued. "He has one book in English—*Ethiopia: The Classic Case*. He speaks very good English."

I checked around. You can't buy the book on Amazon. It's out of print. My secret weapon for those rare books that are unavailable on Amazon—the database of all library books in the world——said there was one copy in the Library of Congress. The only other copy in the world was listed in an Atlanta library. I traveled to Atlanta. When I arrived, they said it existed in another branch in the same city. I then navigated Atlanta traffic in the rain to find that library, and they said it was in some vault in storage. After a long wait, someone finally brought it out for me.

Girma qualified his recommendation: "I don't expect you to believe it or accept it. But it does answer your question: 'Why is the Ark of the Covenant kept in Ethiopia? Why specifically here and not anywhere else?'"

Ermias's rare book did not disappoint. He answers my question squarely and directly. He recounts the monotheism of Ethiopians from Adam through the time of Christ. "The phenomenal attitude of the Ethiopians towards God and finally towards Jesus was in absolute contrast to that of the Jews, whose hatred and rejection of Christ culminated in crucifying Him." He then points to Sheba's visit to Solomon as the key event to begin "the fulfilment of the holy cause of Ethiopianism."

"This meeting was a fundamental turning point for both Ethiopia and Israel," he continues. "Because of this episode in the divine plan, all what was for Israel was transferred to Ethiopia, and all the divine blessings that were for the Israelites were bestowed upon the Ethiopians. The final habitation and entrustment of the subsequent holy covenants that include the seed and the throne of David, the Ark with all its sacred accessories and blessings, such as the faith and teachings of Judaism, its books, worship rites and rituals, as well as the learned and chosen ones from the Israelites were all moved to Ethiopia, entrusted to the Ethiopians, and ultimately Ethiopianized....Incredible as it may seem, these realities remained intact and fully maintained by Ethiopians and are as lively as they were, even to this day."

So, there you have it. Ethiopia is the new Israel, the new Chosen Nation. Any Westerner who attempts to write according to "the Ethiopian perspective" should be prepared for an exciting adventure. This same exceptionalist view is what caused me to be skeptical when writing earlier on Haile Selassie's speech before the League of Nations when he proclaimed: "Apart from the Kingdom of the Lord, there is not on this earth any nation that is superior to any other." Did Haile Selassie, as a devout Ethiopian Orthodox Christian, fully believe those words?

Eritrean historian Michela Wrong, writing from a likely non-Ethiopian perspective, called the Kebra Negast "a radical rewrite of the Bible that substituted Ethiopia for Israel as God's Chosen People." Her take is that it is a legend "justifying a deep-rooted sense of racial and cultural superiority."

Regarding Ermias's assertions, official church publications do not contradict his exceptionalist assertions. Ethiopians are "heirs to the promise made to Abraham," says Lule Melaku. Another publication makes it clear that, when Jesus talks about his second coming, "it would be the Queen of Sheba of Ethiopia whom he would present as the sign of faith." The Kebra Negast makes the point in several places, including in Chapter 95: "The chosen ones of the Lord are the people of Ethiopia."[5]

Elias Gebreselassie, an industrial chemist and a student of professor Girma, told me that he believes the historicity of the Kebra Negast, although it may have some "embellishments and scribal errors."

"The Ark was preserved by Ethiopia because God knew about the eunuch and the coming Christian empire," he told me. "It also prevents the Jews from continuing to worship it and conduct temple practices."

But Elias was quick to tell me, as did many Ethiopian Orthodox experts, that the Ark is now simply a relic. The fulfillment is in Christ. Ermias Kebede agrees with this statement, despite his ardent Ethiopianism: "When the Christian sacraments were instituted, the Ark of the Covenant which contained the tablets bearing the Word of God ceased to be the holy object of worship." He says the tabots, the altar tables for the Eucharist in Ethiopian churches, serve as a new version of the Ark and carry "the engravings of the crucifixion of Jesus Christ with the images of the holy Virgin Mary and Saint John the Disciple, each standing on the right and left sides of the cross respectively, and with the divine names of God inscribed thereon, signifying the incarnation of the Word of God in the womb of Saint Mary.

"Before the day of the inevitable fall of Jerusalem and of the temple approached, God looked around for another people who, in his eyes, were worthy of being trusted to keep his sacred treasures on earth until the appointed time came for the prophetic symbolism of the Ark to be fulfilled in the incarnation of the Word. Alas! He found the Ethiopians well suited for his purpose."[6]

Girma asked me a question during our interview: "Dean, do you remember the word said by our Lord Jesus Christ about the Queen of the South?"

"She would rise up to judge the world?" I suggested.

Then, he offered some hope for the future of the Jews: "Certain church scholars believe Ethiopia and Israel will lead the world at the end of time. Before the coming of Christ, Ethiopia and Israel will govern the whole world. And after that, the Lord will come."

In fact, the Kebra Negast makes a reference to this version of the Eschaton, the final scene for mankind. But like a lot of things related to Ethiopia's larger role, it takes some digging to get to the bottom of it. Harvard- and Oxford-trained G. W. Bowersock says the Kebra Negast teaches that the Ethiopian Orthodox Church will bring the Ark back to Jerusalem at the final coming, when Christ restores all things. The tricky part is that the most common English translation of the Kebra Negast states the exact opposite.

At the end of the Kebra Negast, Chapter 116, the question is asked: Shall the Ark "remain henceforward, to the Coming of Christ...if their Chariot shall remain [in Ethiopia]." Or will it return to Jerusalem? Bowersock says that Wallis Budge, who provided the best-known English version, mistranslated the answer to read: "It shall assuredly not disappear." Bowersock says German translator Carl Bezold gives the correct answer as: "Nein, er wird verschwinden" ("No, it will disappear."). Gérard Colin also gives the correct translation in the French version: "Non, il est destiné â disparaître" ("No, it is destined to disappear").[7]

When getting to the bottom of what God is up to in Ethiopia, the language and cultural barrier is always a challenge. But if Bowersock is right, and the Kebra Negast is to be believed, then the Ark of the

Covenant will finally leave Ethiopia at the end of the age. It will be brought to Jerusalem when Christ fulfills all things. This scenario assumes that the Ark of the Covenant is indeed in Ethiopia, a matter we have discussed throughout, and for which we will reach an objective conclusion. But in this section, we have answered the larger question: Why is the Ark in Ethiopia?

The answer leads to exceptionalism. Girma insisted on clarifying this "blessing" of being a special nation. "God has chosen Ethiopia to be blessed. But what kind of blessing?" he asked. "It depends on how you look at it."

His point was related to Christ's admonition: "From everyone who has been given much, much will be demanded" (Luke 12:48). Another related verse is Hebrews 12:6: "The Lord disciplines the one he loves, and he chastens everyone he accepts as his son." There is a reason, he says, that Ethiopia has seen so much hardship—European invasions, great famines, poverty, Muslim wars and ongoing encroachments for a thousand years, chemical weapons and war crimes, and, finally, torture, rape, and genocide from its own people.

"That is why I say, 'What is a blessing?'" Girma repeated. "We need to define it."

CHAPTER TWENTY-TWO

ECONOMIC POWER FOLLOWS population growth. Ethiopia has become the largest economy in East Africa, according to the *New York Times*, and the second largest market in Africa, according to geopolitical author William Engdahl, who points to a new train built by the Chinese as a sign of the growth.

"Nothing could be more symbolic of the decline of Europe and the rise of Eurasia than the construction of a modern railway from the Ethiopian capital of Addis Ababa to a port on the Red Sea in Djibouti," the Princeton graduate writes. This same route took Emperor Menelik many days by mule to transfer weapons from the coast to Addis. Now it only takes eight hours.

Engdahl points to Ethiopia's "grand infrastructure project" as a hopeful sign, the government's five-year Growth and Transformation Plan. In 2014, the Ethiopian prime minister announced "Ethiopia's great vision to become a manufacturing powerhouse." People power helps. Currently, Ethiopian labor costs one-tenth of what China's workers demand, and China's price is far less than anything in the West. Foreign direct investment into Ethiopia reached $1.5 billion in 2014 and has been increasing by 250 percent each year.[1]

The United Nations investment guide names Ethiopia as the second most improved business environment in the world. A previous edition acknowledged the country's successful transition from the Derg back to its Christian roots: "Ethiopia offers a stable, secure and, exceptionally for a developing country, mostly corruption-free operating environment."[2]

Engdahl also notes that Ethiopia may be sitting on a massive oil reserve. "It lies along the African Great Rift Belt, a tectonic fault line or belt some 6,000 kilometers long from Lebanon's Beqaa Valley to Mozambique in South Eastern Africa. Some geophysicists believe the Ethiopian or East African Rift Belt contains some of the world's richest untapped mineral deposits and potentially Saudi-levels of hydrocarbons—oil and gas." He thinks there may be more than one reason the Chinese have shown so much interest in the country.

Ethiopia is the second most populous nation in Africa, behind Nigeria. But it is Africa itself that provides the most enormous statistics to demonstrate the coming shift in civilization from the West to the continent of the future. Ethiopia serves as the spiritual and cultural leader of this emerging powerhouse, with its permanent hosting of the African Union where ambassadors from every nation gather regularly at Addis Ababa to deliberate on the continent's prospects. Haile Selassie is known as the "Father of Africa." With its ancient Christian and Jewish heritage, Ethiopia brings a cultural depth and a millennia-old script, a tool other sub-Saharan nations only learned to use upon colonization.

Thanks to massive population growth during the past several decades, Asia has emerged temporarily as the new great continent. According to the World Economic Forum: "Africa's population will continue to grow even as Asia—currently the biggest regional driver of economic growth—begins to see its population growth recede." Sadly, the Asian nations, like the West, have begun to imbibe in the "suicide tablet" created by Margaret Sanger. China's 6.4 children per woman in 1965 has plummeted to today's nearly mathematically irreversible 1.5 rate—no country has ever recovered from a rate of 1.3. South Korea has seen a similar plunge during that time from 6.1 to 1.1, and, by some reports, even as low as 0.96.[3]

"Europe will continue to shrink, which is worsening its economic problems," declares the *Washington Post*, which notes that China is also in trouble. "The Asian century could be followed by the African century. As China shrinks, its workforce will get smaller precisely when it needs them most." The *Post* entitled this article, "The amazing, surprising, Africa-driven demographic future of the Earth."

By 2030, one in five people will be African. More than half of the growth on the planet (fifty-four percent) in the next few decades will be Africa's 1.3 billion additional people, more than doubling Africa's current 1.2 billion population. In the next thirty-three years, two billion babies will be born in Africa. In 1950, ten percent of the world's children were African. By 2050, Africa will claim thirty-three percent of children eighteen and under and forty percent of children five and under.[4]

A map of the world's twenty largest cities in 2100 shows two concentrations, one around India–Southeast Asia and the larger concentration in Africa, with Ethiopia's Addis Ababa as one of those cities of the future. None of the cities are in the Americas, Europe, Russia, China, Korea, Japan, or the Middle East. The top four cities are as follows:

Lagos, Nigeria: 88.3 million people (currently 10.6 million)

Kinshasa, Congo: 83.5 million (currently 9.1 million)

Dar Es Salaam, Tanzania: 73.7 million (currently 4.4 million)

Mumbai, India: 67.2 million (currently 20.1 million)

The top three are African cities. New York, Los Angeles, Mexico City, and Moscow make the list today but all disappear by 2100.[5] Economic development in these burgeoning cities follows a different paradigm. Today, access to a mobile phone is available to most people in Africa—now the world's largest market for cellular devices—but far fewer have piped water. More specifically, thirty percent of Africans have sewer service, fifty-four percent have paved roads, sixty-three percent have piped water, sixty-five percent have electricity, and ninety-three percent have cell phone service.

A decade ago, Chinese investors poured $2.4 billion into seventy-five foreign countries. Of those, forty-five percent were Asian and forty-two percent African. Besides investing in their Asian neighbors, these Chinese oligarchs are pouring money into Africa, almost exclusively. According to the World Economic Forum: "Combine the continent's soaring population with technology, improvements in infrastructure, health and education, and Africa could be the next century's economic growth powerhouse."

"Africa is going to be the epicenter of what's happening in the world for years to come," writes investment strategist Doug Casey, a *New York Times* bestselling author. "It's gone from being just an empty space on the map in the nineteenth century, to a bunch of backwater colonies in the twentieth century, to a bunch of failed states that people are only vaguely aware of today. Soon, however, it will be frontpage news."[6]

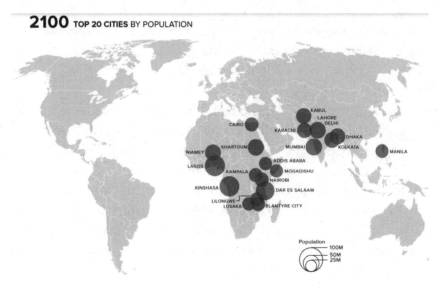

2100 TOP 20 CITIES BY POPULATION

SOURCE: GLOBAL CITIES INST.   MAP: VISUALCAPITALIST.COM

Before we address the mighty efforts of the Bill and Melinda Gates Foundation to prevent Africa from reaching its demographic destiny, the thinking of such elitists and former eugenicists—most specifically their Malthusianism—needs to be squarely debunked once and for all. Thomas Malthus, Margaret Sanger, and more recently, Paul Ehrlich, got it wrong: more people leads to wealth, not poverty.

Firstly, some mental pictures to help overcome the propaganda: today's population, all seven billion, could each have five acres of land for themselves. Of course, not all land can grow food (that problem hasn't been solved yet!), but every person on the planet could have his or her own half-acre of productive land. Living as families of four, the entire world population can fit into Texas, with each family owning a nice house and yard. Standing three feet apart, the entire world can fit into the city of Jacksonville, Florida.[7]

There's plenty of land for everyone, and there will be for a long time. After that, perhaps Elon Musk will provide more opportunities in space.

Secondly, we are not in a unique, unprecedented situation. Demographers estimate that at least twenty billion people lived on earth between 8000 BC and the time of Christ (see Berkeley scientist Kenneth Wachter's *Essential Demographic Methods*). The notion that half of all people who have ever lived are alive currently is a myth.

Thirdly, there is plenty of food. The world grows enough food today for three billion more people than now exist, as Eric Holt-Giménez writes in the *Journal of Sustainable Agriculture*: "We already grow enough food for 10 billion people…and still can't end hunger." Exactly. The Oxford-based humanitarian group Oxfam stated that "famines are not natural phenomena, they are catastrophic political failures." Or, as the Population Research Institute puts it: "'Overpopulation' is not to blame. It's the policy, stupid."[8]

Fourthly, there is plenty of water. Of course, two-thirds of the globe is covered in water and looks blue from outer space. Sure, that's saltwater, but, again, some creative person may figure out a simple way to convert it. Regarding the kind of water you can currently drink, obtainable freshwater has increased sevenfold since 1900, while the world population has increased only fourfold. People tend to figure out a way to garner the abundance of freshwater on our planet, according to scientist Dr. Peter Gleick's piece "A Look at Twenty-First Century Water Resources Development" in *Water International*.[9]

Then, why all this Chicken Little fearmongering about overpopulation? As British historian Paul Johnson noted, for 200 years the Malthusian advocates have spouted "mumbo-jumbo" and have never been taken seriously by the larger public. The big change emerged when Stanford professor Paul Ehrlich wrote a book in 1968 called *The Population Bomb*. It didn't sell that well until his handlers discovered the real secret to success—he appeared on Johnny Carson's *Tonight Show* nearly a dozen times. The book sold two million copies and appeared in several languages. Ehrlich created "the unlikely category of superstar scientist," according to geopolitical analyst James Corbett, who calls Ehrlich a "pseudo-science charlatan."

That sounds rather harsh until you examine the evidence: Ehrlich, in the late 1960s and early 1970s, predicted the following:

"There will never be seven billion people in the year 2000"

"As far as petroleum goes...we're running out rapidly, some estimates are that it will all be gone by the year 2000."

"Sometime in the next fifteen years, the end will come and, by the end, I mean the utter breakdown of the planet to support humanity."

"The collapse of civilization itself is a near certainty in the next few decades."[10]

He also predicted that four billion people would starve in the 1980s, including sixty-five million Americans. In the first line of *The Population Bomb*, he writes: "The battle to feed all of humanity is over. In the 1970s, hundreds of millions of people will starve to death in spite of any crash programs embarked upon now." He also said that "he would take even money" that England would not exist in the year 2000. This one prediction he got right, although he was off by a couple of centuries, and it will happen for the opposite reason. As we have already demonstrated in this book, demographic winter will soon destroy England and all of Europe. The United States will follow, but on a slower pace due to immigration.[11]

Ehrlich's solutions to the so-called "problem" of overpopulation? Forced sterilization and world government. Addressing a student's question on China's one-child policy, he said: "...one of the things that might be good...is to add something to the water supply that makes you have to take an antidote in order to have a baby...In the U.S., you can't even dare discuss it."

The *New York Times* quoted Ehrlich: "The government might have to put sterility drugs in reservoirs and in food shipped to foreign countries in order to limit human multiplication." The *Boca Raton News*, appalled at the idea, called Ehrlich "worse than Hitler." In the 1977 textbook *Ecoscience: Population Resources, Environment* that Ehrlich co-authored with Barak Obama's future science czar, John Holdren, they again suggested a sterilant for the water supply to solve overpopulation, along with forced abortions. These measures "could be sustained under the existing Constitution," they wrote. They call for a "planetary regime" to ultimately control and solve population issues.[12]

Society has had fifty years since Ehrlich's madness—both his predictions and his solutions—to debunk and defame him. Unfortunately, his gamesmanship has barely been exposed. As the adage goes, "repeat a lie often enough, and it becomes the truth." Ehrlich was made a fellow of the Royal Society of London in 2012, received awards from the Swedish Academy of Sciences, the University of Missouri, and the Sierra Club, and is a top professor of Biology at Stanford. He is still consulted today as an expert on population issues.

Contrast Ehrlich with a more credible academic during the same time, economist Dr. Julian Simon, who publicly challenged Ehrlich to a bet regarding so-called overpopulation and its effect on resource scarcity, a contest now known as the "Simon-Ehrlich Wager," which has its own *Wikipedia* page. In libertarian circles, it is known as "the Bet of the Century."

Simon grew up in New Jersey, like Ehrlich. They were both born in 1932. They both attended Ivy League schools. They both advocated for population control measures until Simon decided to examine the real data. "Spurred by doubts about whether population reduction might actually harm humanity rather than save it, Simon (unlike Ehrlich) went back to the data to see if the population hysteria was actually justified," writes James Corbett. "Finding that the data in fact showed the opposite of what doomsayers like Ehrlich were saying, Simon began writing articles arguing against the population control advocates."[13]

Simon tried to get his message out, but his anti-Malthusian message wasn't backed by oligarchs like the Rockefellers, who funded

Margaret Sanger and other Malthusians in the previous generation. He challenged Ehrlich to a debate but was ignored. Dr. Pierre Desrochers, a professor with the University of Toronto system, gives this account of Simon's wager:

"So, Simon is at home watching Ehrlich on the Johnny Carson show when he goes bananas because he sees him all the time, in his opinion, spouting nonsense-things that are not backed up by the data. But then, what are you gonna do? . . . nobody wants to listen to him. He might be, you know, the most prominent anti-Malthusian, but that's kind of like saying that you're the tallest of the seven dwarfs.

"And so, what he does is that he makes a very public bet to Ehrlich to essentially put up or shut up. . . . 'OK, select any five resources of your liking over any period of time of more than a year, and if, as you say, we're heading towards a Malthusian catastrophe, with more mouths to feed [with] finite resources, well, obviously, the price of these resources should go up over time. I mean, that's basic economics. If, on the other hand, the price of these resources decreases while population increases, then it will show you that you're wrong and that humanity is actually able to create resources, not just consume them.'"

Ehrlich consulted with Holdren, the future science czar, and decided to take up Simon on the bet. He chose five resources they were sure would increase in price: copper, chromium, nickel, tin, and tungsten. The ten-year bet was formalized in 1980, with September 29, 1990, as the payoff date.

Ehrlich lost the bet. All five metals decreased in price. It cost him $576.07, based on the calculation of the small wager. Desrochers concludes the story: "Julian Simon finds in his mailbox a check written by Paul Ehrlich with nothing else. Ehrlich never acknowledges that his perspective might have been wrong. He honors his bet, but that's it, and then he goes on saying [about Simon] that, you know 'stupid people can be wrong sometimes. The world will never run out of imbeciles.' And he's very rude to Simon and always refuses to engage him in a public debate."[14]

For his part, Simon hates small-minded thinkers with "the inability to imagine good things that can be created by other people." He says this tunnel vision "feeds into people's fear about population growth and their fear that we are going to run out of copper and of oil. They can't imagine, so many people simply can't conceive, how other people can respond to problems with new ideas and imagination and solutions, which will leave us better off, as if the problem had never arisen."

"The most important resource," says James Corbett, "is not chromium or tin or any other physical commodity, but human ingenuity itself."[15]

Ehrlich also predicted that India would starve, but "Norman Borlaug happened," according to Andrew Garber's documentary *We're All Gonna Starve!* "You may have never heard of him, but he's kinda one of the greatest human beings who ever lived," the documentary explains. Borlaug won the Nobel Prize for developing a more productive strain of wheat. India went from starving to becoming a wheat exporter. The nation issued a national stamp in 1968 celebrating this wheat revolution, the same year Ehrlich's *The Population Bomb* was published, which declared that India would never be able to feed itself. Borlaug is credited with saving a billion lives from starvation.

Elon Musk, a high-profile futurist and CEO of the electric car manufacturer Tesla, sees the real challenge in the days ahead: "I think the biggest problem the world will face in 20 years is population collapse," he said. "*Collapse.* I want to emphasize this. The biggest issue in 20 years will be population collapse—not explosion—collapse," he repeated. "Most people think we have too many people on the planet, but actually this is an outdated view."[16]

So, more people aren't a problem. God's first commandment is to be fruitful and multiply, and the Bible never tells us otherwise. The Ethiopian Orthodox Church has stayed the course up to now, and, for their trust and obedience, have positioned themselves to lead the future of civilization. But this will not happen if the friends of Bill Gates have their way.

The Bill and Melinda Gates Foundation sponsored the opening ceremonies for the International Conference on Family Planning held in Addis Ababa, Ethiopia, on November 12, 2013. With 3,400 attending from 110 countries, the four-day event was hailed as the largest family planning gathering in history.[17]

The conference leaders "celebrated Ethiopia as a model of success," reported *NPR*. "Ethiopia was the largest recipient of family planning assistance in sub-Saharan Africa since 2000." The efforts are working: ". . . the number of women using hormonal birth control has steadily increased, from eight percent in 2000 to twenty-nine percent in 2014." Ethiopia's birthrate has decreased from 7.2 in 1991 to 4.2 in 2019.

Ethiopia's Minister of Health Dr. K. Admasu gave this assessment: "We are lucky that we don't have a strong opposition from the religious institutions." According to *NPR*, that statement is not quite true. "Many, though not all, Orthodox leaders express opposition to the family planning programs. But in authoritarian, one-party Ethiopia, the church can't really openly oppose the state." Admasu clarified it as "a kind of gentleman's agreement we have with the church leaders."

A thirty-five-year-old Orthodox priest at Holy Trinity Cathedral told *NPR*: "The Bible doesn't allow the use of pills." The church only allows natural family planning—abstaining from sex, which includes fast days, up to 250 a year on the Orthodox calendar.

"So, the church works through its own channels," says *NPR*, "advising congregants directly and through sermons that, while managing the family and providing the children is important, the permissible way to limit births is through natural means."[18]

A number of the Ethiopian leaders that I spoke with say Muslims are more forceful at resisting the contraception efforts initiated by the Gates Foundation. They say major financial backers from Saudi Arabia have their own plans to make Ethiopia a majority Muslim country— current numbers hover around forty-five percent Orthodox Christian and thirty-five percent Muslim, with the rest mainly Protestant and a few Catholics. The contraception advocates make more progress with Orthodox Christians and Protestants than with Muslims.

"We cannot compete with them, because they have more than one wife," professor Girma Batu told me. "There are some sponsors behind it—they want to make Ethiopia a Muslim-dominated country."

Girma waited until his thirties to marry and has two children.

"Do you plan to have as many children as God gives you?" I asked him.

"Yes."

He said the effect of modernity on Christians is another major factor for the decreasing birthrate. "They try to be like Westerners. What's happening due to this modernization—at least one child, they say. At most, two. That's enough. It's exactly copying the West."

And yet the West, as we have seen, is on a collision course with disaster. But like a modern-day Samson, who killed his rivals along with himself, the elites of the U.S. and Europe are dead set on handing Africa the suicide pistol of Queen Victoria and bringing Margaret Sanger's suicide tablet to Ethiopia and the rest of the continent. If recent trends continue, they will succeed.

When the world's richest men met in 2009, they each gave fifteen-minute presentations on their primary concerns for the planet. "Taking their cue from Gates, they agreed overpopulation was a priority," according to the report from London's *Sunday Times*. Meanwhile, the staffers of the oligarchs were told that "security briefings" were the reason for their meeting. "We only learned about it afterward," said Stacy Palmer, editor of *The Chronicle of Philanthropy*. "Normally these people are happy to talk about good causes, but this is different— maybe because they don't want to be seen as a global cabal."[19]

Gates's meeting was a great success, as his billionaire friends and all the major foundations decided to contribute to the Gates Foundation's population control efforts. Warren Buffett, the second-richest person at the time behind Gates, shifted $31 billion of his assets to his friend Bill. In an interview with Bill Moyers in 2003, Gates said that "the one issue that really grabbed me as urgent were issues related to population." Then he clarified himself: "...reproductive health."[20]

Most people have a working knowledge of Bill Gates's rise from a teenager in the Seattle suburbs to college dropout, to computer whiz kid who forged an unlikely software partnership with IBM to become the richest man in the world. He is the science type. Smart. Rational. He's not a church-goer. Bill said church represents an inefficient use of his time. According to biographer Ron Chernow, Gates has a staff of thirty people who work on his public image. And that's good, because Gates was in an awkward position as a rich white male speaking publicly about his ambition to use his money to tell women in foreign countries what to do with their bodies. Even so, he forged ahead. "You could tell three things about Bill Gates pretty quickly," said his Microsoft high school partner turned billionaire, Paul Allen. "He was really smart, he was really competitive....and he was really, really persistent."[21]

BILL AND MELINDA GATES

Allen and Gates first met at Lakewood High School in Seattle, the most prestigious in the state of Washington and ranked sixth in the nation. The tuition cost three times more than Harvard's. Bill's PR handlers have done a pretty good job of positioning their boss as a "just above middle-class suburbanite" who hit it big. The news never really got out that his father, who goes by Bill Gates, Sr., was a major corporate lawyer on the national scene and that his mother was even more prominent. Bill's great-grandfather on his mother's side, J. W. Maxwell, founded Seattle's National City Bank in 1906. His fortune left little Bill a trust fund worth millions in today's dollars. His mother was also on the board of the United Way with the chief executive officer of IBM, so a relationship in high places helped that particular computer geek, out of many, to somehow land the nation's largest software deal. Neither Bill nor Paul Allen wrote the code.

Bill is an elitist. His father, William Gates, Sr., is actually William the Third, but, for some unknown reason, he changed his name to Junior. So, the billionaire Bill Gates, who was a multimillionaire at birth, is actually William Henry Gates IV.[22]

The affable Bill Gates, persistent as always, ignored the differences between him and his darker-skinned, poor female constituency and promised to give away ninety percent of his fortune, focusing on health care, contraception, and prevention. "Vaccines" are "something I love," he said during a talk on climate change and overpopulation. He was mixing all those words a little too closely together as he talked about the "magic of vaccines," and he kept messing up in his public addresses. At a 2010 Ted Talk he said the following:

"The world today has 6.8 billion people. That's heading up to about nine billion. Now, if we do a really great job on new vaccines, health care, reproductive health services, we could lower that by perhaps ten or fifteen percent."[23]

First of all, any kind of talk discussing the lowering of population is a little eerie, and sounds like the eugenics of a century ago. This particular quote by Gates sounds a bit like an attempt to use vaccines to lower the population. Surely, there must be an explanation. Then, in a separate interview, he created the same confusion a second time. When asked by CNN's Sanjay Gupta about his Decade of Vaccines initiative, he said: "The benefits [of vaccines] are there in terms of reducing sickness, reducing population growth."

His gaffes were enough to cause suspicion in many places. Dr. Gary Null writes of the "public image of the very likable mild-mannered Bill Gates" and his "ambition to improve the health of the developing world." But his several on-the-record comments suggest "the possibility of other ulterior motives that are contrary to saving lives."[24]

Surely there is an explanation here. It's not like Bill Gates is directly connected to Margaret Sanger and speaking publicly about eliminating "human waste." Surely, Gates's thirty handlers were scratching their heads regarding the repeated gaffes. Perhaps they advised him to find someone else for the face of the franchise. So, what does the very smart, very competitive, very persistent Bill Gates do? Enter Melinda Gates.

CHAPTER TWENTY-THREE

MARRIED TO BILL in 1994, Melinda French brings a savvy that Bill can't quite muster, and she caters to the right demographic. She is younger. She is a woman. First in her high school class and the college valedictorian, she runs marathons and climbs tall mountains. She and Bill get to have three kids—more than the replacement rate—and she was raised in a home of four children who enjoyed having a stay-at-home mother. Their house has twenty-four bathrooms and is valued at $147.5 million, not including a notebook known to reside somewhere inside (when not loaned to museums) belonging to Leonardo da Vinci worth $50 million. But Melinda, raised in an upper-class neighborhood—but lower than her current station—is certainly closer to the target constituency of poor, African females than Bill.

She is also more perceptive than her husband. "Bill readily admits that Melinda understands people better than he does," according to a friendly biopic, likely written by the PR staff. Warren Buffett agrees. "Bill is an awkward guy. He's lopsided, but a little less lopsided since he's with Melinda."[1]

Melinda was quick to explain Bill's strange comments about vaccines as part of a plan to reduce population. "If you allow a child to live, there's a whole group of skeptics who say 'Well, isn't the mother going to keep having seven babies or five babies and we're going to overpopulate the planet? That worried Bill and me, too, quite frankly," she said. "But, thank God the converse is true, that, as a woman and the husband see their children will live into adulthood, the woman naturally brings down her birthrate." Their argument: vaccines improve health. Healthier families decide it's okay to have less children. Thus, population is reduced.[2]

She also addressed other sticky issues: "Some people worry that the real goal of family planning is to control populations. These are all side issues that have attached themselves to this core idea that men and women should be able to decide when they want to have a child." She also dealt head-on with the "lingering concern that if we separate sex from reproduction, we're going to promote promiscuity. And I think that's a reasonable question to be asked about contraception—what is its impact on sexual morality?

"But, like most women, my decision about birth control had nothing to do with promiscuity," Melinda insists. She tells her story of earning a master's degree from Duke University and then becoming one of the youngest female executives at Microsoft. While Bill says less-endearing things like "religion is not very efficient," Melinda attended only Catholic schools as a child and considers herself a Christian and a "practicing Catholic."[3]

Melinda Gates is, without a doubt, an impressive spokesperson for her cause. And with African leaders receiving $43 billion annually from Europe and the United States, no one immediately surfaced with any determination to face off with her in public. Not until, that is, a young Nigerian woman found herself getting angrier and angrier as she watched Melinda Gates speak in a way that she felt misrepresented Africans, and, more specifically, African women.

Obianuju Ekeocha (she goes by "Uju") was born the last of six children. Her grandfather sold coconuts to support the family. Then when her father was six, her grandfather borrowed eighty dollars to send his son to school, who, eventually, earned an accounting degree from Cambridge University. His children, including Uju, followed their father's footsteps and attended college. She looks to education instead of sexual freedom for answers. "What education has done for my family, it can do for other Africans," she says.[4]

Uju works as a laboratory scientist in hematology—formerly at the University of Nigeria Teaching Hospital and now in London. She was a simple lone voice when she was confronted with Melinda

Gates's opposing worldview. She had no personal wealth, no foundation, no publishing company, and no publicists to help her. So she simply uploaded onto the internet "An Open Letter to Melinda Gates."

"In 2012, I stumbled upon Melinda Gates plan to collect pledges for almost $5 billion to ensure that the African woman would be less fertile, less encumbered, and, yes, more 'liberated,'" she writes. "With her incredible wealth she wanted to replace the legacy of an African woman—which is her child—with the legacy of 'child-free sex.' I was so outraged that I wrote a public letter..."[5]

Uju heard Melinda relate her own situation regarding career advancement and birth control. However, Uju notes that Melinda was not married during all those years, and she seems unable to consider the idea of abstinence as an option during one's education years. When the policies pushed by Gates were debated for a UN resolution, Uju observed, "These Western nations could not accept the notion of 'delay of sexual debut' as a way for women to protect themselves," adding that an African delegate turned away saying that "it's all about sex, sex, sex, for them."

Melinda can say that it has nothing to do with promiscuity, but Uju says it doesn't work that way on the ground. She relates the story of Sam Ruteikara, co-chairman of the Ugandan National AIDS-Prevention Committee: "We recognized that population-wide AIDS epidemics in Africa were driven by people having sex with more than one partner. Therefore, we urged people to be faithful," he said. "...our main message was: Stick to one partner. We promoted condoms only as a last resort." However, "when the document draft was published, fidelity and abstinence were missing."

While Melinda insists that population control is "only a side issue," Uju flatly contradicts her. "There are a number of gatherings around the world for the sole purpose of moving Africa toward the Western standard of low fertility rates," she writes. "The Gates Foundation has taken a leadership role in this project, which on its surface is about women but at its core is about population control."[6]

One of those gatherings was in Addis Ababa, the largest event of its kind, sponsored by Bill and Melinda, where Ethiopia was hailed as a "model of success" for lowering an African country's birthrate. Uju was one of the few voices of protest. "We mourn deeply for the destructive seeds of sexual revolution which were sown last week in Addis Ababa," she said. ". . . a handful of people who have access to the greatest material wealth in the world came to us to tell us that what Africans need most is full access to sex without attachments." She said the views of African societies against sex outside of marriage were considered "judgmental" by the speakers and officials at the conference. "Dearest people of the world, this is absurd! This is twisted and distorted!" Uju wrote. "This is heartbreaking for the entire continent of Africa!"

"In my letter to Melinda Gates, I saw her billions of dollars as buying Africans not the real health care that they need but only misery," said Uju. "Needless to say, my letter did nothing to stop the Gates Foundation's full-speed-ahead push for contraceptions."[7]

OBIANUJU EKEOCHA

Melinda, meanwhile, was blessed with the opportunity to give a Ted Talk, one of the most visible speaking platforms in today's world, a year after the conference in Ethiopia, where she again advanced birth control. She talked about a new technology that they developed for women in Ethiopia so that they don't have to take a pill daily; instead, they can get an injection four times a year. "The reason women like it so much in Africa is they can hide it from their husbands, who sometimes want a lot of children." She also spoke of her Catholic school upbringing. "Today, in the Foundation's work, I believe I'm applying the lessons I learned in

296

high school." In another place she spoke of Bill Gates, Sr.: "Bill's dad, thank goodness, has always been there. This family presence is really important in the foundation."[8]

While Melinda was using the world's best platforms, Uju, also a Catholic, kept blogging on the internet. "In that letter, I explained to Gates, a Catholic, that many of the sixty-nine countries she was targeting for her contraceptive campaign had large Catholic populations," she wrote. "With most African women faithfully practicing and adhering to a faith (mainly Christian, or, in some cases, Muslim), there is a high regard for the sexual act as a sacred and private trust between a man and a wife. The trivialization of sex is simply not an acceptable part of African society, at least not yet."[9]

The Gates Foundation marched onward. At a summit in London, with the foundation's help, the government of India pledged to provide birth control to sixty-four million women. India will soon be the most populous nation on the planet, so the Gates Foundation built a national office there. When Melinda traveled to her Catholic high school in Dallas to give a $12 million donation, she mentioned that some of the nuns supported her work. That was enough to cause the bishop overseeing the Dallas area to address the matter publicly: "Human sexuality and sexual expression in marriage are among God's greatest gifts. Artificial contraception violates the meaning of this gift," wrote Bishop Kevin Farrell in a public statement directed at Melinda but without mentioning her. "Every Catholic has a serious responsibility to inform themselves about this teaching and to form their consciences in its light."[10]

Uju named her. The "Open Letter to Melinda Gates" went viral on the internet. It was posted on the website of the Vatican's Pontifical Council for the Laity. In her letter, she noted that African women intuitively understand the importance of the moral teachings that the Catholic Church has championed in the face of bitter modernist attacks in the twentieth century. "Women with little education and wealth have embraced what the average *Vogue*- and *Cosmo*-reading woman in the United States has refused to understand: that when sex and marriage and children are separated, promiscuity, divorce, abortion, prostitution, and pornography spread as never before."

A year after her letter was recognized in Vatican circles, Pope Francis himself released a 2015 encyclical that addressed the issue: "Instead of resolving the problems of the poor and thinking of how the world can be different, some can only propose a reduction in the birth rate," he proclaimed. For a Catholic, being on the wrong side of the Pope is never helpful in a public relations strategy. But at least one Gates was identifying as a card-carrying Christian. Bill, on the other hand, when asked about church, said, "There's a lot more I could be doing on a Sunday morning."[11]

The new face of the foundation franchise spoke about Christianity in a way to attract a larger demographic. But the tension was growing for Melinda regarding her expressed Catholicism and her actions which defied some of the most important teachings of the Catholic Church. The London *Independent* reported her decision to openly admit the contradiction: "Melinda Gates, billionaire philanthropist and practicing Catholic, laid down the gauntlet to the Vatican by vowing to dedicate her life to improving access to contraception for women in the developing world."

"Of course I wrestled with this," Melinda told the *Independent*. "As a Catholic I believe in this religion, there are amazing things about this religion, amazing moral teachings that I do believe in, but I also have to think about how to keep women alive." The article points to her "commitment to reducing unwanted pregnancies in poorer countries, which experts say lead to more than 100,000 women dying prematurely every year."[12]

Uju does not back down from these highly charged arguments. Firstly, she notes that the statistics are used a bit deceptively to promote the contraception agenda. While fewer pregnancies lead obviously to fewer deaths by pregnancies, birth control does not decrease the percentage of deaths per pregnancy. Secondly, she says the true solution is better health care: "...the availability of contraception does not necessarily mean that a country has adequate maternity care. What African nations need is not a massive infusion of contraceptives into their communities but a renewed commitment to building up the various branches of the dilapidated healthcare systems across the continent. Imagine if billions of dollars were invested in that!"

Uju notes that the same types of arguments are used for HIV prevention. South Africa is praised as a role model, where the largest condom distribution program was established to prevent AIDS. "Yet South Africa is among the African countries with the highest incidence rates of HIV, and it has the highest percentage of HIV-infected young women in southern and eastern Africa," she writes. "Think of the exponential spread of HIV and other STDs as men and women with abundant access to contraceptives take up multiple, concurrent sex partners."[13]

Uju's indictment—that Melinda Gates is funding contraception rather than preventing the death and diseases she claims to be addressing—is backed by one of the most prestigious medical journals, *The Lancet.* One article notes that African philanthropy has seen "a heavy bias in funding towards malaria and HIV/AIDS, with relatively little investment into tuberculosis, maternal and child health, and nutrition—with chronic diseases being entirely absent from its spending portfolio." In the same paper, entitled "What has the Gates Foundation Done for Global Health?" Dr. David McCoy says that "the grants made by the Foundation do not reflect the burden of disease endured by those deepest in poverty."

Melinda Gates speaks about the foundation's involvement with other areas besides contraception. "We also need to help small farmers—farmers who plow small plots of land in Africa—so that they can grow enough food to feed their children."[14]

Now, while Melinda does have some credibility as a woman speaking on issues of female contraception, I will suggest that she knows very little about farming or third world economic development. She grew up in the upper-middle-class suburbs of Dallas. We must assume that, in this area, she is simply serving as a talking head for others behind the curtain. And a little investigative work proves this to be true. In fact, the Gates Foundation "is a major shareholder of Monsanto, now Bayer AG," according to Ivy League author William Engdahl. Monsanto is the leading proponent of GMOs (genetically modified organisms), a highly controversial industry that sells seeds to farmers that cannot be used the following year. They are patented. You, therefore, cannot eat an apple, take out a seed, and plant it in your yard. You have to go back to the store and buy more seeds. It's almost like patenting rainwater. Something that was a free gift since the beginning of time is now used to extort fortunes for the wealthy from the struggling masses.

According to *The Guardian* in 2006: "Both Gates and the Rockefeller Foundation...launched the Alliance for a Green Revolution (AGRA), based on the premise that hunger in Africa is mainly the result of a lack of technology and functioning markets." *The Guardian* added that this GMO seed alliance "changed the farming agenda in Africa." Dr. Gary Null and Richard Gale say these changes by the international GMO initiatives funded by Gates "have devastated small cooperative farms that have served as the lifeline of food for centuries and has resulted in the deaths of hundreds of thousands of farmers."[15]

AGRA, this Gates and Rockefeller creation, is involved closely with Monsanto, DuPont, Dow, Syngenta, and other agribusiness giants. "The person from the Gates Foundation responsible for its work with AGRA is Dr. Robert Horsh, a 25-year Monsanto GMO veteran who was on the team that developed Monsanto's Roundup Ready GMO technologies," writes Engdahl. "His job is reportedly to use Gates's money to introduce GMO into Africa." Monsanto is now the world's biggest seed company, according to the *Corbett Report*, citing Monasanto's control of over ninety percent of the cotton soy in India. "They've taken over most of the seed companies in the world," says Indian scholar Vandana Shiva. Founded in 1901, Monsanto began strengthening its ties to the military-industrial complex during World War II, assisting in the development of nuclear weapons. Monanto's infamous contribution to the Vietnam War was its poisonous herbicide-defoliant known as Agent Orange.[16]

As an added bonus for population control enthusiasts, genetically modified corn, the staple in Mexico and other countries, reduces fertility. The president of the field-testing company for the modified corn announced that "we have a hothouse filled with corn plants that make anti-sperm antibodies.... [which] make each sperm so heavy it cannot move forward. It just shakes about as if it were doing the lambada." He said it was a possible solution for "overpopulation."

Problems with conflicts of interest are also present with Gates and vaccines. The giant Global Fund for Children's Vaccine (GAVI), spearheaded by Gates, includes partners like the Rockefellers, the World Bank, private vaccine companies, and the International Federation of Pharmaceutical Manufacturers & Associations. Strangely, while pushing health and sustainability, the Gates Foundation has also been invested in Big Tobacco for years and remains a heavy investor in two of the world's Big Oil companies, Exxon and BP.[17]

Rather than discussing GMOs and Big Pharma, Melinda is at her best talking about contraception and population. When she does, her best angle is to address it in terms of women's rights. She likes to share what her parents told her after she graduated with her master's degree: "Even though you've had this great education, if you decide to get married and have kids right away, that's okay by us too." Adds Melinda: "They wanted me to do the thing that would make me the very happiest. I was free to decide what that would be. It was an amazing feeling."

Uju addresses Melinda's imperial assumption for African women—that they prefer not to get pregnant right away or have many children. But before I share those thoughts, it is worth noting that Melinda, having declared that she actually does not follow official Catholic teachings, now shows that she and Bill really do have their own kind of religion. Princeton law professor Robert P. George, in the clear context of the Gateses and other population control advocates, calls this religion "expressive individualism." He says that Obianuju Ekeocha (Uju) "casts a spotlight on the new colonialism and subjects it to searching critical scrutiny." He says expressive individualism in its extreme "is at the heart of the secular progressive worldview that now functions as the religion of many Western elites."

"It is increasingly clear that it is a militant, evangelizing, and fundamentalist type of 'religion,'" notes George, the McCormick Professor of Jurisprudence at Princeton. "It seeks to embody its core doctrines in law as well as social practices, and it exhibits very little tolerance, or even patience, for dissent or dissenters. It regards 'traditional' beliefs and values—from the sanctity of human life in all stages and conditions, to the ideal of chastity and the idea of marriage as the conjugal union of husband and wife, to the conviction that children are blessings that are far more valuable than personal economic advancement or material possessions and wealth—as retrograde and benighted."[18]

To put it simply, one religion says a woman should be anything she wants to be, regardless of the bigger picture. Another religion says that men and women are to follow God's commandments—the first one being that women are commanded to bear children and that men are commanded to support them in this chief endeavor of mankind. They do not get the choice to do or become whatever they want. Modernity, women's rights, and radical "expressive individualism" cannot exist peacefully with traditional religion and biblical Christianity. In the New Testament, the Apostle Paul cuts to the chase on this key issue. After explaining that men are to be the head of the household, he assures everyone that "women will be saved through childbearing" (1 Tim. 2:15). This worldview may still work in a nation like Ethiopia with over 1,000 monasteries, but it is no longer acceptable in a society where the Bill and Melinda Gates Foundation is the largest and most influential charity.

Uju does not primarily use a religious or scriptural argument to refute Melinda Gates. She meets Melinda on her own ground: the implied, supposedly irrefutable, position that they are helping African women with what they "need" and with what they "want." The Gates Foundation has targeted 220 million women in poor countries who "do not want" to get pregnant. "We are particularly committed to exploring how our family planning efforts can meet the needs of young women and girls," the foundation states on its website.

Says Melinda, articulating her "expressive individualist" religion: "Now, as a mother, what do I want—the very most—for my children? I want them to feel the way I did—like they can do anything they want to do in life. And so, what has struck me as I've traveled the last decade for the Foundation around the world is that all women want the same thing."[19]

But Uju has a different belief on what all African women want. "In the town I come from, a new baby is always welcomed with much joy. In fact, we have a special song reserved for births, a sort of 'Gloria in Excelsis Deo.' The day a baby is born, the entire village celebrates by singing this song, clapping their hands, and dancing. I can say with certainty that Africans love babies.

"I would estimate that I had at least one family member or close friend give birth every single month. So I saw at least twelve babies born in my life every year." She describes the marriage ceremony in her village as "picturesque in every way and so brings to life everything the world romanticizes about Africa—from the kola nuts to the freshly tapped palm wine, from the colorful attires to the skilled drummers and agile dancers moving perfectly to the beat."

"No doubt many Western elites would enjoy attending this event, which is so richly and unabashedly ethnic. When they tout the merits of cultural diversity, they mean native languages, food, clothing, music, and dance.... [But] their tolerance of African cultural heritage does not extend to the deepest thoughts and convictions of Africans," Uju says. "Fertility is considered central, so the entire village publicly prays for it right from the start of a marriage."

Uju cites a 2010 USAID report on the number of children desired across the world, the highest being Africa, ranging from 4.8 children per woman in Ghana to 9.1 in Niger and 9.2 in Chad: "...in a country such as Niger, there is hardly any indication of unwanted fertility." She cites another article that says that women in Niger want an average of nine children, while the men say they want eleven. "In other words, women in Niger consider all their babies as wanted (even when pregnancy is unplanned)."

"Amidst all our African afflictions and difficulties, amidst all the socioeconomic and political instabilities, our babies are always a firm symbol of hope, a promise of life, a reason to strive for the legacy of a bright future.

"These facts call into question the much-lamented crisis of 'unmet need' for family planning," Uju concludes. "'Unmet need' has become the phrase used within Western elite circles to speak about the 'appallingly low' prevalence of contraception use in developing countries. It has become the core of their case for multibillion-dollar contraception projects, the scaffold for their most important policies, and their first and last talking points at every population-themed event."[20]

As articulate as she is, Uju never got an audience with Melinda. We do not know if Melinda ever saw Uju's open letter. We do know that Melinda pressed forward as always. Despite the pressure from Catholics ("even threats from Christians," she claims), she declared that she will continue to fight to bring contraception to women across the world. "This will be my life's work," she said in her small, public relations biography, which ends by saying that Bill and Melinda work together with "intelligence, a ruthless business style, and human compassion to make a difference and change the world for the better."

Melinda continued to push vaccines, her safest subject. In a 2009 *PBS* interview with Charlie Rose, she said that the vaccine programs were "primarily in India" and they want to "bring that program to Africa." Their program in India went so well that she and Bill received the Padma Bhushan award, the country's third-highest civilian honor. Regarding vaccines, Melinda told *PBS*, "we're doing six large scale trials right now in the continent of Africa."[21]

Meanwhile, Uju's boldness and gift of articulation gained her more recognition. She was interviewed on *BBC World News* television in 2017 by Australian-raised female anchor Yalda Hakim, a rather aggressive opponent, who challenged Uju early on regarding hundreds of millions of women who do not have access to contraception but should.

> Uju: Who are you to decide, if you don't mind me saying? There isn't a popular demand, ma'am. If you go to Africa, what people are asking for every day . . . You just speak to any ordinary woman and I think contraception might be the tenth thing she says, if that.
>
> Yalda: But it's a basic human right to have access to it. That's why I say that they should have access. . . . And that's part of that cycle of poverty, and dealing with poverty, and overcoming poverty, is it not?

Uju: Well that's kind of a Western solution, isn't it?...If you speak to the ordinary woman on the streets of Africa, what is she asking for? She's asking for food. She's asking for water. She's asking for basic health care. And contraception continues to be about the last thing they would ever think of.

Yalda: But does not that play into the wider conversation about poverty and food. If they have access to contraception...then it deals with the issues of poverty as well.

Uju: That is the Western solution. Why don't you listen to the people first?...Someone from a Western organization...came and put IUDs into women and said "this is what you need to come out of poverty." That is not what African women need. That is not the single indicator to come out of poverty. What Africans need is education.

Yalda: They do, indeed. It's about education as well, so that they understand their basic human rights. It's not just about the West coming in and imposing something.

Uju: According to you. This is colonial talk. So you better be careful expressing it. According to whom?...My lifeline out of poverty was education. It was not contraception. And there are so many other women who have walked the same path as I have....

Yalda: You're then, also generalizing, speaking on behalf of every woman on the continent.

Uju: Well, so are you....

Yalda: But when the United Nations says that more than 200 million don't have access to [contraception], then that's contradicting what you are saying.

Uju: Those are the calculations of the United Nations. But how many of those 200 million women are actually asking for it? There is a difference between what the United Nations now calls the "unmet need" and the "unmet demand."

Yalda: Perhaps they are unaware.

Uju: Well, for someone like yourself—someone so kind and generous from the West, to come tell them that what they need is contraception to come out of poverty—now you give them contraception, and the next day they still don't have work. The following year they still don't have work. So they turn out to be...

Yalda: [Interrupting] Obianuju, uhhh, I really would like to discuss this further with you. We're just ten seconds to go off the air, so thank you very much for joining us.[22]

The British are skilled at the talking points used by Yalda Hakim. Former Prime Minister David Cameron was quoted in the same *Independent* article where Melinda Gates announced her break with traditional Catholicism: "When a woman is prevented from choosing when to have children it is not just a violation of her human rights," said Cameron, "it can fundamentally compromise her chances in life and the opportunities for her children."

Uju has several responses for these British progressives. Firstly, she refutes the "basic human rights" argument. "I challenged this statement," she said, "knowing that basic human rights include life, liberty, and personal security, even according to the Universal Declaration of Human Rights composed by the United Nations." Contraception is not on the list.

Nor does she suffer the arguments of population density, pointing out that three times more British people live in one square mile than in Ethiopia. "With more than three times the population density of Ethiopia," Uju notes, "Britain has more than enough food to feed its population."

She also tires of the UK's argument for population control based on sustainability and carbon emissions. She reveals that the UK's aggressive initiative "Population Matters" shows on its website that "the carbon emissions in the United Kingdom is more than 13.5 times higher than that in Ethiopia."

"Go ahead," Uju writes, "commandeer the world's resources and live self-indulgently, Population Matters seems to be suggesting, so long as you prevent a poor African from being born."

"We are thirsty and they give us condoms! We are hungry and they offer us contraceptive pills! We are sick and they offer us the most modern techniques of abortion! We are naked and they lead us into the arms of sexual hedonism!"

Although Uju was cut off by the *BBC* and only enjoyed a handful of minutes on screen, her story arc took a steep upward curve soon after. She caught the attention of a major publisher. She was picked up by Ignatius Press, a San Francisco–based establishment considered by many to be the world's top publisher of Catholic books in English, whose titles include works by Pope John Paul II and Pope Benedict.[23] Her book *Target Africa* first appeared in 2018 with the subtitle: *Ideological Neocolonialism in the Twenty-First Century*. Princeton professor of law Robert P. George wrote the foreword and referred to Obianuju Ekeocha as "the great Nigerian human rights activist." Her book is hard-hitting and aims at the jugular vein of what George calls the "expressive individualism."

"Like many of the Africans in the 1950s who longed for independence from their colonial masters, I long for independence from our twenty-first century neocolonial masters so that Africans can rule themselves in a manner that befits their values and aspirations," Uju writes in *Target Africa*. "How does practically sterilizing the poorest women in the world give them control over famine, drought, disease, and poverty? It does not make them more educated or more employable. It does not provide food or safe drinking water. It does not make African women happier or more satisfied in their marriages. No. This extensive contraception project will only make them sterile at the cheapest rate possible. This is certainly not what we African women have asked for," she insists. "But in a world of shocking cultural imperialism, it is what our 'betters' have chosen for us."

Uju's words remind us of the invasions by Italy and their call for "civilizing" the savages and barbarians in Ethiopia. The Abyssinians also endured the "advisory" position of the British that was often an underhanded attempt at colonization. Says Uju: "I call these Western meddlers 'neocolonial masters' of the twenty-first century because, much like the colonials of the nineteenth and twentieth centuries, they have taken strategic positions to advise, direct, persuade, and thereby control other nations and, in the process, destroy the cultures and institutions of the countries they claim to be helping.

"Of course, these individuals and organizations are doing the same work of deconstruction in their own countries, where they are redefining sexual identity and marriage, for example. But their ambition is not limited to their own nations. No, they wish to recreate the entire world. As the feminists, eugenicists, abortion activists, gender theorists, and sexual revolutionaries attempt to remake reality in most parts of the Western world, they are skillfully imposing their will on Africa too," she writes. "These are the same ones who are pushing the movement to normalize lesbian, gay, bisexual, and transgender (LGBT) identity and behavior. They are the same ones implicated in various draconian population-control programs around the globe in the name of saving the world.[24]

"It is becoming increasingly evident that a new design for mankind has been hatched in the imagination of the wealthiest class of social engineers and cultural architects in the Western world," Uju writes. "Africans who resist gender ideology and sexual anarchy are truly countercultural," she adds. "What will become of Africa as the social engineers attempt to redesign the human race? Will Africa be chopped off, knocked down, or just reconditioned to accept the new definitions of 'male,' 'female,' and 'marriage'? Will Africans be punished into submission, as are increasing numbers of men and women who have voiced their concerns or objections in Europe and America?

"If my neighbors lost everything in a fire, and I included some condoms in a package of food and blankets I brought them, they would rightly be offended. So why is it acceptable for wealthy Westerners to send along contraceptives with their humanitarian aid after a hurricane or natural disaster? Trying to stop people in the developing world from having children should be considered appalling, especially since doing so is not a development strategy. It is an invasion strategy, and that is the reason Africa must walk away from aid."[25]

Uju then appeals to all Africans to understand their calling. In fact, *they* are the ones in the position to help save the West, not vice versa: "The most precious gift that Africans can give to the world right now is our inherent culture of life. Most Africans understand, by faith and tradition, the inestimable value of human life, the beauty of womanhood, the grace of motherhood, the blessing of married life, and the gift of children. All these have come under great attack in most of the Western world, where abortion on demand is legal, where fertility is considered inconvenient and treated as if it were a disease, where motherhood is devalued and marriage is redefined. Africa can offer the world a refocused view of the dignity of the human person and the goodness of family life, but to do this, we must be confident that we possess something precious."

Uju was pleadingly sincere in her appeal to Melinda: "I see this $4.6 billion buying us unfaithful husbands. I see it buying us streets devoid of the innocent chatter of children. I see it buying us disease and untimely death," she concludes. "Please Melinda, listen to the heartfelt cry of an African woman and mercifully channel your funds to pay for what we *really* need."[26]

These strong arguments are difficult to debate, and perhaps that is why we have seen little of Uju since her brief appearance on BBC. Instead, we hear the same talking points, the best weapons in the West's arsenal repeated again and again. They were used by former Prime Minister David Cameron, speaking for the likes of Melinda and the BBC, who told the *Independent*: "We're not telling anyone what to do. We're giving women and girls the power to decide for themselves," he said. "We're not talking about some kind of Western-imposed population control, forced abortion, or sterilization."[27]

Cameron highlighted freedom and choice as their key points. However, their best argument took a major hit when international news outlets reported the assertion of Kenyan leaders that 2.3 million women had been sterilized without their knowledge and against their will by a vaccine laced with a contraceptive known as HCG.

KENYA'S BISHOPS AND government health ministry "are locked in a heated battle over the safety of a tetanus vaccine that's being administered to women in the country," reported the *Washington Post* on November 14, 2014. The United Nations insisted that its vaccines are safe, but "the country's Catholic leaders say they have proof that the doses given to Kenyan women since March are 'laced' with a fertility inhibiting hormone."[1]

Nearly twenty-five percent of Kenya is Catholic. The Catholic Church operates fifty-two percent of the health care facilities in the nation including fifty-four hospitals, eighty-three health centers, and seventeen medical and nursing schools. The vaccine scandal emerged when Kenyans raised their concerns regarding who the vaccine was targeting and the unusual dosage. Why were only women age fifteen to forty-nine receiving a vaccination for tetanus when boys and men are more likely to get lockjaw from a rusty nail? Why did the vaccine require three large doses over a few months when normal tetanus vaccinations require one booster per ten-year period?

The church leaders called on their people to boycott the vaccine until the matter could be resolved. The bishops' medical advisors were primarily the Kenya Catholic Doctors Association. Their spokesman, Dr. Muhame Ngare, of the Mercy Medical Centre in Nairobi, pulled no punches in describing the problem to the international media. "We sent six samples from around Kenya to laboratories in South Africa. They tested positive for the HCG antigen. They were all laced with HCG." The World Health Organization (WHO), overseeing the vaccination effort, denied the accusations.

Releasing a bulletin about the laced vaccines on behalf of the doctors association, Dr. Ngare, an obstetrician and gynecologist with an MBA, was adamant in his accusations: "This proved right our worst fears; that this WHO campaign is not about eradicating neonatal tetanus but a well-coordinated forceful population control mass sterilization exercise using a proven fertility-regulating vaccine."[2]

The *Washington Post* printed the denials of the UN organizations: "WHO and UNICEF said the 'grave allegations' were 'not backed by evidence.' The Kenyan government has also denied that the vaccination program is a secret mass sterilization effort."

"Both the bishops and health officials agree that if present, the hormone has no business being in the vaccine doses," the *Post* continued. "Several Western Catholic groups, along with organizations identifying as 'pro-life,' have waded into the matter, as has online debunking site Snopes, which rated the claim 'false.'"

Snopes acted as an arbitrator of sorts between the two sides that were forming, the Catholics and the United Nations. Snopes calls itself "the definitive fact-checking and reference source," and clients have included Facebook and ABC. The effort was started by David and Barbara Mikkelson and is now run out of the Mikkelson home in Tacoma, Washington. Snopes positions itself as unbiased, impervious to money or other temptations, and neither for or against religion or the secularism of the UN. It is simply about the facts.

In its investigation, Snopes squared off against Ngare, a Catholic father of three and one of eleven children from a Presbyterian pastor. He vaccinates his kids. "The Catholic Church has been here in Kenya providing health care and vaccinating for 100 years," he said. Ngare chose a medical career at the age of ten after his dog Tommy had a stomach wound and had to be put down by gunshot. The authorities only shot him in the arm. "He ran back to us," Ngare relates, noting that he could see the dog in the yard but was not allowed to go outside to help him. "I wanted to be a veterinary doctor so a dog wouldn't die like that again."[3]

Snopes began its debunking by addressing the accusations that only childbearing women were being targeted. "Neonatal tetanus resulted in the deaths of 550 Kenyan babies in 2013" and, according to UNICEF, "neonatal tetanus represents a very high proportion of the total tetanus disease." Snopes explained that the women were targeted to prevent babies from being born with tetanus.

Ngare had other questions. "Usually we give a series of three shots over two to three years. We give it to anyone who comes in the clinic with an open wound—men, women or children. If this is intended to inoculate children in the womb, why give it to girls starting at 15 years? You cannot get married until you are 18."

Snopes calls this "a good illustration of fallacious thinking." Since five shots are required, starting three years before a girl is married "makes more sense than exposing women who are married but not yet immunized to losing children to tetanus."

David Mikkelson and Snopes then addressed Ngare's original accusation, that the vaccine was a contraceptive: "Dr. Collins Tabu, the head of immunization at Kenya's Health Ministry, refuted the claim and said women immunized under the program in recent years subsequently conceived, prompting Ngare to respond with: 'Either we are lying or the government is lying.'"[4]

Ngare can perhaps be forgiven for not completely trusting the government or the World Health Organization that was funding the government operation. WHO came under investigation from both the UK and the European Union for falsely predicting a swine flu epidemic in 2009, which led to various nations buying and stockpiling $7 billion worth of swine flu vaccines. In an article entitled "Report condemns swine flu experts' ties to big pharma," *The Guardian* explains that the three scientists advising the World Health Organization were on the payroll of the Big Pharma companies selling the vaccines. The corruption accusations were initially reported in the *British Medical Journal*. Editor Fiona Godlee's comments were printed in the *Washington Post*: "For WHO, its credibility has been badly damaged."[5]

Dr. Ngare referenced an early incidence of the HCG hormone used in a vaccine: "...the last time this vaccination with five injections was used was in Mexico in 1993 and Nicaragua and the Philippines in 1994," he said. "It didn't cause miscarriages till three years later," noting that a recent conception by a Kenyan girl was a meaningless counterclaim if the effect can take three years.

DR. WAHOME NGARE

Ngare said that WHO and the United Nations attempted to bring the same anti-fertility vaccine to Kenya in the 1990s. "We alerted the government and it stopped the vaccination. But this time they haven't done so."[6]

Snopes dismisses the 1993 incidents in Mexico, Philippines, and Nicaragua as "false rumors." The reason given is that WHO denied it. "These rumors, apparently initiated by so-called 'pro-life' groups, are completely untrue," concluded Snopes.

The definitive story of the saga in the Philippines and South America was provided by J. A. Miller in a publications for Human Life International (HLI). "During the early 1990s, the World Health Organization has been overseeing massive vaccination campaigns against tetanus in ... Nicaragua, Mexico, and the Philippines," he wrote in 1995. HLI, which then had 60 world affiliates, one day received a report from its Mexican affiliate workers who observed some highly suspicious procedures. Why women and no men? Why multiple booster shots? HLI "obtained several vials of the vaccine and had them analyzed by chemists," says Miller. "Some of the vials were found to contain human chorionic gonadotropin (HCG)."

HCG is produced by an expecting woman and allows her to provide nutrients to a fertilized egg when the tiny baby attaches to the uterine lining. A positive result of pregnancy is determined when a pregnancy test detects HCG. But when a woman is injected with HCG mixed with the tetanus vaccine toxins, the woman's body also identifies HCG as toxic and does not secrete it. So, future fertilized eggs do not get the nutrients they need and the new life dies. Thus, her pregnancies are terminated immediately.

Miller says Human Life International then warned its worldwide affiliates of the issue. "Soon additional reports of vaccines laced with HCG hormones began to drift in from the Philippines, where more than 3.4 million women were recently vaccinated. Similar reports came from Nicaragua…"[7]

It's all in the details. Did the vaccine actually have HCG? Snopes provides some reasons besides UN denials to argue against it. Citing the organization Reproductive Health Matters (changed in 2019 to "Sexual and Reproductive Health Matters" to highlight their "gender diversity" efforts), Snopes alleges that Catholic workers discovered the presence of HCG using only pregnancy kits, which do not work for testing a vaccine. The test requires laboratory technology. When six labs tested the vaccine "the results clearly showed that the vaccines did not contain HCG."[8]

Miller and HLI tell a different story: "Confronted with the results of laboratory tests which detected its presence in three of the four vials of tetanus toxoid examined, the World Health Organization and the [Kenyan] Department of Health scoffed at the evidence coming from 'right-to-life and Catholic' sources. Four new vials of the tetanus vaccine were submitted by the Department of Health to St. Luke's (Lutheran) Medical Center in Manila—and all four vials tested positive for HCG."

Snopes again quotes Reproductive Health Matters: "The low levels of HCG-like activity seen in some places were the result of false positive reactions." According to UNICEF, any trace of HCG would be "an extremely rare contamination."

Miller said the argument changed from outright denial to "insignificant" amounts of HCG and "false positives," which means that the contamination was derived from the manufacturing process. Another thirty women were tested in the Philippines after being vaccinated and "twenty-six tested positive for high levels of anti-HCG," he wrote. "The WHO and the [department of health] had no answers."[9]

Regarding Dr. Ngare's charges of sterilization attempts in those countries as well as Kenya more recently, Snopes called it "conspiracy theory." But perhaps the dog-loving Ngare can be forgiven for entertaining conspiracy theories when only a year before the tetanus scandal in Kenya, it was revealed that 130,000 Ethiopians living in Israel were subjected to similar forced contraceptive practices.

Forbes magazine discussed the global headlines that said "a report revealing African women immigrating to Israel were subjected to mandatory contraceptive injections, effectively amounting to forced (if temporary) sterilization . . ." The Ethiopian-Israeli population has historically been poor but healthy and growing, although the birthrate decreased twenty percent in the past decade. "Advocacy groups now claim this decline is the result of a birth control program forced upon Ethiopian immigrant women."

"Israel has acknowledged the issue (without admitting any wrongdoing)," said *Forbes*, "and has vowed institutional changes in healthcare for immigrants." The prestigious financial magazine adds: "There is no excuse for depriving women sovereignty over their own reproductive choices." *Forbes* calls the development "shocking." While saying it is not comparable in scale to Jews' past sufferings, *Forbes* also says that "Israel's implicit intent to limit 'burdensome' (read: undesirable) portions of the population recalls the dark eugenics experiments of World War II."[10]

But what about the actual science in Kenya? Do the vaccines contain HCG? Have the tests been done? What does Snopes—dedicated to just the facts and not bias, perspective, worldview, or opinion—tell us about the laboratories and testing?

Before wading into that controversy, let us mention here that Dr. Ngare's call for a boycott extended beyond tetanus. He and the bishops warned against the polio vaccine, the holy grail of all vaccinations.

"Africa will mark one year without polio on Tuesday," reported *NPR*. "But last week...[Kenya's] Catholic bishops declared a boycott of the World Health Organization's [polio] vaccination campaign, saying they needed to 'test' whether ingredients contain a derivative of estrogen. Dr. Wahome Ngare of the Kenyan Catholic Doctors

Association alleged that the presence of the female hormone could sterilize children."

Oddly, *NPR* made no mention of the blazing tetanus vaccine controversy occurring around the same time, a campaign losing steam due to the Catholic boycott. Dr. Ngare's suspicion was raised "by WHO's decision to blanket Kenya with polio vaccines, well over and above routine injections," reported *NPR*. "The WHO says there's no harm in giving extra vaccines to children who are already vaccinated."

In fairness, *NPR* represents Ngare as pro-vaccine in general: "He administers vaccines to his patients in his clinic. His children are vaccinated. 'Regular immunizations are safe and they must continue,' he says. 'You must immunize your child.'"

"He raises the specter of eugenics—sterilizing segments of human populations," writes *NPR* reporter Gregory Warner. "He put forth other objections as well: 'There are all sorts of stories out there,' he told me. 'Vaccines can cause autism. Vaccines have been used for spread of HIV. There are some cancer-causing viruses that you'd find in vaccines. So there are a lot of stories. Some of them we don't know whether they're true or not.'"

Says the reporter Warner: "I pointed out to him that research has shown that claims of vaccines being linked to autism and HIV and cancer are in fact not true. His response: 'We could debate this forever.'"[11]

Once again, Ngare is being positioned, rightly or wrongly, as a "conspiracy theorist." And now he and the bishops are calling off vaccinations for polio, considered, by far, the most effective of all vaccines, created by the most famous of all vaccination doctors, Jonas Salk. Take your choice, the famous inventor who made the cover of *Time* Magazine—the "Father of Vaccines," or an unknown whistleblower in Africa. Dr. Ngare can, perhaps, be forgiven for his conspiracies regarding the polio vaccine if we consider Jonas Salk's own words. Cultural critic Jay Dyer's review of a book by Salk revealed that the Father of Vaccines suggests the possibility of injecting harmful viruses into humans, specifically reproductive organs. Salk writes: "'Mutations' as here defined, would also be produced by the introduction, either naturally or experimentally, of a virus into a sperm or egg cell, the genetic information of which would then be incorporated in either the DNA or the RNA and transmitted. Such new information might be advantageous or disadvantageous."[12]

Salk writes this statement on page 43 of his book with the very eugenic-sounding title: *The Survival of the Wisest*. Who gets to receive Salk's negative viruses? He doesn't say. He does note in the same short book that "relativistic" thinking is better than "anti-evolutionary" value judgments—so he may not care for the Catholics. "Absolutists are extremists who see life exclusively from their own narrow, rigid viewpoint" and "may be destroyed by their own inability to participate in the evolutionary process." If you "resist evolution" it leads to "nonsurvival and nonexistence."

"When we speak of the survival of the wisest," he concludes, "by wisest we mean those who comprehend the survival-evolutionary process, as well as the being-becoming process, and who make choices such as enhance the possibility of existence rather than nonexistence, recognizing evolution as an essential and inexorable continuum of growth and development."[13]

He may have been a great scientist. I don't know, but he was an awful writer—albeit a frightening one. His book is another difficult one to find. I traveled a few hours to see one firsthand.

Regarding the actual testing of the tetanus vaccine in Kenya, the process started with the bishops, the doctors association, and Dr. Ngare sending six samples for testing in South Africa. Their joint statement stated that the vaccine is "laced with the Beta-HCG hormone."

The largest Catholic doctors organization in the world, Mater-Care, based in Canada, backed Ngare and the bishops, calling the vaccination program "evil," according to MaterCare's Harvard-educated founder Dr. Robert Walley. The *Washington Post* printed this important endorsement of Ngare.[14] Snopes cited UNICEF's refutation, saying that the analyzers used were for blood and urine, not for vaccines. But Ngare maintained that a retest was difficult, as the first test required surreptitiously obtaining samples by devout Catholics at the hospital. He said that this vaccine was lacking "the usual fanfare of government publicity" and instead "only a few operatives from the government are allowed to give it out. They come with a police escort."

To resolve the mistrust, both the Catholic doctors and the government's health department agreed to do a second test by a joint committee of Catholic, government, and independent medical experts. But the results were again debated. Dr. Stephen Karanja, another official with the Kenya Catholic Doctors Association, submitted to the committee the new findings of HCG in the vaccine, calling it "nothing short of a scheme to forcefully render women incapable of bearing children." Conversely, the health department submitted its test results to the committee, showing no trace of HCG.[15]

A leader of the committee lamented: "We are at loss about who to believe since both sides have tabled conflicting results." However, MaterCare founder Robert Walley felt like he had seen enough evidence to switch sides. "The bishops did the responsible thing in raising concerns," Walley said. "But I have checked with experts in Australia and America and confirmed the information the Catholic doctors put out was not right."

For Kenya's new joint committee, six laboratories ran results. One lab, Lancet Kenya, run by Dr. Ahmed Kalebi, did not find any HCG. "I've checked results from the other five labs and these give very consistent findings to what we have," he said, "except for two samples…at Pathcare." So once again, the methods of the testing were questioned. Dr. Ngare said the second tests "raise suspicion that the vaccine is laced with HCG, more so the results of Pathcare that were way above the lab cut-off."[16]

Therefore, all parties called for a *third* round of testing. Meanwhile, the secretary general of the teacher's union of Kenya called for a boycott of the tetanus vaccine. "A generation will come when we will not have children to teach," he said. "We will, therefore, end up with no jobs."[17]

The *Washington Post* reported that the Kenyan Parliament itself moved to oversee the third test of the vaccine, causing the newspaper to ask if "the bishops' accusations will hold up to continued scrutiny?" But, in the same breath, it also alluded to the eugenics skeleton in America's past. "Forced, involuntary sterilization—particularly targeting certain groups, such as the poor, the mentally ill or the HIV positive—has a long and shameful history, including in the United States."[18]

Life Site News reported that the tests commissioned by the Kenyan Parliament—the third round of tests—showed that three of the fifty-nine vials of the vaccine samples contained the HCG hormone. "Local news media...reported this [result] as if it resolved the controversial issue [but] the Kenyan Conference of Catholic Bishops issued a 19-point statement questioning the test claims" and insisted no more vaccines be administered until they are proven safe.

The formal statement, signed by the chairman of the conference, Cardinal John Njue, said none of the samples came from the early campaign, where HCG was first detected, thereby giving WHO an opportunity to change the later vaccine samples. The bishops also contended that the third test was to involve equal amounts of samples from the government and the bishops. Of the bishops' nine samples, three contained HCG. When the government saw the results, it added forty more vials to the samples and delayed the committee's report one week to include the extra findings.[19]

Once again, the two groups were at an impasse. Then, Dr. Ngare and his colleague, Dr. Karanja, were summoned to appear before the Preliminary Inquiry Committee of the Kenya Medical Practitioners, which determines licensure. At this same time, one of the labs that detected HCG in the third round of testing, Agriq-Quest Ltd, was stripped of its accreditation. *Business Daily Africa* reported that a former employee, who requested anonymity, claimed that "the lab lacked capacity to carry out the tests it was handling for its clients." Agriq-Quest, according to Snopes, claimed that the government had withheld a large sum for their lab services due to its "refusal to doctor results in favor" of the Department of Health. Snopes said that "no evidence has been offered to suggest that narrative was anything other than a desperate PR move by a business whose accreditation had been revoked."[20]

Health Impact News interviewed a spokesman for Agriq-Quest, which has a headquarters in the Netherlands as well as Kenya. Asked if its labs had the necessary equipment for testing HCG, the spokesman replied: "Yes, the method of choice was HPLC (High Performance

Liquid Chromatography). We have three HPLC machines and we developed and validated the method." This same spokesman said that three of six vials tested had the HCG hormone. "We reported our preliminary findings to the joint committee. The committee was disbanded before the final report was presented."

"Our license was not suspended. We continue to run the laboratory," the Agriq-Quest spokesman added, saying that the news about licensing had to do with "soil and wastewater" issues of a local concern, not the lab. "They suspended the accreditation which we know was due to other influence and we decided we did not require it anymore and withdrew from it."

"We feel we were right in our analysis and that the vaccines were contaminated with beta HCG," the spokesman continued. "No kind of intimidation will hide this and take this scientific fact away. What happened was a systematic scheme to destroy the credibility of the laboratory and cast doubt on the tests since they did not have the capacity to challenge the science and method used to analyze the vaccines." Dr. Ngare agreed. "They only withdrew their local accreditation, which is of little consequence to the functionality of the laboratory. It was most likely a preemptive move to put doubt in the results just in case the results are ever published in a scientific paper as we have done."

Ngare believes that the licensure hearing he and his colleague were summoned to appear before was a similar show trial. They were given "a long lecture on the importance of vaccines" but heard nothing further. "My feeling is that the sermons were used to create a certain impression among the public—that we were summoned by the board for disciplinary proceedings [but] we have never spoken thereafter. A very clever political trick, I must admit."[21]

In 2017, three years after the initial controversy, the former prime minister of Kenya, Raila Odinga, said: "Today, we can confirm to the country that the Catholic Church was right." The story was reported by *Agence de Presse*, the wire service of France, which added: "According to Odinga, the government, for some mysterious reason, was hell bent on misleading the country, while intentionally sterilizing Kenyan girls and women."

Ngare assured the media that the Catholic health providers will continue to test vaccinations "so that they will not poison our people in the future." But MaterCare's Dr. Walley continues to believe the fears are groundless, saying his fellow Catholic doctors "got confused, I think, by the reports from Mexico and India about sterilization campaigns."[22] In fact, two years after the Kenya controversy, India's Health Department cut all ties with the Gates Foundation regarding vaccinations. *The Economic Times* reported that officials in India grew alarmed over conflict-of-interest problems with Big Pharma and Gates after conducting and publishing a study entitled "Philanthropic Power and Development—Who shapes the agenda?" The study warned of "the growing influence of the large philanthropic foundations, especially the Bill & Melinda Gates Foundation." Only two years earlier, Bill and Melinda Gates had been given India's third-highest civilian award. "We have always said foreign influence in our domestic policies must be avoided," said a spokesman for a sovereignty advocacy group in India.[23]

For Dr. Ngare and those concerned about vaccine tampering, various tests and presentations of "evidence" from the other side no longer have much staying power. "Why should anyone be surprised," he said. "They did it in South America." The *Washington Post*'s initial 2014 article said the matter was "unresolved" but did give some resolution by pointing to the "online debunking site Snopes, which rated the claim 'false.'"

Snopes, which updated its report in 2018, has this final word on the Agriq-Quest claim of "foul play" and Kenya's vaccine scandal: "…the claim of a government's mandating doctored results to sell a secret sterilization program has not been ignored by conspiracy-minded websites…"[24] Snopes, of course, refers to itself not as a website that is conspiracy-minded or biased or has malice toward traditionalists, progressives, or any other worldview. It refers to itself as "scholarly and reliable" and added Facebook as a client. However, two years after Snopes's negative assessment of the Catholic bishops and doctors, the *Daily Mail* released a rather embarrassing article with the long but interesting title: "Facebook 'fact checker' who will arbitrate on 'fake news' is accused of defrauding website to pay for prostitutes—and its staff includes an escort–porn star and 'Vice Vixen domme.'"

Snopes founder David Mikkelson found himself on the receiving end of a divorce from cofounder Barbara Mikkelson. Her legal filings, according to the *Daily Mail,* stated that he "embezzled $98,000 of company money and spent it on 'himself and prostitutes.'" His new wife, Elyssa Young, a "long-time escort and porn star," is on staff at Snopes. The *Daily Mail* gives quite a few details of her escort web page. "While David Mikkelson has denied that Snopes takes any political position, his new wife has a background in politics," reports the newspaper. She ran for congress and bashed her Republican opponent, handing out "cards and condoms stamped with the slogan 'Don't get screwed again.'"...But she received "a bad spot of media attention after Young misspelled her Republican opponent's name on her campaign website."

"One of the lead fact-checkers, Kim LaCapria, has also been a sex-and-fetish blogger who went by the pseudonym 'Vice Vixen.'" the *Daily Mail* reported. "She described her blog as a lifestyle website 'with a specific focus on naughtiness, sin, carnal pursuits, and general hedonism.'" She wrote on her blog that she "has posted on Snopes.com while smoking pot."

Regarding financial details of the divorce: "David wanted his salary raised from $240,000 to $360,000—arguing that this would still put him below the 'industry standards' and that he should be paid up to $720,000 a year....So bitter was the dispute, that they even fell out over the arbiter they had appointed to settle disputes, meaning that Facebook's arbiter cannot even agree on its own arbiter."[25]

A writer for *Forbes* balked at Mikkelson's refusal to comment on the *Daily Mail* article because of a pending lawsuit. "In short, when someone attempted to fact check the fact checker, the response was the equivalent of 'it's secret.'"[26]

THE TWO OPPONENTS in Kenya's vaccination scandal have not been able to reconcile. "They are all my good friends on both sides," said the Lancet Lab director. "Now they are [denouncing] each other."

Robert Walley, the Harvard-trained doctor and founder of Mater-Care, who has supported both sides at one time or another, ultimately struggled with the idea of United Nations organizations being involved in a conspiracy to hurt others. "The World Health Organization and UNICEF are intensely regulated organizations, mandated to improve the physical and social well-being of women and children throughout the world," he said. "[They are] therefore unlikely to be involved in giving a contraceptive vaccine disguised as a tetanus vaccine. This would amount to a gross violation of human rights."[1]

This is generally what the argument comes down to. It is almost impossible to believe that "nice" people would do such bad things. Could certain doctors in their benign white jackets perform such dark deeds? What about UN workers called to help the helpless? It doesn't seem possible. What about the billionaire philanthropists whose friendly faces we see on a regular basis? To believe the HCG-laced vaccine story is to open the door to believing other possibilities of sinister actions taken by people who command a tremendous amount of respect and an enormous amount of power.

New York Times columnist Ross Douthat feels your pain. "It's easy for us to look back and pass judgment on yesterday's eugenicists. It's harder to acknowledge what we have in common with them," he writes, listing as shared characteristics a "desire for mastery and control" and "a belief in our own fundamental goodness, no matter to what end our mastery is turned."

"The American elite's pre-World War II commitment to breeding out the 'unfit'—defined variously as racial minorities, low-I.Q. whites, [etc.]—is a story that defies easy stereotypes about progress and enlightenment," Douthat notes. "But these same eugenicists were often political and social liberals—advocates of social reform, partisans of science . . ." He quotes from the recent *Yale Alumni Magazine,* which was attempting to come to terms with a well-known eugenicist alum: "They weren't sinister characters out of some darkly lighted noir film about Nazi sympathizers," the writer explains, "but environmentalists, peace activists, fitness buffs, healthy-living enthusiasts, inventors and family men."

The *New York Times* columnist continues: "From Teddy Roosevelt to the Planned Parenthood founder Margaret Sanger, fears about 'race suicide' and 'human weeds' were common among self-conscious progressives, who saw the quest for a better gene pool as of a piece with their broader dream of human advancement." He provides a final foreboding comment: ". . . the elimination or pre-emption, through careful reproductive planning, of the weaker members of the human species—has become a more realistic possibility than it ever was in the 1920s and '30s."[2]

Douthat encourages us not to look on the mere surface: science types, sustainability activists, heath advocates, wonderful family people—none of those examples should keep us from asking the difficult questions. We should examine the facts and the documentation and draw our own conclusions.

The problem is, in many cases, as we saw in the Kenya vaccine saga, both sides deal with "evidence" and come to different conclusions based on their premises and predispositions—their worldview or their "religion," if you will. When facts and evidence are not enough, where do we look? We look for that inner voice, that message from a place beyond just this sensory world. We go to our "holy of holies."

Where does a Christian like Dr. Wahome Ngare go? We know about the Christian holy of holies. This book has traced the story of the sacred small room in Israel containing the Ark of the Covenant, Ethiopia's claim to be its custodian after Israel fell, and the Ethiopian belief in the ultimate fulfillment of the words of God engraved in stone inside the Ark—Jesus the Word incarnate, born of Mary. Since Jesus has made each of us temples, we pray in our "little holy of holies" in the sense that Christ dwells within us. So for Christians, their holy of holies is Jesus Christ, with the primary referent in terms of land or object being the tabernacle and the Ark.

As is turns out, those with the opposite worldview of Dr. Ngare, those extreme "expressive individualists" identified by Princeton law professor Robert George, the secularists who see the United Nations' programs and its agenda as a fulfillment of their ultimate hopes—they too have a holy of holies.

"This little speck on earth is becoming a holy ground," said Robert Muller, called by some the "philosopher of the United Nations," a forty-year veteran and the UN Assistant Secretary-General. He wasn't referring just to the United Nations building in New York City. The ultimate holy spot is the United Nations' "Meditation Room" housed within the building. This room was commissioned by the UN's first Secretary-General, Trygve Lie, in 1949 and established, developed, and finished by his successor, Dag Hammarskjöld, who received a third of the funding for the room from John D. Rockefeller.[3]

"It is not the center of the house in a physical sense, but it should be the center in the spiritual sense," said Hammarskjöld. Muller tells us, "Dag Hammarskjöld, the rational Nordic economist, had ended up as a mystic. He too held at the end of his life that spirituality was the ultimate key to our earthly fate in time and space." Dag the mystic took great pains to design the room with exact precision. Which was easy. Except for one fresco on the wall, the thirty-by-eighteen foot room has only one object or decoration in the center: a six-ton black rectangular slab of rock with dimensions mirroring that of the

Ark of the Covenant, in a room with similar dimensions to Israel's holy of holies.

The centerpiece in 1955 was originally from Africa, an 800-pound, thirty-seven-inch-wide upright section of an agba tree. Curiously, it was replaced after two years with a Nordic dark-gray block of crystalline iron ore from Sweden—the largest of its kind ever mined. "The stone in the middle of the room reminds us also of the firm and permanent in a world of movement and change," wrote Hammarskjöld. "We may see it as an altar, empty not because there is no God, not because it is an altar to an unknown god, but because it is dedicated to the God whom man worships under many names and in many forms."[4]

What are those names? We will get more specific as we go. But one rather disturbing name has emerged on the internet the past few years. Various bloggers claim that the Meditation Room is maintained and run by the Lucis Trust and that Lucis stands for "Lucifer." This claim is, in fact, a curious rabbit trail that I have been following for over ten years. I went to the LucisTrust.org website. They discuss the issue: "There are comments on the World Wide Web claiming that the Lucis Trust was once called the Lucifer Trust. Such was never the case." A pretty straightforward denial. I'm sure they are nice people. They are in fact related in various ways to the United Nations, as an official NGO (non-governmental agency) and on the Roster of the United Nations Economic and Social Council. Their mission statement calls for "a new and better way of life for everyone in the world based on the fulfillment of the divine plan for humanity." Okay. Not specifically Christian, but they sound rather harmless.[5]

DAG HAMMARSKJÖLD

When I flew from New York to Axum two years ago, I didn't think then about how I was travelling from one type of ark to another. On the last day of my lengthy stay, I decided to take an evening walk from my hotel—a fairly new and nice little place, used by a lot of Western tourists. I decided to head in the direction of St. Mary of Zion Church, the complex where the Ark is kept. Not far into my two-mile walk, I looked up to see a billboard that shocked me. There are not many billboards in Axum in general. You are as likely to see a goat in the street as a nice car. And the tone of the city is strongly Christian. No mosques are allowed by law. The billboard featured an ad for condoms. Three young Ethiopian girls, drawn by an artist, hand each other condoms in secretive fashion. I was surprised to see this in Ethiopia at all, much less the holy city of Axum. I then found out that six months prior, Melinda Gates had been a guest at my very same hotel.

Is Bill Gates evil? Is Melinda Gates evil? This is a difficult question to ask, and the best way to start is to acknowledge my Christian faith, which teaches that all of us struggle with being evil or acting in evil ways at various times. Do I think Bill and Melinda are conspiring in back rooms to depopulate only darker races? I doubt it. (Well, Bill maybe.) Somebody is probably doing that, but my guess is that Bill and Melinda are admirable proponents of an ideology they believe is helping the world. And when they run into a set of facts that challenge their ideology, they do what many of us do at times. They block it out.

But somebody out there may be cooking up evil. Who knows? And how does one catch them? In my quest ten years ago to dig up more on the Lucis Trust, I learned that the Bill and Melinda Gates Foundation is a donor. The Lucis Trust website showed them as a "Financial Partner" with a Lucis subsidiary, the New Group of World Servers. The Lucis website says "Men of goodwill who co-operate form part of the New Group of World Servers which is working to implement the Plan."

What is "the Plan"? They don't specifically say, but "ultimate world unity" is mentioned in the same paragraph. Also, we learn the following: "Behind these leaders and the co-operating men of goodwill are the Custodians of the Plan, 'the inner spiritual Government of the Planet.'" Whatever the unity is, the web page makes a point to say "this kingdom is not a Christian kingdom," but rather "these are the people who are building the new world order." They are also called "Enlightened Ones."[6]

I'm sure Bill and Melinda were flattered. I also suspect their thirty PR staffers got to work scrubbing the site as they are no longer listed as financial partners. In fact, the list no longer exists on the website. Neither does the article thanking "George Soros" and "Bill Gates" and saying "the money energy is beginning to flow into new channels." You can't even find it on the Wayback Machine, the archive of the internet. However, ten years ago, I had an inkling this documentation might disappear, so I took screenshots of all of the information. The files are still in my possession.[7]

Are the Gateses evil? Again, this is a difficult way to phrase the question. Is Planned Parenthood evil? Was Margaret Sanger evil, the eugenicist who founded the largest performer of abortions? For those who believe that abortion is murder, who know it involves killing or dismembering a child in the womb, who detest the idea of population control based on class, ability, or genetic strength—the answer is a resounding yes. Do the people running Planned Parenthood today think they are evil? No. And they dress nicely.

The Gateses also dress well. And they seem to really believe that their efforts are for the good. As you know, the story of Bill Gates is as follows: a middle-class computer geek becomes an overnight billionaire, and one day he wakes up out of nowhere in his forties and decides to take on overpopulation. But his handlers have kept you from the rest of the story. Bill committed another gaffe in 2006 when he gave an interview to Bill Moyers. He said the following:

"When I was growing up, my parents were always involved in various volunteer things. My dad was head of Planned Parenthood. And it was very controversial to be involved with that. And so it's fascinating. At the dinner table, my parents are very good at sharing the things that they were doing. And almost treating us like adults, talking about that."[8]

No, Bill Gates didn't just decide one day later in life to take on overpopulation. He was raised from childhood to believe overpopulation was the key problem for humanity. He was discipled by a disciple of Margaret Sanger.

Overpopulation. "It's an interest he's had since he was a kid," Bill Gates, Sr., told *Salon.com*.[9]

We never hear about this again from Bill Gates. He provides a seven-page interview on his late father in 2015 and did not mention Planned Parenthood, although several other boards his father sat on were named. What did Bill mean exactly by "My dad was head of Planned Parenthood"? Did he mean the local chapter? We learn from *Salon* that Bill Gates, Sr., was a member of the *national* board of directors of Planned Parenthood. Let that sink in. Such a nonprofit empire is controlled by its board of directors. They have more power than Planned Parenthood's president, a position they appoint. This fact means that there was no person on earth with more power over the control, population control efforts, abortion operations, or Planned Parenthood assets ($2.2 billion today) than Bill Gates's father. He shared that power with a handful of others.[10]

What did Bill Jr. mean by "head of Planned Parenthood"? Perhaps his father was chairman of the board for a time. I could find no records to document that fact.

Bill Gates, Sr., as much as any person in the world, had the power and position to advance the legacy of Margaret Sanger, the woman who openly called for using birth control and sterilization to eliminate "human waste" and "create a race of thoroughbreds." In her *Birth Control Review* she promoted Nazi eugenics and white supremacy. Sanger famously said: "The most merciful thing that the large family does to one of its infant members is to kill it." How did Bill Gates's father view Margaret Sanger? According to an official Planned Parenthood history: "Our founder, Margaret Sanger, was a woman of heroic accomplishments, and like all heroes, she was also complex and imperfect."[11]

"My dad was a large presence, both physically and his wisdom," said Bill, noting that Bill Sr. was "good at stepping back and seeing the broad picture." In a tribute video, he said his father was a leader in everything he did. He closed with this comment to Dad: "You really got the foundation going and put it in a direction that's made it incredibly successful."[12]

Now we can see why friendly little Bill Gates was the leader who called together the billionaire oligarchs, the world's richest people, to discuss depopulation. What about the others attending that 2009 meeting, such as David Rockefeller? It goes from bad to worse. The Rockefeller Foundation funded Margaret Sanger in her early years. A little research on the HCG vaccine that sterilizes women also brings to the fore the Rockefeller family. I tracked down the Rockefeller Foundation's 1968 Annual Report. On page 52 it calls for "progress on immunological methods, such as vaccines, to reduce fertility." Their 1988 Annual Report cites a large grant given to India for "a large anti-fertility vaccine for women." Another generous grant is listed on page 56 "for research on a potential contraceptive vaccine based on beta-HCG synthesized bacteria"—just a few years before the 1993 experiments in Mexico, Nicaragua, and the Philippines.[13]

Let's look at one more member of the famous 2009 meeting of oligarchs in Manhattan, home of the Nordic stone ark—Ted Turner. The founder of CNN has been concerned about overpopulation for decades. In 1996 he told *Audubon* magazine: "We're all five billion of us on this little earth swimming around in space, and there's too many of us," he said. His goal is "a much smaller population" where, over time, "we could cut back to 250 million–350 million people."[14]

Turner's longings are memorialized by a monument of huge, druid-like stone tablets that sit atop a rural hill in Elbert County, Georgia, thirty minutes from CNN headquarters. Yoko Ono wrote a musical score with John Cage in three movements to honor these "Georgia Guidestones," which proclaim in eight languages the "Ten Guides" for the six billion people [then] on earth.[15]

The First Guide says in engraved script: "Maintain humanity under 500,000,000 in perpetual balance with nature."

There are no instructions for how to get from several billion down to 500 million people, causing us to wonder what kinds of plans were being made by Turner, Gates, Rockefeller, and the others at their secret meeting in 2009.

The United Nations Environment Program (UNEP) quoted an expert in its *Global Biodiversity Assessment* report: "A reasonable estimate for an industrialized world society at the present North American material standard of living would be 1 billion. At the more frugal European standard of living, 2 to 3 billion would be possible."[16]

Some high-profile figures, however, have called for a deliberate attempt by world leaders to kill off large segments of the population. In a 1991 United Nations publication, world famous oceanographer Jacques Cousteau said: "It's terrible to have to say this: world population must be stabilized, and to do that we must eliminate 350,000 people per day." Prince Philip, royal spouse of Queen Elizabeth, declared his ambition to solve the "population explosion" by being reincarnated as a "particularly deadly virus." Bertrand Russell, the famous atheist philosopher and humanist leader, who is celebrated worldwide by population control institutions, provided a careful, reasoned quote to help understand how rational people just might consider eliminating half of humanity.

"I do not at all pretend that birth control is the only way in which population can be kept from increasing," wrote Russell in *The Impact of Science on Society*. "War so far has had no great effect on this increase... perhaps a bacteriological war may prove more effective. If a Black Death could be spread throughout the world once in every generation, survivors could procreate freely without making the world too full...the state of affairs might be somewhat unpleasant, but what of it? Really high-minded people are indifferent to suffering, especially that of other people's."[17]

Bertrand Russell received the Nobel Prize for Literature. He was, by all accounts, a cordial man. And he dressed nicely.

Again, it is difficult for all of us to imagine "nice" people thinking this way or acting upon it. However, the elite mentality has always been with us, since Plato wrote his *Republic* 2,300 years ago. Every kid studies this book at prep schools like Bill Gates attended. This most famous of Greek philosophers told us that the ruling class is made up of those individuals "whose aim will be to preserve the average of population." He further states: "There are many other things which they will have to consider, such as the effects of wars and diseases and any similar agencies, in order as far as this is possible to prevent the State from becoming either too large or too small."

Plato adds that population control must be done in secret—what you might call a conspiracy. "Now these goings on must be a secret which the rulers only know, or there will be a further danger of our herd...breaking out into rebellion."[18]

In his 2003 memoirs, David Rockefeller does nothing to dispel the notion that Plato's *Republic* is the oligarch's go-to playbook: "Some even believe we are part of a secret cabal working against the best interests of the United States, characterizing my family and me as 'internationalists' and of conspiring with others around the world to build a more integrated global political and economic structure— one world, if you will. If that is the charge, I stand guilty, and I am proud of it."[19]

The Rockefellers have another black mark on their record that is particularly egregious. Dr. Gregory Pincus, who helped Sanger develop the birth control pill, studied and worked with the Rockefeller-funded Kaiser Wilhelm Institute, exposed for sterilizing 600 French African children and closely associating with the Nazi eugenics program. The Kaiser Wilhelm Institute was in fact the primary driver of eugenics in Hitler's Third Reich, overseeing a complex of hospitals and research centers, including the Kaiser Wilhelm Institute of Anthropology, Human Heredity, and Eugenics. Hitler was highly influenced by the first director, Eugen Fischer, and his two-volume *Principles of Human Heredity and Race Hygiene.* Many ideas from this book reappear in Hitler's *Mein Kampf.* Dr. Karin Magnussen conducted experiments at the Kaiser Wilhelm Institute on eye color to prove Nazi racial theories, and her eye specimens were supplied from concentration camps by famous Nazi Dr. Joseph Mengele. When funding began to fall, the Kaiser Wilhelm Institute's eugenics center looked to the Rockefellers, who provided more support.[20]

Hitler is well-known for his obsession with the occult. That obsession led to his quest to find the Ark of the Covenant, a journey made famous by the blockbuster Spielberg-Lucas movie *Raiders of the Lost Ark*. What caused Hitler to be so fascinated with the occult? Many credit Hitler's obsession to nineteenth century author and occultist Helena Blavatsky, a Russian immigrant and self-proclaimed levitating psychic who founded the occult and spiritualist movement called Theosophy, which became wildly popular, especially in Germany. She is "widely considered the 'mother' of New Age spirituality as well as a touchstone in the development of Nazi paganism and the chief popularizer of the swastika as a mystical symbol," writes Jonah Goldberg in *National Review*.[21]

"The occult revival in Germany and in Europe in general in the late nineteenth and early twentieth centuries led to a remarkable growth of Theosophic lodges as well as other occult groups," writes author C. M. Vasey. He says there are "parallels between Blavatsky's esoteric thought and Hitler's racial ideology" and connects Blavatsky's "Cyclopean eye" and the elevation of the Aryan race with themes later championed by Hitler.[22]

Blavatsky hardly concealed the true focus of her occult leanings. In an 1888 book she writes: "It is but natural...to view Satan, the Serpent of Genesis, as the real creator and benefactor, the Father of Spiritual mankind." In another passage she extols "the 'Harbinger of Light,' bright radiant Lucifer," who opened the eyes of Adam.[23]

Blavatsky's Theosophy magazine *The Messenger* was edited by Alice Bailey, who called the levitating admirer of Satan her mentor, dedicating one of her books to Blavatsky, "that great disciple who lighted her torch in the east and brought the light to Europe and America." Bailey went on to found the Lucis Trust, and Blavatsky's works are promoted on the Lucis Trust website. Another follower of Alice Bailey was Robert Muller, mentioned earlier as United Nations Assistant Secretary-General under the first two UN secretary-generals who established the United Nations Meditation Room. He is known as the "father of global education," and his Robert Muller schools are certified UN institutions. Today's Common Core Curriculum is sometimes traced to his work, as he wrote

"The Robert Muller School World Core Curriculum Manual," which earned him a UNESCO prize for Peace Education.

MADAM HELENA BLAVATSKY

The preface to Muller's manual says the following: "The underlying philosophy upon which the Robert Muller School is based will be found in the teachings set forth in the books of Alice A. Bailey, by the Tibetan teacher, Djwhal Khul." (A different version of the curriculum is generally available, but this original version that won him the award, with the infamous preface, is difficult to find. It is not for sale online. Only three libraries list it. I called and had the preface emailed to me.)[24]

So, this man closely related to the United Nations Meditation Room bases his curriculum on writings by the founder of the Lucis Trust, Alice Bailey. The Tibetan teacher that the preface mentions is, in fact, a channeled spirit that Bailey claimed inspired her to write her books using telepathy. Muller also spoke for the Lucis Trust's Arcane School in 1979. The Lucis Trust names as its primary mission advancing the teachings of Alice Bailey, but also includes United Nations support as a key component to their work. The Lucis website displays a great many of Bailey's beliefs on its site. But certain Alice Bailey teachings listed on the site a few years ago are discoverable now only on the Wayback Machine. In 2000, the site noted that Bailey and her followers at Lucis look for the "return of the 'World Teacher,' the Coming One Who will return to lead humanity into a new age and into a heightened consciousness." In 1998 the website had another interesting sentence: "Today the reappearance of the World Teacher, the Christ, is expected by millions, not only by those of Christian faith but by those of every faith who expect the Avatar under other names—the Lord Maitreya, Krishna, Messiah, Imam Mahdi and the Bodhisattva."[25]

The Lucis Trust is headquartered at 866 United Nations Plaza and claims 6,000 members. It is associated with the UN Meditation Room, which the authors of *Spiritual Politics* call "one of the holiest of holies on the planet." A Lucis-affiliated magazine says that "the Charter of the UN is the Ten Commandments of nation-states." What is the official relationship between the United Nations Meditation Room and Lucis? Some say they are the "custodian" of the room. Others say they "maintain" the room. I could not find any documentation, although their site does show that their affiliated meditation groups hold meetings there on a regular basis. Certainly, there is a strong connection between Lucis, Alice Bailey, and Robert Muller, the "philosopher of the United Nations" and the "father of global education." And the Lucis Trust is, of course, an official NGO of the UN and on the Roster of the United Nations Economic and Social Council.[26*]

To say Lucis has an official connection to the UN Meditation Room, without current documentation, might identify someone as a "conspiracist" in the same way the site admonishes those who believe Lucis Trust was once called Lucifer Trust. We printed their statement earlier: "There are comments on the World Wide Web claiming that the Lucis Trust was once called the Lucifer Trust. Such was never the case."

So, who do the Lucis people worship and who is being worshipped in that Meditation Room? Longtime Lucis Trust President Sarah McKechnie discussed the problem of conspiracy theorists in a 2013 interview: "It's only in more recent years with the internet and this sharing of ideas, no matter how cockamamie they might be, that the internet offers, that we hear more and more from people who are concerned about our name."

Elsewhere on the Lucis site, McKechnie writes about "so much confusion and misunderstanding concerning the 'fallen angels' of which Lucifer is the best-known representative."

"Anybody's who's curious about it, you can go to our website lucistrust.org," she says in the interview, "and you will find an article explaining the origins of Lucifer and the history of the Lucis Trust. And that should put it to rest."[27]

Well, I took her up on the challenge. In fact, I did so several years ago, and I kept the screenshots. However, as of this writing, the screenshots are not necessary, because the Lucis Trust's explanation of their name continues to be posted as follows, word for word:

> There are comments on the World Wide Web claiming that the Lucis Trust was once called the Lucifer Trust. Such was never the case. However, for a brief period of two or three years in the early 1920s, when Alice and Foster Bailey were beginning to publish the books published under her name, they named their fledgling publishing company 'Lucifer Publishing Company.' By 1925 the name was changed to Lucis Publishing Company and has remained so ever since. Both 'Lucifer' and 'Lucis' come from the same word root, *lucis* being the Latin generative case meaning *of light*. The Baileys' reasons for choosing the original name are not known to us, but we can only surmise that they, like the great teacher H. P. Blavatsky, for whom they had enormous respect, sought to elicit a deeper understanding of the sacrifice made by Lucifer.[28]

CHAPTER TWENTY-SIX

THIS IS A book about Ethiopia. The First Act told the story of the Battle of Adwa and featured Emperor Menelik as the main character. Acts Two and Three highlighted Emperor Haile Selassie and his epic struggle with Mussolini and later the tragic saga with his own people.

What about Act Four? There is no Ethiopian highlighted. Act Four features the rising human rights activist Obianuju Ekeocha, a Nigerian. Also providing leadership is Kenyan Dr. Wahome Ngare, speaking boldly regarding the proper use of vaccines. No Ethiopian has emerged thus far to lead Africa, much less the world, on these issues of life, human dignity, traditional morality, or the ancient Christian faith. As I argue, Ethiopians are indeed poised to serve as the spiritual and cultural leader of the continent of the future. But will they do so? A battle rages both in Ethiopia and the rest of the continent.

The situation is urgent. *NPR* reported in 2014 the use of birth control among Ethiopian women increasing from eight percent to twenty-nine percent between 2000 and 2014. According to a 2016 Ethiopia National Planning Commission report, those numbers are now at forty-two percent, and the commission forecasts an increase to fifty-two percent of Ethiopian women using birth control by 2020. Ethiopia's birthrate has dropped by almost half in the past twenty years.[1]

The official statistics prove that the decrease is primarily in Christian areas, with the Muslim population maintaining its high birthrate. A 2011 study by ICF International, sponsored by the United Nations, shows that of the ten regions of Ethiopia, the top four in birthrates are Muslim majority, with the Somali ethnic group highest at 7.1 children per woman. Tigray, the historic Orthodox Christian region and home of the Ark, is in the sixth spot with a 4.6 rate. According to the study, Addis Ababa, the largest city in the country, has a birthrate of 1.9 children per woman, below replacement level. Addis is eighty-two percent Orthodox Christian.[2]

Unless the Church and the leaders in the Orthodox world begin to take action, it appears likely the population reduction efforts to keep Ethiopia and Africa from their demographic destiny will win the day, and the great historic Christian and Old Testament nation of Ethiopia will become a majority Muslim nation. A Christian nation that kept out invaders for 3,000 years will finally be defeated by Margaret Sanger's suicide tablet. The Christian bride representing all the gentile nations—"black and beautiful" according to the Song of Solomon—may waver in its historic covenant.

It has been my hope—since my prayer ten years ago to learn where the future of Christendom is headed—that Ethiopia might serve as an ark or refuge for Christians if the West's moral foundation implodes and the civilizational shift is realized. In fact, the Kebra Negast not only refers to the Ark as "Lady Zion" and "mercy-seat," but also calls it "place of refuge," "haven of salvation," and, of most interest, "ship." The Ark of the Covenant is, thus, a type of the ark of Noah. Ethiopia and certain African nations remain the only Christian-dominated countries that enforce moral laws on the books upholding life and family integrity. Could birthrates and godly laws make Ethiopia an "ark," a place of refuge, for Western Christians? If Ethiopia does serve as a refuge for the West based on these two reasons, then a secular commenter on a Doug Casey article looked at it this way: "If nobody nukes Africa, it might be an interesting place."[3]

Apart from nuclear war, the pending demographic and civilizational shift will require the reversing of the current and alarming trend of a decreasing Ethiopian birthrate. However, we know that the Ark of the Covenant had special powers, according to the Old Testament Scriptures. Families and nations associated with the Ark were blessed with unusual fertility. This blessing is something that those concerned about Ethiopia's future can place their hope in, if, indeed, the Ark truly does reside in Ethiopia.

Before we finish the final discussion of the location of the Ark, who are today's leaders in Ethiopia? After the fall of the Derg in 1991, Ethiopia was led by Prime Minister Meles Zenawi and his political party, the Tigray People's Liberation Front. The Orthodox Church was immediately restored to full freedom of worship, but a church faction emerged when the patriarch under the Derg, Abuna Merkorios, was removed and a new one appointed, Patriarch Abuna Paulos. Paulos was previously imprisoned by the Derg and then exiled to America. Even so, he was made archbishop while still studying at Princeton and St. Vladimir's Eastern Orthodox Seminary in New York. A few years after returning to Ethiopia, Paulos was made patriarch, while the outgoing Patriarch Merkorios left for the United States to lead a large grouping of Ethiopian churches there. The two churches excommunicated each other.

After the Derg, the concept of an Ethiopian emperor was destroyed, with no interest to resurrect the millennia-old institution. In fact, the Meles government even resisted the idea of finally giving the legendary Ethiopian leader Haile Selassie a proper funeral and burial. However, grassroots demand for such a ceremony forced the government's hand in 2000, twenty-six years after Haile Selassie's tragic demise. Held at the Ba'ita Orthodox Church in Addis Ababa, Patriarch Paulos officiated. Among the many dignitaries on the stage was the last surviving direct descendent of the emperor, the aging Princess Tenagne-Work.

The procession from the church stopped for a time at St. George's Cathedral, built by Menelik and where Haile Selassie was crowned. The procession moved on to the final place of rest, the Cathedral of the Holy Trinity, where the emperor was buried alongside his wife and the sixty-one leaders assassinated the day after Ras Tafari was arrested. One of those sixty-one was Asserate Kassa, whose son wrote a biography of the emperor and attended the funeral.[4*]

"Some people demonize him as a ruthless dictator, while others revere him as a saint," writes Asfa-Wossen Asserate. He assesses the emperor's life by listing his accomplishments in bringing improvements to the country, noting how the Derg genocide highlighted the positive aspects of Haile Selassie's benign dictatorship. He even makes an appeal for the Church to consider sainthood for the devout Christian monarch. But Asfa-Wossen was not blind to the negative.

"Without diminishing the emperor's merit, I am afraid that by refusing to provide the Ethiopian people with a successor at the right moment and by clinging to power until the very end, history may hold him responsible for the demise of the 3,000-year-old reign of the House of David in Ethiopia." However, "I feel sure that future generations of Ethiopians will judge him far more kindly than my generation has done."

Ethiopia's leader today is Prime Minister Abiy Ahmed, elected in 2018 at the age of 41, after twenty-seven years of controversial leadership by the Tigray-dominated government of Meles Zenawi and his successor Hailemariam Desalegn. Of primary dispute was the little-to-no representation given in government affairs to the Oromo ethnic group, Ethiopia's largest, with both Christian and Muslim adherants. The new prime minister brings a strange brew of diversity. He is the sixth child of his Muslim father's fourth wife. His mother grew up in Christian Tigray but converted to Islam. Abiy's ethnic group is Oromo. He is a devout Pentecostal Christian, along with his wife and four children.[5]

His early administration gained high marks for signing a peace treaty with Eritrea in the north, a country Ethiopia has been at war with for decades after Eritrea's long struggle for independence. Abiy survived an early assassination attempt, and then suffered an attempted coup in June 2019 after the governor of Amhara and the head of the military were assassinated the same day. A year earlier, Abiy added another great achievement by reviving talks between the two divided patriarchs of Ethiopian Orthodox Christianity, the exiled Patriarch Merkorios and the current Patriarch in Ethiopia, Matthias. The two factions enduring the decades-long schism reached an agreement of unity and communion on July 27, 2018. The excommunications were lifted.[6]

Will a united church have the strength to lead a continent, hungry for an ancient foundation, to resist the West in order to reach its destiny? Will Ethiopia's church even have the strength to resist the alarming effects of modernism on its own country? Birthrates are crashing, but current Ethiopian families are still large, and parents can afford to see a son or daughter choose monasticism for his or her calling. So Ethiopia's one thousand monasteries today are still vibrant and full of monks...and they are praying.

Traditional Ethiopian beliefs, especially those promulgated by the monks, are generally ridiculed in modern circles. These views include saints talking with angels, the infant Jesus traveling to Ethiopia (with monasteries forming at each spot the holy family visited), and the book of Enoch's explanation of new technology for mankind being derived from communicating with fallen angels. This book's attempt to portray the nation's history more from an Ethiopian perspective than a Western perspective in many ways comes down to the question of the supernatural. In large part, the beliefs, traditions, stories, and legends of Ethiopia are discounted by modern historians because of the strange supernatural element. I have attempted to do otherwise.

However, along the journey I stumbled into an irony. The "rationalistic" West is not always so rational, and its beliefs can be as supernatural as those found in Ethiopia. As we learned at the beginning of this book, the man who coined the term "British Empire" spent his final years dialoguing with angels. John Dee talked with an angel "Uriel," clearly not the good angel who appears by the same name in the book of Enoch, as Dee's spirit led him into wife swapping to gain secret knowledge. This advisor to Queen Elizabeth who signed his name "007" entitled one of his manuscripts: *"A True & Faithful Revelation of what passed for many years between Dr. John Dee...and some spirits."*

And it's not just Elizabethan thinkers. Scientist Sir William Crookes, the inventor of cathode tubes, which led to the television, received a medal from the Royal Society in 1875. His piece "Researches in the Phenomena of Spiritualism" detailed his lifelong involvement with contacting the dead. He believed the psychic realm was critical for scientific investigation. He also joined something called the "Ghost Club" and followed Madam Blavatsky's theosophy. When he published his views in the *Quarterly Journal of Science*, he was told by some critics that the things described were impossible. Replied Crookes: "I didn't say it was possible. I only said it was true."[7]

Crookes's belief in a connection between scientific discovery and supernatural spirits dovetails with Dee's belief of asking angels for technological insights, a process today known as "Enochian magic." As also noted at the beginning of this book, in a 1967 *NSA Technical Journal* article, the intelligence service refers to "our man Dee," who excelled in mathematics and natural science "and above all in the really rewarding sciences of those days—astrology, alchemy, and psychic phenomenon."[8]

Another perceived champion of science with an occult underbelly was Margaret Sanger. Her daughter Peggy, age five, died on November 6. "After Peggy's death, Margaret became a driven woman," writes biographer Madeline Gray. She also became an occultist, hopping "from one séance to another," hoping to hear from Peggy.[9] She was heavily involved in astrology, watching her calendar carefully based on her horoscope, and was obsessed with numerology, particularly the number six, the day her daughter died. Margaret herself died on Sept. 6, 1966.[10]

SIGMUND FREUD

Similar lifetime involvement with spirits can be seen with the founders of psychology. Carl Jung spent thirty years conducting séances and working in the occult. Known as the founder of analytical psychology, Jung spent years pushing these occult practices on his mentor, Sigmund Freud, founder of psychoanalysis and "generally recognized as one of the most influential and authoritative thinkers of the twentieth century." But Freud was skeptical.

By 1905 Jung had already used eight different mediums. He spoke regularly with a spirit named "Philemon" as well as other "ghostly gurus" as he dubbed them, such as

"Ka," "Elijah," and "Salome." In a session with Philemon, Jung spent three days in a spell of automatic writing, producing his work *The Seven Sermons to the Dead.*[11]

In 1907 Freud had attended a séance but was skeptical, urging Jung to make his Freudian sexual theories "a dogma, an unshakeable bulwark" against "the black tide...of occultism." But Freud mellowed over time as he attended more séances. Then, a strange event occurred within an hour or two of Freud informally anointing Jung as his successor, saying to Jung "[I] adopted you as an eldest son, anointing you as my successor and crown prince." Some kind of explosion emerged from Freud's bookcase. Jung predicted it would happen again, and it did. Freud, alluding to having just become Jung's spiritual father, remarked that the event "then and there divested me of my paternal dignity." He wrote Jung separately to say: "In matters of occultism, I have grown humble...my hubris has been shattered."[12]

Some try to downplay Jung's extreme occultism by quoting him in his early years, such as a 1919 paper where he used the term "unconscious complexes" for the phenomena. "I see no proof whatever," he remarked, "of the existence of real spirits." But in 1948 he revised the paper and added a footnote to that very comment: "After collecting psychological experiences from many people and many countries for over fifty years, I no longer feel as certain as I did in 1919, when I wrote this sentence. To put it bluntly, I doubt whether an exclusively psychological approach can do justice to the phenomenon in question." Or, as he said it in 1946, "...the spirit hypothesis yields better results..."[13]

So Western "scientists" are not always as rational as they seem. They may wear white lab coats, but that doesn't mean they don't believe in spirits and angels. In fact, in some cases, they heavily rely on them. Angels need to be taken into account for any worldview.

A specific angel was named in the previous chapter by the name of Lucifer. Most Christians would agree that Lucifer, also known as Satan, is behind the abortion industry. But in this day of massive population control, why would he be so interested in preventing the conception of human beings? Let's start with the premise that angelic beings are everywhere, by the billions, maybe trillions. Daniel 7:10 speaks of "ten thousand times ten thousand." In other words, too many to count. In his commentary on Ezekiel, John Calvin says that "all creatures are animated by angelic motion," so that would mean an angel for every man, woman, animal, and insect and anything else that moves.[14*]

If the earth has fallen to the Evil One, then all or many of those angels are fallen angels. This fact adds more meaning to God's command to Adam to be fruitful and multiply and also to take dominion over the entire earth. This will require a lot of people. "Do you not know that we will judge angels?" Paul asks the Corinthians (1 Cor. 6:3). One way to look at the overall purpose of human history is the changing of the guard from angels to men. The book of Revelation captures the transfer from the old to the new. In the early chapters, the angelic cherubim and seraphim are in the throne room with "ten thousand times ten thousand" angels in the audience (Rev. 5:11). In Chapter 14, we instead see a host of tens of thousands of people in the air with Christ. Angels are less prominent and people increase as the book moves forward.

"He sat down at the right hand of the Majesty in heaven," we are told in the book of Hebrews, "so he became...superior to the angels..." (Heb. 1:3–4). And we follow Christ to this superior position over the angels. More saints and more godly Christians moving into the throne room make for a transfer of leadership that surprises but pleases the good angels. Yet it must terrify the angels who hate mankind and are willing to use all attempts to prevent mankind from entering this throne room—or better yet, prevent them from being conceived in the first place.

After my many interviews with Girma Batu, I shared my honest feelings about the many claims of the Ethiopian Christians. I told him that it's all a bit overwhelming. I shared with him a story of an Orthodox church I attended in Pennsylvania with a large contingent of believers from the Caucasus. They believe that their nation was where Noah landed. It is also the location of the Garden of Eden, they say. Hebrew is derived from their native tongue.

"Is what I'm hearing just another example of a nationalistic people claiming everything is derived from their land?" I asked.

He laughed and I laughed. He took no offense. He knows the claims are difficult to believe.

"Most historians, most researchers believe after seeing archeological findings, research work, anthropological works, and so on," Girma said. "But we must ultimately rely on traditions and the position of the Church."

On this we agreed. Then, he asked a great question.

"Have you heard of any other country which claims to have the Ark of the Covenant?"

In fact, I have not. Several theories exist about what may have happened to the Ark. Some theorists say it is still hidden in a labyrinth underneath the Western Wall of the Temple in Jerusalem. Others speak of a cave in the wilderness. The Harrison Ford movie suggests it resides in a massive warehouse in Washington, D.C. But no other country has a long, historic tradition of guarding and preserving the Ark of the Covenant. Only Ethiopia.

And it is no small tradition. The national spirit and culture in many ways centers around the Ark. The worship of Jesus Christ is conducted from the ark replica altar table in every one of the tens of thousands of churches in the nation. From the most sophisticated person to the common laborer to the simple farmer, proponents of the Kebra Negast story are in abundance. Due to this overwhelming tradition, I believe the Ark is in Ethiopia. No other country makes this claim. As scholar Sergew Hable Selassie says: "Let us not deny all the ancient traditions in Ethiopia if we are not able to put anything better in their place."[15]

Yes, this belief is based mostly on oral tradition. But so was the work of Homer, whose history of Ancient Greece was dismissed by scholars until only recently. The earliest fully extant manuscript we have of Homer's *Iliad*, the *Venetus A* in Venice, was copied in the tenth century AD—a full 1,700 years after Homer wrote his epic in the eighth century BC. In addition, the historical events that Homer describes took place in the twelfth century BC, 400 years before Homer penned them. Until around 150 years ago, people assumed that the stories of Homer were myth. But Heinrich Schliemann, a German businessman turned archeologist, set out to prove Troy and the Trojan Wars were historical fact. "When Schliemann told people this they laughed at him," writes E. H. Gombrich in Yale University Press's *A Little History of the World.* "But he didn't give up." Now, most scholars believe Homer describes a world similar to what actually existed in history. And so with time we may learn more about the truth of Ethiopia's extraordinary claims.[16]

While my belief is strong that the Ark resides in Ethiopia, there is a problem. Unfortunately, I cannot agree with certain key premises of the Kebra Negast story. I say *unfortunately*, because, of course, I do not want to disappoint my Ethiopian friends. However, they may be pleased to know that my problem with the story of the Ark at the time of Sheba and Menelik is not related to a refusal to believe in stories of a fantastic and supernatural nature. As my Ethiopian friend Elias put it, Bible-supporting Christians believe in a talking donkey, so why not? With God, anything is possible. Yes, I believe in "crazy" supernatural phenomenon—just like Jung, Freud, Crookes, and Dee!

I also agree with Girma's admonition that "we must ultimately rely on traditions and the position of the Church," not scientific or rationalistic arguments. And this is the root of the problem: I am an Eastern Orthodox Christian. And like the Ethiopians, and unlike the Protestants, we include in our Bible the books between the Old and New Testaments, what we call the deuterocanonical books, popularly known as the Apocrypha—such works as Baruch, Esdras, Tobit, Judith, the Wisdom of Solomon, Sirach, and—for the Eastern Orthodox—the Maccabees. These books have been a part of the Church's canon of the Bible since the beginning.

Protestants, while pointing to the ancient church as the authority for what books Christians place in the Bible, curiously cut out the ancient church's deuterocanonical books, in Thomas Jefferson–like fashion. That decision leaves a Protestant free to accept the Kebra Negast with no biblical contradiction. However, for the Orthodox (and

Roman Catholics), the Second Book of Maccabees, chapter two, says the following:

> In the records it will be found that Jeremiah the prophet…ordered that the tent and the ark should accompany him, and how he went to the very mountain that Moses climbed to behold God's inheritance. When Jeremiah arrived there, he found a chamber in a cave in which he put the tent, the ark, and the altar of incense; then he sealed the entrance (2 Macc. 1, 4–5, NABRE).[17]

This passage clearly states that the famous prophet Jeremiah placed the Ark in a cave in Mount Sinai, the same mountain that Moses climbed. Jeremiah lived 300 years after the time of Solomon, Sheba, and Menelik. So the Ark could not have been in Ethiopia. Like the passage about Josiah calling for the Ark to be brought to the temple—verses I could not overcome for a long time—this passage seems to leave me no wiggle room for an alternative explanation. Perhaps I will come across an explanation someday. But, for now, I must defer to the revealed religion that I have ascribed to, over and against that portion of the Kebra Negast's teaching. I submit to my tradition, and I hope Ethiopians can respect that stance.

How do Ethiopians handle this passage? Quite easily. Although we agree on most of the Deuterocanon as part of the Bible, the Ethiopians do not include the Maccabees. Instead they have 1, 2, and 3 Meqabyan, which similarly provides a history between the Old and New Testaments but do not discuss the Maccabee family and do not include the passage about Jeremiah and the Ark. Simply put, Ethiopians do not believe that passage is scriptural.

But as for my position reflecting an "Ethiopian perspective," all is not lost. I do believe that the Ark is in Ethiopia. I do believe that Sheba and Solomon had a son, and it makes sense to me that he returned to his country, perhaps with an entourage of princes and priests, and began the tradition of Old Testament Yahweh worship in Ethiopia. For me, the spirit of the Kebra Negast is maintained, although not the letter. And on this point, it is worth mentioning that the Kebra Negast, although greatly revered, is not read aloud in the churches of Ethiopia, the act which determines whether a book is officially Scripture.

So, if the Ark is in Ethiopia, and it did not come by way of the first Menelik stealing the Ark from Solomon in the tenth century BC, then how did it make its way to the land of Sheba? Just as there are no nations like Ethiopia which claim to have historically preserved the Ark, neither are there many options for choosing what event or migration might have brought the Ark to Ethiopia sometime after Jeremiah hid it in a cave in Mount Sinai in the seventh century BC. This book has already discussed the solid evidence for an ancient tradition of Old Testament religion in northern Ethiopia. The historical evidence is backed by several verses in the Bible that confirm a Jewish presence in Ethiopia as early as the eighth century, if not earlier. We know that the Ark was swifted away from Jerusalem before the fall of Jerusalem in 587 BC. According to 2 Maccabees, Jeremiah placed it at Sinai, but might it have been taken somewhere else later? Where might that be? In fact, scholars agree that there are only two or three occurrences in history of Jewish temples that were built outside Jerusalem. The reason that there are so few is that a temple is only supposed to be built for the Ark. This fact suggests that one of those temples may have actually housed the Ark.

It is along this line of reasoning that Graham Hancock, author of the runaway bestseller *The Sign and the Seal*, constructed his well-reasoned theory that the Ark came to Ethiopia in either the fifth or fourth century BC by way of a Jewish temple built curiously on a remote island. The small island is called Elephantine and sits in the Nile River in southern Egypt on the way from Jerusalem to Ethiopia.

When I began this book, I was open to all theories on the existence of the Ark and how it may have reached Ethiopia. After concluding that the Ark did not travel to Axum until after Jeremiah placed it in a cave sometime in the seventh century BC, I looked more closely at Hancock's Elephantine Island theory.

I had already come across hints of the theory. Sergew Hable Selassie references the views of a European scholar, considered one of the foremost authorities on ancient Ethiopian languages, who suggests the possible Elephantine migration of Ethiopia's black Jews. "Wolf Leslau holds the view that the Falashas are Hamites who were converted to Judaism by Israelites from Elephantine in Egypt or from South Arabia…the question remains open," writes Sergew.[18] I also learned from a top scholar on African Judaism, Dr. Richard Hull, that such a school of thought does indeed exist on the Falasha Jews. "Other scholars speculate that their faith may have trickled down from Elephantine via the Nile River valley and Meroe after the destruction of their temple. Perhaps, then, the Elephantine Jews fled southwards into Ethiopia." Hull acknowledges that Hebrew University scholar Stephen Kaplan doubts this theory, but Kaplan does admit that the Jews in Northern Ethiopia are "almost unique among Jewish groups in their practice of animal sacrifice outside the land of Israel," thus acknowledging a unique correlation between the temple Jews of Israel and Ethiopia. Animal sacrifice was not practiced apart from the temple.[19]

So I knew Graham Hancock's theory was not something he had created out of thin air.

Primary sources show a rather substantial amount of scholarship on this anomalous Jewish Temple that appears on the Nile not long after 2 Maccabees records the Ark being hidden in a cave. Knowledge of this temple derives from a large amount of correspondence found on broken pieces of pottery and a great many papyri manuscripts, some still untranslated. I was able to obtain the works of one of the scholars cited by Hancock on Elephantine, Dr. Bezalel Porten. He tells us that, besides Elephantine, there are only a few nominees in history for a temple that could house the Ark: "[Besides Elephantine], two and perhaps three other Jewish temples are known to have existed outside of the one in Jerusalem: the Temple of Onias at Leontopolis in Egypt, the Samaritan Temple on Mount Gerazim, and perhaps the [Transjordan palace] of Hyrcanus."

The last mention, nearly discounted by Porten himself, is the Samaritan city and temple taken over by Hazmonean King John Hyrcanus in 120 BC. But neither Hyrcanus nor the Samaritans are a good option, as the Samaritan temple had no real chance of ever containing the Ark. From the Bible, we know the Hyrcanus site as a heretical temple with a golden calf built a century before the time of Jeremiah (1 Kings 12:25–33). If devout Jews were custodians of the Ark, the Samaritans would never be considered for preserving it. The remaining option is a temple built by a Syrian Jewish prince named Onias, who fled to Leontopolis, Egypt and was granted permission by the Ptolemy king to build a temple in 155 BC. However, we know of no larger migration from Leontopolis to Ethiopia, and this temple is in Northern Egypt, much further away from Ethiopia than Elephantine. The final tipping point: Porten tells us the Elephantine temple, compared to the others, was "unusually lavish."[20]

Thanks to the papyri manuscripts, we have an enormous amount of information on the Elephantine temple. It had a cedar roof, like Solomon's temple, and its dimensions were ninety feet by thirty feet, the exact dimensions for the temple in the Bible. Oxford and Harvard scholar Tudor Parfitt notes the similarities: "It was the closest thing to the Jerusalem Temple on the face of the earth."[21]

Documents show this temple was destroyed in exactly 410 BC. It was built perhaps 100 to 200 years before, a window of time that fits nicely with Jeremiah's seventh century reference to the Ark and the emergence of established Jewish settlements in Ethiopia. According to Porten, Elephantine Jews prayed to "Yahweh, Lord of heaven" and a few sources reference Yahweh "Lord of Hosts." Hancock believes this phrase only occurs when the Ark is present. As Porten says: "To the Elephantine Jews, the 'Lord of hosts'—no doubt heavenly hosts as well as military—was the 'God of Heaven' who 'dwelt in Elephantine.'"[22]

In dealing with any theory championed by Graham Hancock, a few hurdles must be overcome. Firstly, while he and I agree on the Elephantine theory, we disagree on the Queen of Sheba, who I believe was Ethiopian while Hancock suggests a Yemeni origin, or perhaps she is a legend only. Secondly, he does not believe everything in the Bible. Regarding the Bible's teaching that God and the Ark killed people, Hancock says the Old Testament was simply incorrect. To believe the Bible would make God "a psychopathic killer." So he concludes that the Bible is only sometimes right. In another place, he goes out of his way in the book to take Christ's name in vain, not an endearing quality.

His interest is less in biblical truth and more about mystical and mysterious phenomena and the origins of the universe. And Hancock sells a lot of books discussing these matters.[23]

Thirdly, he's kind of an odd one. In 2005, he wrote *Supernatural: Meetings with the Ancient Teachers of Mankind, an investigation of shamanism and the origins of religion.* Like Melinda Gates, he was granted the privilege of giving a Ted Talk. But TEDx removed him from its YouTube channel. It turns out that he doesn't just talk about shamanism, he promotes altered states of consciousness to improve the world, and he makes trips to South America to take a hallucinogenic drug called "ayahuasca" from the shamans themselves.[24]

These credentials don't help with the fourth problem I have with Graham Hancock: some scholars viscerally dislike him, as we discussed in an earlier chapter. He even talks about smoking marijuana for years while writing past books, including *The Sign and the Seal.* But for my part, I don't dislike him. In fact, I'm a fan of his writing style and even some of his scholarship. But I'll pass on the writing enhancements.[25]

Hancock's old friend, Edward Ullendorff, the scholar whose criticisms we discussed earlier (including calling Graham a "parvenu"), reappears when it comes to the crucial Elephantine theory. The venerable Oxford scholar told the *Los Angeles Times* that it was impossible for Jews to migrate from Elephantine to Ethiopia, as no evidence exists that Africa was ever penetrated by that route. "The Nile's not navigable," he snapped.[26]

Again, it seems Ullendorff's judgment gets clouded by his disdain for Hancock. Before reading Graham's book, I had already come across information contradicting Ullendorff's allegation, this time from the "Father of History," fifth century BC Greek scholar Herodotus. "Ethiopians inhabit the country immediately above Elephantine and one half of the island; the other half is inhabited by Egyptians," the ancient Greek scholar tells us, already establishing a connection between the Egyptian island and Ethiopia. He then explains the journey: "...sail for forty days...then you will arrive at a large city, called Meroe..."[27]

I'm not sure how Ullendorff missed this passage. Hancock adds more important details from Herodotus. First, he notes that the journey described by Herodotus goes fifty-six days *beyond* Meroe (Khartoum, Sudan), which describes rather well the time it would take to reach Northern Ethiopia. More importantly, Hancock addresses Ullendorff's contention that the Nile is "not navigable." Herodotus writes: "You will then disembark and travel along the bank for forty days, for there are sharp rocks in the Nile and many reefs through which you will be unable to sail." Clearly, everybody back then knew it wasn't navigable for long stretches. They portaged their boats, like any good adventurer, and finished the journey with success and regularity.[28]

If you read *The Sign and the Seal*, you may agree with the critics. As the *Los Angeles Times* put it, Hancock "has lately been backpedaling from some of his more bizarre assertions, including one that the ark is really the Holy Grail of medieval legend and that it has been the object of a secretive search over the centuries by the Knights Templar and the Masons, societies that have been warhorses of paranoid conspiracy theorists since ancient times." Indeed, the book has all that. But as I mentioned previously, Hancock is careful to note where he is having fun with conjecture and where he is offering more serious scholarship. I love his writing, and I get it. As it turns out, his response to the *L.A. Times* confirmed my suspicions: "The Grail, the Templars, in those areas I'm definitely out on a limb," Hancock admitted. "The speculation about what the ark may actually be is entirely personal. But the area of the book I feel strongest about is the argument about how the ark got to Axum. The evidence for it is strong, makes sense, and explains a lot of anomalies."[29]

I agree.

After all that work to establish Hancock's Elephantine theory for how the Ark of the Covenant found its way to Ethiopia, there is one little curious note that deserves a second look. The critical 2 Maccabees passage seems pretty clear. Then again...

Let's look one more time at the larger passage and especially the two highlighted phrases:

In the records it will be found that Jeremiah the prophet ordered the deportees to take some of the fire with them as indicated...[and] he exhorted them that the law should not depart from their hearts. *The same document also tells* how the prophet, in virtue of an oracle, ordered that the tent and the ark should accompany him, and how he went to the very mountain that Moses climbed to behold God's inheritance. When Jeremiah arrived there, he found a chamber in a cave in which he put the tent, the ark, and the altar of incense; then he sealed the entrance (2 Macc. 1,4–5, NABRE; emphasis added).[30]

On its face this passage seems to end the argument. It says Jeremiah put the Ark in a cave. But, it doesn't quite say that. It says "in the records." Other translations say: "According to the archives."

Why add this? Why is this phrase in this passage along with "the same document also tells..."? Does the Bible use this kind of language regarding Moses parting the Red Sea—"In the records it will be found" that Moses parted the Red Sea? No. Does it say: "According to the archives," David killed Goliath? No. It just states as fact what actually happened.

So, why did the writer of Maccabees feel compelled to add this clarification? I could not find a phrase like this one anywhere else in the Scriptures. Is it because the records or archives may not have been exactly accurate? As a writer, I know how to quote with some finesse and dexterity, and that would be a clever little trick without being untrue. Could it be that the writer of Maccabees was intentionally trying to throw people off the scent regarding the true location of the Ark? To me this interpretation does not seem likely. But I believe it is worth mentioning.

One more thing. The rest of the Maccabees passage I find quite interesting:

The place is to remain unknown until God gathers his people together again and shows them mercy. Then the Lord will disclose these things, and the glory of the Lord and the cloud will be seen, just as they appeared in the time of Moses and of Solomon when he prayed that the place might be greatly sanctified (2 Maccabees 2:7–8, NABRE).

This prophecy, to me, is in line with what the Kebra Negast teaches about what will happen with the Ark throughout history—nothing!—and how no one will see it, not until it reappears at the end of history.

Until then, the people of Ethiopia face strong headwinds. I do believe that the Ark is preserved there today and has been for many centuries. I can take confidence in that fact, considering the many trials and challenges now facing the great Ethiopian people. Will they succumb to modernism? Will a great people who have never been conquered finally give way to the sinister suicide tablet of the West? The Ark itself has always been associated with the blessing of fertility. I must believe that God will continue to honor those who preserve the Ark—and, more importantly, those who honor the fulfilment of the Ark.

This challenge is not their first. In the days of Emperor Menelik, a great army rose up to defeat the invading Europeans, and an army carrying the Ark or a tabot replica achieved Africa's greatest military victory over Europe. When a morally depraved Mussolini invaded a half-century later, the devout and faithful Haile Selassie served as an inspiration to a people who never stopped fighting until a defeated Italian army left once again. In Haile Selassie's disappointing later reign, a revolutionary movement formed that led to Ethiopians slaughtering a million of their own ranks. Nevertheless, the people of the Ark continued to follow the first commandment to be fruitful and multiply. A generation later, they are a vibrant people, in a position to lead the continent of the future.

Yes, the challenges are real. But so is their historic faith and their ancient commitment to repelling the snakes that enter beyond the gate. I am keeping a watchful eye, for it seems the story of Ethiopia and its future may be, in some real but mystical way, the story of us all.

EPILOGUE

THE BAREFOOT ETHIOPIAN ran one pace ahead of his Moroccan opponent, Rhadi Ben Abdesselam, in the final stretch of the 1960 Olympic marathon as they raced down the Appian Way, the most famous highway of ancient Rome.

"The little Abyssinian," said an Australian journalist, "races along with his thin sinewy legs like some long-distance runner of biblical times, nimble as a deer."[1]

At a point near the end of the race, Rhadi and Ethiopian Abebe Bikila ran past an obelisk on their right, the very one Mussolini had stolen in 1937 and taken back to Rome, now called the "Obelisk of Axum." The stela stood 80 feet tall, was made of 160 tons of granite, and was nearly 2,000 years old. Both runners were in a position to win the Olympic marathon, the most famous of all athletic competitions. The race began at the Arch of Constantine directly beside the Colisseum and ended in the same spot. As they approached the finish line, the lights of the arch were turned on to illuminate the historic landmark. With 1,000 yards to go, Bikila found the inner strength to pull ahead. He went out in front alone by several yards.

"Thousands cheered," wrote the *New York Times*. Biographer Paul Rambali said Bikila looked up and "thanked his God."[2]

The unimaginable happened. He became the first black African to win an Olympic gold medal—and he was running with no shoes, in bare feet. He broke the world record, running the fastest marathon ever. Abebe Bikila accomplished arguably the greatest feat in the history of all sports.

He became the most popular man in Africa. For many in the rest of the world, he was the first African they had ever heard of. Bikila became "a symbol of the new Africa in its years of decolonization," wrote biographer Tim Judah. As he stood on the pedestal by the Colosseum to receive his medal, the band struggled to play the Ethiopian national anthem. New Zealand's bronze medalist Barry Magee congratulated him: "You did it," he said. "Never mind the shoes."[3]

When he returned to Ethiopia, Emperor Haile Selassie pinned onto him the Order of Menelik II. An Ethiopian filmmaker noted that the monarch grew concerned over how much attention Bikila was receiving. An *Associated Press* article said, "Only the Emperor Haile Selassie has greater stature among his people—and not much." The writer added that the famous runner now "lives the life of a king—not just a king's bodyguard." He became the new symbol for Ethiopia, the nation claiming to be in covenant with God for millennia.

"He was very polite, very humble," said his trainer, Onni Niskanen. "From the bottom of his heart he was a good man." Bikila went on to win the 1964 Olympic Marathon in Tokyo—but this time wearing shoes. "After 1964, things slowly changed again. Bikila grew up," wrote Judah.

"Bikila walks the streets as a national hero," said the *New York Times*. "He now lives the life of a celebrity and a rich man.... He moves in the highest society. He has everything he wants." The newspaper also called him "a devoted family man."

"He was affected by fame," said Niskanen, his trainer. "Before Tokyo he may have had some relations with women, but now it became open. He was found drunk many times—and almost everywhere around town. It was sad. The whole nation was concerned." A family friend believed Bikila's wife Yewibdar knew of the affairs but was left to suffer in silence.[4]

Though still training for the upcoming marathon in Mexico, he was drinking five or six glasses of whiskey every night. But he remained confident. "Of course, I will win in Mexico," he told reporters. "Nobody can beat me for some time to come." However, at the fifteen-kilometer mark of the 1968 Olympic Marathon in Mexico, Bikila was forced to drop out of the race due to severe leg pain.

Nine months later, on March 22, 1969, he drove his Volkswagen toward the area where his mother lived after visiting a bar around 9 p.m. On a wet road forty-five miles from Addis Ababa, the car flipped, and he was trapped inside. He was found early the next morning and rushed to the hospital. His seventh vertebre had been dislocated. Abebe Bikila would never walk again.[5]

Flown to London, he received the best medical attention in the world. He was visited by the Queen of England, and President Nixon sent him a letter. Bikila's daughter noted that visitors "couldn't help but cry or express their sadness in grim silence." She remembered a moment when her father finally bowed his head and began to cry. One of his attendants spoke of his great desire to walk. "Because he had a strong religious faith, he thought he would have a miracle." But she reported the hard truth that, in fact, he needed help to reach the toilet.

With his indomitable spirit, Bikila could not be held down. For the next three years, he became a champion for the Games for Wheelchair Sportsmen, similar to the Paralympic Games, competing in archery and table tennis and placing first in sleigh-riding. Bikila attended the 1972 Olympics in Munich, Germany, as a guest and received a standing ovation from the arena on opening day.

A year after his accident, Bikila went back home to live with his wife and four young children. He grew a beard and gained a few pounds. Life was difficult. "Every day is a real struggle. Much more difficult than the marathon," Bikila told a French reporter. "I am certain that if I did not believe in the Lord, I would not have the courage to survive."

Then he added: "In the end, only the Lord knows what will happen to me."

Not long after, in 1973, Abebe Bikila died of a brain hemorrhage. He was 41. The famous runner was buried six days later with full military honors and the emperor in attendance. A family friend who gave the eulogy remarked that "it is not only Ethiopia which is in mourning, but the whole of Africa."[6]

No one will ever forget the great day that the barefoot Ethiopian runner defeated the rest of the nations in the Olympic marathon.
However, Bikila himself did not consider winning the 1960 marathon
his happiest moment, nor even his second victory in 1964. According
to his biographer, Bikila believed "the happiest day of his life had nothing to do with winning the race." The day before winning the Tokyo
marathon, he lost his gold wedding ring in the shower. A Tokyo house-
wife, who was cleaning the athletes' showers, found Bikila's wedding
ring, the symbol of his covenant, and returned it. That, he said, was his
happiest day.[7]*

Abebe Bikila of Ethiopia (center), gold medalist in 1960 Olympic marathon. Left: Rhadi Ben Abdesselam, Morocco (silver). Right: Barry Magee, New Zealand (bronze).

ACKNOWLEDGMENTS

THIS BOOK BEGAN with a trip to Nairobi, Kenya, with my daughter, Tabitha, and son, Jaime, funded by my mother to visit her sister, Jony, a longtime artist there and an enthusiastic fan of all things Ethiopian. Fascinated by that strange and ancient Christian country, I slipped away from Kenya for a week to visit Ethiopia on my own.

My initial guide was Misgana Lemma, whom I met when he was a seventeen-year-old exchange student with the Bowling family in Chattanooga years before. (He is now Dr. Misgana.) His family in Nazret was kind and hospitable. Near the end of the trip, Misgana helped me find the Orthodox seminary in Addis Ababa, and I had lunch with professor Girma Batu just before my flight departed. That providential relationship was key to this book venture.

I must also thank many others besides Girma who are associated with Holy Trinity Theological College, including Archbishop Themotewos, Solomon the administrator, Professor Jacob Jossi (now in India), and students Elias Gebreselassie, Bazien Abei, and Fre Salib. On my second trip I visited Axum and met on the plane the translating angels Tadu and Tsega, who took me to visit their relatives and helped me make good decisions in a foreign culture. The best decision was shaking off my initial tour guide who oversold himself at the airport. I eventually hired Yirga Fisseha, who has in subsequent trips displayed professional, academic, and spiritual integrity. He also pointed me to *The Sign and the Seal* by Graham Hancock, correctly noting that it was a solid piece of work despite the critics.

Thanks also for the kindnesses from Dr. Ahmed Hassen, director of the Institute of Ethiopian Studies. Magic doors opened for me thanks to Todd Womack, chief of staff for U.S. Senator Bob Corker, and the senator himself, chairman, at the time, of the prestigious Senate Foreign Relations Committee.

My colleagues at Partners for Christian Media, Bob and Justin, along with the encouraging staff, have been important partners in this project. My church friends at St. Tikhon Orthodox Mission are too many to name. Thanks to all of you. Our Archbishop Alexander, Chancellor Marcus, and Fathers David, Jonas, Peter, Stephen, Thomas, and Seth have been extremely encouraging regarding all things Ethiopian.

My longtime editor Dan Bockert got a well-deserved promotion just as this project commenced. Nevertheless, he generously added his keen skill and professional eye as a general editor and consultant in the midst of a very busy schedule. He is a true talent. Peter Selgin designed a fabulous cover. Najdan Mincic is a solid professional with interior design. Jeremy Milford helped with graphics. IV Whitman pushed me to find a better title. Dr. Austin Martin provided numerous copy edits in just the nick of time. Paul, father of nine, helped me with last-minute adjustments. Robert Kwasnik sent me a great article just before the deadline. T. J. Johnson, as is his wont, contributed constant encouragement and enthusiasm during the process, in word and deed.

Publisher Joel Belz called me out of the blue one day regarding a previous book and complimented my unique way of adding asterisks to endnote reference numbers for further commentary. That confidence-booster led to continuing that practice here. Let me also mention several libraries that have been helpful: University of Chattanooga, Covenant College, Cleveland State Community College (TN), Chattanooga Bicentennial Library, as well as Morehouse and Emory Universities in Atlanta. Librarians, as preservationists, are often longsuffering with my bent to imperfectly exploit what is perfectly preserved. Shout out to Doug Flynn who traveled to D.C. to look up an article for me at Howard University Library. Early readers helped me find my way to clarity: Caleb, Zach, Bill, Keff, Bobbie, T. J., Kevin the skeptic (who became a fan), and several others. A place to write offsite was enabled by Todd, Rocki, Boo, and Mike Hunter. Kevin Kettenring provided numerous writing enhancements. David Morgan fixed both doors in my home office, allowing me to concentrate for long periods of time.

Regarding the text itself, authors whom I relied on heavily in certain sections should be recognized. For Part One, Raymond Jonas's *The Battle of Adwa* was enormous. What a great book—an important contribution to history and the future. For Parts Two and Three, Asfa-Wossen Asserate provides a scholarly, readable, and sobering account of the life of Haile Selassie, a Shakespearian tragedy. As a friend and fellow aristocrat, Asfa-Wossen has every reason to withhold details on the emperor's failings but insists on sharing the hard truth. Regarding the central Eden section, I am a personal fan of Gert Muller's theory and persuasive writing. I also want to recognize with gratitude my friend "Alex" in that section who must, for good reasons, remain anonymous. Part Four was less dependent on certain authors, but journalist Steve Weatherbe with *Life Site News* should be mentioned as well as the faithful archivers of every issue of Margaret Sanger's *Birth Control Review* at Life Dynamics.

Many others I could acknowledge related to the text but they are already quoted, mentioned, or cited in the book, and I trust that will serve as proper recognition. I am sure I have missed a few.

Many have departed since my previous major book project, including Gordon Wetmore, Dalton Roberts, Scottie Probasco, Mike Goodman, Mary Lou Henderson, Kevin, Ezra, and Tinsley. I miss my friend Dr. Smartt.

Warren Caterson led me to Orthodoxy. Doug Daugherty and Charles Wysong played a major role in my formation as a pro-lifer and advocate for the first commandment. Much of the premise of *Unknown Empire* was inspired twenty years ago by Pat Buchanan's book *The Death of the West*. I have read nearly all his columns and most of his books, but his material on demographics changed my view of the future. This book is a result.

BIBLIOGRAPHY

INTERVIEWS

Father Abraham, scholar at Abba Garima Monastery. Interview by Dean W. Arnold in Adwa, Ethiopia, May 2017. Translated by Yirga Fesseha. Transcript, archives of Dean W. Arnold, Chattanooga, TN.

Bazien Abai and Elias Gebreselassie, graduate students at Holy Trinity Theological College. Interviewed together in Addis Ababa, Ethiopia, January 2018. Transcript, archives of Dean W. Arnold, Chattanooga, TN.

Elias Gebreselassie, graduate student, Holy Trinity Theological College. Separate interview by Dean W. Arnold in Addis Ababa, Ethiopia, January 2018. Transcript, archives of Dean W. Arnold, Chattanooga, TN.

Girma Batu, Vice Academic Dean, Holy Trinity Theological College. Interview by Dean W. Arnold in Addis Ababa, Ethiopia, May 2016, and January 2018. Transcript, archives of Dean W. Arnold, Chattanooga, TN.

Father John, priest in the village of Mulle. Interview by Dean W. Arnold in Tigray region, Ethiopia, January 2018. Translated by Bazien Abai. Transcript, archives of Dean W. Arnold, Chattanooga, TN.

Father Kiros, scholar at Debre Damo Monastery. Interview by Dean W. Arnold in Tigray, Ethiopia, May 2017. Translated by Yirga Fesseha. Transcript, archives of Dean W. Arnold, Chattanooga, TN.

Megabe Hadis Yilma Chernet, Komos Aba Zekarias Bogale, and Dr. Yohannes Endeshaw, officials at the Dagimawi Qulbi Debre Bisrate St. Gabriel Weabune Tecklehaimanot Ethiopian Orthodox Tewahedo Church. Interview by Dean W. Arnold, Atlanta, Georgia, February 14, 2019. Translated by Yohannes Endeshaw. Recording in archives of Dean W. Arnold, Chattanooga, TN.

Teclehaimanot Gebreselassie, Chairman Emeritus, Department of History, Addis Ababa University. Interview by Dean W. Arnold at Institute of Ethiopian Studies, Addis Ababa, Ethiopia, May 2017. Transcript, archives of Dean W. Arnold, Chattanooga, TN.

Tsagazam GeliGiyorgis, spokesman for Gororo village church. Interview by Dean W. Arnold in Tigray, Ethiopia, January 2018. Translated by Bazien Abai. Transcript, archives of Dean W. Arnold, Chattanooga, TN.

Yirgalem Fisseha, history guide, Axum and Tigray Region, Ethiopia. Conversations with Dean W. Arnold in Tigray, Ethiopia, May 2016, May 2017, and January 2018. Recordings and notes in archives of Dean W. Arnold, Chattanooga, TN.

"Yosef" (pseudonym used), guide for National Museum of Ethiopia. Interview by Dean W. Arnold in Addis Ababa, Ethiopia, January 2018. Transcript, archives of Dean W. Arnold, Chattanooga, TN.

BOOKS AND JOURNALS:

*Ethiopian authors are alphabetized by first name.

Abraham Buruk Woldegaber and Mario Alexis Portella. *Abyssinian Christianity: The First Christian Nation? The History and the Identity of the Ethiopian and Eritrean Christians.* Pismo Beach, CA: BP Editing, 2012.

Asfa-Wossen Asserate. *King of Kings: The Triumph and Tragedy of Emperor Haile Selassie I of Ethiopia.* London: Haus Publishing, 2015.

Baker, Jean H. *Margaret Sanger: A Life of Passion.* New York: Hill and Wang, 2012.

Baldovin, John F. *The Urban Character of Christian Worship: The Origins, Development, and Meaning of Stational Liturgy.* Ann Arbor, MI: UMI Dissertation Services, 2005.

Barker, A. J. *The Rape of Ethiopia, 1936.* Edited by Barrie Pitt. New York: Ballantine Books, 1971.

Blaut, J. M. *The Colonizer's Model of the World: Geographical Diffusionism and Eurocentric History.* New York/London: The Guilford Press, 1993.

Bowersock, G. W. "Helena's Bridle and the Chariot of Ethiopia" in *Antiquity in Antiquity: Jewish and Christian Pasts in the Greco-Roman World,* Edited by Gregg Gardner and Kevin L. Osterloh. Tubingen: Mohr Siebeck, 2008.

Buchanan, Patrick J. *The Death of the West: How Dying Populations and Immigrant Invasions Imperil Our Country and Civilization.* New York: Thomas Dunne Books, 2002.

Buchanan, Patrick J. *Suicide of a Superpower: Will America Survive to 2025?* New York: St. Martin's Press, 2011.

Cannistraro, Philip V. and Brian R. Sullivan. *Il Duce's Other Woman.* New York: William Morrow and Company, 1993.

Chase, Allan. *The Legacy of Malthus: The Social Costs of the New Scientific Racism.* New York: Alfred A. Knopf, 1977.

Chilton, David. *The Days of Vengeance: An Exposition of the Book of Revelation*. Ft. Worth, TX: Dominion Press, 1987.

Crutcher, Mark, Carole Navielli, and Renee Hobbs, "Racial Targeting and Population Control," *Life Dynamics Incorporated*, 2011.

Diodorus Siculus. *Book III*, "Ethiopia and the Gold Mines of Egypt," The Library of History of Diodorus Siculus, published in Vol. II of the Loeb Classical Library edition, 1935.

Ehrlich, Paul. *The Population Bomb*. Cutchogue, NY: Ballantine Books, 1968.

Ekeocha, Obianuju. *Target Africa: Ideological Neocolonialism in the Twenty-First Century*. San Francisco: Ignatius Press, 2018.

Ermias Kebede Wolde-Yesus, *Ethiopia : the classic case: a biblical nation under God that survived great trials for 7490 years of its existence and ordained to invoke divine judgment and condemnation upon the world! : will the present generation of humanity hearken this time to the divine warning in order to avert another imminent universal cataclysm? : the message*. Washington, D.C.: Ethiopia: The Kingdom of God Services, 1997.

Ferguson, Niall. *Civilization: The West and the Rest*. New York: Penguin Books ebook, 2011.

Fermi, Laura. *Mussolini* (Chicago and London: University of Chicago Press, 1961.

Germanus of Constantinople. *On the Divine Liturgy*. Crestwood, NY: St. Vladimir's Seminary Press, 1984.

Glass, D. V. *Population Policies and Movements in Europe*. Oxford: Clarendon Press, 1940.

Goldberg, Jonah. *Liberal Fascism: The Secret History of the American Left, From Mussolini to the Politics of Change*. New York: Doubleday, 2007.

Goldman, David P. *It's Not the End of the World, It's Just the End of You: The Great Extinction of the Nations*. New York: RVP Publishers, 2011.

Gordon, Linda. *Woman's Body, Woman's Right: Birth Control in America*. New York: Penguin Books, 1990.

Grant, George. *Grand Illusions: The Legacy of Planned Parenthood*. Nashville: Cumberland House Publishing, 2000.

Grant, George. *Killer Angel: A Biography of Planned Parenthood's Founder Margaret Sanger*. Franklin, TN: Ars Vitae Press, 1995.

Gray, Madeline. *Margaret Sanger: A Biography of the Champion of Birth Control.* New York: Richard Marek Publishers, 1979.

Grombrich, E. H. *A Little History of the World.* Yale University Press: New Haven & London, 2008.

Haas, Christopher. "Mountain Constantines: The Christianization of Aksum and Iberia." *Journal of Late Antiquity,* Spring 2008.

Haile Selassie, *My Life and Ethiopia's Progress,* Volume 2. Addis Ababa: Frontline Distribution, 1966.

Hancock, Graham. *The Sign and the Seal: The Quest for the Lost Ark of the Covenant.* New York, London: Touchstone, 1992.

Hitler, Adolph. *Mein Kampf.* New York: Reynal Hitchcock, 1940.

Hubbard, David Allan. *The Literary Sources of the Kebra Nagast.* PhD Dissertation. University of St. Andrew's, 1957.

Hull, Richard. *Jews and Judaism in Africa.* Princeton, NJ: Markus Wiener Publishers, 2009.

Jonas, Raymond. *The Battle of Adwa: African Victory in the Age of Empire.* Cambridge: The Belknap Press of Harvard University Press, 2015.

Jones, E. Michael. *Beyond the Bomb: Werner Heisenberg and Jewish Science.* South Bend, IN: Fidelity Press, 2019.

Jones, E. Michael. *Libido Dominandi: Sexual Liberation and Political Control.* South Bend, IN: St. Augustine's Press, 2005.

Jones, A. M. H. and Elizabeth Monroe. *A History of Abyssinia.* Clarendon Press, 1935.

Josephus. *The Life and Works of Flavius Josephus.* Translated by William Whiston. New York: Holt, Rinehart and Winston, 1957.

Judah, Tim. *Bikila: Ethiopia's Barefoot Olympian.* London: Reportage Press, 2008.

Jung, Carl G. and Roderick Main. *Jung on Synchronicity and the Paranormal.* Princeton NJ: Princeton University Press, 1999.

Kebra Nagast. Translated by Sir. E. A. Wallis Budge, under the title: *The Queen of Sheba and Her Only Son Menyelek.* Cambridge, Ontario: In Parenthesis Publications, 2000.

Kessis Kefyalew Merahi. *The Covenant of Holy Mary Zion with Ethiopia*. Addis Ababa: 1997.

Kessis Kefyalew Merahi. *The Meaning of Quine: The River of Life*. Addis Ababa: 2006.

Kessis Kefyalew Merahi. *The Order of Marriage and Social Ethics*. Addis Ababa: 1990.

Leeman, Bernard. "The Ark of the Covenant: Evidence Supporting the Ethiopian Traditions." Queen-of-Sheba-University.org, Academia.edu., 2011.

Louv, Jason. *John Dee and the Empire of Angels: Enochian Magick and the Occult Roots of the Modern World*. Rochester, VT; Toronto, Canada: Inner Traditions, 2018.

Lule Melaku. *History of the Ethiopian Orthodox Tewahedo Church, Part I*. Addis Ababa: 2008.

Marcus, Harold G. *The Life and Times of Menelik II: Ethiopia 1844-1913*. Lawrenceville, NJ: Red Sea Press, 1995.

Means, Sterling. *Ethiopia and the Missing Link in African History*. Chicago: Lushena Books, 2001.

Melake Mikr Kefyalew Merahi. *Christianity in Ethiopia III*. Addis Ababa, April 2012.

Messay Kebede. "Gebrehiwot Baykedagn: Eurocentrism, and the Decentering of Ethiopia." *Journal of Black Studies*, July 2006.

Muller, Gert. *Eden: The Biblical Garden Discovered in East Africa*. London: Pomegranate Publishing, 2013.

Mussolini, Rachele. *Mussolini: An Intimate Biography by his Widow*. New York: William Morrow and Company, 1974.

Olla, Roberto. *Il Duce and His Women*. Richmond, UK: Alma Books–Kindle edition, 2011.

Origen. *The Song of Songs: Commentary and Homilies*. Edited by R. P. Lawson. New York, NY: Newman Press, 1988.

Pankhurst, Richard. *Travellors in Ethiopia*. London: Oxford University Press, 1965.

Parfitt, Tudor. *The Lost Ark of the Covenant: Solving the 2,500 Year Old Mystery of the Fabled Biblical Ark*. New York: HarperOne, 2008.

Porten, Bezalel. *Archives from Elephantine: the Life of an Ancient Jewish Military Colony*. University of California Press, Berkeley, Los Angeles, 1968.

Price, Randall. *Searching for the Ark of the Covenant*. Eugene, OR: Harvest House Publishers, 2005.

Prunier, Gerad and Eloi Ficquet, ed. *Understanding Contemporary Ethiopia: Monarch, Revolution, and the Legacy of Meles Zenawi*. London: Hurst & Company, 2015.

Quine, Maria Sophia. *From Malthus to Mussolini: The Italian Eugenics Movement and Fascist Population Policy, 1890-1938*. Dissertation: University College London, 1990.

Reich, David. *Who We Are and How We Got Here: Ancient DNA and the New Science of the Human Past*. New York: Pantheon Books, 2018.

Reich, William. *Passion of Youth: An Autobiography, 1897-1922*. New York: Farrar, 2013.

Rogers, J. A. *The Real Facts About Ethiopia*. Black Classic Press, 1936.

Rose, Seraphim. *Genesis, Creation, and Early Man: The Orthodox Christian Vision*. St. Herman of Alaska Brotherhood, 2011.

Roza, Greg. *Bill and Melinda Gates: Digital Age Philanthropists*. New York: Britannica Educational Publishing, 2015.

Saffarti, Margherita. *My Fault: Mussolini As I Knew Him*. Edited by Brian Sullivan. New York: Enigma Books, 2014.

Salk, Jonas. *The Survival of the Wisest*. New York: Harper & Row, 1973.

Sanger, Margaret. *My Fight for Birth Control*. New York, NY: Farrar & Rhinehart, 1931.

Sanger, Margaret. *The Pivot of Civilization*. New York: Brentano's Publishers, 1922.

Sanger, Margaret. *Woman and the New Race*. New York: Truth Publishing Company, 1920.

Sergew Hable Selassie. *Ancient and Medieval Ethiopian History to 1270*. Addis Ababa: Haile Selassie University, 1972.

Snowden, Jr., Frank M. *Before Color Prejudice: The Ancient View of Blacks*. Cambridge, MA: Harvard University Press, 1991.

Spencer, John H. *Ethiopia at Bay: A Personal Account of the Haile Selassie Years*. Algonac, MI: Reference Publications, 1984.

Spenser, Robert. "The United Nations Meditation Room—Friends of the Meditation Room." *The Cult of the All-Seeing Eye*. Palmdale, CA: Omni Publications, 1960.

Tadesse Tamrat, *Church and State in Ethiopia, 1270-1527.* Hollywood, CA: Tsehai Publishers, 2009.

Ullendorff, Edward. *Ethiopia and the Bible: The Schweich Lectures.* Published for the British Academy by The Oxford University Press, 1967.

Wrong, Michela. *I Didn't Do It for You: How the World Betrayed a Small African Nation.* HarperCollins ebooks, 2006.

SELECT ARTICLES AND AUDIO:

Casey, Doug. "Doug Casey on Africa." Interview and edited by Louis James. *Casey Daily Dispatch*, February 22, 2012.

Corbett, James. "Meet Paul Ehrlich, Pseudoscience Charlatan." Episode 338. *The Corbett Rep*ort, June 5, 2018.

Danzig, Allison. "Barefoot Bikila First at Rome in Fastest Olympic Marathon." *New York Times*, September 10, 1960.

Douthat, Ross. "Eugenics, Past and Future." *New York Times*, June 9, 2012.

England, Christina. "Mass Sterilization of Millions of African Girls through Tetanus Vaccine Scandal Broadens as Kenyan Laboratory Attacked." *Health Impact News*. August 2018.

Gaestel, Allyn and Allison Shelly. "Ethiopians Seeking Birth Control: Caught Between Church and State." NPR, December 30, 2014.

Gale, Richard and Gary Null. "Death by Vaccination: The Gates Foundation and the New Eugenics." *Progressive Radio Network*, September 22, 2010.

Jordan, James B. "Book of Revelation." Collection of 203 mp3 Podcasts. Biblical Horizons, 1999.

Jordan, James B. "The Book of Ruth." Part 7, mp3 podcast. *Wordmp3.com*, 1992.

Kirsch, Jonathan. "Book Review: Speculation Ladled On With a Heavy Hand, The Sign and the Seal: A Quest for the Lost Ark of the Covenant by Graham Hancock." *Los Angeles Times*, April 1, 1992.

Lakhani, Nina. "Catholic Melinda Gates Defies the Vatican over Birth Control Funds." *Independent*, July 12, 2012.

Mikkelson, David. "Is Tetanus Vaccine Spiked with Sterilization Chemicals? Catholic bishops in Kenya asserted that a tetanus vaccine campaign was really a secret effort to sterilize young women." *Snopes*, November 10, 2014. Updated April 18, 2018.

Miller, J. A. "Are New Vaccines Laced with Birth-Control Drugs?" *Human Life International Reports*, June/July 1995, Vol. 13, No. 8.

Ohiheiser, Abby. "The tense standoff between Catholic bishops and the Kenyan government over tetanus vaccines." *Washington Post*, November 14, 2014.

Raffaele, Paul. "Keepers of the Lost Ark: Christians in Ethiopia have long claimed to have the ark of the covenant. Our reporter investigated." *Smithsonian Magazine*, December 2007.

Stevens, Christopher. "Mussolini the Insatiable." *The Daily Mail*, February 24, 2017.

Weatherbe, Steve. "'A mass sterilization exercise': Kenyan doctors find anti-fertility agent in U.N. tetanus vaccine." *Life Site News*, November 6, 2014.

COLLECTIONS:

Archives and Papers of Dean W. Arnold, Chattanooga, Tennessee. Relevent screenshots at http://deanslist.info/lucis

Institute of Ethiopian Studies. Library and Manuscript Collection. Addis Ababa University Campus, Addis Ababa, Ethiopia.

The Margaret Sanger Papers Project. New York University. nyu.edu/projects/sanger

Sophia Smith Collection, Smith College. Northampton, MA. libex.smith.edu/omeka

"Archives of the American Holocaust." Life Dynamics. *Birth Control Review*, Entire Collection, February 1917–January 1940. lifedynamics.com/library/#birth-control-review.

NOTES AND COMMENTS

Prologue

1   Girma Batu, Vice Academic Dean, Holy Trinity Theological College, interview
     by Dean W. Arnold in Addis Ababa, Ethiopia, May 2016, and January 2018. All
     quotes in this book from Girma Batu are sourced from these two interviews.

Chapter 1

1   Homer, *The Iliad*, Book II, Section 1, cited in Frank M. Snowden, Jr., *Before Color
     Prejudice: The Ancient View of Blacks* (Cambridge, MA: Harvard University Press,
     1991), 69.

2   Tim Judah, *Bikila: Ethiopia's Barefoot Olympian* (London: Reportage Press, 2008),
     78–79.

3   Allison Danzig, "Barefoot Bikila First at Rome in Fastest Olympic Marathon," *New
     York Times*, Sept. 10, 1960.

4   G. B. Luciano, "Colonizzazione e ordimento militare nell'Eritrea," *L'esplorazione
     commerciale*, 6 (1891), 115, cited in Harold G. Marcus, *The Life and Times of
     Menelik II: Ethiopia 1844–1913* (Lawrenceville, NJ: Red Sea Press, 1995), 122–
     123.

5   *very polite*   Judah, *Bikila*, 66.

     Christ gave them to me   Michela Wrong, *I Didn't Do It for You: How the World
     Betrayed a Small African Nation* (HarperCollins ebooks, 2006), chap. 2, loc. 541.

     eight men   Raymond Jonas, *The Battle of Adwa: African Victory in the Age of
     Empire* (Cambridge: The Belknap Press of Harvard University Press, 2015),
     134–135.

6   *invader*   Diodorus Siculus, "Ethiopia and the Gold Mines of Egypt," *Book III,*
     Section 2, cited in The Library of History of Diodorus Siculus, published in Vol.
     II of the Loeb Classical Library edition, 1935, http://penelope.uchicago.edu/
     Thayer/E/Roman/Texts/Diodorus_Siculus/3A*.html (Retrieved April 11, 2019).

     the Land of God   John A. Wilson, *The Culture of Ancient Egypt* (The University of
     Chicago Press, 1958), 169, 176, https://oi.uchicago.edu/sites/oi.uchicago.edu/files/
     uploads/shared/docs/culture.pdf (Retrieved April 28, 2019).

     church appoved publication   Melake Mikr Kefyalew Merahi, *Christianity in Ethiopia
     III* (Addis Ababa, April 2012), 1, 10.

7   "It is said," according to Richard Pankhurst, that Muhammad wrote the following: "'Yonder lieth a country wherein no one is wronged. A land of righteousness. Depart thither; and remain until it pleaseth the Lord to open your way before you.' When the Arab persecutor requested the return of these Muslim refugees, Emperor Armah allegedly responded: 'If you were to offer me a mountain of gold, I would not give up these people who have found refuge with me.'" Regarding these letters, Sergew Hable Selassie says their "authenticity is dubious." (Richard Pankhurst, *Travellers in Ethiopia* [Oxford University Press, 1965], v; Sergew Hable Selassie, *Ancient and Medieval Ethiopian History to 1270*, [Addis Ababa: Haile Selassie University, 1972], 17).

8   Judah, *Bikila*, 6, 77, and highlighted quote on unnumbered page in front matter.

9   *Bethlehem*   Lule Melaku, *History of the Ethiopian Orthodox Tewahedo Church, Part I* (Addis Ababa: 2008), 32.

     mob scene   Allison Danzig, "Barefoot Bikila First at Rome in Fastest Olympic Marathon," *New York Times*, Sept. 10, 1960.

10   Michiko Kakutani, "King Leopold's Ghost: Genocide With Spin Control," *New York Times,* August 30, 1998.

11   *modern king Leopold*   Doug Casey, "Doug Casey on Africa," interviewed by Louis James, *Casey Daily Dispatch*, Feb. 22, 2012, comment 9/3/18 at 18:48.

     work ethic   Doug Casey, "Doug Casey on China's Exploitation of Africa," *Casey Daily Dispatch*, Aug. 31, 2018.

     statement of the obvious   Niall Ferguson, *Civilization: The West and the Rest* (New York: Penguin Books ebook, 2011), loc. 561.

12   Sergew Hable Selassie, *Ancient and Medieval Ethiopian History to 1270* (Addis Ababa: Haile Selassie University, 1972), 1.

13   "50 stunning Olympic moments. No. 24: Abebe Bikila runs barefoot into history," *The Guardian*, April 25, 2012.

Chapter 2

1   Graham Hancock, *The Sign and the Seal: the Quest for the Lost Ark of the Covenant* (New York, London: Touchstone, 1992), 202.

2   *Enoch and Melchizedek*   Girma Batu, interview by Dean W. Arnold in Addis Ababa, Ethiopia, May 2016 and January 2018.

     Ethiopians generally go by their first names. If they give two names, the second is the first name of their father. If they give three, the third is the first name of their grandfather. This practice is difficult at present to standardize, as many Western books and bibliographies use the second name in the Western style, while many Ethiopian books use the first name. This book leans toward using the first name, although exceptions are made for a few Ethiopians who have been heavily covered in Western media such as Abebe Bikila.

1,000 monasteries   This is a number the author heard often repeated in Ethiopia. Certainly, there are hundreds of monasteries, but I could find no objective census. However, the African Studies Center at Michigan State University states: "There are many monasteries found in Ethiopia (one island alone—in Lake Tana—has twenty)—they spread from the islands to isolated mountain tops." (http://exploringafrica.matrix.msu.edu/module-twenty-two-activity-three [Retrieved April 17, 2019]).

3   *Shakespeare*   Marcus, *Menelik II*, 13.

4   *Vanity Fair*   Jonas, *Battle of Adwa*, 4, 271.

5   *Menelik means son of the king*   Abba Abraham Buruk Woldegaber and Mario Alexis Portella, *Abyssinian Christianity: The First Christian Nation? The History and the Identity of the Ethiopian and Eritrean Christians* (Pismo Beach, CA: BP Editing, 2012), 63.

  confirmed by the Church   Lule Melaku, *History of the Ethiopian Orthodox Tewahedo Church, Part I* (Addis Ababa, 2008), 27.

  loved me as a son   Guglielmo Massaja, *I miei trentacinque anni di missione nell'alta Etiopia* (Tivoli, 1928), ix. 28, cited in Marcus, *Menelik II*, 23.

6   *end of castration*   Jonas, *Battle of Adwa*, 14.

  bamboo rods   Marcus, op. cit., 25.

  chained and severely treated   Donald Crummey, *Priests and Politicians, Protestant and Catholic Missions in Orthodox Ethiopia 1830–1868* (Hollywood: Tsehai, 2007), 137, cited in Wikipedia: Charles Duncan Cameron.

7   Jonas, *Battle of Adwa*, 15–16.

8   Marcus, *Menelik II*, 24, 28.

9   *without a God*   Snowden, Jr., *Before Color Prejudice*, 69.

  second nation after Israel   Abraham and Portella, *The First Christian Nation?* x.

  at the Vatican   "Patriarch Encourages Bishops in Africa Synod; Says Religious Leaders Have Key Role on Continent," *Zenit.org*, Vatican City, Oct. 6, 2009, reprinted in https://www.johnsanidopoulos.com/2009/10/patriarch-abuna-paulos-addresses.html (Retrieved March 16, 2019).

10   *we don't need proof*   Paul Raffaele, "Keepers of the Lost Ark: Christians in Ethiopia have long claimed to have the ark of the covenant. Our reporter investigated,"

Smithsonian Magazine, December 2007.

only European man is rational J. M. Blaut, *The Colonizer's Model of the World: Geographical Diffusionism and Eurocentric History* (New York/London: The Guildford Press, 1993), 104, 144.

For his characterization of Jung, Blaut sources Farhad Salal, "The Racism of Jung," (1988). Blaut also quotes Jung disciple Eric Neumann, *The Origins and History of Consciousness* (1954): "The evolution of consciousness as a form of creative evolution is the peculiar achievement of Western man...in primitive societies...the earliest stages of man's psychology predominate" (p. xviii-xix). Blaut quotes Jung himself from *Psychological Types: The Collected Works of C. G. Jung* (1971): "If we go right back to primitive psychology, we find absolutely no trace of the concept of the individual" (p. 10).

11   *inscription* Sergew Hable Sellassie, *Ancient and Medieval Ethiopian History*, 103.

    coins Abraham and Portella, *The First Christian Nation?*, 17; Sergew Hable Sellassie, *Ancient and Medieval Ethiopian History*, 102–103.

    in this cross, you will conquer G. W. Bowersock, "Helena's Bridle and the Chariot in Ethiopia," in *Antiquity in Antiquity: Jewish and Christian Pasts in the Greco-Roman World*, eds. Gregg Gardner and Kevin L. Osterloh (Tubingen: Mohr Sieback, 2007), 390.

12   Matthew Bryan, "The Curious Case of Ethiopian Christianity," *Conciliar Post*, Aug. 4, 2016, see Constantius's letter, http://www.newadvent.org/fathers/2813.htm (Retrieved Aug. 1, 2019).

Young Emperor Ezana learned about Christ in the early AD 300's from a Greek-speaking Syrian named Frumentius. His story is provided to us by fourth century historian Rufinus, a generally trusted scholar monk in Italy, who said that Frumentius and another boy were taken on a trip to India by their relative, a philosopher named Meropius. They stopped at an Ethiopian port, and as Rome's treaty with the region had been broken, the "barbarians" rushed the ship and put everyone to the sword.

"The boys were found studying under a tree and preparing their lessons," said Rufinus. They were taken to the king, who was familiar with Greek—he [had] used it in an inscription—and saw the great value of two educated, Greek-speaking boys. He later appointed Frumentius as his secretary and treasurer. His companion, Aedesius, was made cupbearer. The king died early while his son was still an infant. In his will, he pronounced Frumentius and Aedesius as free men, but the queen begged them to stay and help train the young prince, who grew to become the future Emperor Ezana, founder of the first Christian empire.

Rufinus called Aedesius "simple," but said the more sagacious Frumentius focused much of his time growing churches in his adopted country. Rufinus described the Christian communities as outposts of Roman Christians, merchants scattered around the coast as a result of trade and travel—an important point for the Egyptian Copts, whose position benefited from no existing indigenous Christians before Frumentius's missionary efforts.

When Ezana became of age, he allowed the two Syrians to return to their homes. Aedesius left for the Mediterranean city of Tyre, where they both originated, but Frumentius headed to Alexandria, Egypt, to meet with Athanasius, the Patriarch of Alexandria, to discuss his concerns for the Ethiopian Christians. Known as St. Athanasius the Great, he was the famous champion of Trinitarianism at the Council of Nicea and defender of the faith against the heresy of Arianism. Frumentius shared with Athanasius the great need for a bishop to oversee this new Christian people. Patriarch Athanasius then declared to Frumentius before a council of priests: "What other man shall we find in whom the Spirit of God is, as in thee?" So, he consecrated Frumentius as bishop, then and there, and sent him back to oversee Ethiopia. "Miracles were wrought" and "barbarians were converted," according to Rufinus, who claimed he received the entire narrative from Aedesius himself, simple as he was. (Sergew Hable Sellassie, *Ancient and Medieval Ethiopian History*, 98–99).

13   Armenia is often cited as the first Christian nation, with the date AD 301 given as the year of conversion. I have been careful to use the phrase "first Christian empire" for Ethiopia. Armenia was not an empire and was subject to the Romans. According to *Armenica.org*, "[For Rome], it was not essential who sat on the Armenian throne, as long as he was loyal to the Roman Empire and would agree to receiving his throne from the hand of the Roman emperor."

Beyond the distinction just mentioned, the date for Armenian conversion has been questioned by recent scholarship. The traditional date derives solely from the account of a monk named Agathangelos, a secretary to the Armenian king, who claims to have been an eyewitness of the baptism of King Tiridates III in AD 301 in the Arsenias River. Textual critics lay bare several problems with Agathangelos's *History of the Armenians*, landing on a date for his work closer to AD 450. The original manuscript is written in Armenian, and the Armenian script was not invented until c. AD 405, making it impossible for the writer to be an eyewitness to the king's baptism. According to *Encyclopaedia Iranica*, "The *History* of Agathangelos is not of great value as a historical document."

Also, beyond Agathangelos's unreliable account, there are no other supporting sources for an early baptism of an Armenian king. Ethiopia's Ezana, however, is sourced directly from his still-existing inscription and the coins he minted with Christian crosses, along with the more reliable history of St. Frumentius discipling the young prince before he became emperor. In fact, Rufinus's account of the parents allowing such early catechesis could move the date of the Ethiopian court accepting Christianity far earlier than AD 330 and approach the AD 301 date of the Armenian claim. Beyond that, at the alleged conversion, Armenia "became a nominally Christian kingdom," according to Peter

Brown (*The Rise of Western Christendom*, 277). Ethiopia, on the other hand, had seen a popular Christian movement for centuries, beginning with the Ethiopian eunuch and a visit from the Apostle Matthew (see endnote 11 for Chapter 8.), to the point that Origen (c. AD 250) provided a clarification to the great movement that not *all* the Ethiopians had yet been converted.

Origen Sergew Hable Sellasie, *Ancient and Medieval Ethiopian History*, 97.

subject to Rome "History of Armenia," *Armenica.org*, 55, http://www.armenica. org/cgi-bin/armenica.cgi?467864590376361=1=1=55=5==1=3=A (Retrieved July 20, 2019).

not of great value "Agathangelos," *Encyclopaedia Iranica*, http://www.iranicaonline. org/articles/agathangelos [Retrieved July 20, 2019].

See also Abba Abraham Buruk Woldegaber and Mario Alexis Portella, *Abyssinian Christianity: The First Christian Nation? The History and the Identity of the Ethiopian and Eritrean Christians*, (Pismo Beach, CA: BP Editing, 2012), ix–xii.)

14 Jason Louv, *John Dee and the Empire of Angels: Enochian Magick and the Occult Roots of the Modern World* (Rochester, VT; Toronto, Canada: Inner Traditions, 2018), 252, 332.

15 Louv, *John Dee and the Empire of Angels*, 36, 2–3.

Chapter 3

1 For raw data on birthrates in every country, 1960–2016, see World Bank statistics, https://data.worldbank.org/indicator/SP.DYN.TFRT.IN (Retrieved March 16, 2019).

alarming .096 rate "South Korea's fertility rate set to hit record low of 0.96," *The Guardian*, Sept. 3, 2018, https://www.theguardian.com/world/2018/sep/03/ south-koreas-fertility-rate-set-to-hit-record-low (Retrieved March 16, 2019); Linda Poon, "South Korea is trying to boost its birth rate. It's not working," *Citylab.com*, Aug. 3, 2018, https://www.citylab.com/life/2018/08/south-korea-needs-more-babies/565169 (Retrieved March 16, 2019).

2 *Russia struggling to recover* Anatoly Karlin, "The 'Normalization' of Russia's Demographics," *The Unz Review*, Nov. 25, 2014, *http://www.unz.com/akarlin/ normalization-of-russias-demographic* (Retrieved March 16, 2019); "Russia May Have Turned the Corner in Demographic Crisis," *Breitbart*, June 14, 2017 https:// www.breitbart.com/national-security/2017/06/14/russia-may-turned-corner-demographic-crisis (Retrieved March 16, 2019); "Russia's rising birth rate gives new life to health care providers," *Reuters*, March 20, 2017, https://www.reuters. com/article/russia-md-medical-group-results-idUSL5N1GX2AU (Retrieved March 28, 2019); Nick Gutteridge, "'We're OUTBREEDING you!' Putin taunts West as

he unveils drive to boost Russian birth rate," Nick Gutteridge, *London Express*, Dec. 1, 2016, https://www.express.co.uk/news/world/738910/Vladimir-Putin-Kremlin-leader-Russia-outbreeding-Europe-West (Retrieved March 16, 2019).

no country has ever recovered   Report from Chinese Academy of Social Sciences, CGTN TV of *China Media Group*, https://youtu.be/nmjbV7PxZmc (Retrieved April 19, 2019).

3   Muslim vs. Christian birth rates by region: *Ethiopia: Demographic and Health Survey*, 2011, Report by Central Statistical Agency Addis Ababa, Ethiopia ICF International, Calverton, Maryland, USA March 2012, https://dhsprogram.com/pubs/pdf/FR255/FR255.pdf (Retrieved March 16, 2019), 71.

4   Kate Kelland, "Africa's rapid population growth puts poverty progress at risk, says Gates," *Reuters*, Sept. 18, 2018, https://uk.reuters.com/article/uk-health-global-gates/africas-rapid-population-growth-puts-poverty-progress-at-risk-says-gates-idUKKCN1LY0GQ (Retrieved March 16, 2019)

5   Marcus, *Menelik II*, 30.

6   *bevy of ancient treasures was seized*   Volker Matthies, *The Siege of Magdala: The British Empire Against the Emperor of Ethiopia* (Princeton, New Jersey: Markus Weiner Publishers, 2010), cited in Wikipedia: Expedition to Abyssinia.

we do not come to conquer   Marcus, *Menelik II*, 29.

7   *elephants*   Alan Moorehead, *The Blue Nile* (New York: Harper and Row, 1972), 309ff, cited in Wikipedia: Expedition to Abyssinia.

8   Augustus Blandy Wilde, *Modern Abyssinia* (London: Methuen, 1891), 472–473, cited in Jonas, *Battle of Adwa*, 40.

9   Orazio Antinori, letter dated Liche Nov. 13, 1876, printed in "Spedizione italiana," *Bollettino della Societa Geographica Italiana*, 13 (1876), 669–672; Memorie di G. Chiarini sulla storia recente dello Scioa, della morte ki Sahli Selassie sino ad oggi (Nov. 1877), in "Spedizioni italiana nell'Africa Equitoriale, *Memorie della Societa Geografica Italiana*, 1. (1878), 150, cited in Marcus, *Menelik II*, 47.

10   *a Christian empire in a region of Islam*   Michela Wrong, *I Didn't Do It for You: How the World Betrayed a Small African Nation*, HarperCollins ebooks, 2006), chapt. 2, loc. 541.

odor   Asfa Yilma, *Haile Selassie Emperor of Ethiopia: With a Brief Account of the History of Ethiopia* (London: Sampson Low, Marston, 1936), 104–105, cited in Jonas, *Battle of Adwa*, 21–22.

devoutly Orthodox   Paul de Lauribar, *Douze ans en Abyssinie* (Paris, 1898), 575, cited in Marcus, *Menelik II*, 72–73.

11 *3 a.m.* Lord Edward Gleichen, *With the Mission to Menelik, 1897* (London, 1898), 153, cited in Asfa-Wossen Asserate, *King of Kings: The Triumph and Tragedy of Emperor Haile Selassie I of Ethiopia* (London: Haus Publishing, 2015), 14.

ugliest Massimo Romandini, "Ferdinando Martini ad Addis Ababa," *Miscellanea di storia delle esplorazioni geografiche*, IX, Genoa, 1984, 201–243, cited in Michela Wrong, *I Didn't Do It for You*, chap. 3, loc. 1074.

12 *deeply pitted* Jonas, *Battle of Adwa*, 9.

intelligent and kind Alphonse Aubrey, "Une mission au Choa et dans les pays Galla," *Comte rendu des seances de la societe de geographie* (1886), 323, in Jonas, op. cit., 10.

rare quick wit Nicola D'Amato, *Da Adua ad Addis-Abeba ricordi d'un prigioniero* (Salerno: A. Volpe, 1898), 72, in Jonas, op. cit., 22.

Taytu was feared Jonas, op. cit., 22.

sounding board Harold Marcus, *Menelik II*, 73.

13 Guglielmo Massaja, "Corrispondenza da Scioha," *Bollettino della Societa Geographica Italiana*, 10 (1873), 33, cited in Marcus, op. cit., 37.

14 Enid Starkie, *Arthur Rimbaud in Abyssinia* (Oxford: Clarendon Press, 1937), 88, cited in Jonas, op. cit., 76.

15 *cannons thundered* Marcus, *Menelik II*, 55, quoting Atme, "Ya-galla Tarik," (Unpublished manuscript), ii, 94.

I only wish Yohannes to Queen Victoria, Debra Tabor, Sept. 20? (1887), "Correspondence respecting Mr. Portal's Mission to Abyssinia," in Great Britain, House of Commons, *Accounts and Papers*, 45, c. 5431 (London, 1888), No. 45, enclosure, cited in Marcus, op. cit., 98.

16 *we are liars* Cesare Correnti, addressing the Italian Geographical Society, April 18, 1875, Maria Carazzi, "La Societa Geografica Italiana e l'esplorazione coloniale in Africa," (1867–1900)," *La Nuova Italia*, 1972, 144–157, cited in Michela Wrong, *I Didn't Do It for You*, chap. 2, loc: 745.

717,000 Italians left Ferdinando Martini, *Nell'Affrica Italiana*, Fratelli Treves, Editori, Milan, 189;1, both cited in Michela Wrong, op. cit., chap. 2, loc: 577.

land hungry Ibid., chap. 2, loc. 509, 573.

17 *50 acres… three percent loan* Jonas, *Battle of Adwa*, 97–98.

one inch of land Portal to Baring, Jan. 1, 1888, "Correspondence respecting Mr. Portal's Mission to Abyssinia," in Great Britain, House of Commons, *Accounts and Papers*, 45, c. 5431 (London, 1888), No. 65, enclosure 1, cited in Marcus, *Menelik II*, 98.

more like a brown Englishman   Augustus Wylde, *Modern Abyssinia*, 149, cited in Jonas, op. cit., 45.

18   *understood the gravity*   Traversi to Dalla Vedova, Entotto, March 22, 1887, in "Estratti di lettere dallo Scioa," *Bollettino della Societa Geographica Italiana*, 24 (1887), 497–498, cited in Marcus, *Menelik II*, 87.

    baptize with blood   "[Gondarine] Ge'ez Manuscript," Institute of Ethiopian Studies, Addis Ababa, 170, in Marcus, op. cit., 41.

    fanatic for weapons   Antonia Cecchi, *Da Zeila alla frontiere del Caffa*, (Rome, 1886), i., 161–163, in Marcus, op. cit., 47. See also Marcus, 101, 48.

19   Ibid., 93–112

20   Menelik to King Umberto, Addis Ababa, Nov. 20, 1889, *Documents Diplomatiques Francais*, XCIV, 1, No. 63, cited in Marcus, op. cit., 117.

21   Michela Wrong, op. cit., loc. 638, 639, 647.

22   Queen Victoria to Menelik, Osbourne, Feb. 20, 1890, United Kingdom, Public Record Office, Foreign Office Archives, 97/751, cited in Marcus, *Menelik II*, 124; Carlo Zaghi, *Crispe e Menelich nel Diario inedito del conte Augusto Salimbeni* (Torino, 1956), 152, in Marcus, op. cit., 114.

Chapter 4

1   *Menelik is a myth*   Francesco Lemmi, ed., *Lettere e diari d'Africa, 1895–1896* (Rome: Edizioni Roma, 1936), 41, cited in Jonas, *Battle of Adwa*, 111.

    black snake   Oreste Baratieri, *Memories d'Afrique, 1892–1896* (Paris, Ch. Delagrave, 1899), 75, cited in Marcus, *Menelik II*, 154.

2   *Yohannes never wanted to cede*   Carlo Zaghi, *Crispe e Menelich nel Diario inedito del conte Augusto Salimbeni* (Torino, 1956), 152, cited in Marcus, op. cit., 126.

    entice the enemy   Marcus, op. cit., 159.

    whether he could be bought   Jonas, op. cit., 48.

3   *place in the sun*   Michela Wrong, *I Didn't Do It for You*, chap. 3, loc. 1110.

    licked his chops   J. A. Rogers, *The Real Facts About Ethiopia* (Black Classic Press, 1936), 10.

    childlike emotion   Blaut, *The Colonizer's Model of the World*, 96.

4   "The Misfortune of a Race," *The Atlanta Constitution*, March 2, 1896, cited in Jonas, op. cit., 5.

5   *Field of Hunger" and "one race must replace another*   Massimo Romandini, "Da Massaua ad Asmara: Ferdinando Martini in Eritrea nel 1891," *La Conoscenza dell'Asia e dell'Africa nel XIX Secolo*, vol. III, 1989, 911–933, cited in Michela Wrong, op. cit., chap. 2, loc. 676, 745.

6   Michela Wrong, Ibid., loc. 745, 779.

7   Jonas, op. cit., 112, 91, 113.

8   *30,000 troops were the most*   Marcus, op. cit., 162.

    help me by prayer   Richard Pankhurst, "Special Issue on the Battle of Adowa," *Ethiopian Observer*, 1, 1957), 346, cited in Marcus, op. cit., 160.

    I am black   Carlo Zaghi, "l'Italia e Etiopia alla vigilia di Adua nei dispacci segreti di Luigi Capucci," *Gli annali Africa italiana* 4, no. 2. (1941), 553, cited in Jonas, op. cit., 112.

9   Carlo Zaghi, *Crispe e Menelich nel Diario inedito del conte Augusto Salimbeni* (Torino, 1956), 254, cited in Marcus, op. cit., 130.

10 Alfonso Riguzzi, *Macalle: diario 45 giorni di Assedio* (Palermo: Fratelli Marsala, 1901), 31, cited in Jonas, *Battle of Adwa*, 136–137.

11 *brilliant gamesmanship*   Jonas, op. cit., 138, 2.

    never in history   George F. H. Berkeley, *The Campaign of Adowa and the Rise of Menelik* (Westminster: Archibald Constable & Co., Ltd., 1902), 119, 126, cited in Marcus, op. cit., 163.

12 *many, many*   Vico Mantegazza, *La Guerra in Africa* (Florence: Le Monnier, 1896), 450, cited in Jonas, op. cit., 125.

    prove my loyalty?   Rapporto del cavaliere Pietro Felter, Asmara, 8 avrile 1896, in Archivio storico del Ministero Africa Italiana, pos. 3/10, fasc. 69, in Jonas, op. cit., 140.

    This is my faithful subject   Pietro Felter, *La vicenda affricana, 1895–1896* (Brescia: Giulio Vannini, 1935), 37–38, in Jonas, op. cit., 141.

Chapter 5

1   Christopher Muscotto, "History of Coffee: Facts & Timeline," *Study.com*, https://study.com/academy/lesson/history-of-coffee-facts-timeline.html (Retrieved March 22, 2019).

2   *we really don't believe differently*   "Unity with the Ethiopian Orthodox after 1500 years? Some hopeful talk on communion (Interview with Archbishop Alexander),"

Dean W. Arnold, *Global Storyline*, Aug. 5, 2017, http://globalstoryline.com/home/2017/1/21/unity-with-ethiopia (Retrieved Sept. 2, 2019).

their mysteries are invalid "Copts and Orthodoxy," Orthodox Christian Information Center http://orthodoxinfo.com/ecumenism/copts_orth.aspx (Retrieved Sept. 2, 2019).

3   This book tells interesting stories and focuses on the similarities of the Eastern Orthodox and Oriental Orthodox in terms of being traditional Christian institutions, churches rooted in the ancient Church Fathers, whose common stance against modernism brings hope for the future. As I will discuss later in the book, I am committed to the Eastern Orthodox tradition and am happy to follow the teachings handed down to me. My prayer is for unity one day between the two ancient churches. How that unity takes place, I am not sure. If it requires one side to fully repent of their theological error, than I hope and pray for that miracle.

A detailed description of the split between the Eastern Orthodox and Oriental Orthodox is worthy of an entire chapter. In fact, a book needs to be written. For this treatment, I have an audience who is likely interested in about as much as what I provided—a page or two. For more extensive commentary on the split, see *Saint Cyril of Alexandria and the Christological Controversy* by John McJunkin and *Imperial Unity and Christian Divisions* by John Meyendorff.

4   Author's conversations with Archbishop Themotewos and Dr. Jacob Jossi, January 2018, Holy Trinity Theological College, Addis Ababa, Ethiopia.

5   *shrewd strategist* Jonas, *Battle of Adwa*, 147.

some kind of version of the Ark at Adwa Raymond A Silverman, *Painting Ethiopia: The Life and Word of Qes Adamu Tesfaw* (Los Angeles: UCLA Fowler Museum of Cultural History, 2005), 84; Guebre Sellassie, *Chronique du regne de Menelik H, roi des rois d'Ethiopie, ed. Maurice de Coppet*, trans. Tesfa Sellassie (Paris: Maisonneuve, 1930), 243, both cited in Jonas, op. cit., 183.

6   *similar chest with winged cherubim* Graham Hancock, *The Sign and the Seal*, 292, 289.

7   *Egyptian chest resembled a small ship* Hancock, op. cit., 290.

Ark-like cases to hold Torah scrolls Randall Price, *Searching for the Ark of the Covenant*. Eugene, OR: Harvest House Publishers, 2005), 206–207.

belly of a ship "Kebra Negast": *The Queen of Sheba and Her Only Son Menyelek* (Kebra Negast), trans. Sir. E. A. Wallis Budge (Cambridge, Ontario: In Parenthesis Publications, 2000), chap. 17, https://30bjgl1bdznn2o37ol2y4jex-wpengine.netdna-ssl.com/wp-content/uploads/2018/06/kebra_budge.pdf (Retrieved Sept. 2, 2019), hereafter "Kebra Negast."

8   *existence of Ethiopia*   Melake Mikr Kefyalew Merahi, *Christianity in Ethiopia III*, 17.

    psyche… 20,000 churches   Kaye Corbett, "Found: The Ark of the Covenant," *Worldnetdaily*, Dec. 30, 1998, cited in Price, *Searching for the Ark of the Covenant*, 111.

    since time immemorial   Edward Ullendorff, *Ethiopia and the Bible: The Schweich Lectures* (Published for the British Academy by The Oxford University Press, 1967), 82.

9   *especially chosen*   Lule Melaku, *History of the Ethiopian Orthodox Tewahedo Church, Part I* (Addis Ababa, 2008), 36.

    62-years-old… 100 percent convinced   "Is the Ark of the Covenant in Ethiopia?" *Aleteia*, May 22, 2016, https://aleteia.org/2016/05/22/is-the-ark-of-the-covenant-in-ethiopia (Retrieved March 27, 2019).

10 Edward Ullendorff, *Ethiopia and the Bible*, 140; Kebra Negast, chap. 91.

11 These quotes and the next section all from Kebra Negast, chap. 30–56.

12 Kebra Negast, chap. 30–56.

13 Ullendorff, *Ethiopia and the Bible*, 133.

14 St. Germanus of Constantinople, *On the Divine Liturgy* (Crestwood, NY: St. Vladimir's Seminary Press, 1984), 59.

15 *sparks*   Louis Ginzberg, *Legends of the Jews,* Jewish Publications Society of America, Philadelphia, 1911, vol. III, 210, cited in Hancock, op. cit., 276.

    six being born   Ginzberg, op. cit., 275, in Hancock, op. cit., 284.

16 Hancock, op. cit., 19, 22.

17 Kebra Negast, chap. 94.

18 Ibid., chap. 53.

19 Hancock, op. cit., 194–197.

20 Fre A. Salib, Discussion in Facebook group "Ask About the Tewahedo Orthodox Faith," August 8, 2018, https://www.facebook.com/search/top/?q=adwa&filters=eyJycF9hdXRob3IiOiJ7XCJuYW1lXCI6XCJhdXRob3JfbWVcIixcImFyZ3NcIjpcIlwifSJ9 (Retrieved Aug. 8, 2018).

Chapter 6

1   *recent radiocarbon dating*   Abba Abraham Buruk Woldegaber and Mario Alexis Portella, *Abyssinian Christianity: The First Christian Nation? The History and the Identity of the Ethiopian and Eritrean Christians* (Pismo Beach, CA: BP Editing, 2012), 24, 38–40.

   was not allowed inside   "Exploring the Ancient Gospels of Ethiopia," *Marginalia*, Los Angeles Review of Books, Dec. 22, 2017, http://marginalia.lareviewofbooks. org/discoveries-ethiopian-desert (Retrieved March 16, 2019).

2   Father Abraham (scholar at Abba Garima Monastery), interviewed by Dean W. Arnold, trans. Yirga Fesseha, Adwa, Ethiopia, May 2017.

3   *change our religion*   Richard Pankhurst, "Special Issue on the Battle of Adowa," *Ethiopian Observer*, 1, 1957), 346, cited in Marcus, *Menelik II*, 160.

   civilizing mission   Michela Wrong, *I Didn't Do It for You*, chap. 2, loc. 573.

   cultural infrastructure   Jonas, *Battle of Adwa*, 107.

   scamper off   Alessandro Sapelli, *Memorie d'Africa* (Bologna: Zanichelli, 1935), 103, cited in Jonas, op. cit., 164.

   effeminate   Emilio Bellavita, *Adua: i precedent—la battaglio—la conzegenze 1881–1931* (Genoa: Rivista di Roma, 1931), 322, in Jonas, op. cit., 168.

   testicles   Francesco Frisina, *L'Italia in Abissinia e nel Sudan: dall'acquisto di Assab, 1869, alla cessione di Cassala, 1897* (Alexandria: Molco Petrini, 1919), 202 in Jonas, op. cit., 233.

4   *road to hell*   Alfonso Riguzzi, *Maccalle: diario 45 giorni di Assedio* (Palermo: Fratelli Marsala, 1901), 21–22, cited in Jonas, op. cit., 136

   morale   Guido Moltedo, *L'Assedio di Maccale: campagna d'Africa 1895–96* (Rome: Dante Alighieri, 1901), 89, in Jonas, op. cit., 136, 181.

   you're not afraid, are you?   Ridolfo Mazzucconi, *La Giornata di Adua (1896)* (Milan: Mondadori, 1935), 225, in Jonas, op. cit., 181.

5   *delay is rightly questioned*   Chris Prouty, *Empress Taytu and Menelik II: Ethiopia, 1883–1910* (London: Ravens, 1986), 155, Jonas, op. cit., 182, note 26.

   communion and the start of the battle   Jonas, op. cit., 182–183 and Marcus, *Menelik II*, 172.

   communion on the field   Ibid.

6   *don't give an inch*   Asfa-Wossen, *King of Kings*, 16.

   Hotchkiss cannon   Jonas, *Battle of Adwa*, 363, fn 78.

   impossible they are not Europeans   Guido Moltedo, *L'Assedio di Maccale:*

campagna d'Africa 1895–96 (Rome: Dante Alighieri, 1901), 135, cited in Jonas, op. cit., 139.

spears Author's email exchange with Raymond Jonas, Aug. 29, 2018; For this section, see also Jonas, op. cit., 142, 150, 196.

7   *slaughterhouse* Giavanni Tedone, *Angera: I ricordi di in prigionieri di Menelik* (Milan: Giordano, 1964), 8, cited in Jonas, op. cit., 201.

Viva l'Italia Giuseppe Menarini, *La brigala Dabormida alla battaglia d'Adua,* 13, in Jonas, op. cit., 205.

betrayed Gherardo Pantano, *Ventitre anni di vita Africana* (Florence: Casa editrice militare italiana, 1932), 97, in Jonas, op. cit., 321.

8   For casualties, Marcus, *Menelik II*, 173. For this section, see also Jonas, Jonas, op. cit., 201, 213, 215, 302.

colossal slaughter "Vittorie sopra vittorie," *L'Italia*, March 7, 1896, in Jonas, op. cit., 302.

9   Raymond Jonas quotes, 233, 3, 228.

colonial farce Emilio Bellavita, *Adua: i precedent—la battaglio—la conzegenze (1881–1931)*, 310, cited in Jonas, Jonas, op. cit., 169.

10   William E. B. Du Bois, "The Pan-African Movement," in George Padmore ed., *History of the Pan-African Congress: Colonial and Coloured Unity, a Programme of Action* (London: Hammersmith Bookshop, 1963), cited in Jonas, op. cit., 184.

J. A. Rogers, *The Real Facts About Ethiopia*, 16.

11   See Jonas, *Battle of Adwa*, 320, 302–303, 194.

Bring them back to me alive Nicola D'Amato, *Da Adua ad Addis-Abeba ricordi d'un prigioniero* (Salerno: A Volpe, 1896), 8, in Jonas, op. cit., 240.

Turks Carlo Diotti, Prigioniero d'Africa: La attaglia di Adua e 'limpresa coliniale del 1895–1896 nel diario di un caporale italiano (Como: Nodolibri, 2006), 71–72, in Jonas, op. cit., 244.

odor Tedone, *Angera*, 71, in Jonas, op. cit., 244.

12   See Jonas, op. cit., 243, 246.

Two lateral cuts Tedone, *Angera*, 27–28, in Jonas, op. cit., 222.

13   See Jonas, *Battle of Adwa*, 227, 259, 225.

one of ours Luigi Goj, *Adua e prigionia fra i galla* (Milan: Scuola Tip. Salesiana, 1901), 28, cited in Jonas, op. cit., 223.

ignoble practice J. G. Vanderheym, *Une expedition avec le negous Menelik: vingt mois en Abyssinie* (Paris: Hatchette, 1896), 71, in Jonas, op. cit., 223.

kindness   Jonas, op. cit., 249.

14   *definitely annulled*   Carlo Rossetti, *Storia diplomatica durante il regno di Menelik II* (Torino, Societa Tipografica—Editrice Nazionale, 1910), 181, cited in Marcus, *Menelik II*, 176–77.

longest-lived independent Christian nation   Richard Hull, *Jews and Judaism in Africa* (Princeton, NJ: Markus Wiener Publishers, 2009), 190.

15   *Arimondi's body… offered a mass*   Francesco Frisina, *L'Italia in Abissinia e nel Sudan*, 183, cited in Jonas, op. cit., 289.

476,000 men   Asfa-Wossen, *King of Kings*, 114.

we shall never make that mistake   Michela Wrong, *I Didn't Do It for You*, chap. 3, loc. 1143 (author's emphasis).

Chapter 7

1   Girma Batu (Vice Academic Dean, Holy Trinity Theological College), interview by Dean W. Arnold in Addis Ababa, Ethiopia, May 2016 and January 2018; Elias Gebreselassie (student, Holy Trinity Theological College), interview by Dean W. Arnold in Addis Ababa, Ethiopia, January 2018.

2   St. Athanasius of Alexandria, *Homily of the Papyrus of Turin*, 71:216 (ante AD 373) in MCF, 206, cited in Brian Forrest Roberts, *Dear Brother* (Lulu: 2006), 213. See also *Luigi S. M. Gambero, Mary and the Fathers of the Church: The Blessed Virgin Mary in Patristic Thought* (San Francisco: Ignatius Press, 2006). For a scholarly assessment of the veracity of this quote, see "A Discourse on 'The Discourse on the Holy Theotokos'" by Paul Hoffer, *Spes Mea Christus!* April 10, 2009, http://capriciousness.blogspot.com/2009/04/discourse-on-discourse-on-holy.html (Retrieved March 29, 2019).

3   *15,000 churches*   Melake Mikr Kefyalew Merahi, *Christianity in Ethiopia III*, 16.

Portugese… neighboring country Egypt   Girma Batu, interview by Dean W. Arnold.

the manna…   Kebra Negast, chap. 98.

'overshadowing' the Ark   Steve Ray, "Mary, the Ark of the New Covenant," *Catholic Answers*, Oct. 1, 2005, https://www.catholic.com/magazine/print-edition/mary-the-ark-of-the-new-covenant (Retrieved June 22, 2019).

4   Zwingli Opera, Corpus Reformatorum (Berlin, 1905), v. 1, 424;
Wesley: "Letter to a Roman Catholic" *In This Rock*, Nov. 1990, p.25;
Luther: Weimar edition of Martin Luther's Works, English translation edited by J. Pelikan (Concordia: St. Louis), Volume 51, 128–129;

John Calvin also failed to refute the doctrine of Mary's perpetual virginity and warned against disputing it: "It is said that Joseph knew her not till she had brought forth her first-born son: but this is limited to that very time. What took place afterwards, the historian does not inform us. Such is well known to have been the practice of the inspired writers. Certainly, no man will ever raise a question on this subject, except from curiosity; and no man will obstinately keep up the argument, except from an extreme fondness for disputation." (John Calvin's Commentary on Matthew 1:25

5   Or, as British journalist and humorist Malcolm Muggeridge put it bluntly: "The orgasm has replaced the cross as the focus of longing and the image of fulfillment." Muggeridge, *Tread Softly for you Tread on my Jokes* (London and Glasgow: Collins–Fontana, 1969), 46.

6   *the Bride of Heaven and her chariot*   Kebra Negast, chap. 113.

Tharbis was the daughter of the king   Flavius Josephus, *The Genuine Works of Flavius Josephus the Jewish Historian, containing 20 Books of the Jewish Antiquities*, ed. William Whiston (London, 1737), Book 2, chap. 10, http://penelope.uchicago.edu/josephus/ant-2.html (Retrieved March 29, 2019).

Interpreters of Scripture differ on how to reconcile Josephus's account—and the account of Moses's Cushite wife in Numbers 12—with the account in Exodus 2 of Moses marrying the Arab Zipporah, a Midianite. Some interpreters argue for Zipporah being "Arabian Cush" rather than Ethiopian Cush (see index entry "Arabian Cush" for pages later in this book that address the subject). Others say Moses had two wives, not difficult to believe as Moses was age 40 when the biblical account of his adult life begins and he meets Zipporah. For those embracing the two wives hypothesis, some accept the implied polygamy and say Moses married again in exile while his first wife remained in Egypt. Others say Tharbis stayed in Ethiopia when young Moses returned to Egypt and years later joined the famous Moses in the wilderness. Still others believe Zipporah died in the wilderness (as did almost all the adult Israelites) and Moses subsequently remarried an Ethiopian.

7   *Ethiopian bride*   St. Iranaeus, *Against Heresies*, Book IV, chap. 20, section 12, *NewAdvent.org*, http://www.newadvent.org/fathers/0103420.htm (Retrieved March 29, 2019).

having become the first-fruits   Eusebius, *Church History*, Book II, Section 13, *NewAdvent.org*, http://www.newadvent.org/fathers/250102.htm (Retrieved March 29, 2019).

I am black and beautiful   Origen, *The Song of Songs. Commentary and Homilies*, ed. R. P. Lawson (New York, NY: Newman Press, 1988), 90–105.

8   James B. Jordan, "Book of Revelation," Collection of 203 mp3s, Biblical Horizons ministries. mp3 no. 178, "Millennium 2" and mp3 no. 31, "The Coming of the Lamb," http://www.wordmp3.com/product-group.aspx?id=79 (Retrieved March 29, 2019).

Chapter 8

1   A. J. Barker, *The Rape of Ethiopia, 1936*, ed. Barrie Pitt (New York: Ballantine Books, 1971), 14, 15.

2   Asfa-Wossen, *King of Kings*, 32.

3   Ibid., 14–15.

4   Michela Wrong, *I Didn't Do It for You*, chap. 7, loc. 2344.

5   John H. Spencer, *Ethiopia at Bay: A Personal Account of the Haile Selassie Years* (Algonac, MI: Reference Publications, 1984), 134, cited in Wrong, op. cit., chap. 7, loc. 2347.

6   Cf. Eloi Ficquet, Taurin Cahagne, Encyclopedia Aethiopica, ed. Siegbert Uhlig, vol. 1, 664ff, cited in Asfa-Wossen, op. cit., 23.

7   *charges against Iyasu*   Gobeze Tafeta, *Abba Tena Iyasu* (Addis Ababa, 1996), 149ff; Marse Hasan Wolde Qirqos, *YeZaman Tarik Tezetaye BaNegesta Negestat Zawditu Zamana Mangist* (Addis Ababa, undated), 166, cited in Asfa-Wossen, op. cit., 26–27.

     political lightweight   Asfa-Wossen, op. cit., 29.

8   Harold Marcus, *Haile Selassie I: The Formative Years, 1892–1936* (Berkeley, Los Angeles, London, 1987), 3ff, cited in Asfa-Wossen, op. cit., 40.

9   Spencer, *Ethiopia at Bay*, 354.

10   Mahatma-Selassie Wolde-Maskal, *Zekra Nagar*, 725, cited in Asfa-Wossen, op. cit., 74.

     full name   "King of Kings: the Life and Death of Haile Selassie I," *The Daily Star* (Dhaka, Bangladesh), Jan. 21, 2016, https://www.thedailystar.net/shout/the-greatest-story/king-kings-the-life-and-death-haile-selassie-i-204853 (Retrieved March 29, 2019).

11   Why did it take so long for the first Christian empire to gain its own patriarch? Ethiopian church history has a glaring gap between the two highly documented events of (1) the life of Frumentius who Christianized Ezana, Ethiopia's first emperor, and (2) the conversion of the Ethiopian eunuch in the Book of Acts, 300 years before Frumentius. Ancient historian Rufinus, in his definitive account of Frumentius, describes the Christian communities in Ethiopian ports of that day as outposts of Roman Christians, merchants scattered around the coast as a result of trade and travel—an important point for the Egyptian Copts, whose position overseeing Ethiopia benefited from the understanding that indigenous Christians in Abyssinia did not exist before Frumentius's missionary efforts.

Unlike the Coptic version of the founding of Christianity in Abyssinia, Ethiopians believe Bacos the eunuch returned to his country and the new gospel he shared grew organically over the centuries. In fact, the greatest early church historian, Eusebius, confirms this view, saying Bacos "is said to have been the first on returning to his country to proclaim the knowledge of God." Church Father John Chrysostom mentions early Ethiopian Christianity, and Origen implies that a healthy chunk of the population converted before the days of Frumentius: "The gospel is not said to have been preached to *all* the Ethiopians, especially to such as live beyond the river." (For citations regarding Eusebius, Chrysostom, and Origen, see Sergew Hable Sellasie, *Ancient and Medieval Ethiopian History*, 97.)

Apart from these few quotes, one must ask why no other documentation exists. I brought this question to a ranking scholar in the Ethiopian church, who asked to remain anonymous. "There were many written documents, but they were deliberately snatched and destroyed by the Egyptians," he told me. "You know why? They needed Frumentius to be the first Ethiopian church leader. That way there is no chance for Ethiopia to have its own diocese. To do so, they destroyed all the historical documents and historical traditions.

"Also, there were many monasteries under the leadership of Ethiopian monks in those days. But today there is no way to get access to the rooms that have the historical documents and parchments. A person who had lived there seven years came to Ethiopia and gave a presentation to us. He said the monasteries have areas that are restricted from Ethiopians. Why are they restricted, especially from Ethiopians?"

This scholar also said the Egyptians brought back from the Council of Nicea a forged version of the agreed upon canons that decreed the nation to be under Egypt's patriarch. "It is an historical fallacy," he told me. "The church corrected that." The Ethiopian Church's official website confirms this. "The Egyptians therefore inserted the forty-second Pseudo-Canon of the Council of Nicea, prohibiting Ethiopians from occupying hierarchical positions…Thus, an Egyptian bishop always remained at the head of the Ethiopian church from its foundation up to the second half the twentieth century. This is a unique phenomenon in the history of the Christian Church." Haile Selassie's longtime goal for an independent church was realized at the instillation of Abuna Basileos on Jan. 13, 1951, the first patriarch of Ethiopia. ("Pseudo-Canon": Church Organization, *The Ethiopian Orthodox Tewahedo Church Faith and Order,* https://www.ethiopianorthodox.org/ english/ethiopian/prechristian.html (Retrieved June 27, 2019).

Actually, the Coptic-appointed Frumentius is not the only Ethiopian hierarch discussed in Abyssinian history. There are two more that are highly documented in church tradition. However, the Ethiopian church itself denies the accounts, at least partially.

First century Ethiopian King Fulvianus is an official saint for the Eastern Orthodox. His virgin daughter Ephigenia is a Catholic saint. Church hagiography teaches that the Apostle Matthew preached and ministered in Ethiopia and was martyred by King Fulvianus, who later converted. According to the official story of the Eastern Orthodox Church: "When the holy apostle was fervently entreating God for the conversion of the Ethiopians the Lord Himself appeared to him in the form of a youth. He gave him a staff, and commanded him to plant it at the doors of the church. The Lord said that a tree would grow from this staff and it would bear fruit, and from its roots would flow a stream of water. When the Ethiopians washed themselves in the water and ate the fruit, they lost their wild ways and became gentle and good."

After Matthew healed the queen and prince from evil spirits, the still-pagan King accused Matthew of sorcery and ordered his execution by fire. In an episode resembling the fiery furnace story in the book of Daniel, Matthew was not burned at all but the flames leaped out toward the King. "The frightened Ethiopian turned to the saint with an entreaty for mercy, and by the prayer of the martyr the flame went out. The body of the holy apostle remained unharmed, and he departed to the Lord."

Like Gideon, the king needed one more sign. Matthew's body was thrown out to sea in an iron coffin. If it returned unharmed, the king would believe. "That night the Apostle Matthew appeared to Bishop Platon in a dream, and commanded him to go with clergy to the shore of the sea and to find his body there."

The king converted. We know nothing about this "Bishop Platon," and might assume, with his Greek name (derived from *Plato*) that he was a companion of the Apostle Matthew. "Upon the death of Bishop Platon, Matthew appeared to [Fulvianus] and exhorted him to head the Ethiopian Church. Having become a bishop, Saint Fulvian-Matthew toiled at preaching the Word of God." ("St. Frumentius, Archbishop of Abyssinia, Ethiopia," *Orthodox Church of America*, https://www.oca.org/saints/lives/2019/11/30/103451-saint-frumentius-archbishop-of-abyssinia-ethiopia)

We learn from this account, held in total or part by the Greek Orthodox, Russian Orthodox, and Roman Catholic traditions, that Ethiopia had at least three other hierarchs 300 years before Frumentius: (1) the Apostle Matthew himself; (2) King Fulvianus, also known as Bishop Fulviun-Matthew, and; (3) the unknown Bishop Platon. Why do Ethiopians fail to embrace this tradition? No mention of a King Fulvian or Fulvianus is named in their secular or church history. In fact, the church officially rejects the teaching that Matthew was martyred in Ethiopia.

Firstly, the Orthodox and Catholic accounts derive from the ancient *Apochryphal Acts of the Apostles, Vol. II* (London: Williams and Norgate, 1871), which describes the people that martyred Matthew as cannibals (p. 93). The Eastern Orthodox story of Fulvianus repeats this. Ethiopians consider themselves, while not all Old Testament believers before Christ, to have been monotheists—sun worshippers like Sheba—and certainly not cannibals. Secondly, the Ethiopian church teaches that Ethiopians did not shed apostolic blood. They believe the people saturated in the

Old Testament, like the Ethiopian eunuch, were prepared for the message of Christ when Bacos returned to share the good news. Fitting these criteria, the Ethiopian Church believes Matthew visited and ministered in Ethiopia, but did not die there.

"According to Rufinus and some other historians, the Apostle Matthew came to Ethiopia," said the scholar I interviewed who has suspicions of the Egyptians. He noted that Matthew was not martyred there. "What happened after that? We don't know. When you discuss this with Coptic fathers, when you mention any unique features of Ethiopian Christianity, they have many reservations. When you mention the Ark of the Covenant, they have reservations."

Frumentius is a saint in the Ethiopian, Eastern Orthodox, and Catholic churches. But he is not a saint in the Coptic church.

12   See Asfa-Wossen, op. cit., 93, 62; *New York Times*, Nov. 3, 1930, cited in Asfa-Wossen, op. cit., 90.

13   Richard Greenfield, *Ethiopia. A New Political History* (London: F. A. Praeger, 1965), 158, cited in Asfa-Wossen, op. cit., 58.

14   *New York Times*, May 5, 1924, cited in Asfa-Wossen, *King of Kings*, 59.

   Gospels   Baron von Waldthausen, dispatch to the German foreign office, Oct. 22, 1930, AA R77856, in Asfa-Wossen, op. cit., 83.

   Zakok anointed King David   Zawde Retta, Yakadamawi Haile-Selassie Mengest (Delhi, 2012), 18–45, in Asfa-Wossen, op. cit., 84.

15   Jonah Goldberg, *Liberal Fascism: The Secret History of the American Left, From Mussolini to the Politics of Change* (New York: Doubleday, 2007), 35.

16   Roberto Olla, *Il Duce and His Women* (Richmond, UK: Alma Books-Kindle edition, 2011), 135–137.

17   Margaret Sanger, *My Fight for Birth Control* (New York, NY: Farrar & Rhinehart, 1931), 76–77, https://archive.org/stream/in.ernet.dli.2015.219268/2015.219268. My-Fight_djvu.txt (Retrieved March 30, 2019).

18   *ruthless logic*   Pietro Nenni, *Lucifero* journal, May 3, 1914, cited in Roberto Olla, *Il Duce and His Women*, 134.

   stabbings   Benito Mussolini, *My Life from 29th 1883 to 23rd November 1911* in Volume 33 of *Opera Omnia*, eds. Edoardo Susmel and Duilio Susmel, (Forence, La Fenice 1951–63). 248, in Olla, op. cit., 32–33.

19   Mussolini, *My Life*, in Vol. 33 *Opera Omnia*, 245, 251, cited in Olla, *Il Duce and His Women*, 34, 62, 54; Renzo De Felice, *Mussolini il Rivoluzionario* (Turin: Einaudi, 1965), 35, cited in Olla, op. cit., 62.

20   Ibid., 79, 82.

21 *took her virginity* Claretta Petacci, *Mussolini segreto*, ed. Mario Suttora (Milan: Ruzzoli, 2009), 8, cited in Olla, op. cit., 86–87.

whatever I want to do Silvio Bertoldi, *Mussolini tale e quale* (Milan: Longanesi, 1973), 43, in Olla, op. cit., 95.

liked to ridicule Jesus Jonah Goldberg, *Liberal Fascism*, 32.

22 *beat his wife* Laura Fermi, *Mussolini* (Chicago and London: University of Chicago Press, 1961), 117.

brandished a gun Rachele Mussolini, *Mussolini privato* (Milan: Mondadori, 1980), 28, cited in Olla, op. cit., 93.

holding a revolver Cesari Rossi, Mussolini Com'era (Rome: Ruffolo, 1946), 203, in Olla, op. cit., 170.

read Nietzsche and the Koran Fermi, *Mussolini*, 121.

23 *she's used to my infidelities* Reda Rafanelli, *Una donna el Mussolini* (Milan: Rizzoli, 1946), 131–132, cited in Olla, op. cit., 132.

the only beautiful woman in my life Rachele Mussolini, *Mussolini privato*, 80, in Olla, op. cit., 64.

fist fights Ibid., 79, 148.

24 Olla, *Il Duce and His Women*, 100–101, 2–5;

He is a Man Simonetta Falasca-Zamponi, *Fascist Spectacle: The Aesthetics of Power in Mussolini's Italy* (Berkeley: University of California Press, 2000), 51, cited in Goldberg, *Liberal Fascism*, 33.

armed squads Edvige Mussolini, *Mio fratello Benito* (Florence: La Fenice, 1957), 100, in Olla, op. cit., 207

25 *create his own ideology* Hannah Arendt, *Le Origini del Totalitarismo* (Milan: Edizioni di Comunita, 1967), 234–5; Fermi, *Mussolini,* 72.

26 *a genius* Sanger, *Pivot of Civilization*, 182–3.

tyranny/undermine the Christian churches/downfall Walter Adolphe Roberts, "Birth Control and the Revolution," *Birth Control Review*, ed. Margaret Sanger, Volume I, Number 6 (June 1917), 7, https://lifedynamics.com/app/uploads/2015/09/1917-06-June.pdf (Retrieved May 1, 2019).

a new sex morality Sanger, *Woman and the New Race* (New York: Truth Publishing Company, 1920), 167.

spiritual illumination Sanger, *Pivot of Civilization*, 271.

multiple sex partners Gray, *Margaret Sanger*, 61, 71, 163, 224, 227, 487.

three times a day about right Ibid., 227–228.

27   *Saturnalia*   Madeline Gray, *Margaret Sanger*, 59

28   Scholars share concern that much of Nietzsche's work was reinterpreted by his sister who edited the primary sources through a Nazi lens. Researchers claim this selection is from a work not edited by his sister. See "Nietzsche's influence on Nazis," https://en.wikipedia.org/wiki/Talk%3AFriedrich_ Nietzsche%2FArchive_1#Nietzsche's_influence_on_Nazis (Retrieved April 6, 2019). Nietzsche's quotes from Friedrich Nietzsche, *Nachgelassene Fragmente Anfang 1880 bis Sommer 1882*, 189, in Giorgio Colli and Mazzino Montinare, eds., *Nietzsches Sämtliche Werke* (Munich, 1980), Vol. 9, 250, cited in Michael Burleigh and Wolfgang Wippermann, *The Racial State: Germany, 1933–1945* (New York: Cambridge University Press, 1991), 34, 35.

      the crucified one   Peter Kreeft, "The Pillars of Unbelief–Nietzsche," *peeterkreeft.com,* http://www.peterkreeft.com/topics-more/pillars_nietzsche.htm (Retrieved April 5, 2019).

      syphilis   Bernd Magnus, "Frederick Nietzsche," *Brittanica.com*, https://www. britannica.com/biography/Friedrich-Nietzsche (Retrieved April 5, 2019).

29   "100 years after death, Nietzsche's popularity keeps growing," *Stanford News Service*, June 5, 2001, https://news.stanford.edu/pr/01/nietzsche66.html (Retrieved April 2, 2019); Adolph Hiter, *Mein Kamp* (New York: Reynald Hitchock, 1940), 349, 396.

30   *subhumans*   Martin A. Ruehl, "In defense of slavery: Nietzsche's dangerous thinking," *Independent*, Jan. 2, 2018, https://www.independent.co.uk/news/long_ reads/nietzsche-ideas-superman-slavery-nihilism-adolf-hitler-nazi-racism-white-supremacy-fascism-a8138396.html (Retrieved April 2, 2019), see also *Quality of Life: The New Medical Dilemma*, eds. James J. Walter, Thomas Anthony Shannon (Mahwah, NJ: Paulist Press, 1960), 63.

      human waste   Sanger, *Woman and the New Race*, 4.

      raising of human thoroughbreds   Sanger, *Pivot of Civilization*, 145.

      masthead   Margaret Sanger, ed., *Birth Control Review*, November 1921. For an image of this magazine and masthead, see https://gerardnadal.com/2010/01/05/ sanger-targets-the-lower-classes/ (Retrieved April 6, 2019) See also https:// lifedynamics.com/app/uploads/2015/09/1921-11-November.pdf (Retrieved May 1, 2019).

31   *International Aspects of Birth Control: The International Neo-Malthusian and Birth Control Conference* (New York: American Birth Control League, 1925), v, cited in George Grant, *Killer Angel: A Biography of Planned Parenthood's Founder Margaret Sanger* (Franklin, TN: Ars Vitae Press, 1995), 80. This same quote can be found in "The Function of Sterilization: Part of an address delivered by Margaret Sanger before the Institute of Ethenics at Vasser College August 5th," *The Margaret*

Sanger Papers Project, New York University, https://www.nyu.edu/projects/sanger/webedition/app/documents/show.php?sangerDoc=304387.xml (Retrieved April 3, 2019).

32   *weeding out the unfit*   Sanger, *Woman and the New Race*, 229.

    the strong and the fit…a higher race of men   Sanger, *Woman and the New Race*, 160–161.

33   *mothers' hearts cling*   Sanger, *Woman and the New Race*, 160.

34   Jean H. Baker, *Margaret Sanger: A Life of Passion* (New York: Hill and Wang, 2012), 147.

35   Maria Sophia Quine, *From Malthus to Mussolini: The Italian Eugenics Movement and Fascist Population Policy, 1890–1938* (Dissertation: University College London, 1990), 7, 8, http://discovery.ucl.ac.uk/1317873/1/294923.pdf (Retrieved April 5, 2019).

36   *yes, they are!*   Bruce Strang, *On the Fiery March* (New York: Praeger, 2003), 21.

    racial equanimity   George Grant, *Grand Illusions: The Legacy of Planned Parenthood* (Nashville: Cumberland House, 2000), 43.

    negroid aboriginal tribes   Lothrop Stoddard, "Population Problems in Asia," *Birth Control Review*, ed. Margaret Sanger, Vol. V, Number 12 (Dec. 1921), 11, https://lifedynamics.com/app/uploads/2015/09/1921-12-December.pdf (Retrieved May 1, 2019).

37   *favorable review…White supremacy*   Havelock Ellis, "The World's Racial Problem," *Birth Control Review*, ed. Margaret Sanger, Oct. 1920, Vol. IV, No. 10, 15–16, https://lifedynamics.com/app/uploads/2015/09/1920-10-October.pdf (Retrieved May 1, 2019).

    segregation or sterilization   Margaret Sanger, "A Plan for Peace," *Birth Control Review*, April 1932, Vol. XVI, No. 4, 108, https://lifedynamics.com/app/uploads/2015/09/1932-04-April.pdf (Retrieved May 1, 2019).

    Nazis   Ernst Rudin, "Eugenic Sterilization: An Urgent Need," *Birth Control Review*, ed. Margaret Sanger, April 1933, Vol. XVII, No. 4, 102, https://lifedynamics.com/app/uploads/2015/09/1933-04-April.pdf (May 2, 2019).

38   *Opera Omnia*, Vol. 28, 321, cited in Roberto Olla, *Il Duce and His Women*, 372.

Chapter 9

1   Olla, *Il Duce and His Women*, 123, 177.

2   *we remain neutral*   Emil Ludwig, *Nine Etched from Life* (Ayer Company Publishers, 1934, 1969), 321.

nationality exists…assassinate the party   Jasper Ridley, *Mussolini: A Biography* (New York: St. Martin's, 1997), 71, cited in Goldberg, *Fascism and Mussolini*, 45.

3   *women prefer*   Rossi, *Mussolini Com'era*, 209, cited in Olla, *Il Duce*, 286.

very bones   Margherita G. Sarfatti, *The Life of Benito Mussolini*, trans. Frederic Whyte (New York: Stokes, 1925), 263, cited in Goldberg, op. cit., 45.

4   *attacked the Avanti! offices*   Olla, op. cit., 215.

quite violent   Charles Delzel, *Mediterranean Fascism 1919–1945* (New York: Harper & Row, 1971), 4.

ruthless and energetic   Christopher Hibbert, *Rome: The Biography of a City* (Penguin Books, 2001), p. 427.

5   Goldberg, op. cit., 50.

6   Olla, op. cit., 207, 271, 361.

Hitler…emulates   see video "Mussolini Dead! Historic newsreel tells of dictator's demise," embedded in Christopher Stevens, "Mussolini the Insatiable," *The Daily Mail*, Feb. 24, 2017, https://www.dailymail.co.uk/news/article-4257958/Mussolini-violent-lover-demanded-sex-constantly.html (Retrieved April 9, 2019).

7   *sent by Providence*   Robert Andrews, "In Defense of Il Duce," *The Telegraph*, July 2, 2003, https://www.telegraph.co.uk/culture/books/3597570/In-defence-of-Il-Duce.html (Retrieved April 9, 2019).

8   *Fascism is a religion*   Goldberg, *Mussolini and Fascism*, 40.

sublime perversity…Nietzschean superman   Fermi, *Mussolini*, 72.

9   Goldberg, op. cit., 50.

10   Asfa-Wossen, *King of Kings*, 104.

11   Ibid., 52.

12   Robert Andrews, "In Defense of Il Duce."

13   Philip Cannistraro and Brian Sullivan, *Il Duce's Other Woman* (New York: William Morrow and Company, 1993), 462–463.

14   *married to all Italian women*   Goldberg, op. cit., 33.

violinist…a great lover   Olla, op. cit., 47.

the Churchills' comments   Christopher Stevens, "Mussolini the Insatiable," *The Daily Mail*, Feb. 24, 2017.

15   Roosevelt to Long, June 15, 1933, *Breckinridge Long Papers*, Library of Congress, Box 105, cited in Cannistraro and Sullivan, op. cit., 409.

16   *quoting Rudyard Kipling*   Theodore Roosevelt, Jr., to mother, August 13, 1933, *Theodore Roosevelt, Jr., Papers*, Library of Congress, container 20, cited in Cannistraro, op. cit., 411.

   I need peace   "Mussolini Willing to Guarantee Enforcement of an Arms Treaty," *The New York Times*, April 14, 1934, in Cannistraro, op. cit., 430.

17   Francamaria Trapani, "Mia madre Margherita Sarfatti, la grande passione di Mussolini," *Gente*, Sept. 10, 1982, III, 58, cited in Cannistraro, op. cit., 474.

18   *worthy of a brothel*   see *Il Popolo d'Italia*, No. 297, Dec. 12, 1922, 20, cited in Olla, op. cit., 232.

   since she was a toddler   Margharita Saffarti, *My Fault: Mussolini As I Knew Him* (New York: Enigma Books, 2014), ed. Brian Sullivan, 247.

   in love with the daughter   Ercole Boratto, *Diario sul Duce*, file JZX–6220, National Archives, Washington, sent by Agent CB–55 (X-2, Oss, Roma), 1946, cited in Olla, op. cit., 297–298.

19   *sex on the carpet…gonorrhea and syphilis*   Olla, op. cit., 64, 77, 129, 261–262, 286.

20   *Viagra-like drug*   Silvio Bertoldi, *Gli Arricchiti all'ombra di Palazzo Venezia* (Milan: Ugo Mersia Editore, 2009), 34–35, cited in Olla, op. cit., 45–47.

   spasms   Sarfatti, *My Fault*, 299.

   smells   Fermi, *Mussolini*, 119.

   more than two in the room…terrible smell   Claretta Petacci, *Mussolini segreto*, ed. Mario Suttora (Milan: Ruzzoli, 2009), 101, 75–76, in Olla, op. cit., 233–234.

Chapter 10

1   "Ethiopia is an outlier in the Orthodox Christian world," *Pew Research Center*, Nov. 28, 2017, https://www.pewresearch.org/fact-tank/2017/11/28/ethiopia-is-an-outlier-in-the-orthodox-christian-world (Retrieved June 28, 2019).

2   Melake Mikr Kefyalew Merahi, *Christianity in Ethiopia III* (Addis Ababa, April 2012), 1, 10.

3   Blaut, *The Colonizer's Model of the World*, 47; Sergew, *Ancient and Medieval Ethiopian History to 1270*, 51, 55.

   futilely   Blaut, op. cit., 50.

   hurried their own downfall   Melake, op. cit., 17.

4   Ermias Kebede, *Ethiopia: The Classic Case*, 20.

5   "Italian Quests for Ethiopia's legends," *historicmysteries.com*, Feb. 11, 2010, https://www.historicmysteries.com/italian-quests-for-ethiopias-legends (Retrieved April 9, 2019).

6   Olla, *Il Duce and His Women*, 365; Cannistraro and Sullivan, *Il Duce's Other Woman*, 474–475.

7   A. J. Barker, *The Rape of Ethiopia, 1936*, ed. Barrie Pitt (New York: Ballantine Books, 1971), 14, 18.

8   *trust is in our Creator*   Asfa-Wossen, *King of Kings*, 120.

     barbarity   Olla, op. cit., 367.

     peace for all…not as civilized   Barker, op. cit., 131, 51.

9   Ibid., 56.

10   *lose control*   Cannistraro, op. cit., 476.

     savages   Barker, op. cit., 22.

11   *burning, deadly rain*   Angelo Del Boca, *Yperit-Regen. Der Giftgas*krieg [Yperit Rain. Chemical Warfare] in *Der erste faschistische Vernichtungskrieg. Die italienische Aggression gegen Athiopien 1935–1941*, eds. Asfa-Wossen Asserate and Aram Mattioli (Cologne: 2006), 53, cited in Asfa-Wossen, op. cit., 118.

     nurse   Leo Van Bergen, *Before My Helpless Sight: Suffering, Dying and Military Medicine on the Western Front, 1914–1918* (Ashgate Publishing, 2009) p. 184, cited in Wikipedia: Sulfur mustard: Physiological effects, https://en.wikipedia.org/wiki/Sulfur_mustard#Physiological_effects (Retrieved April 10, 2019).

12   *hospitals bombed*   Michela Wrong, *I Didn't Do It for You*, chap. 3, loc. 1155.

     veritable hell   Marcel Junod, *Kampfer Beiderseits der Front* (Zurich, Vienna, 1947), 64, cited in Asfa-Wossen, op. cit., 119.

     sirens sounded…   Barker, op. cit., 23, 61–62.

13   *1000 tons*   Asfa-Wossen, *King of Kings*, 119.

     Mussolini's sons   Cannistraro, op. cit., 483.

     with or without the Ethiopians   Barker, op. cit., 69.

14   Cannistraroop. cit., 481.

15   *150,000*   Asfa-Wossen, op. cit., 127.

     oil companies   Olla, op. cit., 365.

     fait accompli   Barker, op. cit., 93, 95.

Chapter 11

1   *howitzer*   Spencer, *Ethiopia at Bay*, 24.

    made a vow   Asfa-Wossen, *King of Kings*, 122.

    not a morsel of food…flatly refused   Barker, *Rape of Ethiopia,* 106, 125.

2   *there was no time to lose…to no avail*   Asfa-Wossen, op. cit., 123, 125.

    Vigor had left his face   George Steer, *Caesar in Abyssinia* (London: 1936), 367, cited in Asfa-Wossen, op. cit., 124–126.

    emperor does not leave his country   Spencer, *Ethiopia at Bay*, 64.

    above all his dignity   Extracts from Reports of Proceedings of H.M. Ships *Enterprise* and *Diana*, "Concerning the Evacuation of the Emperor of Abyssinia from Djibuti," Dispatch by Murray to the Foreign Office, London, June 30, 1936, FO 371/20197, in Asfa-Wossen, op. cit., 124–126.

3   *lions…artist Martini*   Cannistraro and Sullivan, *Il Duce's Other Woman,* 494.

    Ethiopia belongs to Italy!   Olla, *Il Duce*, 368.

4   *35ᵗʰ son of Adam*   Sterling Means, *Ethiopia and the Missing Link in African History* (Chicago: Lushena Books, 2001), 19.

    legend of King Arwe   Sergew, *Ancient and Medieval Ethiopian History to 1270*, 95.

5   Father Kiros (scholar at Debre Damo Monastery), interview by Dean W. Arnold in Tigray, Ethiopia, May 2017.

6   Frederich Hegel, *The Philosophy of History* (New York: Dover, 1956), 103, cited in Messay Kebede, "Gebrehiwot Baykedagn: Eurocentrism, and the Decentering of Ethiopia," *Journal of Black Studies*, July 2006, 818.

    childlike   Blaut, *The Colonizer's Model of the World,* 96.

7   Messay Kebede, "Gebrehiwot Baykedagn: Eurocentrism, and the Decentering of Ethiopia," *Journal of Black Studies*, July 2006.

8   Messay, "Eurocentrism, and the Decentering of Ethiopia," 825.

9   Bazien and Elias quotes from Bazien Abai and Elias Gebreselassie (graduate students, Holy Trinity Theological College), interview by Dean W. Arnold in Addis Ababa, Ethiopia, January 2018.

10   *faith does not go well*   Stuart Munro-Hay, *The True History of the Tablets of Moses* (I.B Tauris & Co., 2005), 39, cited in Abraham and Portella, *The First Christian Nation?*, 75.

    Ullendorff, Edward, *Ethiopia and the Bible: The Schweich Lectures* (Published for the British Academy by The Oxford University Press, 1967), 134.

11   Diodorus Siculus, *Book III*, "The coasts of the Arabian Gulf: animals," Section 36–37, cited in The Library of History of Diodorus Siculus, published in Vol. II of the Loeb Classical Library edition, 1935, http://penelope.uchicago.edu/Thayer/E/Roman/Texts/Diodorus_Siculus/home.html (Retrieved April 11, 2019).

12   Michela Wrong, *I Didn't Do It for You*, chap. 5, loc. 1678.

13   *Regardless of what is in the Axum chapel*   Randall Price, *Searching for the Ark of the Covenant* (Eugene, OR: Harvest House Publishers, 2005), 177.

       Randall Price credentials   Price, Searching for the Ark, About the Author; *Israel My Glory* magazine, Friends of Israel Gospel Ministry, https://israelmyglory.org/authors

       Jews were a threat…replacement theology   Price, *Searching for the Ark*, 107–108, 192.

14   *supports a midieval date*   Price, *Searching for the Ark*, 108.

       is a fact…they know nothing of the Babylonian captivity   Samuel Mercer, "The Falashas," *Aethiops*, 3 1939, 50–51, cited in Sergew Hable Selassie, *Ancient and Medieval Ethiopian History*, 96.

       eligible for the Law of Return   Graham Hancock, *Sign and the Seal*, 26.

       600 years old at the most   see *Jerusalem Post International*, Oct. 3, 1992, 9, cited in Price, *Searching for the Ark*, 107.

15   "Obituary: Professor Edward Ullendorff," *The Telegraph*, April 17, 2011, https://www.telegraph.co.uk/news/obituaries/culture-obituaries/books-obituaries/8457104/Professor-Edward-Ullendorff.html (Retrieved May 9, 2019).

16   Ullendorff, op. cit., 83. Ullendorff's attribution of authorship to Abu Salih has since been corrected by newer discoveries. See Johannes den Heijer, "The Composition of the History of the Churches and Monasteries of Egypt. Some Preliminary Remarks," dans D. W. Johnson (éd.), *Acts of the 5th Intern. of Coptic Studies* (Washington, 1992), vol. 2, 208–213, cited in Wikipedia: Abu al-Makarim.

       difficult to imagine…boast of Jewish descent   Ullendorff, op. cit., 25.

Chapter 12

1   *BR…Hebrew script*   Bernard Leeman, "The Ark of the Covenant: Evidence Supporting the Ethiopian Traditions," Queen-of-Sheba-University.org, *Academia.edu.*, 2010, https://www.academia.edu/32962122/THE_ARK_OF_THE_COVENANT_EVIDENCE_SUPPORTING_THE_ETHIOPIAN_TRADITIONS.

     Kebra Negast…had long been known   Ullendorff, *Ethiopia and the Bible*, 75 (author's emphasis).

2   Bernard Leeman, "The Ark of the Covenant: Evidence Supporting the Ethiopian Traditions."

Randall Price, *Searching for the Ark of the Covenant* (Eugene, OR: Harvest House Publishers, 2005), 106–107.

Ullendorff, *Ethiopia and the Bible*, 133–134.

3   Jonathan Kirsch, "Book Review: Speculation Ladled On With a Heavy Hand, The Sign and the Seal: A Quest for the Lost Ark of the Covenant by Graham Hancock," *Los Angeles Times*, April 1, 1992, http://articles.latimes.com/1992-04-01/news/vw-29_1_graham-hancock (Retrieved April 15, 2019).

4   Randall Price, op cit., 106.

Chapter 13

1   *British royalty avoid*   Asfa-Wossen, *King of Kings*, 132.

Lion Incognito   in *Time* magazine, June 8, 1936, cited in Asfa-Wossen, op cit., 132.

compromise his imperial dignity   "Answering Ethiopia," *Time* magazine, July 13, 1936, in Asfa-Wossen, op cit., 133.

2   Haile Selassie, *My Life and Ethiopia's Progress* Volume 2 (Addis Ababa: Frontline Distribution, 1966), 5, 12.

3   *Hitler's admiration*   Cannistraro and Sullivan, *Il Duce's Other Woman*, 483.

fear of imminent war … I will not lose hope   Haile Selassie, *My Life*, 62–64, 25, 64–65.

4   *sacred duty*   "Answering Ethiopia," *Time* magazine, July 13, 1936, cited in Asfa-Wossen, op cit., 134.

Haile Selassie stood before the microphone … what reply   Barker, *The Rape of Ethiopia*, 132–3.

5   *great speech*   "Answering Ethiopia," *Time*, op cit.

crack of the firing squad   Barker, *The Rape of Ethiopia*, 140.

Mussolini began to jeer   Haile Selassie, *My Life*, 6.

without effect   "Answering Ethiopia," *Time*, op cit.

pathetic faith   Barker, op cit., 29, 133.

6   *International morality … superior to any other*   Haile Selassie, Speech to the General Assembly of the League of Nations, June 30, 1936, http://www.mtholyoke.edu/acad/intrel/selassie.htm (Retrieved April 10, 2019), cited in Asfa-Wossen, op cit., 134–135.

7   *declared war on me*   Kwame Nkrumah, *Ghana: The Autobiography of Kwame Nkrumah* (Edinburgh: Thomas Nelson and Sons, 1957), cited in Michela Wrong, *I didn't Do it For You*, chap. 6. loc. 1894.

　　Czech spectator had shot himself   Anthony Eden, *Facing the Dictators: The Eden Memoirs* (London, 1962), 388, cited in Asfa-Wossen, op cit., 136.

　　release your claim over Ethiopia…I rejected whatever gifts   Haile Selassie, op cit., 43–44, 11.

8   *occupy and pacify*   Barker, op cit., 137.

　　historic obelisk…camps as prostitutes   Haile Selassie, op cit., 26.

9   *Look!*   Barker, op cit., 98–99.

　　"scepter of Solomon…sticks and stones…gangrene…he killed the white man   Haile Selassie, op cit., 89, 76, 71, 79.

10 *day of my wedding…surrendered our arms*   Ibid., 78, 76.

　　total destruction   Michael Mann, *The Dark Side of Democracy: Explaining Ethnic Cleansing* (Cambridge University Press, 2005), 309.

　　not be exterminated   Barker, op cit., 132.

　　Archbishop of Canterbury   Selassie, op cit., 14–15.

11 *Opera Omnia* Vol 28, eds. Edoardo Susmel and Duilio Susmel (Florence, La Fenice 1951–63), 312–321, cited in Olla, *Il Duce and His Women*, 372 (author's emphasis).

Chapter 14

1   Sanger letter to Dr. C. J. Gamble, Dec. 10, 1939, Sophia Smith Collection, Smith College (Northampton, MA), https://libex.smith.edu/omeka/files/original/d6358bc3053c93183295bf2df1c0c931.pdf (Retrieved March 16, 2019).

2   Clarence Gamble, Sophia Smith Collection, Smith College (Northampton, MA), undated memo, "but probably November or December 1939," according to Linda Gordon, *Woman's Body, Woman's Right: Birth Control in America* (New York, NY: Penguin Books, 1990), 329.

3   Margaret Sanger, *Woman and the New Race* (New York, NY: Truth Publishing Co., 1920), 63, online version, https://pdfbooks.co.za/library/MARGARET_SANGER-WOMAN_AND_THE_NEW_RACE.pdf (Retrieved March 16, 2019), 27.

　　The title of Chapter Five containing this quote is "The Wickedness of Creating Large Families." Larger quote: "Many, perhaps, will think it idle to go farther in demonstrating the immorality of large families, but since there is still an abundance of proof at hand, it may be offered for the sake of those who find difficulty in adjusting old-fashioned ideas to the facts. The most merciful thing that the large family does to one of its infant members is to kill it. The same factors which create the terrible infant mortality rate, and which swell the death rate of children between the ages of one and five, operate even more extensively to lower the health rate of the surviving members. Moreover, the overcrowded homes of large families reared in poverty further contribute to this condition. Lack of medical attention is still another factor, so that the child who must struggle for health in competition with other members of a closely packed family has still great difficulties to meet after its poor constitution and malnutrition have been accounted for."

4   *lower types…must be rigorously curtailed*   Havelock Ellis, "The World's Racial Problem," *Birth Control Review*, ed. Margaret Sanger, Oct. 1920, Vol. IV, No. 10, 15–16, https://lifedynamics.com/app/uploads/2015/09/1920-10-October.pdf (Retrieved May 1, 2019).

   blacks decreased…Hispanics   "Population of the United States by Race and Hispanic/Latino Origin, Census 2000 and 2010," *InfoPlease*, https://www.infoplease.com/us/race-population/population-united-states-race-and-hispaniclatino-origin-census-2000-and-2010 (Retrieved May 2, 2019).

   43 percent…black women   Health Services Administration of the City of New York, *Report on First 18 Months of Legal Abortions*, Feb. 20, 1982, cited in Allan Chase, *The Legacy of Malthus: The Social Costs of the New Scientific Racism* (New York: Alfred A. Knopf, 1977), 411.

5   Mark Crutcher, Carole Navielli, and Renee Hobbs, "Racial Targeting and Population Control," *Life Dynamics Incorporated*, 2011, see especially "Analysis & Conclusion," 22, https://www.klannedparenthood.com/wp-content/themes/trellis/PDFs/Racial-Targeting-Population-Control.pdf (Retrieved May 2, 2019).

   The authors add that Planned Parenthood attempted to refute the results of their report, claiming a study showing "only 1 in 10 Planned Parenthood clinics is located in a minority community." But the authors' rebuttal is that Planned Parenthood did not list the many referring clinics in minority neighborhoods (p. 1–2).

6   *NFL Player*   "Benjamin Watson: Planned Parenthood Was Created to 'Exterminate Blacks,'" *Fox News*, Aug. 6, 2016, https://insider.foxnews.com/2016/08/06/benjamin-watson-planned-parenthood-was-created-exterminate-blacks (Retrieved May 2, 2019).

7   *It is not true!*   "Il discorso dell'Ascensione," *Scritti e Discorsi dal 1927 al 1928* (Milan: Scritti e Discorsi di Benito Mussolini, VI, 1934), 42–46, cited in D. V. Glass, *Population policies and movements in Europe* (Oxford: Clarendon Press, 1940), 220.

   Italy's cribs lay empty   Maria Sophia Quine, *From Malthus to Mussolini: The Italian Eugenics Movement and Fascist Population Policy, 1890–1938* (Dissertation: University College London, 1990), 7.

8 Paul Johnson, *A History of the English People* (New York: Harper and Row, 1985), 276, cited in George Grant, *Grand Illusions*, 36–37.

9 *reproductive war* Quine, *From Malthus to Mussolini*, 8.

far from bringing misery Achille Loria, *La legge di popolazione e il sistema sociale* (Siena: 1882), 60, cited in Quine, op cit., 42–43.

10 Ibid., 51, quoting Corodo Gini, *I fattori demografici della evoluzione delle nazioni* (Turin: 1912), 46–52.

11 *bachelors* D. V. Glass, op cit., 236.

prolific mothers…eunuch race Quine, op cit., 130, 9, 21, 42.

12 *Sanger and Mussolini exchange* "What Margaret Sanger Thinks of Mussolini," *Plain Talk Magazine*, May 25, 1927, Margaret Sanger Papers, *Library of Congress* (131:0310), http://www.nyu.edu/projects/sanger/webedition/app/documents/show.php?sangerDoc=143477.xml (Retrieved April 12, 2019).

scholars suggest D. V. Glass, op cit., 263–4.

13 A. J. Barker, *Rape of Ethiopia, 1936*, 143–145.

14 *1500–2000 killed* Angelo del Boca: Graziani Massacre, *Encyclopedia Aethiopica*, 2, 878, cited in Asfa-Wossen, *King of Kings*, 129.

exterminated…burned to the ground Haile Selassie, *My Life*, 159.

will not be allowed to live…Our life in Bath…used to help the exiles…British film company Haile Selassie, op cit., 75–76, 36.

Imperial silver Katalog Brunn Rasmussen Kunstauktioner: Fine Arts + Antiquities International Auction 841, June 4–13, 2013, Copenhagen, Catalogue No. 841/244, 192f, cited in Asfa-Wossen, op cit., 139.

15 *willing to buy you a palace…the emperor refused* Haile Selassie, op cit., 43–44.

a single grate Asfa-Wossen, op cit., 139.

16 Tim Judah, *Bikila: Ethiopia's Barefoot Olympian*, 29, 30.

17 Paul Rambali, *Barefoot Runner: The Life of Marathon Champion Abebe Bikile* (London: Serpent's Tail, 2008), 150.

18 Ibid., 138–139.

19 Judah, op cit., 76–77.

Chapter 15

1   This citing of Genesis 2:10–14 is from the King James Version. The most accessible translation of this passage for my purposes is the Common English Version (CEV) which uses the words "Ethiopia," "Tigris," and "Euphrates." (KJV uses Hiddekel rather than Tigris.) However, the KJV translates the original wording of this passage more literally than the CEV, which fails to capture how the "whole land" of Ethiopia is encompassed by the Nile.

The CEV for Gen. 2:10–14 is as follows: "From Eden a river flowed out to water the garden, then it divided into four rivers. The first one is the Pishon River that flows through the land of Havilah, where pure gold, rare perfumes, and precious stones are found. The second is the Gihon River that winds through Ethiopia. The Tigris River that flows east of Assyria is the third, and the fourth is the Euphrates River."

2   Marwa Eltagouri and Avi Selk, "How a white nationalist's family came to blows over a trailer tryst," *Washington Post*, March 14, 2018, https://www.washingtonpost.com/news/post-nation/wp/2018/03/13/white-nationalist-leader-matthew-heimbach-arrested-for-domestic-battery/?utm_term=.5848c1337e20 (Retrieved April 12, 2019).

3   Allie Conti, "White Nationalist Matthew Heimbach is Going to Jail," *Vice.com*, May 15, 2018, https://www.vice.com/en_us/article/mbkadb/matthew-heimbach-the-white-nationalist-in-that-bizarre-love-triangle-is-going-to-jail (Retrieved April 12, 2019).

4   "Cushan," *Easton's Bible Dictionary*, http://eastonsbibledictionary.org/944-Cushan.php (Retrieved April 28, 2019), cited in Gert Muller, *Eden: The Biblical Garden Discovered in East Africa* (London: Pomegranate Publishing, 2013), 32.

5   *KAS KASH KSH*   Sergew Hable Selassie, *Ancient and Medieval Ethiopian History to 1270*, 2, 45.

Buhen Stela   "Ancient Kush or 'Ethiopia,'" *Ta Neter Foundation*, www.taneter.org/ethiopia.html (Retrieved April 15, 2019).

6   "Cush," *Easton's Bible Dictionary*, http://eastonsbibledictionary.org/943-Cush.php (Retrieved April 28, 2019).

"Ethiopian Woman," *New Bible Dictionary*, Second edition, ed. J. D. Douglas (Wheaton, IL: Tyndale House Publishers, 1982), 355.

Muller, *Eden*, 30–31.

7   Isaiah 7:14 and Psalm 22:16. See Fr. John A. Peck, "Masoretic Text vs. Original Hebrew," *Preacher's Institute*, Aug. 31, 2015, https://preachersinstitute.com/2015/08/31/masoretic-text-vs-original-hebrew (Retrieved April 12, 2019).

8   *were the first of all men*   Diodorus Siculus, *Book III*, "Ethiopia and the Gold
    Mines of Egypt," Section 2, cited in The Library of History of Diodorus Siculus,
    published in Vol. II of the Loeb Classical Library edition, 1935, http://penelope.
    uchicago.edu/Thayer/E/Roman/Texts/Diodorus_Siculus/3A*.html (Retrieved April
    11, 2019).

    manifest histories   Sergew, op. cit., 47.

9   This quote and translation from Muller, *Eden*, 131. Similar translation of "terraces
    of myrrh" and "God's land" from John A. Wilson, *The Culture of Ancient Egypt*
    (The University of Chicago Press, 1958), 169, 176, https://oi.uchicago.edu/sites/
    oi.uchicago.edu/files/uploads/shared/docs/culture.pdf (Retrieved April 28, 2019).

10 Homer, *The Iliad*, Book II, Section 1, lines 424–425, http://perseus.uchicago.
    edu/perseus-cgi/citequery3.pl?dbname=GreekTexts&query=Hom.%20Il.%20
    1.400&getid=2 (Retrieved May 3, 2019).

    Homer, *The Odyssey*, Section 1, Lines 20–15, http://perseus.uchicago.edu/perseus-
    cgi/citequery3.pl?dbname=GreekTexts&query=Hom.%20Od.%201.22&getid=2
    (Retrieved May 3, 2019).

    Herodotus, *Book II*, Section 29, https://archive.org/stream/historiesofherod00herorich/
    historiesofherod00herorich_djvu.txt (Retrieved May 3, 2019).

11 Diodorus Siculus, *Book III*, "Ethiopia and the Gold Mines of Egypt," Section 3, 4.

12 Owen Jarus, "Baboon mummy analysis reveals Eritrea and Ethiopia as location of
    land of Punt," *Independent*, April 26, 2010, https://www.independent.co.uk/life-
    style/history/baboon-mummy-analysis-reveals-eritrea-and-ethiopia-as-location-of-
    land-of-punt-1954547.html (Retrieved April 28, 2019).

13 Diodorus Siculus, *Book III*, "Ethiopia and the Gold Mines of Egypt," Section 12.

14 *Zaila*   Eugene Arnaud, *La Palestine ancienne et moderne* (Berger–Levrault, 1868), p. 32.

    Jewish traveler   Elkan Adler, *Jewish Travelers* (Routledge, 2014), p. 61, cited in
    Wikiwand: Havilah, http://www.wikiwand.com/en/Havilah (Retrieved April 12,
    2019).

    Furra   Seyoum Hameso, "Furra Legend in Sidama traditions," *The Oromo
    Commentary*, Vol. 7, No. 2, 1997, https://oromocommentary.files.wordpress.
    com/2010/08/the-furra-legend-in-sidama-traditions.pdf (Retrieved April 12,
    2019).

    Cain and Abel   Hal Markovitz, *Modern Middle East Nations and Their Strategic
    Place in the World* (Yemen: 2004), cited in Wikipedia: Aden (Retrieved April 12,
    2019).

15 *French rabbi Rishi*   Shaul Wolf, "Where Are the Four Rivers that Come from
    Eden?" *Chabad.org*, https://www.chabad.org/parshah/article_cdo/aid/3082157/

jewish/Where-Are-the-Four-Rivers-that-Come-from-Eden.htm (Retrieved Aug. 30, 2019).

as the Blue and White Nile "The Four Rivers of Paradise," *Jewish Heritage Online Magazine* in Wayback Machine, Feb. 18, 2005, https://web.archive.org/web/20050218184401/http://www.jhom.com/topics/rivers/eden.htm, cited in Muller, *Eden*, 29.

16   Muller, *Eden: The Biblical Garden Discovered in East Africa* (London: Pomegranate Publishing, 2013), 73, 18.

17   *dispersion or flower* Josephus, *The Life and Works of Flavius Josephus*, trans. William Whiston (New York: Holt, Rinehart and Winston, 1957), 33.

Haddakel Abarim Publications, http://www.abarim-publications.com/Meaning/Haddakel.html#.XNR0ntNKgUs (Retrieved May 9, 2019).

Euphrates becomes the Nile W. H. S. Jones, trans., *Pausanius Description of Greece* (London: William Heinemann, 1918), 273, cited in Muller, op. cit., 66–68.

18   "Tsagazam GeliGiyorgis" (lay leader for Gororo village church), interview by Dean W. Arnold in Tigray, Ethiopia, January 2018.

19   *material rivers…rivers spiritual* John Chrysostom, "Homilies on the Gospel of St. John," 46:4, *The Fathers of the Church: A New Translation* (Washington D.C.: Catholic University of America Press, 1947), 33, 470, http://www.newadvent.org/fathers/240146.htm (Retrieved Aug. 30, 2019).

Blessed Moses…similar mythologies John Chrysostom, Homilies on Genesis, 13.3–4, *The Fathers of the Church: A New Translation*, 74, 175–176, cited in Seraphim Rose, *Genesis, Creation, and Early Man: The Orthodox Christian Vision* (St. Herman of Alaska Brotherhood, 2011), 221–222.

Chrysostom says in another place: "Perhaps one who loves to speak from his own wisdom here also will not allow that the rivers are actually rivers, nor that the waters are precisely waters, but will instill in those who allow themselves to listen to them, that they (under the names of rivers and waters) represented something else. But I entreat you, let us not pay heed to these people, let us stop up our hearing against them, and let us believe the Divine Scripture, and following what is written in it, let us strive to preserve in our souls sound dogmas." (Homilies on Genesis, 13.4, *The Fathers of the Church: A New Translation*, 74, 177–178, cited in Rose, *Genesis*, 224–225).

St. John of Damascus provides similar commentary: "Some have imagined Paradise to have been material, while others have imagined it to be spiritual. However, it seems to me [to be] a twofold aspect of being perceptible both to the senses and to the mind.…While in his body [Adam] lived on the earth in the world of sense, in his spirit he dwelt among the angels . . ." Slightly related, St. John Damascus notes that "some Holy Fathers state that even before the fall

Paradise was in an elevated place, being 'higher than all the rest of the earth.'" (St. John Damascene, *On the Orthodox Faith* 2.11, 2.30, *The Fathers of the Church: A New Translation* 37, 232, 265, 230, cited in Rose, *Genesis*, 228–229, 224).

20   *dark red gemstone*   St. Pachomius Library Translation of the Septuagint, *Commentary on Genesis 2:12*, 1948, cited in Muller, op. cit., 76.

     garnet lantern   Garnet: The warm red of the garnet illuminated Noah's Ark, *International Colored Gemstone Association*, https://gemstone.org/education/gem-by-gem/154-garnet (Retrieved April 14, 2019), cited in Muller, op. cit., 79.

     malachite   Muller, op. cit., 92–95.

21   *Jewish scholars…concluded*   Muller, op. cit., 166.

     Liturgy of St. James   John F. Baldovin, *The Urban Character of Christian Worship: The Origins, Development, and Meaning of Stational Liturgy* (Ann Arbor, MI: UMI Dissertation Services, 2005), 26.

22   Muller, op. cit., 146.

23   *spring at Gish Abbai*   Muller, op. cit., 64.

     Giyon   R. E. Cheesman, *Lake Tana and the Blue Nile: An Abyssinian Quest* (London: Cass, 1936), 71, 75, cited in Graham Hancock, *The Sign and the Seal*, 450.

     to the people in these villages   "The Blue Nile: Ethiopia's Sacred Waters," *National Geographic*, December 2000, cited in Muller, op. cit., 64.

Chapter 16

1   Stephen Strong with Andy Whitely, "DNA Evidence Debunks the 'Out-of-Africa' Theory of Human Evolution," *Wake Up World*, https://wakeup-world.com/2013/12/16/dna-evidence-debunks-the-out-of-africa-theory-of-human-evolution/ (Retrieved April 12, 2019).

2   Anatole A. Klyosov and Igor L. Rozhanski, "Re-Examining the 'Out of Africa' Theory and the Origin of Europeoids (Caucasoids) in the Light of DNA Genealogy," *Advances in Anthropology*, Vol. 2. No. 2, 2012 , 80–86, https://file.scirp.org/Html/19566.html (Retrieved April 12, 2019).

3   *vertebra of a baboon*   Colin Baras, "Baboon bone found in famous Lucy skeleton," *New Scientist*, April 10, 2015, https://www.newscientist.com/article/dn27325-baboon-bone-found-in-famous-lucy-skeleton (Retrieved April 12, 2019).

     knee joint two miles away   "Problems with Lucy and Skull 1470," David A. Plasted's page at University of North Carolina, http://www.cs.unc.edu/~plaisted/ce/lucy.html (Retrieved April 11, 2019).

lived in a tree   Jack Stern and Randall Susman, "The Locomotor Anatomy of Australopithecus afarensis," *American Journal of Physical Anthropology*, March 1983, 279–313, https://onlinelibrary.wiley.com/doi/abs/10.1002/ajpa.1330600302 (Retrieved April 12, 2019).

4   Muller, *Eden*, 10–14.

5   David Reich, *Who We Are and How We Got Here: Ancient DNA and the New Science of the Human Past* (New York: Pantheon Books, 2018), xvi, xiii.

     Alan Wilson and Rebecca Cann, "The Recent African Genesis of Humans," *Scientific American*, April 1992.

6   Reich, *Who We Are*, xvi.

7   The video by Reich is embedded in the article: "The Genomic Ancient DNA Revolution: A conversation with David Reich, *Edge.org*, Feb. 1, 2016, https://www.edge.org/conversation/david_reich-the-genomic-ancient-dna-revolution (Retrieved April 13, 2019).

     quotes from Novembre and Cunliffe   "Ancient DNA Tells Tales of Humans' Migratory History," *Howard Hughes Medical Institute*, Feb. 21, 2016, https://www.hhmi.org/news/ancient-dna-tells-tales-of-humans-migratory-history (Retrieved April 13, 2019).

8   Reich, op. cit., xvi, 22, 5, 15.

9   Clive Cookson, "Who We Are and How We Got Here by David Reich—Out of Africa and back again?" *Financial Times*, March 23, 2018, https://www.ft.com/content/824635cc-2c60-11e8-a34a-7e7563b0b0f4 (Retrieved April 13, 2019).

     "David Reich has doubts on Africa as the origin of Anatomical Modern Humans," *Antrogenica: Genetics and Anthropology Discussion Forum*, March 27, 2018, https://anthrogenica.com/showthread.php?13840-David-Reich-has-doubts-on-Africa-as-the-origin-of-Anatomical-Modern-Humans/page4 (Retrieved April 13, 2019) 4.

     Neanderthals … quadrillion   Reich, op. cit., 13, 35–36.

10   "Yosef" (pseudonym used), guide for National Museum of Ethiopia, interview by Dean W. Arnold in Addis Ababa, Ethiopia, January 2018.

11   The story of the journey to the "unplugged village" is based on actual events. One name was changed to perserve anonymity.

12   Father John, priest in the village of Mulle, interview by Dean W. Arnold in Tigray, Ethiopia, January 2018.

Chapter 17

1   Haile Selassie, *My Life*, 68, 41, 87.

2   Barker, *Rape of Ethiopia*, 149, 87.

     an axis around   Cannistraro and Sullivan, *Il Duce's Other Woman*, 480, 496.

     Blackshirts!   Opera Omnia, Vol. 28, 253, cited in Olla, *Il Duce and His Women*, 384.

     Asfa-Wossen, *King of Kings*, 143.

3   *not in today's special chapel*   Rick Drewsbury, "Will this be the first time the world sees the Ark of the Covenant?" *Daily Mail*, Dec. 5, 2011, https://www.dailymail.co.uk/news/article-2069765/Ark-Covenant-revealed-leaking-roof-Ethiopian-chapel.html (Retrieved April 15, 2019).

     substitute another ark   Sergew, *Ancient and Medieval Ethiopian History to 1270*, 42.

     No king or patriarch   Raffaele, "Keepers of the Lost Ark: Christians in Ethiopia have long claimed to have the ark of the covenant," *Smithsonian Magazine*, December 2007.

4   Jonathan Kirsch, "Book Review: Speculation Ladled On With a Heavy Hand, The Sign and the Seal: A Quest for the Lost Ark of the Covenant by Graham Hancock," *Los Angeles Times*, April 1, 1992, http://articles.latimes.com/1992-04-01/news/vw-29_1_graham-hancock (Retrieved April 15, 2019).

5   *fine timber*   I Kings 10: 11–12, New English Translation (NET).

6   Ullendorff, *Ethiopia and the Bible*, 134–135.

7   *Origen*   Frank Snowden, *Before Color Prejudice: The Ancient View of Blacks*, 102.

     Gregory of Nyssa… Theologian   David Hubbard, *The Literary Sources of the Kebra Nagast* (Ph. D. Dissertation, University of St. Andrew's, 1957), 434.

     let us not deny   Sergew, op. cit., 43.

8   *palace not sufficiently old enough*   Hancock, *Sign and the Seal*, 17; Roger Boyes, "German Archeologist on Trail of Ark of the Covenant," *Foxnews.com*, May 13, 2008, https://www.foxnews.com/printer_friendly_story/0,3566,355264,00.html (Retrived April 15, 2019).

     sure that this is the palace   "Archeologists find Queen of Sheba's palace at Axum, Ethiopia," *nazret.com*, May 7, 2008, http://nazret.com/blog/index.php/2008/05/07/archaeologists_find_queen_of_sheba_s_pal (Retrieved April 15, 2019).

9   *only Jews to continue to practice animal sacrifice*   Richard Hull, *Jews and Judaism in Africa*, 186.

last surviving practitioners   Hancock, *Sign and the Seal*, 139.

 Old Testament practices   Hull, op. cit., 187 and Abraham and Portella, *The First Christian Nation?*, 45.

pig bones   Christopher Haas, "Mountain Constantines: The Christianization of Aksum and Iberia," *Journal of Late Antiquity*, Spring 2008, 110 fn 29.

10   "Marcus Daoud": Abraham and Portella, op. cit., 45.

Ullendorff, op. cit., 73–74 fn 85, 16.

Sergew, op. cit., 40, 43.

date of Psalm 68   "Probable Occasion on Which Each Psalm was Composed," *Blueletter Bible*, https://www.blueletterbible.org/study/parallel/paral18.cfm (Retrieved April 15, 2019).

Chapter 18

1   *Mr. Strong left the coast*   Barker, *Rape of Ethiopia*, 154–155.

Churchill   Anthony Mockler, *Haile Selassie's War* (Oxford: 1984), 312, cited in Asfa-Wossen, *King of Kings*, 149.

 we took the risk…leave behind only infamy   Haile Selassie, *My Life,* 100–101, 103, 105.

2   *Wingate*   Leonard Mosley, *Haile Selassie: The Conquering Lion* (London: 1964), 258, cited in Asfa-Wossen, op. cit., 148, see also Asfa-Wossen, 151, 158, 153.

3   Haile Selassie, op. cit., 113, 160–161.

4   Ibid., 163–165.

5   Christopher Stevens, "Mussolini the insatiable," *Daily Mail*, Feb. 24, 2017, https://www.dailymail.co.uk/news/article-4257958/Mussolini-violent-lover-demanded-sex-constantly.html (Retrieved April 15, 2019).

6   *Giuseppina Petacci…thinking of prostitutes*   Stevens, "Mussolini the insatiable," *Daily Mail*, Feb. 24, 2017.

scarf   Magda Fontanges (Madeleine Coraboeuf) *Love Affair with Mussolini* (Liberty, 1940), cited in Olla, *Il Duce*, 370.

7   Cannistraro and Sullivan, *Il Duce's Other Woman*, 541.

8   Stevens, op. cit.

9   *Rhadi came from nowhere…Bikila fasted every Wednesday*   Paul Rambali, *Barefoot Runner*, 139, 5.

determination and heroism   "Abebe Bikila: August 7, 1932–October 25, 1973," *The Running Deo*, http://www.deorunner.com/2012/01/bikila-barefoot-and-appendix.html (Retrieved April 16, 2019).

10   Judah, *Bikila*, 69–76. His daughter's name is Tsige Abebe.

11   Rambali, op. cit., 139.

Chapter 19

1   *West's richest men met*   "Billionaire club in bid to curb overpopulation" *The Times*, May 24, 2009, https://www.thetimes.co.uk/article/billionaire-club-in-bid-to-curb-overpopulation-d2fl22qhl02 (Retrieved Aug. 31, 2019).

sixty million Italians never reached   According to *worldometers.com,* Italy's population grew until 2010 to 59,730,000 and is now steadily decreasing. See http://www.worldometers.info/world-population/italy-population (Retrieved April 16, 2019).

oldest in Europe world's second-oldest   "Italy to be oldest country after Japan," *ANSA*, Oct. 3, 2017, http://www.ansa.it/english/news/general_news/2017/10/03/italy-to-be-oldest-country-after-japan_e06776ae-d0d1-437d-9bf7-ca9f0459558e.html (Retrieved Sept. 10, 2019).

will cease as a country   David P. Goldman, *It's Not the End of the World, It's Just the End of You: The Great Extinction of the Nations* (New York: RVP Publishers, 2011), 16, 26.

2   *German language*   David P. Goldman, op. cit., 15.
Patrick J. Buchanan, *The Death of the West: How Dying Populations and Immigrant Invasions Imperil Our Country and Civilization* (New York: Thomas Dunne Books, 2002), 23–24.

3   J. M. Blaut, *The Colonizer's Model of the World: Geographical Diffusionism and Eurocentric History*, 67.

Niall Ferguson, *Civilization: The West and the Rest* (New York: Penguin Books ebook, 2011), loc. 475, 516.

4   *Europe…12 percent*   Jack Goldstone, "The New Population Bomb: The Four Megatrends That Will Change the World," *Foreign Affairs*, Jan./Feb. 2010, 32–33, cited in Patrick Buchanan, *Suicide of a Superpower* (New York: St. Martin's Press, 2011), 164.

Western Civilization 2.0   Ferguson, op. cit., loc. 741.

difficult to reverse "Can Policies boost Birth Rates?" Policy Brief, Organization for Economic Cooperation and Development, Nov. 2007, cited in Buchanan, *Suicide of a Superpower*, p. 166–167.

5   *pyramid standing on its point* Russell Shorto, "No Babies," *New York Times Magazine*, June 29, 2008, 71, cited in Buchanan, op. cit., 172.

Russia struggling to recover "Russia Demographics Are Now Reasonably Healthy. Birth Rate the Highest in Europe," *Russia Insider*, March 22, 2016; Anatoly Karlin, "The 'Normalization' of Russia's Demographics," *The Unz Review*, Nov. 25, 2014, http://www.unz.com/akarlin/normalization-of-russias-demographic (Retrieved March 16, 2019).

incentive for children… Order of Parental Glory "Russia May Have Turned the Corner in Demographic Crisis," *Breitbart*, June 14, 2017.

make a baby day Wikipedia: Day of Conception (Retrieved Aug. 31, 2019).

it is still a rise "'We're OUTBREEDING you!' Putin taunts West as he unveils drive to boost Russian birth rate," *London Express*, Dec. 1, 2016; Russia's rising birth rate gives new life to health care providers," *CNBC*, March 20, 2017.

not one Ibid.

6   *undermine the authority of the Christian Churches* Walter Adolphe Roberts, "Birth Control and the Revolution," *Birth Control Review*, ed. Margaret Sanger, Volume I, Number 6, June 1917, 7, https://lifedynamics.com/app/uploads/2015/09/1917-06-June.pdf (Retrieved May 1, 2019).

7   *hundreds of children* Helga Kuhse and Peter Singer, *Bioethics: an anthology* (Wiley-Blackwell, 2006), 232, cited in Wikipedia: Kaiser Wilhelm Institute/ Eugenics (Retrieved April 16, 2019).

43 percent Ben J. Wattenberg, *The Real America* (Garden City, NY: Doubleday & Company, 1974), 158, cited in Buchanan, *The Death of the West*, 26.

suicide tablet Ibid.

8   Obianuju Ekeocha, *Target Africa: Ideological Neocolonialism in the Twenty-First Century* (San Francisco: Ignatius Press, 2018), 45, 227, 237.

9   Story told by Ethiopian author Mammo Wudineh, Nov. 2000, to author Asfa-Wossen Asserate, *King of Kings*, xv.

10   Memorandum of Dec. 9, 1940, National Archives, Kew, London FO 371/24645/306, cited in Asfa-Wossen, op. cit., 160.

11   *free and independent state* Ibid., 163.

our true friend… Brigadier Maurice Lush Haile Selassie, *My Life*, 162, 172.

12 *protectorate* U.S. State Dept. Memorandum, June 18, 1941, National Archives, SD 884.001 Selassie 1372, cited in Asfa-Wossen, op. cit., 164.

13 "February 1945," Franklin D. Roosevelt Day by Day: A Project of the Pare Lorentz Center at the FDR Presidential Library, http://www.fdrlibrary.marist.edu/daybyday/resource/february-1945-13 (Retrieved Sept. 9, 2019).

Spencer, *Ethiopia at Bay*, 160–161.

14 Asfa-Wossen, op. cit., 172, 166.

15 *apartheid* Michela Wrong, *I Didn't Do It for You,* chap. 3, loc. 1212.

tedious Richard Pankhurst, "The Legal Question of Racism in Eritrea during the British Military Administration," *Northeast African Studies*, Vol. 2, Part 2, 1995, in Wrong, op cit., chap. 5, loc. 1565.

16 Nelson Mandela, *Long Walk to Freedom: Autobiography* (London: 1995), 349, cited in Asfa-Wossen, op. cit., 247–249.

17 *my son, I beg you* Berekat Habte Selassie: *The Crown and the Pen: The Memories of a Lawyer Turned Rebel* (Trenton, NJ, 2007), 186ff, cited in Asfa-Wossen, op cit., 254.

Father of Africa...African giant Ibid., 254, xvi.

"Queen...red carpet": Ibid., 193.

18 The archbishop gives firsthand testimony on this video: "Bob Marley's Christian conversion - Archbishop Abuna Yesehaq," https://youtu.be/WXiPllReCBI (Retrieved April 17, 2019). See also Christopher Stefanick, "Redemption Songs: The Christian Conversion of Bob Marley, *Catholic Online*, May 17, 2011, https://www.catholic.org/news/ae/music/story.php?id=41433 (Retrieved April 17, 2019).

19 *"rain began to pour...rain ended...We are not God* Asfa-Wossen, op. cit., 258–259.

20 *considered blasphemous* Ermias Kebede Wolde-Yesus, *Ethiopia : the classic case: a biblical nation under God that survived great trials for 7490 years of its existence and ordained to invoke divine judgment and condemnation upon the world! : will the present generation of humanity hearken this time to the divine warning in order to avert another imminent universal cataclysm? : the message* (Washington, D.C.: Ethiopia: The Kingdom of God Services, 1997), 94, 153.

lost it in the classroom Messay Kebede, "Gebrehiwot Baykedagn: Eurocentrism, and the Decentering of Ethiopia," *Journal of Black Studies*, July 2006, 827.

10,000 students Asfa-Wossen, op. cit., 266–267.

indoctrination...Western philosophy Ermias Kebede, op. cit., 153.

21 Melissa Twigg, "Is the Ark of the Covenant in Ethiopia?" *Daily Beast*, Jan. 1, 2019,

https://www.thedailybeast.com/is-the-ark-of-the-covenant-in-ethiopia (Retrieved April 17, 2019).

22   Krzysztof Piotr Blazewicz, "Ethiopian Monasticism," Institute of Oriental Studies, Warsaw University, XII/2/1999, 45.

Chapter 20

1   *called God*   William Reich, *Ether, God and Devil: Cosmic Superimposition* (New York: Farrar, Strauss, and Giroux, 1973), 39ff.

I did this every day   William Reich, *Passion of Youth: An Autobiography, 1897–1922* (New York: Farrar, 2013), p. 22, http://www.pseudology.org/psyhology/Reich-the-passion-of-youth-1897-1922-1928a.pdf (Retrieved April 17, 2019).

Full quote: "One day I grew so excited looking at the animals that I took a whip with a smooth grip, turned it around, and thrust the handle into the vagina of a mare. The animal was surprised at first but then seemed to enjoy it. She spread her legs wide and began to urinate while I had an orgasm (without ejaculation). From then on, I did this every day and extended my activities to other mares as well, although I never could understand why their reactions were so varied."

2   Lasha Darkmoon, "Masters of Porn: The Systematic Promotion of Sexual Deviancy and Mass Demoralization," *Culture Wars*, January 2013, http://culturewarsmagazine.com/2013/Darkmoon.htm (Retrieved July 30, 2019).

3   E. Michael Jones, *Libido Dominandi: Sexual Liberation and Political Control* (South Bend, IN: St. Augustine's Press, 2005), 259.

4   Jonas E. Alexis, "Psychoanalysis, the Illuminati, and Sexual Liberation Are Concentric Circles," *Veterans Today*, March 14, 2016, https://www.veteranstoday.com/2016/03/14/psychoanalysis-the-illuminati-and-sexual-liberation-are-concentric-circles-part-i (Retrieved July 30, 2019).

5   E. Michael Jones, *Beyond the Bomb: Werner Heisenberg and Jewish Science* (South Bend, IN: Fidelity Press, 2019), 55, 56.

6   *led to cruelty in German adults*   Ibid., 56.

suppression of the natural sexuality in the child   William Reich, *The Mass Psychology of Fascism* (New York: Orgone Institute Press, 1946), cited in Myron Sharaf, *Fury on Earth: A Biography of Wilhelm Reich* (Da Capo Press, 1994), p. 163. See also Wikipedia: The Mass Psychology of Fascism.

7   Richard Greenfield, *Ethiopia: A New Political History* (London: 1965), 373, cited in Asfa-Wossen, op. cit., 225.

8   Asfa-Wossen, op. cit., 225, 316.

9   Berhanu Assres, *Men yenagar yanabara—yatahasu gereger ena mazazu* (Addis Ababa: 2013), 143ff, cited in Asfa-Wossen, op. cit., 223.

10   James Perloff, "Do Americans Face a Red Terror?" *jamesperloff.com*, March 11, 2014, https://jamesperloff.com/2014/03/11/do-americans-face-a-red-terror (Retrieved April 17, 2019).

11   *Get up!* Asfa-Wossen, op. cit., 233.

     Tewodros has taught me something! Greenfield, *Ethiopia: A New Political History*, 317, cited in Asfa-Wossen, op. cit., 235.

12   *amend Article V* Asfa-Wossen, op. cit., 184.

     there will be no change "Selassie Pledges Unchained Rule," *New York Times*, Dec. 21, 1960, cited in Asfa-Wossen, op. cit., 236.

13   Hans Wilhelm Lockot, *The Mission: The Life, Reign, and Character of Haile Selassie I* (London: 1989), 53ff, cited in Asfa-Wossen, op. cit., 203.

14   Spencer, *Ethiopia at Bay*, 135, 355. *five aristocratic leaders* *The Reporter*, April 7, 2003, cited in Asfa-Wossen, op. cit., 239.

     already been on the throne Spencer, *Ethiopia at Bay*, 317.

15   *President Nixon* Report from the American Ambassador to Ethiopia to the U.S. State Department, Addis Ababa, Dec. 16, 1960, SD 775.00/12–1660, in Asfa-Wossen, op. cit., 272.

16   *Kissinger…most boring toasts* Theodore Vestal, *The Lion of Judah in the New World: Emperor Haile Selassie of Ethiopia and the Shaping of Americans' Attitudes toward Africa* (Santa Barbara, Denver, Oxford: 2011), 184, cited in Asfa-Wossen, op. cit., 274.

17   Spencer, *Ethiopia at Bay*, 345.

18   The student is the emperor's future biographer, Asfa-Wossen Asserate, author of *King of Kings: The Triumph and Tragedy of Emperor Haile Selassie I of Ethiopia*, xx, xxi, 280.

19   *40,000…starved…revolutionary movement* Asfa-Wossen, op. cit., 282, 299.

20   Spencer, *Ethiopia at Bay*, 340–341.

21   Ibid, 242

22   This quote is a combination of the following two sources, both of which name the emperor's butler Eshetu Tekle-Mariam as the witness: Alden Whitman, "Haile

Selassie of Ethiopia Dies at 83," *New York Times*, Aug. 28, 1975, cited in Asfa-Wossen, op. cit., 308 and Michela Wrong, op. cit., chap. 11, loc. 3619.

23   *crudest way*   Ibid. chap. 11, loc. 3619.

what Lenin did   Christopher Andrew and Vasili Mitrokhin, *The Mitrokhin Archive II: The KGB and the World* (Penguin, 2006), 467–468, cited in Wikipedia: Qey Shibir (Retrieved April 18, 2019).

raping…torture…necktie   Deirdre McQuillan, "Ethiopia still haunted by memory of Derg genocidal regime," *The Irish Times*, May 6, 2011, https://www.irishtimes.com/news/ethiopia-still-haunted-by-memory-of-derg-genocidal-regime-1.563626 (Retrieved April 18, 2019).

24   *1,000 children*   Stephane Courtois, *The Black Box of Communism: Crimes, Terror, Repression* (Harvard University Press, 1999), 691, cited in Wikipedia: Qey Shibir (Retrieved April 18, 2019).

Amnesty International   Red Terror Martyrs Memorial Monument, *Red Terror Martyrs' Family and Friends Association,* https://rtmmm.org/redterror.html (Retrieved April 18, 2019).

one million   Michael Johns, "A U.S. Strategy to Foster Human Rights in Ethiopia," *The Heritage Foundation*, Feb. 29, 1989, https://www.heritage.org/middle-east/report/us-strategy-foster-human-rights-ethiopia (Retrieved April 18, 2019).

harvest was weeds   Ermias Kebede, *Ethiopia: The Classic Case*, 153.

sink no further   Asfa-Wossen, *King of Kings*, 317.

25   *convicted of war crimes*   "Court sentences Menghistu to death," *BBC News*, May 26, 2008.

the chattering classes   David P. Goldman, *It's Not the End of the World*, 25.

26   For a lengthy treatment on the Orthodox Church's historic stance against birth control, see the author's article: Dean W. Arnold, "Saving the West: 17 Reasons to have married sex with no pills or condoms," deanslist.info, Nov. 4, 2017, http://deanslist.info/saving-the-west-17-reasons-to-have-married-sex-with-no-pills-or-condoms (Retrieved Aug. 3, 2019).

27   *7.1 to 7.2*   World Bank statistics: Fertility Rates - Ethiopia, https://data.worldbank.org/indicator/SP.DYN.TFRT.IN?locations=ET (Retrieved April 19, 2019).

27 to 51 million   Population Statistics: Ethiopia, http://www.populstat.info/Africa/ethiopic.htm (Retrieved April 19, 2019).

Italy 2.4 to 1.3   World Bank statistics: Fertility Rates - Italy, https://data.worldbank.org/indicator/SP.DYN.TFRT.IN?locations=IT (Retrieved April 19, 2019).

no country has ever recovered   Report from Chinese Academy of Social Sciences,

CGTN TV of China Media Group, https://youtu.be/nmjbV7PxZmc (Retrieved April 19, 2019).

28   *Ethiopia has double Italy's population*   For Ethiopia's and Italy's population by year see Population Statistics: Ethiopia, http://www.populstat.info/Africa/ethiopic.htm and for Italy, http://www.populstat.info/Europe/italyc.htm (Both retrieved April 19, 2019).

enemy's capacity to reproduce   J. G. Vanderheym, *Une expedition avec le negous Menelik: vingt mois en Abyssinie* (Paris: Hatchette, 1896), 71, cited in Jonas, *Battle of Adwa*, 223, 249.

continue to depopulate Africa   Massimo Romandini, "Da Massaua ad Asmara: Ferdinando Martini in Eritrea nel 1891," *La Conoscenza dell'Asia e dell'Africa nel XIX Secolo*, vol. III, 1989, 911–933, cited in Michela Wrong, op. cit., chap. 2, loc. 676, 745.

29   *Britain's numbers...pale to its African rivals*   Britain's birthrate: https://data.worldbank.org/indicator/SP.DYN.TFRT.IN?locations=GB (Retrieved April 19, 2019).

elected to pass out of existence   David P. Goldman, op. cit., 15.

30   Ibid., 15, 16, 25.

Chapter 21

1   *in Jerusalem since the 12ᵗʰ century*   Richard Pankhurst, *Travellors in Ethiopia* (London: Oxford University Press, 1965), vi.

small chapel...in the Old City   Graham Hancock, *Sign and the Seal*, 105.

daily encounters with Ethiopian monastics   Jerome, Epistle 107:2, *New Advent*, http://www.newadvent.org/fathers/3001107.htm (Retrieved April 20, 2019).

2   *continuous presence in Jerusalem...Melchizedek*   Ermias Kebede, *Ethiopia: The Classic Case*, 36, 37.

points to the source of the Nile   Gert Muller, *Eden*, 108.

3   *'to uncover feet' is a sexual expression*   The VOICE Bible translation, Ruth 3:5–7, special note on "to uncover the feet," https://www.biblegateway.com/passage/?search=Ruth+3%3A5-7&version=VOICE (Retrieved Aug. 31, 2019).

euphemistic rather than the literal   James Jordan, The Book of Ruth, Part 7, http://www.wordmp3.com/details.aspx?id=8477 (Retrieved Aug. 31, 2019).

4   *Don't call us Jews!*   Kebra Negast, chap. 70, 108.

flesh-eating hyenas   Richard Hull, *Jews and Judaism in Africa*, 195.

5   *holy cause of Ethiopianism*   Ermias Kebede, op. cit., 48

all that was for Israel was transferred to Ethiopia   Ibid., 49.

radical rewrite...racial and cultural superiority   Michela Wrong, *I Didn't Do It for You*, chap. 5, loc. 1623.

heirs to the promise   Lule Melaku, *History of the Ethiopian Orthodox Tewahedo Church, Part I* (Addis Ababa: 2008), 25.

Sheba...the sign of faith   Melake Mikr Kefyalew Merahi, *Christianity in Ethiopia III* (Addis Ababa, April 2012), 13–14.

6   *God knew about the eunuch...now simply a relic*   Elias Gebreselassie, graduate student, Holy Trinity Theological College, interview by Dean W. Arnold in Addis Ababa, Ethiopia, January 2018.

ceased to be object of worship...God looked around   Ermias Kebede, op. cit., 51, 48.

7   G. W. Bowersock, "Helena's Bridle and the Chariot of Ethiopia" in *Antiquity of Antiquity: Jewish and Christian Pasts in the Greco-Roman World*, eds. Gregg Gardner, Kevin Osterloh (Mohr Seibeck, 2008), 387, 385 fn.

Chapter 22

1   William F. Engdahl, "China Railway Links Ethiopia to Red Sea," *New Eastern Outlook*, April 13, 2016, https://journal-neo.org/2016/04/13/china-railway-links-ethiopia-to-red-sea (Retrieved April 20, 2019).

2   "An Investment Guide to Ethiopia," *United Nations Conference on Trade and Development*, March, 2004, http://unctad.org/en/pages/PublicationArchive.aspx?publicationid=466 (Retrieved April 20, 2019).

3   *massive oil reserve*   William F. Engdahl, op. cit.

African populations numbers grow even as Asia recedes   John McKenna, "Six numbers that prove the future is African," *World Economic Forum*, May 2, 2017, https://www.weforum.org/agenda/2017/05/africa-is-rising-and-here-are-the-numbers-to-prove-it (Retrieved April 22, 2019).

China's...nearly irreversible 1.51 rate   Chinese and South Korean birthrate numbers from World Statistics Pocketbook 2016, United Nations, https://unstats.un.org/unsd/publications/pocketbook/files/world-stats-pocketbook-2016.pdf and World Bank statistics: Fertility Rates – China, South Korea, https://data.worldbank.org/indicator/SP.DYN.TFRT.IN?end=2016&locations=IT-CN-KR&start=1960&view=chart (Both retrieved April 22, 2019).

South Korea...0.96   Linda Poon, "South Korea is trying to boost its birth rate. It's not working," *Citylab.com*, Aug. 3, 2018, https://www.citylab.com/life/2018/08/south-korea-needs-more-babies/565169 (Retrieved March 16, 2019).

4   Max Fisher, "The amazing, surprising, Africa-driven demographic future of the Earth, in 9 charts," *Washington Post*, July 16, 2013, https://www.washingtonpost.com/news/worldviews/wp/2013/07/16/the-amazing-surprising-africa-driven-demographic-future-of-the-earth-in-9-charts (Retrieved Aug. 11, 2019).

by 2030, one in five people will be African   John McKenna, "6 numbers that prove the future is African."

5   *world's 20 largest cities in 2100*   "Mapping the World's 20 Most Populous Cities by 2100," *Zero Hedge*, June 28, 2017, https://www.zerohedge.com/news/2017-06-27/mapping-worlds-20-most-populous-cities-2100 (Retrieved April 21, 2019). See also Daniel Hoornweg and Kevin Pope, "Socioeconomic Pathways and Regional Distribution of the World's 101 Largest Cities," Jan., 2014, *Global Cities Institute* (Working Paper No. 04), http://media.wix.com/ugd/672989_62cfa13ec4ba47788f78ad660489a2fa.pdf (Retrieved April 22, 2019).

6   Doug Casey, "Doug Casey on China's Exploitation of Africa," *Casey Daily Dispatch*, Aug. 31, 2018.

7   *five acres of land…half-acre of productive land*   Anne Roback Morse and Steven W. Mosher,"Debunking the Myth of Overpopulation," *Population Research Institute*, Oct. 1, 2013, https://web.archive.org/web/20180117155654/https://www.pop.org/debunking-the-myth-of-overpopulation (Retrieved April 22, 2019).

fit into Texas   "No way everyone could fit in Texas…," Episode 1: Overpopulation: The Making of a Myth," https://overpopulationisamyth.com/episode-1-overpopulation-the-making-of-a-myth (Retrieved July 31, 2019).

fit into Jacksonville, FL   "Jacksonville": http://www.city-data.com/forum/jacksonville/1537655-worlds-population-could-fit-jacksonville-2.html (Retrieved July 31, 2019).

8   Anne Roback Morse and Steven W. Mosher, "Debunking the Myth of Overpopulation."

9   Ibid, fn 2.

10   *never 7 billion*   Dr. Paul Ehrlich at ISU Armory on April 24, 1970, *Special Collections Iowa State University Library*, https://youtu.be/WMhR79EQQqg (Retrieved April 22, 2019).

petroleum gone by 2000   "WOI-TV Interviews Dr. Paul Ehrlich on April 24, 1970," *Special Collections Iowa State University Library*, https://youtu.be/YZWiRaIkXxg (Retrieved April 22, 2019).

sometime in the next 15 years   "Population Bomb: the Dire Prediction that Fell Flat," *RetroReport.org*, June 1, 2015, https://www.retroreport.org/transcript/the-population-bomb (Retrieved April 22, 2019).

next few decades Damian Carrington, "Paul Ehrlich: 'Collapse of civilization is a near certainty within decades,'" *The Guardian*, March 22, 2018, https://www.retroreport.org/transcript/the-population-bomb (Retrieved April 22, 2019). See also "Meet Paul Ehrlich, Pseudoscience Charlatan," Episode 338, *The Corbett Report*, June 5, 2018, https://www.corbettreport.com/ehrlich/ (Retrieved April 22, 2019).

11   *4 billion … 65 million Americans* *The Progressive*, April 1970, cited in "Meet Paul Ehrlich, Pseudoscience Charlatan," *The Corbett Report*, June 5, 2018.

hundreds of millions of people will starve Paul Ehrlich, *The Population Bomb* (Cutchogue, NY: Buccaneer Books, 1968), xi.

England would not exist Bernard Dixon, "In praise of prophets," *New Scientist and Science Journal*, Sept. 16, 1971, 606.

12   *add something to the water supply* Transcript of "GST, Gonski, Population and Diversity," *ABC.net*, Nov. 2, 2015, https://www.abc.net.au/qanda/gst-gonski-population-and-diversity/10653806#transcript (Retrieved April 22, 2019); Gladwin Hill, "A Sterility Drug in Food is Hinted," *New York Times*, Nov. 24, 1969.

worse than Hitler William J. Cook, "Expert on population pleased by response," *Boca Raton News*, June 16, 1972. This article was part of the Newsweek Feature Service, cited in Climate Depot, https://www.climatedepot.com/2010/02/19/1972-article-unearthed-worse-than-hitler-population-bomb-author-paul-ehrlich-suggested-adding-a-forced-sterilization-agent-to-staple-food-and-water-supply (Retrieved April 22, 2019).

sterilant for the water supply Screenshots of *Ecoscience* at "John Holdren, Obama's Science Czar, says: Forced abortions and mass sterilization needed to save the planet," *ZombieTime.com*, July 10, 2009, http://zombietime.com/john_holdren (Retrieved April 22, 2019).

13   James Corbett, "Meet Paul Ehrlich, Pseudoscience Charlatan," Episode 338, *The Corbett Report*, June 5, 2018.

14   James Corbett, "Pierre Desrochers Explains the Bet of the Century," Episode 1107, *The Corbett Report*, Nov. 6, 2015, https://www.corbettreport.com/interview-1107-pierre-desrochers-explains-the-bet-of-the-century (Retrieved April 22, 2019).

15   *new ideas and imagination* The PRC Forum—Julian Simon (2 of 6), https://youtu.be/xSQw4X5ET-o (Retrieved April 22, 2019).

human ingenuity itself James Corbett, "Meet Paul Ehrlich, Pseudoscience Charlatan," Episode 338, *The Corbett Report*, June 5, 2018.

16   Andrew Garber, *We're All Gonna Starve!* A freethink original series, Aug. 17, 2017, https://www.facebook.com/freethinkwrong/videos/109428766440237/

UzpfSTY2ODMzODYzOToxMDE1NTg0NDEyODA1MzY0MA (Retrieved April 22, 2019).

Elon Musk…population collapse   Pete Baklinski, "Tesla's Elon Musk: 'Population collapse' (not overpopulation) is 'biggest problem' facing world," *Live Action*, Sept. 5, 2019, https://www.liveaction.org/news/musk-population-collapse-problem/?fbclid=IwAR0_00tG-azkZK4NFo_4fEoFXmCYjlm7f_6zX4VrD IE_mRo4Xk6MGyPoyDA (Retrieved Sept. 9, 2019).

17   *sponsored by Gates*   "Gates' sponsor opening ceremonies": International Conference on Family Planning, Nov. 12-15, 2013, http://fpconference. org/2013/program/auxiliaryevents/on-site-auxiliary-events/ (Retrieved April 22, 2019);.

3400 attending from 110 nations   International Conference on Family Planning, http://2018.fpconference.org/about.

Largest family planning event in history   "Obianuju Ekeocha Calls out Melinda Gates for Turning up the Heat on Population Control in Africa," *Catholic Online*, Nov. 23, 2013, https://www.catholic.org/news/international/africa/story. php?id=53208 (Retrieved April 22, 2019).

18   *from 7.2. to 4.2*   "Ethiopia's birthrate has decreased from 7.2 in 1991 to 4.2 today": World Bank statistics: Fertility Rates – Ethiopia, World Bank statistics: Fertility Rates - Ethiopia, https://data.worldbank.org/indicator/SP.DYN.TFRT. IN?locations=ET

a model of success…gentleman's agreement   Allyn Gaestel and Allison Shelley, "Ethiopians Seeking Birth Control: Caught Between Church and State," *NPR*, Dec. 30, 2014, https://www.npr.org/sections/ goatsandsoda/2014/12/30/301425396/ethiopians-seeking-birth-control-caught-between-church-and-state (Retrieved Aug. 11, 2019).

19   John Harlow, "Billionaire club in bid to curb overpopulation" *The Times*, May 24, 2009, https://www.thetimes.co.uk/article/billionaire-club-in-bid-to-curb-overpopulation-d2fl22qhl02 (Retrieved April 22, 2019).

20   *the one issue that really grabbed me*   Transcript – Bill Moyers interviews Bill Gates, NOW, PBS/WTCI, May 09, 2003, https://www.pbs.org/now/printable/ transcript_gates_print.html (Retrieved April 25, 2019); Video clip: "Bill Gates: My Father Headed Planned Parenthood," *InfoWars*, https://www.pbs.org/now/ printable/transcript_gates_print.html (Retrieved April 25, 2019).

21   *church represents an inefficient use of his time*   "The Gates Operating System," *Time*, Jan. 13, 1997.

a staff of 30 people   Michael Fitzgerald, "A tale of two titans: Gates and John D. Rockefeller," July 1, 1998, *ZDNet*, https://www.zdnet.com/article/a-tale-of-two-titans-gates-and-john-d-rockefeller (Retrieved April 22, 2019).

persistent   Greg Roza, *Bill and Melinda Gates: Digital Age Philanthropists* (New York: Britannica Educational Publishing, 2015), 19.

22   *sixth in the nation*   2018 Best High Schools in America, *Niche.com,* https://web. archive.org/web20180614194819/http://www.niche.com/k12/search/best-high-schools/ (Retrieved April 22, 2019).

three times more…J. W. Maxwell…trust fund…CEO of IBM   Philip Greenspun, "How to Become as Rich as Bill Gates," 1998, https://philip.greenspun.com/bg (Retrieved April 22, 2019).

changed his name   Greg Roza, *Bill and Melinda Gates*, 9.

23   *magic of vaccines*   Ibid., 40.

something I love…lower that by perhaps 10 or 15 percent   2010 Ted Talk transcript, https://www.ted.com/talks/bill_gates/transcript?language=en ; 2010 Ted Talk video, "Innovating to Zero!" https://www.ted.com/talks/bill_gates?language=en (Retrieved April 22, 2019).

24   *reducing population growth*   Bill Gates 2011 interview with CNN's Dr. Sanjay Gupta, (28 second mark), https://youtu.be/U_Gi6cf-jiI see also, https://jasperandsardine.wordpress.com/2015/06/05/pro-vaccine-fanatic-bill-gates-funds-predictive-model-showing-33-million-people-dead-from-spanish-flu-pandemic.

likable, mild mannered…ulterior motives   Richard Gale and Gary Null, "Death by Vaccination: The Gates Foundation and the New Eugenics," *Progressive Radio Network*, Sept. 22, 2010, http://prn.fm/wp-content/uploads/2017/01/10-Death ByVaccinationGatesFoundation.pdf (Retrieved April 22, 2019).

Chapter 23

1   *three kids…awkward…lopsided*   Roza, *Bill and Melinda Gates*, 25–26.

mansion   Sean Keeley and Sarah Anne Lloyd, "25 Facts about Bill Gates Medina Mansion," Feb. 23, 2018, *Seattle Curbed,* https://seattle.curbed. com/2017/2/16/14637668/bill-gates-medina-mansion (Retrieved April 23, 2019).

2   Charlie Rose interviews Melinda Gates, *CharlieRose.com*, Nov. 16, 2009, https://charlierose.com/videos/15330 (Retrieved April 22, 2019).

3   *real goal is to control populations*   Melinda Gates, *TEDxChange*, April 2012, https://www.ted.com/talks/melinda_gates_let_s_put_birth_control_back_on_the_agenda?language=en (Retrieved April 23, 2019).

Religion is not very efficient   Walter Isaacson, "In Search of the Real Bill Gates," *Time,* Jan. 13, 1997, http://content.time.com/time/magazine/article/0,9171,1120657-8,00.html (Retrieved April 24, 2019).

practicing Catholic   Nina Lakhani, "Catholic Melinda Gates Defies the Vatican over Birth Control Funds," *Independent,* July 12, 2012. The *Independent* calls her a "practicing Catholic" while Melinda refers to herself as a "practicing Christian." Roza, *Bill and Melinda Gates,* 41–42.

4   *$43 billion*   Obianuju Ekeocha, *Target Africa: Ideological Neocolonialism in the Twenty-First Century* (San Francisco: Ignatius Press, 2018), 178–179.

grandfather borrowed $80   Ibid., 22.

5   Ibid., 41. See also Obianuju Ekeocha, "Nigerian Woman writes to Melinda Gates: We Don't Need Your Contraception," *Catholic Online,* Aug. 20, 2012, https://www.catholic.org/news/national/story.php?id=47264 (Retrieved April 23, 2019).

6   Obianuju Ekeocha, *Target Africa,* 186, 188, 44.

7   *Mourn…absurd…heartbreaking*   Obianuju Ekeocha, "Obianuju Ekeocha Calls out Melinda Gates for Turning up the Heat on Population Control in Africa," *Catholic Online,* Nov. 23, 2013, https://www.catholic.org/news/international/africa/story.php?id=53208 (Retrieved April 23, 2019).

not real health care…only misery   Obianuju Ekeocha, *Target Africa,* 42–43.

8   Melinda Gates, *TEDxChange,* April 2012, https://www.ted.com/talks/melinda_gates_let_s_put_birth_control_back_on_the_agenda?language=en (Retrieved April 23, 2019.

Charlie Rose interviews Melinda Gates, *CharlieRose.com,* Nov. 16, 2009.

9   Obianuju Ekeocha, op. cit., 41.

10   Bruce Tomoso, "Melinda Gates, Ursuline graduate and lifelong Catholic, parts ways with church on issue of birth control," *The Dallas Morning News,* May 2012, https://www.dallasnews.com/news/news/2012/05/14/melinda-gates-ursuline-graduate-and-lifelong-catholic-parts-ways-with-church-on-issue-of-birth-control (Retrieved Aug. 11, 2019).

11   *average Vogue and Cosmo-reading woman*   Obianuju Ekeocha, "An African Woman's Open Letter to Melinda Gates," *Pontifical Council for the Laity,* http://www.laici.va/content/laici/en/sezioni/donna/notizie/an-african-woman-s-open-letter-to-melinda-gates.html - see also Obianuju Ekeocha, *Target Africa,* 41.

pope   "Encyclical Letter Laudato Si' of the Holy Father Francis on Care for our Common Home," *The Vatican,* May 24, 2015, Item 50, http://w2.vatican.va/content/francesco/en/encyclicals/documents/papa-francesco_20150524_enciclica-laudato-si.html (Retrieved May 9, 2019).

there's a lot more I could be doing on a Sunday morning   Walter Isaacson, "In Search of the Real Bill Gates," *Time,* Jan. 13, 1997, http://content.time.com/time/magazine/article/0,9171,1120657-8,00.html (Retrieved April 24, 2019).

12   Nina Lakhani, "Catholic Melinda Gates Defies the Vatican Over Birth Control Funds," *Independent*, July 12, 2012, https://www.independent.co.uk/life-style/health-and-families/health-news/catholic-melinda-gates-defies-the-vatican-over-birth-control-funds-7936386.html (Retrieved April 24, 2019).

13   Obianuju Ekeocha, op. cit., 43, 44, 66, 199.

14   *chronic diseases being entirely absent*   Richard Gale and Gary Null, "Death by Vaccination: The Gates Foundation and the New Eugenics," *Progressive Radio Network*, Sept. 22, 2010, http://prn.fm/wp-content/uploads/2017/01/10-DeathBy VaccinationGatesFoundation.pdf (Retrieved April 22, 2019).

     we also need to help small farmers   Melinda Gates, *TEDxChange*, April 2012, https://www.ted.com/talks/melinda_gates_let_s_put_birth_control_back_on_the_ agenda?language=en (Retrieved Aug. 11, 2019).

15   *a major shareholder of Monsanto*   F. William Engdahl, "Is Gene Editing the New Name for Eugenics," *New Eastern Outlook*, June 22, 2018, https://www.journal-neo.org/2018/06/22/is-gene-editing-the-new-name-for-eugenics (Retrieved April 24, 2019).

     Gates and Rockefeller launched AGRA   John Vidal, "Are Gates and Rockefeller using their influence to set agenda in poor states?" *The Guardian*, Jan. 15, 2016, https://www.theguardian.com/global-development/2016/jan/15/bill-gates-rockefeller-influence-agenda-poor-nations-big-pharma-gm-hunger (Retrieved April 24, 2019).

     devastated small cooperative farms   Richard Gale and Gary Null, "Death by Vaccination."

16   *use Gates money to introduce GMO into Africa*   Mariam Mayet, "Africa's Green Revolution rolls out the Gene Revolution, African Centre for Biosafety", ACB Briefing Paper No. 6/2009, Melville, South Africa, April 2009, cited in F. William Engdahl, "Bill Gates talks about 'vaccines to reduce population,'" *Voltairenet.org*, March 5, 2010, https://www.voltairenet.org/article164347.html (Retrieved Sept. 2, 2019).

     largest seed company in the world   "Bayer + Monsanto = A Match Made in Hell," *The Corbett Report*, June 23, 2018, www.corbettreport.com/bayer (Retrieved April 24, 2019.

17   *corn plants that make anti-sperm antibodies*   Robin McKie, "GMO Corn Set to Stop Man Spreading His Seed", London, *The Observer*, 9 September 2001, cited in cited F. William Engdahl, "Bill Gates talks about 'vaccines to reduce population.'"

     GAVI…Big Oil…Big Tobacco   Roy Schestowitz, "Gates Foundation Retreats After Being Exposed as Funder of Big Tobacco," *Techrights.org*, April 19, 2010; Roy Schestowitz, "Bill Gates Invests Heavily in Deception about Global Warming and in Abusive Monopolies," *Techrights.org*, February 22, 2010, cited in Richard Gale and Gary Null, "Death by Vaccination: The Gates Foundation and the New Eugenics."

18 *amazing feeling* Melinda Gates, TEDxChange, April 2012.

expressive individualism Obianuju Ekeocha, op. cit., 22.

fundamentalist type of religion Foreword by Robert P. George, Obianuju Ekeocha, *Target Africa: Ideological Neocolonialism in the Twenty-First Century* (San Francisco: Ignatius Press, 2018).

19 *220 million…we are committed* Family Planning Strategy Overview: The Challenge, Bill & Melinda Gates Foundation, https://www.gatesfoundation.org/What-We-Do/Global-Development/Family-Planning (Retrieved Aug. 4, 2019).

all women want the same thing Melinda Gates, TEDxChange, April 2012.

20 *in exelsius deo…their first and last talking points* Obianuju Ekeocha, op. cit., 38–40, 119–120.

21 *threats…ruthless business style* Greg Roza, *Bill and Melinda Gates: Digital Age Philanthropists* (New York: Britannica Educational Publishing, 2015), 40–42.

India…large scale trials Charlie Rose interviews Melinda Gates, CharlieRose.com, Nov. 16, 2009, https://charlierose.com/videos/15330, (Retrieved April 22, 2019).

22 Obianuju Ekeocha, interview by Yalda Hakim, BBC World News, July 11, 2017, https://www.youtube.com/watch?v=FutdOaDXOg0 (Retrieved Aug. 4, 2019).

23 *Cameron* "Catholic Melinda Gates Defies the Vatican Over Birth Control Funds," Nina Lakhani, Independent, July 12, 2012, https://www.independent.co.uk/life-style/health-and-families/health-news/catholic-melinda-gates-defies-the-vatican-over-birth-control-funds-7936386.html (Retrieved April 24, 2019).

Universal Declaration…population density…carbon emission…go ahead Obianuju Ekeocha, op. cit., 33, 149, 185.

We are thirsty "Obianuju Ekeocha Calls out Melinda Gates for Turning up the Heat on Population Control in Africa," *Catholic Online*, Nov. 23, 2013, https://www.catholic.org/news/international/africa/story.php?id=53208 (Retrieved April 23, 2019).

Pope John Paul and Pope Benedict "AD2000 to distribute Ignatius Press titles in Australia from July," AD2000.com, July 2003, https://web.archive.org/web/20080413151205/http://www.ad2000.com.au/articles/2003/jul2003p6_1370.html (Retrieved April 24, 2019).

24 Obianuju Ekeocha, *Target Africa*, 55, 138, 47.

25 Ibid., 120–121, 179–180.

26 Ibid., 189, 200. See also Obianuju Ekeocha, "Nigerian Woman writes to Melinda Gates: We Don't Need Your Contraception," *Catholic Online*, Aug. 20, 2012, https://www.catholic.org/news/national/story.php?id=47264 (Retrieved April 23, 2019).

27   "Catholic Melinda Gates Defies the Vatican over Birth Control Funds,"
     Independent, July 12, 2012.

Chapter 24

1   Abby Ohiheiser, *Washington Post*, "The tense standoff between Catholic bishops
     and the Kenyan government over tetanus vaccines," Nov. 14, 2014, https://
     www.washingtonpost.com/news/worldviews/wp/2014/11/14/the-tense-standoff-
     between-catholic-bishops-and-the-kenyan-government-over-tetanus-vaccines

2   Steve Weatherbe, "'A mass sterilization exercise': Kenyan doctors find anti-
     fertility agent in U.N. tetanus vaccine," *Life Site News*, Nov. 6, 2014, https://web.
     archive.org/web/20080413151205/http://www.ad2000.com.au/articles/2003/
     jul2003p6_1370.html (Retrieved April 24, 2019).

3   *rated the claim false*   David Mikkelson, "Is Tetanus Vaccine Spiked with
     Sterilization Chemicals?" *Snopes*, Nov. 10, 2014 (Updated April 18, 2018), https://
     www.snopes.com/fact-check/tetanus-vaccine-sterilization (April 24, 2019).

     vaccinating for 100 years   Steve Weatherbe, "'A mass sterilization exercise.'"

     his dog Tommy   Game Changer: Interview with Dr. Wahome Ngare, *KTN News Kenya*,
     https://www.youtube.com/watch?v=BZybTGoHzMA (Retrieved April 24, 2019).

4   David Mikkelson, "Is Tetanus Vaccine Spiked with Sterilization Chemicals?"
     Snopes, Nov. 10, 2014.

     Press Statement by the Catholic Health Commission of Kenya—Kenya Conference
     of Catholic Bishops on the National Tetanus Vaccination Campaign scheduled for
     13th-19th October 2014, *Kenya Conference of Catholic Bishops*, Oct. 7, 2014, http://
     www.kccb.or.ke/home/news-2/press-statement-5/ (Retrieved April 24, 2019).

     Steve Weatherbe, "'A mass sterilization exercise.'"

5   Randeep Ramesh, "Report condemns swine flu experts' ties to big pharma," *The
     Guardian*, June 3, 2010, https://www.theguardian.com/business/2010/jun/04/
     swine-flu-experts-big-pharmaceutical (Retrieved April 24, 2019).

     Rob Stein, "Reports accuse WHO of exaggerating H1N1 threat, possible ties to
     drug makers," *Washington Post*, June 4, 2010, http://www.washingtonpost.com/
     wp-dyn/content/article/2010/06/04/AR2010060403034.html (Retrieved April
     24, 2019).

6   Steve Weatherbe, "'A mass sterilization exercise.'"

7   J. A. Miller, "Are New Vaccines Laced with Birth-Control Drugs?" *Human Life
     International Reports*, June/July 1995, Vol 13, No. 8, http://www.whale.to/vaccine/
     miller5.html (Retrieved April 24, 2019).

8   *using only pregnancy kits*   Julie Milstien, P David Griffin and J-W Lee, "Damage to Immunisation Programmes from Misinformation on Contraceptive Vaccines," *Reproductive Health Matters,* Vol. 3, No. 6, Nov., 1995, 24–28.

     name change   "Reproductive Health Matters becomes Sexual and Reproductive Health Matters," *SRHM.org,* Feb. 26, 2019, https://web.archive.org/web/20190226185627/http://www.srhm.org (Retrieved April 25, 2019).

9   *all four vials tested positive…WHO had no answers*   J. A. Miller, "Are New Vaccines Laced with Birth-Control Drugs?" *Human Life International Reports,* June/July 1995.

     result of false positive reacions   "Damage to Immunisation Programmes," *Reproductive Health Matters.*

     rare contamination   Abby Ohiheiser, "The tense standoff between Catholic bishops and the Kenyan government over tetanus vaccines," *Washington Post,* Nov. 14, 2014.

10   Elise Knutsen, "Israel Forcibly Injected African Immigrants with Birth Control, Report Claims," *Forbes,* Jan. 28, 2013, https://www.forbes.com/sites/eliseknutsen/2013/01/28/israel-foribly-injected-african-immigrant-women-with-birth-control/#7e99e37c67b8 (Retrieved April 25, 2019).

11   Gregory Warner, "Catholic Bishops in Kenya Call For A Boycott of Polio Vaccines," *NPR,* Aug. 9, 2015, https://www.npr.org/sections/goatsandsoda/2015/08/09/430347033/catholic-bishops-in-kenya-call-for-a-boycott-of-polio-vaccines (Retrieved April 25, 2019).

12   Jonas Salk, *The Survival of the Wisest* (New York: Harper & Row, 1973), 42–43. For a full review of this book, see Jay Dyer's video/audio podcast, "Why does the Father of Mass Vaccinations Jonas Salk want to Kill Everyone?" *JaysAnalysis.com,* Jan. 29, 2019, https://jaysanalysis.com/2019/01/29/why-does-the-father-of-mass-vaccinations-jonas-salk-want-to-kill-everyone-partial (Retrieved April 25, 2019).

13   Jonas Salk, *The Survival of the Wisest,* 69–70, 52.

14   *joint statement…Matercare*   Abby Ohiheiser, "The tense standoff between Catholic bishops and the Kenyan government over tetanus vaccines."

15   *police escort*   Steve Weatherbe, "'A mass sterilization exercise'.'"

     a scheme…no trace   "Kenyan gvmt launches probe into claim UN is using vaccines for 'mass sterilization,'" *Life Site News,* Nov. 12, 2014, https://www.lifesitenews.com/news/kenyan-gvmt-launches-probe-into-claim-un-is-using-vaccines-for-mass-sterili (Retrieved April 25, 2019).

16   *switched sides…was not right*   Steve Weatherbe, "Kenyan debate over lab results shows need for new tests on UN tetanus vaccine," *Life Site News,* Nov. 25, 2014,

https://www.lifesitenews.com/news/kenyan-debate-over-lab-results-shows-need-for-new-tests-on-un-tetanus-vacci (Retrieved April 25, 2019).

except for two samples Steve Weatherbe, "'A mass sterilization exercise'.'"

17 Steve Weatherbe, "Kenyan gvmt launches probe."

18 "The tense standoff between Catholic bishops and the Kenyan government over tetanus vaccines," *The Washington Post*," Nov. 14, 2014.

19 *3 of 59 vials* Steve Weatherbe, "Kenyan bishops still wary despite new tests showing no sterilizing agent in UN vaccines," *Life Site News*, Jan. 16, 2015, https://www.lifesitenews.com/news/kenyan-bishops-still-wary-despite-new-tests-showing-no-sterilizing-agent-in (Retrieved April 25, 2019).

40 more vials…delayed the report "Kenya Catholic Bishops: 'We insist that no further mass tetanus vaccination campaigns should be undertaken in Kenya,'" *Outbreak News Today*, Jan. 18, 2015, http://outbreaknewstoday.com/kenya-catholic-bishops-we-insist-that-no-further-mass-tetanus-vaccination-campaigns-should-be-undertaken-in-kenya-18049 (Retrieved April 25, 2019).

20 Christina England, "Mass Sterilization of Millions of African Girls through Tetanus Vaccine Scandal Broadens as Kenyan Laboratory Attacked," *Health Impact News*. Feb. 12, 2018, https://healthimpactnews.com/2018/mass-sterilization-of-millions-of-african-girls-through-tetanus-vaccine-scandal-broadens-as-kenyan-laboratory-attacked (Retrieved April 25, 2019).

"License of Industrial lab Agriq-Quest Suspended," *Business Daily Africa*, Jan. 12, 2017, https://www.businessdailyafrica.com/Corporate-News/Licence-of-industrial-lab-Agriq-Quest-suspended/539550-3515280-j78flcz (Retrieved April 25, 2019.

David Mikkelson, "Is Tetanus Vaccine Spiked with Sterilization Chemicals?" *Snopes*, Nov. 10, 2014 (Updated April 18, 2018);

21 "Mass Sterilization of Millions of African Girls through Tetanus Vaccine Scandal Broadens as Kenyan Laboratory Attacked," *Health Impact News*. Feb. 12, 2018.

22 *intentionally sterilizing* "Kenya – Thousands infertile after gov't sponsored vaccination – Odinga," *Agence de Presse Africaine*, Sept. 11, 2017, http://apanews.net/en/pays/kenya/news/kenya-thousands-infertile-after-govt-sponsored-vaccination-odinga (Retrieved April 25, 2019).

will continue to test…fears are goundless Steve Weatherbe, "Kenyan bishops still wary…," *Life Site News*, Jan. 16, 2015.

23 Anhubhuti Vishnoi, "Centre shuts health mission gate on Bill & Melinda Gates Foundation," *The Economic Times*, Feb. 9, 2017, https://economictimes.indiatimes.com/news/politics-and-nation/centre-shuts-gate-on-bill-melinda-gates-foundation/articleshow/57028697.cms (Retrieved April 25, 2019).

24   *they did it in South America*   Steve Weatherbe, "Kenyan bishops still wary…."

unresolved   "The tense standoff between Catholic bishops and the Kenyan government over tetanus vaccines," *The Washington Post*," Nov. 14, 2014.

conspiracy-minded   David Mikkelson, "Is Tetanus Vaccine Spiked with Sterilization Chemicals?" *Snopes*, Nov. 10, 2014 (Updated April 18, 2018).

25   Alana Goodman, "Facebook 'fact checker' who will arbitrate on 'fake news' is accused of defrauding website to pay for prostitutes - and its staff includes an escort-porn star and 'Vice Vixen dome,'" *Daily Mail*, Dec. 21, 2016, https://www.dailymail.co.uk/news/article-4042194/Facebook-fact-checker-arbitrate-fake-news-accused-defrauding-website-pay-prostitutes-staff-includes-escort-porn-star-Vice-Vixen-domme.html (Retrieved April 25, 2019).

26   Kalev, Leetaru, "The Daily Mail Snopes Story And Fact Checking The Fact Checkers," *Forbes*, Dec. 22, 2016, https://www.forbes.com/sites/kalevleetaru/2016/12/22/the-daily-mail-snopes-story-and-fact-checking-the-fact-checkers/#60754448227f (Retrieved April 25, 2019).

Chapter 25

1   "denouncing" is actually the word *rubbishing*. "Kenyan bishops still wary despite new tests showing no sterilizing agent in UN vaccines," *Life Site News*, Jan. 16, 2015.

2   Ross Douthat, "Eugenics, Past and Future," *New York Times*, June 9, 2012, https://www.nytimes.com/2012/06/10/opinion/sunday/douthat-eugenics-past-and-future.html (Retrieved April 25, 2019).

3   *holy ground*   Robert Muller, *New Genesis: Shaping a Global Spirituality* (Garden City, NY: Doubleday & Co., 1982), 46, cited in Wagner and Carbone, *Fifty Years After the Declaration: The United Nations' Record on Human Rights* (Washington, D.C.: Lanham, 2001), 97.

a third of the funding   See *The Layman's Movement Review*, May-June 1960, cited in Robert Spenser, "The United Nations Meditation Room—Friends of the Meditation Room," *The Cult of the All-Seeing Eye* (Palmdale, CA: Omni Publications, 1960), 12.

4   *the center in a spiritual sense*   Roger Lipsey, *Hammarskjold: A Life* (Ann Arbor: University of Michigan Press, 2016), 325.

ended up a mystic   Leo Zonneveld and Robert Muller, *The Desire to be human: a global reconnaissance of human perspectives in an age of transformation written in honor of Pierre Tellhard de Chardin* (Netherlands: Wassenaar Mirananda, 1983), 304.

details of room and ark/rock   Robert Spenser, "The United Nations Meditation Room," 8–20.

altar to an unknown god   Dag Hammarskjold, "'A Room of Quiet' The Meditation Room, United Nations Headquarters," *United Nations*, 1957, https://www.un.org/Depts/dhl/dag/meditationroom.htm (Retrieved April 25, 2019).

5   *such was never the case*   "The Esoteric Meaning of Lucifer," *Lucis Trust*, https://www.lucistrust.org/arcane_school/talks_and_articles/the_esoteric_meaning_lucifer (Retrieved April 25, 2019).

Roster, United Nations: Economic and Social Council (as of Sept. 1, 2018), http://csonet.org/content/documents/E.2018.inf.5.pdf (Retrieved April 25, 2019).

a new and better way of life   Home Page (Welcome-Mission Statement), *Lucis Trust*, https://www.lucistrust.org (Retrieved April 25, 2019).

6   "The New Group of World Servers," *Lucis Trust*, https://www.lucistrust.org/world_goodwill/key_concepts/the_new_group_world_servers3 (Retrieved April 25, 2019).

7   The Archives and Papers of Dean W. Arnold, Chattanooga, Tennessee. Screenshots available online at http://deanslist.info/lucis (Retrieved Aug. 6, 2019).

8   Transcript – Bill Moyers interviews Bill Gates, NOW, PBS/WTCI, May 09, 2003, https://www.pbs.org/now/printable/transcript_gates_print.html (Retrieved April 25, 2019); Video clip: https://www.youtube.com/watch?v=H2OkIua8iEU (Retrieved Sept. 2, 2019).

9   Andrew Leonard, "Is Bill Gates a closet liberal?" *Salon.com*, Jan. 30, 1998, https://www.salon.com/1998/01/29/feature_349 (Retrieved April 25, 2019).

10   *$2.2 billion in assets*   2017-18 Annual Report, Planned Parenthood, 26, https://www.plannedparenthood.org/uploads/filer_public/4a/0f/4a0f3969-cf71-4ec3-8a90-733c01ee8148/190124-annualreport18-p03.pdf (Retrieved April 25, 2019).

11   *human waste*   Margaret Sanger, *Woman and the New Race*, 4.

raising of human thoroughbreds   Margaret Sanger, *Pivot of Civilization*, 145.

masthead   Margaret Sanger, ed., *Birth Control Review*, Nov., 1921. For an image of this magazine and masthead, see https://gerardnadal.com/2010/01/05/sanger-targets-the-lower-classes (Retrieved April 6, 2019). See also https://lifedynamics.com/app/uploads/2015/09/1921-11-November.pdf (Retrieved May 1, 2019).

Nazi eugenics   Ernst Rudin, "Eugenic Sterilization: An Urgent Need," *Birth Control Review*, April 1933, Vol. XVII, No. 4, 102, https://lifedynamics.com/app/uploads/2015/09/1933-04-April.pdf (May 2, 2019).

White supremacy   Havelock Ellis, "The World's Racial Problem," *Birth Control Review*, Oct. 1920, Vol. IV, No. 10, 15–16, https://lifedynamics.com/app/uploads/2015/09/1920-10-October.pdf (Retrieved May 1, 2019).

Most merciful…to kill it   Margarite Sanger, *Woman and the New Race* (New York, NY: Truth Publishing Co., 1920), 63. For online version of book and the quote, see https://pdfbooks.co.za/library/MARGARET_SANGER-WOMAN_AND_ THE_NEW_RACE.pdf (Retrieved March 16, 2019), 27).

complex and imperfect   "Margaret Sanger – Our Founder," *100 Years Strong*, https://www.plannedparenthood.org/files/9214/7612/8734/Sanger_Fact_Sheet_ Oct_2016.pdf (Retrieved April 25, 2019).

12   "Celebrating My Father's 90th Birthday," *gatesnotes*, Bill Gates YouTube Channel, Nov. 29, 2015, https://www.youtube.com/watch?time_ continue=152&v=a2mKUoYc9OE (Retrieved April 25, 2019).

13   *Rockefellers funded Sanger*   "[Sanger's first] clinic received extensive funding from John D. Rockefeller, Jr. and his family, who continued to make anonymous donations to Sanger's causes in subsequent decades." Wikipedia: Margaret Sanger, sourcing Ellen Chesler, *Woman of Valor: Margaret Sanger and the Birth Control Movement in America* (New York: Simon and Schuster, 2007), 277, 293, 558.

grant for a large anti-fertility vaccine   "President's Five-Year Review & Annual Report," *The Rockefeller Foundation*, 1968, 52, 22, 56, https://assets. rockefellerfoundation.org/app/uploads/20150530122242/Annual-Report-1968. pdf (Retrieved April 25, 2019).

14   Bruce Stutz, "Ted Turner Turns it On," *Audubon*, November–December 1991. Vol. 93, No. 6), 113. See screenshot at https://notunlikelee.wordpress.com/tag/ audubon-magazine (Retrieved April 25, 2019).

15   Randall Sullivan, "American Stonehenge: Monumental Instructions for the Post-Apocalypse," *WIRED*, April 20, 2009, https://www.wired.com/2009/04/ff- guidestones/?currentPage=1 (Retrieved April 26, 2019).

16   *Global Biodiversity Assessment*, UNEP (United Nations Environment Program), Section 9, phase One Draft, Section 9.2.3.2, 108 - see also Global Biodiversity Assessment (Cambridge: Cambridge University Press, 1995), 773), cited in Henry Lamb, "The Rise of Global Governance," *Institute for Agriculture & Trade Policy*, https://www.iatp.org/sites/default/files/Global_Governance_Why_How_When. htm#91 (Retrieved April 26, 2019).

17   *Cousteau*   "Interview: Jacques-Yves Cousteau," *The UNESCO Courier*, Nov. 1991, 13, https://joseywales1965.files.wordpress.com/2014/06/0003_jacques_ couteau.pdf (Retrieved April 25, 2019).

Prince Philip   "Foreword by Prince Philip," Fleur Cowles, *If I Were an Animal* (New York: Morrow, 1987), cited in *Wikiquote*: Prince Philip, Duke of Edinburgh, https://en.m.wikiquote.org/wiki/Prince_Philip,_Duke_of_Edinburgh (Retrieved April 26, 2019).

Bertrand Russell   Bertrand Russell, *The Impact of Science Upon Society* (New York: AMS Press, 1968), 103–104, https://ia600300.us.archive.org/0/items/ TheImpactOfScienceOnSociety-B.Russell/TheImpactOfScienceOnSociety-B. Russell.pdf (Retrieved April 26, 2019).

18   Plato, *The Republic*, Book V, in *The Dialogues of Plato* , Vol II (New York: Charles Scribner and Company, 1871), 285.

19   David Rockefeller, *Memoirs* (New York: Random House, 2003), 406.

20   *studied and worked with Kaiser*   "Dr. Pincus, Developer of the Birth Control Pill, Dies," *New York Times*, Aug. 23, 1967, https://archive.nytimes.com/www. nytimes.com/learning/general/onthisday/bday/0409.html (Retrieved April 26, 2019).

sterilizing 600 French African children   Helga Kuhse and Peter Singer, *Bioethics: An Anthology* (Wiley-Blackwell, 2006), 232, cited in Wikipedia: Kaiser Wilhelm Institute of Anthropology, Human Heredity, and Eugenics, https://en.wikipedia. org/wiki/Kaiser_Wilhelm_Institute_of_Anthropology,_Human_Heredity,_and_ Eugenics (Retrieved April 26, 2019).

Hitler highly influenced by   A. E. Samaan, *From a Race of Masters to a Master Race: 1948 To 1848* (A.E. Samaan/ CreateSpace, 2014), p. 539, https://books.google.com/ books?id=JkXJZtI9DQoC&printsec=frontcover#v=onepage&q&f=false (Retrieved April 26, 2019).

Eye experiments   Hans-Walter Schmuhl, *The Kaiser Wilhelm Institute for Anthropology, Human Heredity and Eugenics, 1927–1945* (Wallstein Verlag: Gottingen, 2003), 410, cited in "Eugenics - Karin Magnussen," *Esther M. Zimmer Lederberg Memorial Website,* http://www.estherlederberg.com/Eugenics%20 %28CSHL_List%29/Karin%20Magnussen.html (Retrieved April 26, 2019).

Rockefellers provided more support   Edwin Black, "Eugenics and the Nazis—the California connection," *San Francisco Chronicle*, Nov. 9, 2003, https://www. sfgate.com/opinion/article/Eugenics-and-the-Nazis-the-California-2549771.php (Retrieved April 26, 2019).

21   *Hitler…Blavatsky*   Eric Kurlander, *Hitler's Monsters: A Supernatural History of the Third Reich* (New Haven, CT: Yale University Press, 2017);.

development of Nazi paganism   Jonah Goldberg, "Nazis and Christianity," *National Review*, June 17, 2009, https://www.nationalreview.com/liberal-fascism/ nazis-christianity-contd-jonah-goldberg (Retrieved April 26, 2019).

22   C. M. Vasey, *Nazi Ideology* (Lanham: Hamilton Books, 2008), 67.

23   H. P. Blavatsky, *The Secret Doctrine* (Wheaton, IL: Theosophical Publishing House, 1978), 243.

24   *editor of Theosophy magazine*   Bruce Campbell, *Ancient Wisdom Revived: A History of the Theosophical Movement* (Berkeley: University of California Press), 1980, 151.

dedicated book to Blavatsky   Alice Bailey, *A Treatise on Cosmic Fire* (New York: Lucis Publishing Co., 1962), Dedication page.

Blavatsky's works promoted on website   see https://www.lucistrust.org/store/item/helena_blavatsky_the_secret_doctrine_vol_i_and_vol_ii_1 (Retrieved April 26, 2019).

father of global education… UNESCO Prize   Robert Muller—Biography, *robertmuller.org,* http://www.robertmuller.org/rm/R1/Biography.html (Retrieved April 26, 2019).

based on Alice Bailey and Tibetan teacher   Robert Muller, *The Robert Muller School World Core Curriculum Manual* (Arlington, TX: Robert Muller School, 1986), preface. Screenshots of preface available online at http://deanslist.info/lucis (scroll to bottom) - (Retrieved Aug. 6, 2019).

25   *telepathically*   Alice Bailey, *The Unfinished Autobiography* (New York: Lucis Publishing Co, 1994). See also Wikipedia: Alice Bailey – Influence on women in religion, https://en.wikipedia.org/wiki/Alice_Bailey#Influence_on_women_in_religion (Retrieved April 27, 2019).

United Nations support as a key   Lucis Trust, "Support of the United Nations," https://www.lucistrust.org/about_us/support_un (Retrieved April 27, 2019).

spoke for the Lucis Trust Arcane School   Robert Muller, *New Genesis: Shaping a global spirituality* (Anacortes, WA: World Happiness and Cooperation, 1991), 125, cited in David Cloud, "The United Nations and the New Age," *Way of Life Literature,* Jan. 13, 2009, https://www.wayoflife.org/database/unandnewage.html (Retrieved April 27, 2019).

return of the 'World Teacher'   Lucis Trust, 2000, "The Reappearance of the Christ," https://web.archive.org/web/19990220185701/http://lucistrust.org/goodwill/Wg1.htm#prep (Retrieved April 27, 2019).

under other names—the Lord Maitreya   see Lucis Trust, "Objectives of World Goodwill," https://web.archive.org/web/19990220185701/http://lucistrust.org/goodwill/Wg1.htm#prep (Retrieved April 27, 2019). Screenshots of Wayback Machine/Lucis quotes available online at http://deanslist.info/lucis (Retrieved Aug. 6, 2019).

26   *866 United Nations Plaza*   see Lucis Trust, "Contact Us," https://www.lucistrust.org/contact_us (Retrieved April 27, 2019).

6,000 members   see *Academic Dictionaries and Encyclopedias*, "Lucis Trust," https://enacademic.com/dic.nsf/enwiki/6202657 (Retrieved April 27, 2019).

one of the holiest of holies   Corinne McLaughlin and Gordon Davidson, *Spiritual Politics: Changing the World from the Inside Out* (New York: Ballantine Books, 1994).

Ten Commandments   Aquarian Age Community, "Meditation and the United Nations," http://www.aquaac.org/un/medatun.html (Retrieved April 27, 2019).

philosopher of the United Nations   Laura Batten and Tricia

Robertson, "3 to be honored for contributions to music, medicine, humanities," 4A, *Wilmington Morning Star*, Wilmington, NC, Vol. 126, Number 132, March 17, 1993, https://news.google.com/newspapers?id=964sAAAAIBAJ&sjid=wRQEAAAAIBAJ&pg=2740%2C841277 (Retrieved April 27, 2019).

affiliated meditation groups hold meetings there   The Lucis website links to the Intuition In Service meditation group newsletter which says: "On the 1st Thursday of the month the Caucus invites friends to sit in silence for 30 minutes in the newly renovated Meditation Room at UN Headquarters in New York." Newsletter: *Please Hold the Light*, April 2018, http://www.intuition-in-service.org/newsletter/April18.html (Retrieved April 27, 2019). Intuition In Service founder Steve Nation "worked for almost 20 years at the London office of World Goodwill and Lucis Trust." ("United Nations Days and Years Meditative Services," *Intuition In Service* website, http://www.intuition-in-service.org/stevenation.cfm [Retrieved April 27, 2019]). In listing meditation groups across the world, Lucis makes this disclaimer on their website: "The Lucis Trust does not sponsor the listed groups in any way. They are entirely the responsibility of the individuals who decide they want to serve the Plan in this way. Because of our knowledge of the location of such groups, we act only in a referral capacity." (*Lucis Trust*, "Worldwide Network: List of Groups," https://www.lucistrust.org/worldwide_network/list_groups [Retrieved April 27, 2019]).

27   *no matter how cockamamie*   "Lucis Trust: Interview with President Sarah McKechnie," Produced and Hosted by Angela McKenzie, *Initiative Radio*, week of Dec. 9, 2012 (see minute mark 21.20), https://archive.org/details/Ir-10-38LucisTrust (Retrieved April 27, 2019). See also https://www.youtube.com/watch?v=akflUtK21_4 (Retrieved Sept. 2, 2019).

so much confusion   Sarah McKechnie, *The Beacon*, Sept–Oct, 1989, reprinted at *Lucis Trust*, "Talks and Articles: Descent and Sacrifice," https://www.lucistrust.org/arcane_school/talks_and_articles/descent_and_sacrifice (Retrieved April 27, 2019).

28   "The Esoteric Meaning of Lucifer," *Lucis Trust,* https://www.lucistrust.org/arcane_school/talks_and_articles/the_esoteric_meaning_lucifer (Retrieved April 27, 2019).

Chapter 26

1   *from 8 to 29 percent*   "Ethiopians Seeking Birth Control: Caught Between Church and State," *NPR*, Dec. 30, 2014.

52 percent by 2020   Federal Democratic Republic of Ethiopia: Growth and

Transformation Plan II (GTP II) 2015/16=2019/20, National Planning Commission, May 2016, Addis Ababa, Ethiopia, 61, 190, https://europa.eu/capacity4dev/resilience_ethiopia/document/growth-and-transformation-plan-ii-gtp-ii-201516-201920 (Retrieved April 27, 2019).

2   *top four most fertile regions are Muslim*   "Muslim vs. Christian birth rates by tribe. Ethiopia: Demographic and Health Survey," 2011. Report by Central Statistical Agency Addis Ababa, Ethiopia *ICF International*, Calverton, Maryland, USA March 2012, https://dhsprogram.com/pubs/pdf/FR255/FR255.pdf (Retreived March 16, 2019), 71.

1.9 percent birth rate   "Fertility Decline Driven by Poverty: The Case of Addis Ababa, Ethiopia," *Journal of Biosocial Science*, May 2008, https://www.researchgate.net/publication/5660299_Fertility_Decline_Driven_by_Poverty_The_Case_of_Addis_Ababa_Ethiopia (Retrieved April 27, 2019).

82 percent Orthodox Christian   "Addis Ababa Population 2019," World Population Review, http://worldpopulationreview.com/world-cities/addis-ababa-population (Retrieved April 27, 2019).

3   *ship*   Kebra Negast, chap. 104.

if nobody nukes Africa   "Doug Casey on Africa," *Casey Daily Dispatch*, Feb. 22, 2019, comment Sept. 4, 2018, 18:39.

4   "funeral": Asfa-Wossen, *King of Kings*, 312.

One reason Asfa-Wossen Assserate's biography of Haile Selassie was chosen as a primary source for this book is due to the current trend by most to only criticize Haile Selassie, while a few others blindly lionize him. Asfa-Wossen, a personal friend of the emperor and fellow aristocrat, provides unimpeachable credibility when he includes searing criticism along with appropriate appreciation for this complex world leader.

5   "Dr. Abiy Ahmed's diversity portfolio," *Satenaw News*, April 1, 2019, https://www.satenaw.com/dr-abiy-ahmeds-diversity-portfolio (Retrieved April 28, 2019).

6   "Ethiopia-Eritrea border boom as peace takes hold," *BBC*, Jan. 9, 2019 https://www.bbc.com/news/world-africa-46794296 (Retrieved April 28, 2019).

attempted coup   Dawn Endeshaw and David Lewis, "Twin attacks threaten new Ethiopian government's reforms," *Reuters*, June 27, 2019.

"Decades-Old Schism in the Ethiopian Church Mended," *Ethiopicist.com*, July 30, 2018, https://ethiopicist.com/blog/decades-old-schism-in-ethiopian-church-mended/?fbclid=IwAR3zZWRUmoHg7WWn7lRaMh32iSaNt7hGYwcXBGa3voeTJYf3nZPZUzQfxVg (Retrieved April 28, 2019).

7   *John Dee…secret knowledge…007*   Jason Louv, *John Dee and the Empire of Angels: Enochian Magick and the Occult Roots of the Modern World* (Rochester, VT; Toronto, Canada: Inner Traditions, 2018), 252, 332, 36.

    lifelong involvement with contacting the dead   Rosemary Ellen Guiley, *The Encyclopedia of Ghosts and Spirits* (New York: Facts on File, 2009), reprinted in "Ghost Miscellaneous: Crookes, Sir William," *Occult World*, http://occult-world.com/ghost-miscellaneous/crookes-sir-william (Retrieved April 28, 2019).

    Theosophy and Ghost Club   Janet Oppenheim, *The Other World: Spiritualism and Psychical Research in England, 1850–1914* (Cambridge University Press, 1988), 343–347.

8   Jason Louv, *John Dee and the Empire of Angels*, 36, 2.

9   Madeline Gray, *Margaret Sanger: A Biography of the Champion of Birth Control*, 113, 112.

10 Jean H. Baker, *Margaret Sanger: A Life of Passion*, 103.

11 *seances…Elijah, Ka*   Carl Jung, *Memories, Dreams, Reflections* (London: Routledge & Paul, 1963), 184–5, cited in Sylvester Wojtkowski, "Jung's 'Art Complex,'" https://aras.org/sites/default/files/docs/00028Wojtkowski.pdf (Retrieved April 28, 2019), see also *SCP Journal* (Spiritual Counterfeits Project), vol. 9, 2, 56 and *ATRI News Magazine*, June 1995, cited in John Ankerburg and John Weldon, "Who are the Leading Voices of the New Age Movement?" 2001, https://www.jashow.org/articles/who-are-the-leading-voices-of-the-new-age-movement (Retrieved April 27, 2019).

    a spell of automatic writing   Pravin Thevathasan, "Carl Gustav Jung: Enemy of the Church," *Christian Order*, Dec. 1988, reprinted in *Theotokos Books,* http://www.theotokos.org.uk/pages/churpsyc/cgjung.html (Retrieved April 27, 2019).

12 *the black tide*   Carl Jung, *Memories, Dreams, Reflections*, 147–148; "paternal dignity": Letter from Sigmund Freud to Carl Jung, Vienna IX Berggasse ig, April 16, 1909, *The Freud/Jung Letters: The Correspondence Between Sigmund Freud and C. G. Jung* (Princeton, NJ: Princeton University Press, 1994), 218-220.

    my hubris has been shattered   Letter from Sigmund Freud to Carl Jung, Vienna IX Berggasse ig, June 15, 1911, in (abridged) *The Freud/Jung Letters: The Correspondence Between Sigmund Freud and C. G. Jung* (Princeton, NJ: Princeton University Press, 1994), 187.

13 *I see no proof whatever*   Carl Jung, "The Psychological Foundations of Belief in Spirits," *Collected Works*, vol. 8, *The Structure and Dynamics of the Psyche*, 2nd ed. (London: Routledge & Kegan Paul, 1969), p 318.

    no longer feel as certain as I did   Ibid., footnote added to 1948 revision.

spirit hypothesis yields better results   Carl Jung, *Letters 1: 1906–1950, Vol 1* (London: Routledge, 1973), 431. For this entire passage on Jung, see also C. G. Jung and Roderick Main, *Jung on Synchronicity and the Paranormal* (Princeton NJ: Princeton University Press, 1999), available online, https://www.bibliotecapleyades. net/ciencia/ciencia_synchronicity05.htm (Retrieved Sept. 2, 2019).

14   John Calvin, *Commentaries on the First Twenty Chapters of the Book of the Prophet Ezekiel* (Grand Rapids: Baker Book House, 1979), Vol. 1, 334ff.

Calvin went on to say: "While men move about and discharge their duties…yet there are angelic motions underneath, so that neither men nor animals move themselves, but their whole vigor depends on a secret inspiration." Calvin's assertions were so strange that "he was attacked by his own translator"—according to a footnote in David Chilton's magnificent and rational commentary on Revelation (one of the author's all-time favorite books). Chilton adds in his offhand remarks that Calvin did not live to finish his commentary on Ezekiel, which Chilton called "one of the most fascinating volumes I have ever read." (David Chilton, *The Days of Vengeance: An Exposition of the Book of Revelation* (Ft. Worth, TX: Dominion Press, 1987), 156, fn 22, available online, https://www.garynorth. com/freebooks/docs/pdf/days_of_vengeance.pdf (Retrieved Aug. 15, 2019).

15   Sergew, *Ancient and Medieval Ethiopian History to 1270*, 43.

16   E. H. Grombrich, *A Little History of the World* (Yale University Press: New Haven & London, 2008), 32–33.

17   The New American Bible, Revised Edition (NABRE), available online at United States Conference of Catholic Bishops, http://www.usccb.org/bible/2mc/2 (Retrieved April 28, 2019.

18   Sergew, op. cit., 96.

19   Both quotes from Richard Hull, *Jews and Judaism in Africa*, 187–188.

20   *perhaps three other Jewish temples*   Bezalel Porten, *Archives from Elephantine: The Life of an Ancient Jewish Military Colony* (University of California Press, Berkeley, Los Angeles, 1968), 116.

unusually lavish   Jonathan Kirsch, "Book Review: Speculation Ladled On With a Heavy Hand, The Sign and the Seal: A Quest for the Lost Ark of the Covenant by Graham Hancock," *Los Angeles Times*, April 1, 1992, http://articles.latimes. com/1992-04-01/news/vw-29_1_graham-hancock (Retrieved April 15, 2019).

21   Tudor Parfitt, *The Lost Ark of the Covenant: Solving the 2,500 Year Old Mystery of the Fabled Biblical Ark* (New York: HarperOne, 2008), 166.

22   *exactly 410 BC…Lord of Hosts*   Graham Hancock, *The Sign and the Seal*, 437, 440. *who dwelt in Elephantine*   Porten, *Archives from Elephantine*, 110, 299, 109.

23   Graham Hancock, op. cit., 401–402, 285–286, 210.

24   *altered states of consciousness*   "Visions for Transitions: Challenging existing paradigms and redefining values (for a more beautiful world) – Graham Hancock," *TEDx White Chapel*, Jan. 12, 2013 - online at "The War on Consciousness, Banned Ted Talk," https://www.youtube.com/watch?v=Y0c5nIvJH7w (Retrieved April 28, 2019).

25   Graham Hancock, "Giving up the Green Bitch: Reflections on Cannabis, Ayahuasca and the mystery of plant teachers," *grahamhancock.com*, Jan. 21, 2013, https://grahamhancock.com/giving-up-the-green-bitch-hancock (Retrieved April 28, 2019).

26   Jonathan Kirsch, "Book Review: Speculation Ladled On With a Heavy Hand, The Sign and the Seal."

27   Herodotus, "The Nile," Book II, *The Histories of Herodotus* (New York: Appleton and Company, 1899), online version, https://archive.org/stream/historiesofherod00herorich/historiesofherod00herorich_djvu.txt (Retrieved April 28, 2019). See also "Ancient Nubia": *Ta Neter Foundation*, http://www.taneter.org/nubia.html (Retrieved April 15, 2019).

28   Hancock, op. cit., 448.

29   Jonathan Kirsch, "Book Review: Speculation Ladled On With a Heavy Hand."

30   The New American Bible, Revised Edition (NABRE), http://www.usccb.org/bible/2mc/2 (Retrieved April 28, 2019).

Epilogue

1   Tim Judah, *Bikila*, 80.

2   Allison Danzig, "Barefoot Bikila First at Rome in Fastest Olympic Marathon," *New York Times*, Sept. 10, 1960.

3   Judah, op. cit., 18; Paul Rambali, *Barefoot Runner*, 146.

4   Judah, op. cit., 66–67, 134–138.

5   Ibid., 140, 153–4.

6   Ibid., *Bikila*, 156–159.

7   Ibid., *Bikila*, 132.

Tracking down the source of Bikila's lost ring and his claim that it was the greatest day in his life is a story unto itself. I learned of it first from Tim Judah, Bikila's biographer, but he provides no direct quotes from either Bikila or any other reference or source. The paragraph in the book that discusses the incident only mentions the *Ethiopian Herald* in passing, without writers' names or dates. No searches for Bikila and the *Ethiopian Herald* provided any results.

Judah's book has some loose ends. For example, he identifies bronze medalist Barry Magee throughout as an Irishman, not a New Zealander. Seeing that this anecdote of Bikila finding his ring and calling it his greatest day had become the final metaphor for my book, I felt it important to document the story. That meant tracking down copies of the *Ethiopian Herald*. My searches showed that it was archived in only two places: the Library of Congress and Howard University Library in Washington, D.C. I corresponded with the Library of Congress, and they could not find any articles for me on Bikila.

My attempts to contact Howard University Library brought no responses, so I emailed Tim Judah himself. He said it was too long ago to track down. His book came out over ten years ago and he actually wrote it ten years before it was published.

I asked my followers on social media if anyone lived near D.C. and could go to the Howard Library for me. Doug, a childhood friend who now lives nearby in Maryland, contacted me. Although he works a real job and is raising eight kids, Doug found some time somehow to visit Howard. We talked on the phone with a bad connection while he scrolled through microfilm. Then he found an article about Bikila in the *Ethiopian Herald* dated Nov. 29, 1964, a month or two after the Tokyo Olympics, about Bikila finding his lost ring. (Bikila went on to win a second Olympic marathon in Tokyo in 1964.)

This discovery seemed like a cause to celebrate, but Doug's sleuthing presented two new problems: (1) the article mentions Bikila finding his ring after losing it, but makes no mention of it being "his greatest day," and (2) the article does not call it a wedding ring. "The ring was given to Lt. Bikila by His Imperial Majesty Haile Selassie," the *Herald* reports. However, the publication provided one lifeline of hope for further research. The *Herald* said it got the story from "the mass circulation newspaper 'Mainichi.'"

Mainichi is a Japanese news source in Tokyo. Internet searches for *Mainichi* were also fruitless. I did find a library in Indiana that held bound hardcopies of every *Mainichi* issue, so I ordered a volume through interlibrary loan. A few days later, I got the prize: 500 pages of tiny print in Japanese. I asked locals on social media if anyone could read Japanese. The silence was deafening. I turned to my good friend, Todd, a lover of languages who had just moved to Thailand from my hometown to teach ancient church history. As circumstances would have it, he was actually in Tokyo, where he met his Japanese wife years ago. Fluent in Japanese, Todd skyped me and we carefully looked through the difficult-to-read pages for references to Bikila. There were none. He did find an article later in the *Kyodo News*, and also found a couple of articles in the *Mainichi* after visiting a library in Japan. But these sources also make no mention of Bikila finding his ring as his greatest day.

As a last attempt, I put out a $100 reward on Craigslist, New York City, for anyone who could find the article, and I set a two-week deadline. A number of excited researchers took the bait, emailing me with questions. But they found nothing. (A couple of them did tell me they found a book online with all the information I was looking for…but it turned out to be *this* book! I had placed online a private advance review copy of my manuscript, not thinking the google robots could find it.)

A few days after my deadline for the Craigslist researchers had passed, I concluded my quest had failed. Then I got an email from James Payne in New York asking me if anyone had found the article.

"No," I responded.

"I believe I have located it."

I had heard this before. "There are various articles out there about him finding a ring, I said. "But does he call it the greatest day of his life?"

"Yeah, I have that."

"You sure it's not *my* book that found its way onto the internet?"

"No, it's from the 1970s."

So, hoping I wasn't being scammed, I sent him $100. James Payne had earned his keep. He sent me the quote, the source, and a great deal of documentation on the magazine that cites Bikila saying that the day he found his "wedding ring" was his "happiest day," which "had nothing to do with gold medals." (James gave me permission to use his name. He's an author as well, on the web at jamespayne.info)

A digital snippet of the quote is available online through Google Books under a secondary publisher, the *Africa Journal Limited*, 1973, that released a year's worth of the magazine's issues. The original article was entitled, "Tribute to Abebe Bikila," in *Africa: An International Business, Economic and Political Monthly*, 28 (December 1973), 85. James happens to sell rare and uncommon magazines and said this is a "fairly rare magazine."

This particular account, and some others, refers to a wedding ring. Other accounts say it is an imperial ring from Emperor Haile Selassie. Perhaps Bikila used it as a wedding ring. Certain aspects of this anecdote remain blurry, but the story of Abebe Bikila, who considered the recovery of his wedding ring as the "greatest day" of his life, helps me as a writer to make a point about the larger story of Ethiopia. I want the story to be true. Ironically, the story of the story also serves as a metaphor for much of the discussion in this book about tradition and oral history. How much is true. How firmly can we believe it? Will further information confirm the reports? In this case, the adage "seek and ye shall find" proved to take us a considerable way toward reaching the truth.

Index

I

J

ABOUT THE AUTHOR

DEAN W. ARNOLD is an author and filmmaker whose books include *Old Money, New South* and *The Cherokee Princes*, an Eric Hoffer Award winner. His full feature documentary *Harriet's Secret* premiered at the Chattanooga IMAX Theater and his screenplay on J. R. R. Tolkien and C. S. Lewis was endorsed by the Oxford C. S. Lewis Society. He has also been endorsed by a *Newsweek* editor, Pulitzer winner, and U.S. Senator. However, Arnold's favorite endorsement comes from readers who say "I read it one day" and "I couldn't put it down."

Three generations of family members have lived and worked in East Africa. He is tonsured as "The Reader Gabriel" by the Orthodox Church in America.

Order books and contact the author at deanarnold.org

For information on joining the author on a trip to Ethiopia during the summer of 2020, visit deanslist.info/trip